Basic Language Skills through Films

BASIC LANGUAGE SKILLS THROUGH FILMS

An Instructional Program
for Secondary Students

By

Bruce McDonald
Leslie Orsini
Thomas J. Wagner
Lynne Birlem

LIBRARIES UNLIMITED, INC.

Littleton, Colorado
1983

LIBRARIES UNLIMITED, INC.
P. O. Box 263
Littleton, Colorado 80160-0263

Library of Congress Cataloging in Publication Data

Main entry under title:

Basic language skills through films.

    Includes index.
    1. Language arts (Secondary)--Film catalogs.
I. McDonald, Bruce, 1934-   .
LB1631.B35   1983   420'.7'12   83-14901
ISBN 0-87287-368-4

Libraries Unlimited books are bound with Type II nonwoven material that meets and
exceeds National Association of State Textbook Administrators' Type II nonwoven
material specifications Class A through E.

TABLE OF CONTENTS

Introduction. 7

I. WRITING SKILLS. 11

Critical Thinking. 11
    Categories and Classification 11
    Definition 20
    Comparison 32
    Chronology 42
    Process 53
    Cause and Effect. 62
Techniques of Exposition 78

II. PERSUASION. 88

Sender—Message—Receiver Relationships. 88
    Attention-Getting Devices, Assertions, and
        Audience Assumptions. 89
    Voice 100
    Irony 108
    Persona 122
Persuasion Strategies 134
Signs. 152
A Sign Model: Biography 176
    Character. 176
    Life Structure. 183

III. REFINING THE MESSAGE 198

Focus, Emphasis, and Pacing. 198
Originality 207
Appropriateness of Structure, Details, and Transitions 215

IV. READING COMPREHENSION (SAT SKILLS). 224

Main Idea. 224
Tone. 232
Opinion. 241
Purpose 249
Directly Stated Facts 258
Inference/Implication. 266

V. RESEARCH SKILLS 275

General Reference Sources 276
The Humanities. 283
Social Studies. 291
Pure and Applied Science 298

Film Titles Index. 305

Language Skills Terms Index 309

INTRODUCTION

The thesis of this book is that most of the basic skills in language arts can be taught through film. Film libraries in media centers are sometimes attacked because films are thought to be "mere frills" used by teachers to "goof off." Actually, films can be used in the classroom to introduce and refine basic skills before they are applied in more difficult reading and writing assignments. A large number of educational films from social studies, science, and language arts collections can be used to teach such basic communications skills as outlining, asserting, persuasion, tone of voice, library research, and creative writing. Even reading comprehension as it is tested on the SAT can be taught through films. The approach could be used by media specialists to reinforce curriculum objectives that are of prime importance in any school system.

The 166 films in this book provide the student with basic information in the following areas:

WRITING SKILLS

Today's young people are heavily exposed to TV, which stresses a type of illogic antithetical to clarity in thinking and writing. They are accustomed to meaningless comparisons, facile cause-and-effect relationships, definition only through example, and overgeneralized opinions. In order to write an effective paragraph, the student must therefore gain a fundamental understanding of these tools of logic: categorization and classification, definition, comparison, chronology, process, and cause and effect. Short subject films in Chapter I introduce these skills quickly and simply.

PERSUASION

Any act of communication is an attempt to persuade. Therefore, students must see writing as forming a strategy: finding out about one's audience, adopting an appropriate persona, and employing the necessary persuasion devices. The opening films in Chapter II examine the overall sender—message—receiver relationship. Subsequent films explain how the sender can attract an audience, craft a meaningful assertion, modulate his or her tone of voice, adopt the correct persona, and use signs and persuasion devices to convey a message. A special section on biography shows the various ways this genre can be used to persuade.

REFINING THE MESSAGE

Even the most accomplished writer will admit that style is not polished in the first draft; rather, it is something that only careful editing and rewriting produce. The young person must learn the art of patiently reshaping the original. Films in Chapter III show how to improve the emphasis, pacing, and focus of an essay until they are just right. Other concerns are also addressed, such as how many details are needed, how the transitions between paragraphs can be smoothed, and even how the overall writing can be made more original.

READING COMPREHENSION (SAT SKILLS)

Believe it or not, even the six major reading comprehension skills that a student needs to score well on the SAT can be introduced and refined through film study. Social studies and science films, which are as densely packed with factual information as any SAT passage, can be used to teach students to find main ideas, directly stated facts, inferences, implications, etc.

RESEARCH SKILLS

Too often, young people are expected to do research without being shown how to use the library. Chapter V uses films to teach students what materials would be the most helpful to complete an assignment, how to footnote, how to keep bibliography cards, and how to collect factual information.

Within each chapter, an introduction explains the specific skill to be treated, defines key terms, and, where needed, offers pre-film activities to make the concept clearer to the student. The teacher is then presented with between 5 and 15 films to choose from. The heading of each film includes the distributor, the running time, whether the film is in color, in black and white, or tinted, and the year of release. The summary of each film explains how it can be used to teach the skill at hand. In other words, the teacher gets a plot summary *and* a teaching strategy. Following some films and after each subsection are activities for the student that will reinforce the objective. When appropriate, activities are written directly to the student so that they can be copied and distributed. Full-length books or essays are occasionally recommended for further study.

The films in this book were chosen because of their high quality and their usefulness in teaching language arts objectives. Teachers should not hesitate, however, to substitute films owned by their school systems whenever possible. Teachers should also feel free to pick and choose from this book, teaching one subsection here, another there. The ordering of the book's chapters and subsections is not crucial. Within sections, however, the films are ordered according to their difficulty; the easier ones come first in each subsection.

Finally, the films were selected to create a book with the following characteristics: 1) It includes films from a wide range of subjects, including career education, sociology, history, art, folklore, consumer information, psychology, science, biography, music, fiction, and aspects of technology. 2) In accordance with Title IX of the Education Amendments of 1972, the films deal with both sexes and most races, colors, national origins, and ages. 3) The bulk of the films are modern; that is, released between 1960 and the present. A few earlier "classics," such as *The Plow That Broke the Plains* and *Metropolis*, are included because we feel the technical and artistic superiority of the films makes them timeless. 4) Many of the films are already owned by school systems or can easily be rented. We have tried to limit ourselves to those films listed in *Educational Film Locator of the Consortium of University Film Centers and R. R. Bowker Company*, 2nd edition (New York, 1980). 5) The films, for the most part, can be used in grades 7 through 12, basic to advanced tracks.

I

WRITING SKILLS

CRITICAL THINKING

Categories and Classification

Organizing the continuum of reality into domains or categories with clearly marked boundaries is essential to communication and understanding. Any body of information or experience can be classified into categories, subcategories, and details. Any system of classification identifies the similarities and differences among items in a body of information or experience, differentiates their functions, and establishes a recognizable pattern to the whole.

Consider the large category, "U.S. Federal Government." It can be classified into three branches or subcategories: executive, judicial, and legislative. The legislature, in turn, has two subsections: the House of Representatives and the Senate. Each section can be further divided into smaller, more distinct parts, the representatives and senators who compose it, the duties they perform, the requirements for being elected to those positions, etc. This classification allows the federal government to deal with a wide range of functions (the legislature makes the laws; the executive branch enforces the laws; the judicial branch interprets the laws). The classification identifies among the branches and their personnel similarities (all members of government are concerned with the law) and differences (members of the legislature are elected, while members of the judicial and executive branches, except for the president and vice-president, are appointed). Knowledge of this system enables citizens to understand their government and interact with it (they must appeal to the legislature for the passage of laws, to the judicial branch for judgment on a question of law). The following is a taxonomy (or classification) of that system:

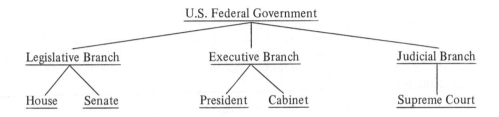

Classification is essential to writing. The writer must identify the topic (or large category) of the essay and determine the subtopics (or subcategories). At that point, an outline can be constructed. The outline will enable the writer to order paragraphs and to develop a topic sentence for each. Under each subcategory, detail is then added to offer clarity and to make the category more concrete for the reader. A portion of an outline for an essay on the three branches of the U.S. federal government might look something like this:

Three Branches of the U.S. Federal Government
- I. The Legislative Branch
  - A. Composition
    - 1. House of Representatives
      Representatives elected for two-year terms
    - 2. Senate
      Senators elected for six-year terms
  - B. Duties
    - 1. Law Making
      - a. Proposals for laws drafted
      - b. Proposals debated
      - c. Proposals voted on
- II. The Executive Branch

An essay, like any act of communication, depends on organization to be effective. A writer must make information as clear as possible for the reader. A knowledge of classification according to category, subcategory, and detail will enable the writer to succeed in that task.

PRE-FILM ACTIVITIES:

1. For each of the following lists, have the students identify the appropriate category terms. Then have them make up their own lists and challenge their classmates to name the categories.
   a. Coke, Sprite, Dr. Pepper, Pepsi (Answer: sodas)
   b. Tab, Pepsi Light, Fresca (Answer: diet sodas)
   c. baseball, football, basketball, hockey (Answer: sports)
   d. Memorial Day, Fourth of July, Labor Day, Christmas (Answer: holidays)
   e. eggs, ham, bacon, cereal (Answer: breakfast foods)
   f. Apollo, Zeus, Athena, Thor (Answer: gods)
   g. ballad, sonnet, ode, elegy (Answer: poetry)
   h. stove, refrigerator, dishwasher, trash compactor (Answer: kitchen appliances)

2. Have the students look through a chapter in a history or science text and list the topic of the chapter and the subcategories used to divide the chapter. Then have them outline the information offered in one of the subcategories.

3. The following list contains details for the category "Employment." The list can be broken into four subcategories. Find those category terms and arrange the items under them.

secretary	letter of application
employment agency	high school transcript
vacation time	workmen's compensation
sick leave	references
gas station attendant	personnel director
classified ads	auto mechanic

working papers   social security number
cashier   union affiliation
resume   guidance department
file clerk   starting salary
insurance coverage   overtime
salesperson   minimum wage

Answer: these suggested category labels are not mandatory.

Jobs	Benefits
secretary	vacation time
gas station attendant	sick leave
salesperson	insurance coverage
cashier	overtime
file clerk	union affiliation
auto mechanic	minimum wage
	starting salary
	workmen's compensation

Job Hunting	Requirements for Job Interview
employment agency	working papers
classified ads	resume
personnel director	letter of application
guidance department	high school transcript
	references
	social security number

4. The process of classifying items in established categories is called a *taxonomy*. A taxonomy is always shown in a hierarchy or ladder of successive ranks or grades much like a family tree. Usually, the most general category is at the top, followed by increasingly specific categories, or in the case of the theater crew taxonomy shown below, from most powerful to least powerful. Have the students look carefully at this example to note how it is structured.

Structure of a Production Staff for a Theater

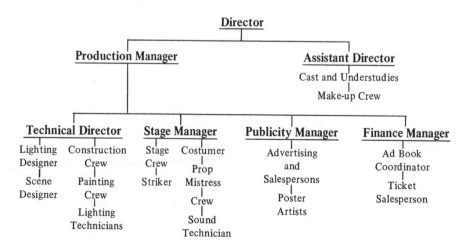

Have students draw up a taxonomy for all the personnel in their high school (including students). Make sure they identify subcategories (such as "maintenance staff"), then even more specific subcategories (such as "electrician" for the "maintenance staff").

5. Once the teacher has chosen the format for an assignment (a paragraph, an essay, a term paper, a 15-minute oral report) and the general subject, the student must narrow the subject accordingly; moving toward increasingly specific categories and subcategories. If the student were to write one paragraph on "entertainment," the narrowing of the topic might look like either of the following:

Notice that only on the last step of the chain has the student reached a subcategory small enough to develop in a single paragraph. Have the students make category-term chains for some or all of the following topics:

sports	energy	magic
jobs	military	his/her hometown
cars	crime	
fashion	literature	

Have students write an assertion for each narrowed topic.

The following films will serve to demonstrate the points indicated in the introduction to this unit on categories and classification. *Decisions, Decisions!* classifies the more than 20,000 jobs available to high school graduates who are willing to continue their education but who do not want to go to a four-year college. *Basic Law Terms* breaks down the legal system of the United States into categories so that its audience will be able to make some sense of a system composed of volumes of statutes, regulations, and precedents. *The Amish: A People of Preservation* is a study of the culture of the Old Order Amish of Lancaster County, Pennsylvania; it manages this difficult task by focusing on various categories of their culture. *A Set of Slides* provides a similar study for Victorian England; it is primarily concerned with the many occupations and the social structure of England during that time. *Frank Film* presents all the images that have been important to the filmmaker Frank Mouris, from birth to the time of the film, while classifying and explicating them through voice-over narration.

DECISIONS, DECISIONS! (Churchill Films: 25 min./color/1973)

For the high school graduate who has decided not to continue his or her education at a four-year college, charting a course for the future is difficult. According to this film, there are over 20,000 professions, trades, and vocations to choose from in the United States that do not require a college degree. *Decisions, Decisions!* uses category terms in an effort to classify and clarify this information.

The film divides the types of career education available into five basic categories: private specialty schools, correspondence schools, armed forces programs, adult education, and junior or community colleges. It looks at some specific training programs, gives some comments of students and graduates, and lists the advantages and disadvantages of each type of career education. For example, a student in an electronics course at a private specialty school emphasizes the sophistication of the equipment such schools possess and the intensive nature of the training. Correspondence schools, the film tells us, offer the advantage of programs that may not be available everywhere and a great deal of individual attention. They require, however, self-discipline on the part of the student who may be forced to pay the entire tuition even if he or she discontinues studies before completing the course.

Decisions, Decisions! uses categories for their most basic function: to make order out of confusion, to break up the continuum of reality into understandable parts. In addition, it compares the categories so that each student can decide which is the most appropriate training program for him or her. Since there are no value judgments on any of the types of career education discussed, the film serves as an excellent introduction to the study of categories.

ACTIVITIES FOR THE STUDENT
1.   While watching the film, identify the five categories of career education that do not require a person to complete a four-year program. List, under each, all the specific jobs that are mentioned.

BASIC LAW TERMS (Pyramid Films: 18 min./color/1973)

The law, for most people, is frightening and confusing. Much of the fear and confusion results because it is generally understood only by those who are involved with it professionally. *Basic Law Terms* attempts to simplify the law by breaking the domain into two general category terms: criminal law and civil law. Criminal law is subdivided into procedures of arrest and rights of the accused. Civil law is composed of torts and contracts. The film presents details of actual legal issues: larceny in criminal law; assault and battery, slander, and negligence in torts; and point of agreement in contracts.

Dramatizations are used to demonstrate each term. Criminal law, defined in the film as that branch of law concerned with wrongs against the public, is demonstrated through the fictional story of a man falsely accused of larceny after he has dropped off a hitchhiker who leaves stolen watches in the car. Civil law, defined in the film as that branch of law concerned with private wrongs, is explored through such fictional stories as the defamation of character of one girl by another, the injury of a boy as a result of horseplay on a rooftop with a friend, and an argument between two girls over whether or not a contract has actually been agreed on for the sale of a guitar. In each case, there are careful definitions of law terms, and the film's narrator discusses whether or not a law actually has been broken.

The film is particularly effective for the study of categories because it defines each of the terms and follows a general-to-specific pattern (from category to subcategory). Thus, it allows the students to see how they can easily structure and understand a domain that is muddled in the minds of most people.

ACTIVITIES FOR THE STUDENT

1. Construct a taxonomy chart that contains the legal terms used in the film. As with any taxonomy, this chart should proceed from the general to the specific. For the teacher: the completed chart should look something like the following:

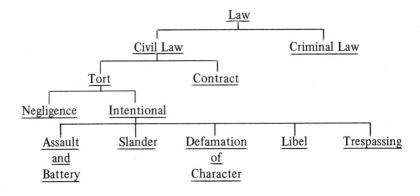

THE AMISH: A PEOPLE OF PRESERVATION (Encyclopaedia Britannica: 28 min./color/1976)

The "people of preservation" reject modern technology, luxuries, and values in favor of a lifestyle based on simplicity. They are different from mainstream American culture in terms of technology, architecture, religion, education, clothing, family structure, and community activity. The differences in each category are deliberate: they are intended to promote a literal following of the words of the Bible, simple and uncluttered living, and a distrust of progress and the hectic pace it brings.

There is no question that the lifestyle of the Old Order Amish of Lancaster County, Pennsylvania, is radically different from that of most social groups within the United States. These people till and harvest their fields with horse-drawn equipment, they use gas lamps in their homes, and they allow no radios, televisions, or record players. Dams and windmills, perhaps the most pervasive forms of technology on Amish farms, stress the belief that nature is a friend. The straight lines and plain design of their homes stress utility over appearance and allow for the evolution of a composite architecture—rows of houses joined together so that a young man and his bride may live on his father's farm in the spirit of the transgenerational family. Religious services are conducted in the homes of the faithful by ministers selected from the laity by lot; such a system places importance on a community gathered together rather than on a formal and imposing church. They send their children to one-room schoolhouses where instruction is limited to basic reading, writing, and arithmetic. Amish dress is of simple colors, the most common being an austere black, emphasizing a seriousness of purpose and conformity within the group. The young marry only if the girl's parents approve and if the boy agrees to adhere to Amish religious principles. The community gathers together as a whole to raise a barn when a neighbor's has been burned to the ground, and all argue about critical questions of values and morals.

But Amish culture and values are in danger. Suffering from the competition of modern, technological agriculture, Old Order farmers have been forced to make concessions. Many now use rudimentary, machine-powered threshers; milking machines allow the Amish to compete for profit with automated dairies; the bulk milk pan, once rejected outright as one of the excesses of progress, is now being considered for the storage of large quantities of milk for increased profits. Teenage boys are now allowed a period to experiment with category choices different from those of the community, and many ride in cars and listen to radios. Tourists now flock to Lancaster County in order to get a look at the old way of life, and shops sell mass-produced mementos while nearby motels offer air conditioning, color televisions, and pools for the hot and weary visitors.

ACTIVITIES FOR THE STUDENT
1. For each of the following subcategories, indicate the details offered by the film:

   a. dress
   b. machinery and technology
   c. architecture

   d. the family and community
   e. religious practices and beliefs
   f. education

A SET OF SLIDES (Wombat Films: 30 min./b&w/1975)
This film displays the social classes and occupational hierarchy of Victorian England while managing to capture the mood of the era. Since British society of that time placed great importance on social structuring, *A Set of Slides* is particularly useful for a study of categories. Still photographs from the era, in combination with voice-over narration, are used to contrast life in the city with life in the country and to make clear distinctions about conditions among the rich, the workers, and the unemployed.

The railway serves as a paradigm for the analysis of Victorian society. We discover that passage on the trains was arranged according to social classes. Members of the royal family had personal cars. Queen Victoria's car, for example, was lavishly fitted with the ornate furniture preferred by the wealthy and the privileged at the time. The aristocracy traveled in well-appointed, first-class coaches, while the working class and the poor contented themselves with the crowded second- and third-class sections of the trains, respectively. Railway builders, the last great mass of migrant laborers in England, spread the rails from London and other cities to the most remote corners of the isle, all the while living in hastily built, makeshift towns of shacks, which lacked even the most basic amenities. Described as "hard living, hard drinking, hard fighting, and hard working," they managed the awesome task of narrowing the width of all the tracks in England from 7 feet to 4 feet 8½ inches, yet received little more than a basic subsistence wage for their efforts. Employees of the railroads arranged themselves, almost as if by nature, into hierarchies, though there were debates as to which groups of workers should be given the greatest power and prestige. Did the ticket taker have the right to command the porter? Over which group did the conductor hold sway, and to whom was he expected to be submissive?

Victorian love of social hierarchy and occupational class distinctions was clearly displayed in London. The rich, in their finest dress, cavorted in Regents Park, Hyde Park, and Oxford Street, while the masses were to be found more appropriately in Picadilly Circus. On holidays, the rich enjoyed travel through parks in their sumptuous carriages as the working men walked or lounged on the lawns. The poor, distinguished by their shabby dress, found labor as errand boys, news vendors, flower sellers, and organ grinders, but the most unfortunate among them could do nothing more than beg for their daily bread. The working class, dressed in somewhat better attire, toiled as mill workers, shipbuilders, taxi drivers, horse grooms, hotel porters, clerks, and street cleaners. As if to mock this excessive need for social categories, the city streets were a confusion of crowds, carriages, taxis, and vehicles of commerce, and the railways and subways were stuffed with bodies.

Life in the country was just as strictly categorized. The aristocracy there was composed of well-dressed, country gentlemen whose only purpose in life was to amuse themselves. The poor lived as hoboes and gypsies; the working class, little better off, labored as saddlers, woodcutters, shepherds, beekeepers, warreners, snake catchers, butchers, dairymen, shoeshine boys, knife sharpeners, etc.

Victorian life was filled with vivid contrasts and contradictions that were perhaps exaggerated by an excessive need to categorize. In an era bustling with technological advances, scientific discoveries, expanding cities, and societal innovations, perhaps this compulsion to divide society into numerous, rigid classes was an attempt to impose order. Such a system of strict classification may have hidden a fear of disorder, of social chaos, but no doubt actually exacerbated class injustices and eventually forced changes. For the British of Victorian times, it led to some amusing hypocrisies, such as in the thinking of some concerned citizens who, alarmed by the excessive consumption of alcohol by Britishers, joined together to encourage laws prohibiting drinking—by the poor.

ACTIVITIES FOR THE STUDENT

1. The film mentions a number of jobs in Victorian England. Organize them into social class categories. For the teacher: the following is a list of some of the jobs arranged into social classes.

City

the poor	working class	aristocracy
errand boy	mill worker	Queen
news vendor	shipbuilder	Lord
flower seller	insurance man	statesman
organ grinder	taxi driver	factory owner
beggar (unemployed)	horse groom	man of leisure
	hotel porter	
	trolley pusher	
	booking clerk	
	businessman	
	street cleaner	

Country

working class and poor		aristocracy
minister	saddler	country gentleman
shepherd	woodcutter	
warrener	beekeeper	
butcher	snake catcher	
baker	seamstress	
dairyman	candlestick maker	
dustman	shoeshine boy	
laborer	knife sharpener	

FRANK FILM (Pyramid Films: 10 min./color/1973)

Filmmaker Frank Mouris' autobiography, *Frank Film*, shows the images that have been important in his life from birth to the present. As they flash onto the screen, two voices—one speaking for the polite, societal side of his personality, the other for his subconscious—offer simultaneous comments on their significance. The result may seem confusing at first, but a careful look at the categories into which Mouris separates the animated images soon reveals that the film is an orderly study of the evolution of a youth into a mature artist.

Mouris' images are common to the everyday experience of almost anyone who has grown up in the United States since the 1940s. The categories for them are, among other things, the religious pictures and idols of his early years, the material objects of his middle-class upbringing, his favorite automobiles as a teenager, and the most important aspects of his college life. Taken by themselves, they seem to suggest that there is little to distinguish the filmmaker from any of us.

It is, however, the reaction of the artist to these common images that distinguishes him from the average person. That reaction is depicted by the two voices of the narration. Mouris' polite, societal voice discusses the images with calmness and naiveté, giving the impression that he was just a typical "good" boy growing up in Middle America. But the images themselves and the voice of his subconscious often demur. When, for example, the societal Mouris tells us that college was a time when he liked "to be with people socially," the film screen is filled with row after row of alcoholic beverages. Similarly, as Mouris talks innocently of his early encounters with girls, the voice of his subconscious recites a long list of female names. The result is often humorous and is consistently suggestive of the intense and highly personal feelings that lie under the surface personality of the artist.

Frank Film shows its audience that the ordinary images and experiences of day-to-day life form the creative mind. In the surface confusion of voices and animations and in their categories, the filmmaker manages to depict the haphazard and free-flowing manner in which that mind evolves.

ACTIVITIES FOR THE STUDENT

1. A way to make order out of the surface confusion of *Frank Film* is to identify the categories for the images the author employs, then to note specific subcategories listed by each of the two voices. Construct a chart that organizes the information of the voices for three categories. The model:

Category	Specific Subcategories of Polite, Societal Voice	Specific Subcategories of Subconscious Voice

You may need to see the film a second time to complete this activity.

FOLLOW-UP ACTIVITIES

1. Each school system has its own philosophy on how the young should be educated and on what environment is most conducive to learning. The system's

values will be reflected in your own school by the category choices in the program of studies, extracurricular activities, and the building's facilities. In an essay, describe the categories of learning in your own school system. In your summary paragraph, determine the system's beliefs and ideals as reflected in the categories you have identified. (For added insight, you may want to examine the school system's budget.)

2. Newspapers traditionally break up the "news" into categories. The category choices and the number of examples indicate the attitudes and values of the editors, or at least their assessment of what their audience values. (Major league pitcher Bill Lee, for example, once observed that Boston's newspapers often placed sports news on the front pages while Montreal's placed theirs near the end.) In an essay, discuss the values of your local newspaper as revealed in the category choices its editors have made. (Does, for example, the number of pages devoted to the arts indicate something about those values?) In your summary paragraph, offer an assessment of the categories chosen by the local editors. Do you agree with them? Do the editors stress categories you feel are important?

3. In an essay, describe the job of your dreams, offering the categories that make it ideal. Do not consider solely the pay, but all possible factors (vacation time, hours, benefits, the types of fellow employees you want to work with, etc.). Be certain to explain why these factors are necessary to make the job perfect.

4. Most stores categorize their products. No two stores will offer exactly the same goods. Investigate a local record store, drugstore, supermarket, bookstore, or newspaper and magazine stand. In an essay, identify the categories the store's shelves are divided into and the amount of merchandise in each. Is the store popular? What does this analysis tell you about the owner's marketing strategies and the store's customers? Look especially for unusual or specialty products. (Your local drugstore may, for example, have a section devoted to "toys.")

5. Review a local restaurant using specific criteria or categories in your essay. Do not just consider the meal (its size, ingredients, taste), but such categories as the menu's offerings, service, decor, clientele, etc.

Definition

To give students the benefit of the doubt for a moment, the dictionary can seem fairly obnoxious. We do not like to have our use or understanding of a word corrected by other people, let alone by a book. Even the dictionary's format—with its smug list of foreign roots in parentheses, its disdain for slang, its pedantic usage distinctions, and the pompous ring of classical quotations—smacks of elitism. Being introduced to *Webster's* at the peak of one's anti-authority figure phase and at the depth of one's spelling acumen really must seem like too much.

No one would argue, of course, against the dictionary in theory; certainly we need a standard collection of definitions if we are to maintain the questionable level of communication we achieve already. But no one should argue that the dictionary's way of defining is the only way, or the best way, or even a very elegant way. Words can be defined by the genus/species (or category/subcategory) method, the synonym method, the etymological approach, or the operational approach, through simile or through negation, in an extended fashion or in a tautology. (Lest anyone think that only students use the last method, consider, for a moment, the *American Heritage* entry: "vicissitudinous: Characterized by or subject to vicissitudes.") All these forms of definition are legitimate. Each has its appropriate use; each facilitates thinking and will be called for in writing sooner or later.

Before launching into a description of each definition method, the teacher should make a distinction between "concrete" words and "abstract" words. This is useful because some of the methods are best suited to defining concrete words, while others work best with abstract ones. (Concrete words vary a great deal in definiteness, some being far more specific and exact in meaning than others.) According to the textbook, *Ideas and Expression* ([Glenview, IL: Scott, Foresman, 1960] p. 4), "concrete words are symbols that stand for things that actually exist or once existed, persons and places and objects that can be sensed—seen, touched, heard, smelled, tasted." Because they stand for things in the objective world, we generally have little trouble agreeing on their meaning. Abstract words, on the other hand, which "are symbols for ideas that exist only in people's minds," differ widely in what they mean to all of us.

PRE-FILM ACTIVITIES

1. *Category/Subcategory/Details Definition.*

   Defining common concrete words, even those words that students know well, can be difficult for them. The reason is almost always organizational—they know what the word means, but they just do not know how to go about explaining it. The best way to proceed is to begin with the general and work toward the specific. The genus/species/details or category/subcategory/details method commonly used in dictionaries does just this. The four-step process is illustrated below.

   a. pizza:
Category:	Pizza is a *food.* (general category term)
Subcategory:	Pizza is an *Italian* food. (more specific subcategory)
Details:	Pizza is made with *dough, tomato sauce,* and *cheese.* Pizza is *baked* in the oven. Pizza is usually *round* and is *eaten with the hands.* (most specific details)
Full Sentence Definition:	Pizza is an Italian food made with dough, tomato sauce, and cheese. It is baked in the oven, is usually round in shape, and is eaten with the hands.

   b. Boston:
Category:	Boston is a *large city.* (general category term)
Subcategory:	Boston is a large *New England* city. (more specific subcategory)
Details:	Boston is a *major seaport.* Boston is the *capital of Massachusetts.* (most specific details)
Full Sentence Definition:	Boston is a large New England city which is a major seaport and the capital of Massachusetts.

Students may need practice determining what category and subcategory to assign some words. If this is the case, activities such as the one that follows (and others, *see* "Categories and Classification," page 11) can be designed to accommodate them. The teacher may wish to limit such charts to concrete words only or to include both concrete and abstract ones.

WORD	CATEGORY	SUBCATEGORY
1. vodka	a liquor	a clear liquor
2. a wink	a gesture	a facial gesture
3. a movie	a form of entertainment	a visual form of entertainment
4. a magazine	a publication	a subscription publication
5. an auto		
6. a skirt		
7. a caterpillar		
8. a carpenter		
9. *Gone With the Wind*		
10. basketball		
11. blue jeans		
12. aspirin		

2. *Operational Definition.*

The operational definition can be used to define general or abstract terms within a specific situation for a specific purpose. For example, a scientist may want to talk about intelligence in rats. "Intelligence" is obviously a very general word and can mean many different things to many different people, but the scientist can make the word clear for the purpose of communicating with other scientists by using an operational definition. The scientist might say: "In my experiment, intelligence means the ability of a rat to run through two or more mazes correctly." The definition is clear because it is limited to specific actions or measurements, but this advantage would become a disadvantage were we to try to apply it to some situation other than the one the scientist is working with. It would be inappropriate, for example, to try to discuss the intelligence of students in terms of their maze-running abilities. Operational definitions are only useful, then, in the context of limited and appropriate situations.

The student's ability to write operational definitions can be tested in a chart such as the one that follows.

WORD	SITUATION	OPERATIONAL DEFINITION
1. coordinated	basketball	A person is coordinated if he or she can complete a turn-around jump shot from the foul line of a regulation basketball court.
2. boredom	classroom	One is bored if one yawns three times in the half-hour lecture delivered by a teacher.
3. famous	small town, U.S.A.	A person is famous if he or she is recognized by three or more strangers when he or she walks through the downtown business district (Main Street).
4. peace		
5. fear		
6. misbehavior		
7. drunken driving		
8. obnoxious		
9. beautiful		
10. cool		

3. *Extended Definition.*

An extended definition is a short essay devoted to the discussion of a single word. The key to this kind of assignment for students is categories. If they can be taught to approach an abstract or general term by dividing it into several subcategories, they should have little trouble discussing each one in a paragraph or two. Teachers who wish to pursue extended definition with their students might try these activities (more follow the films).

a. Beginning with general but concrete terms such as "automobile," "music," "architecture," "sports," "fashion," etc., have students proliferate subcategories for each that could be discussed in a paragraph or two. More general and abstract terms, especially ones used by sociologists and psychologists, such as "adolescence," "civilization," "paranoia," and "family dynamics," could also be discussed in the same fashion.

b. Have students scan newspapers, magazines, books, and nonfiction anthologies for extended definitions. Some interesting examples we have found include: the extended definitions in local newspapers on topics of current interest; two definitions of "democracy," one by E. B. White, one by Carl Becker in *The Norton Reader, An Anthology of Expository Prose*, 3rd ed. (New York: W. W. Norton, 1973); a two-page definition of "the baseball" by Roger Angell from the opening paragraphs of his book *Five Seasons: A Baseball Companion* (New York: Simon and Schuster, 1977); and an extended definition of "migraine headache" by Joan Didion in her essay "In Bed" (*The White Album* [New York: Pocket Books, 1979]). Students should list the category terms used by these authors to define the terms they have chosen. They can then compare the extended definitions with their dictionary equivalents. Here a discussion of objectivity (barring the influence of emotion, surmise, or personal prejudice) and subjectivity (including the influence of personal prejudice, emotion, and surmise) can be held. Students can label the parts of each extended definition as either objective or subjective, determine the purpose of each, and evaluate its success. Teachers may wish to have the students compare each extended definition with their own personal definitions of the same term.

4. *Synonym and Simile.*

Two definition strategies—synonym and simile—should be explored with students to determine their place in the writer's arsenal. Synonyms can play a small but significant role in essay writing. The jargon of literary criticism has produced some infamously vague terms, such as: plot, theme, dynamic and static character, mood, etc. The author who offers the reader a synonym for a jargon word increases clarity. Students can practice defining, with a synonym, terms such as these the first time they are used in an essay. For example: "In the book *Horse's Mouth*, the theme, or message, concerns the role of the artist in society."

The use of similes also can bring emotional impact to an essay, despite the belief held by some that they are the province of poetry alone. In the process of teaching students that their essay conclusions should contain a summation and a closing statement rich in implication, the usefulness of the simile can be made clear. For example,

> In looking at the book *Horse's Mouth*, we have explored
> the complexity and depth of the protagonist by showing

> his change. The key to Gulley's dynamism may lie in the
> author's use of ambiguity, however. Is the painter
> wily like a con man or guileless as a saint? By making
> him a little of both, author Joyce Cary has ensured that
> his character will remain enigmatic and fascinating.

Drilling the students on these two fine points of writing may not be necessary. Monitoring their essays and showing the class good examples from their own definitions by simile and synonym may provide sufficient reinforcement.

5.   *Etymology and Negation.*

Etymology and negation can play a broader role in certain writing assignments. One way to expand the definition of a term is to examine its various meanings over time, beginning with the earliest and concluding with the most recent. A student could, for example, write an extended definition of the term "paranoia" to show that it once described a serious psychological disorder, but now has become synonymous with "jittery," "suspicious," and "nervous." Numerous implications about the ways in which language changes over time could be drawn from the definition.

Defining by negation can be a valuable way to begin an extended definition, especially if one's subject is related closely to other similar but different entities or if it has already received some bad press in the community. Let us say, for instance, that one wishes to define the work of a new fantasy writer. It may be wise to delay a discussion of the author's originality until one first makes it clear how he or she differs from other scribblers in the field. An example:

> Italo Calvino is not an inveterate borrower of myth tale-
> types and motifs like J. R. R. Tolkien; his stories are not
> based relentlessly on esoteric philosophical theories like
> those of Jorge Luis Borges; nor does he, like Ursula K.
> LeGuin, write allegories about chic causes, such as the
> destruction of the ecosystem or the sexual roles of
> men and women. Unlike his competitors in the field,
> Calvino ....

a.   To practice etymology and negation, assign students an extended defini-tion of a new social program launched by any of the local government agencies or political boards. Insist that they begin the essay with a discus-sion of how the new program differs from others like it, both those in operation now and those completed in the past.

b.   Send students to the library to research in the *Oxford English Dictionary* words that may or may not reflect male chauvinism as it has existed throughout history. Insist that their essay take a stand on this issue and that they use as proof the etymologies of such words as: "woman," "man," "male," "female," "masculine," "feminine," etc.

By the end of this unit, students should be able to write an extended definition on almost any topic. To help them toward this goal the seven films that follow show how definitions can be extended in a number of ways. *Kudzu* surveys a wide variety of people to determine what the word "kudzu" means to them. *Chick, Chick, Chick* describes a normal day in the life of some chickens to show how they feed, sleep, exercise, play, interact with other domestic animals, flee from predators, etc. *Leisure* defines an abstract term by examining what the word has meant to mankind through the ages. *The Middle Years* offers us an operational definition of average human behavior during middle age, then shows us people's lives that illustrate the definition. *Mr. Gimme, L'Adolescence*, and *Les Mistons* suggest different operational definitions of the word "adolescence." *Mr. Gimme* defines "adolescence" in terms of its egocentrism, *L'Adolescence* in terms of its vulnerability, and *Les Mistons* in terms of its sexuality.

KUDZU (Pyramid Films: 16 min./color/1977)

The richness of the definition in *Kudzu* will delight any student who is consistently disappointed with the dictionary, which often fails to give the student a working knowledge of a word's meanings and uses. If every dictionary entry reviewed the regional, personal, poetic, historical, and scientific meanings of a word as *Kudzu* does, students would no doubt consult the dictionary more readily and build vocabularies faster.

The film offers an extended definition of kudzu, a green, leafy vine imported into the American South from Japan in the nineteenth century to cover and bind the sandy, southern soil, which is highly susceptible to erosion. No definitive viewpoint or definition of the plant is accepted by the filmmakers, however. Rather, they survey a broad spectrum of people to find out what kudzu means to them.

Unlike lexicographers, the filmmakers accept any definition, no matter how whimsical or personal. Among the definitions, presidential candidate Jimmy Carter tells us the plant is beautiful; poet James Dickey describes it as "a vegetal form of cancer"; a Japanese botanist says that in his country kudzu is an important source of medicine and clothing; to the members of the "Kudzu" rock 'n' roll band, the plant is funky; to Martha Jane Stewart Wilson, kudzu means the fleeting fame she enjoyed in her youth as the Kudzu Queen during the 1930s.

Kudzu allows the viewer to participate in the information-gathering process lexicographers use to define a new word. They collect written passages from magazines, books, and newspapers that contain the new word and from these distill a series of objective, category/subcategory/details definitions. Although dictionary makers would never rely on this film's popular, verbal responses to the term "kudzu," the overall meaning that emerges is far from inaccurate and perhaps richer and more powerful for students because it combines literal, objective, and serious meanings with figurative, subjective, and humorous ones. The film is also valuable as a teaching device because it provides students with data they can use to write an extended definition of their own.

ACTIVITIES FOR THE STUDENT

1. For starters, while watching the film, briefly catalog the reaction of each speaker to kudzu. Using a chart like the one on page 26, indicate the speaker's attitude toward the plant, the remark, and the aspect (or category) of kudzu he or she discusses.

KUDZU CHART

speaker	reaction	remark	aspect (category)
Jimmy Carter	(+)	It's beautiful.	appearance
Japanese botanist	(+)	useful in production of cloth and medicine	practical uses
resource manager	(-)	covers land but makes it useless	effect on land
James Dickey	(-)	a vegetal form of cancer	(1) growth rate (2) atmosphere it creates

2. Once the chart has been completed, prepare an outline for a two-page extended definition of the term "kudzu." Name the five or six subcategories you will use in the essay. Under each subcategory (or heading), list the speakers in the film whose testimony could be used as proof material.

3. Identify the speakers who view "kudzu" as a concrete term and those who see it as an abstract word. Write a category/subcategory/details definition of "kudzu" that mentions the mystical and supernatural properties that some in the film attribute to the plant.

4. Imitating the manner of the film *Kudzu*, interview a variety of people, asking them to define any concrete phenomenon indigenous to your section of the country, state, or county. You could pick a "nor'easter" if you live in New England, the "Bermuda Triangle" if you live on the eastern seaboard, or "smog" if you live in southern California. Or you might select any manmade or natural landmark that has become famous or infamous in your community. Once the survey is complete, either play lexicographer and submit the various replies on citation cards along with one or two category/subcategory/details definitions that synthesize the information, or, after generating from the replies several categories or aspects, write an extended definition of the term.

CHICK, CHICK, CHICK (Churchill Films: 12.30 min./color/1975)

This film offers an uncommon extended definition of a common word: chicken. Although not a word is spoken in the film, we discover more about chickens in 12 minutes than most of us have learned in a lifetime. The filmmakers follow a group of roosters, hens, and chicks in a typical day on the farm. We are shown how chickens sleep, signal sunrise, feed, relate to other barnyard animals, flee from natural predators, drink water, nest, and even hatch.

The film ingeniously packages information that could easily have seemed dry and mundane. The camera gives us dramatic closeups of these animals, but even more importantly, it looks from the ground up to simulate a chicken's-eye view of the world. A wide variety of musical genres and rhythms also are used to suggest the industry of running and feeding chicks, the mystery of a chick's hatching, and the tension caused when a hawk circles over the barnyard.

The structure chosen for the film also makes the information seem interesting and important. The camera follows the chickens from sunup until sundown showing each of their actions in the context of a typical day. The filmmakers also employ a motif that the camera returns to time and time again. At the start of the film, one hen remains on her nest as the day begins, then leaves it when the farmer arrives with the morning allotment of chicken feed. From that point on, the camera returns at intervals to witness the slow hatching of a newborn chick. The mystery of the birth is thus juxtaposed with the conventional operations of a single day, and the audience thereby witnesses the whole world of this animal—its industry, its simplicity, its vulnerability—firsthand.

ACTIVITIES FOR THE STUDENT
1. Discuss the artistry of the film: its camera work, its music, its motifs, and its chronological structure. Identify the information about chickens given the audience through each technique.
2. Prepare an outline for a two-page extended definition of the word "chicken." Name five or six subcategories you will use in the essay.
3. Write an extended definition of a family pet, such as a dog, cat, hamster, etc. Each essay should contain a discussion of at least four subcategories, one per paragraph. Try to imitate the playful tone of the film.

LEISURE (Pyramid Films: 14 min./color/1976)
This film traces the history of mankind from the cave to the city in an effort to define what the abstract term "leisure" has meant. The narrator gives us the history in a sarcastic tone of voice while a cartoon stick figure, representing Man, wrestles with each change brought forth by civilization.

The narrator tells us, with tongue in cheek, that in the beginning original Man had little to do but sit and dream and that he was therefore dull and bored. Soon, however, he had to struggle for food, against fears, and to solve problems. All this work stimulated his mind, but left him with little leisure time. Eventually, the industrial revolution arrived, or as the narrator says, "In order to make life more certain, man took up industry." This development led to the class system, which meant that some groups worked all the time and some played all the time. This was followed by democracy and the declaration that leisure was for everybody. Leisure itself became industrialized, according to the narrator. Playthings such as movies, cars, planes, and phonographs were manufactured to entertain Man at leisure. Man then moved into the cities en masse, and the population also exploded. These developments left life cramped, work strenuous, and relaxation a rare commodity. Sociologists studied Man's malaise while he resorted to drugs, alcohol, and self-expression during his few leisure hours. Urban planners and industrialists then tried to facilitate the enjoyment of what little leisure time Man had. Streets were converted to shopping plazas, car parks to food markets and factory grounds to running tracks. Experiments gave Man the option of a staggered work day and a flexible work week. Soon, an important question occurred to Man: did he want to devote most of his life to work with some leisure time to relax, or did he want to devote most of life to leisure with some time to work for the money that would support his leisure pursuits?

The question, of course, is left unanswered. The narrator does, however, leave us with a definition of the term in question, although he clearly suggests that his is only one way to define this ever-changing, abstract term. "Leisure," he concludes, "is a human having choices of things to do, ranging from nothing to pulling a cartilage for his country (presumably in an Olympic contest) as near as possible to any time a human wishes."

Because of the narrator's ironic tone of voice and the kaleidoscopic nature of the film's jaunt through history, students should be prepared for the film with several warm-up activities. A dictionary definition of "leisure" might best serve as a jumping-off point. Then, in discussion, students should offer their own operational definitions of "leisure." Once these have been compared, the teacher should prepare students for some of the film's ideas by asking if their definition of "leisure" would tend to differ from their parents' and grandparents'. Ask them: Is one's definition of "leisure" determined by one's generation, religion, ethnic group, social class, and nationality? Could one have too much leisure time? Will their definition of leisure change when they graduate from school?

ACTIVITIES FOR THE STUDENT
1. Some black leaders have maintained that language in its definitions and connotations has picked up white people's prejudicial attitudes. Agree or disagree with this claim by researching in the OED and a thesaurus the etymology and synonyms of the words "black" and "white." Add to this research a look at the various names that blacks have chosen for themselves, or that have been chosen for them throughout history. Present your information in a chronology as in *Leisure*, then draw your conclusions in the summary.
2. Try an extended definition of an abstract term, such as "freedom."

THE MIDDLE YEARS (Films, Inc.: 23 min./color/1973)
This film is based on the life cycles theory presented by Gail Sheehy in her book *Passages* (New York: E. P. Dutton, 1976). The film posits that our lives between the ages of 22 and 50 will be shaped by a series of crises and consolidations. According to the filmmakers, between our twenty-second and twenty-ninth years we optimistically build our lives around our adolescent dreams. From ages 29 through 32 we endure a crisis during which we are forced to review our identity and goals more realistically. From age 32 until age 39 we consolidate our gains or make peace with our new selves and the world. At age 39 and until age 43 we suffer a crisis again, this time brought on by a realization that we are mortal, that time is running out. From age 43 until age 50 we again consolidate. Wiser now as a result of life's experiences, we become reconciled to our fate whatever it may be.

To illustrate its theory, the film juxtaposes actual people who have emerged healthier and happier from midlife crises with a fictive couple whose marriage has deteriorated badly in middle age. We see this couple, quite miserable in each other's company, wake up and share breakfast. They speak little and then either miscommunicate or criticize. During the day, the husband is shown attending a funeral, which reminds him of his own mortality. Later, he secretly meets his lover. His wife, meanwhile, prepares a dinner she ends up eating alone. When the husband finally returns, he finds himself locked out for the night.

Against this couple, the filmmakers place several people who have rearranged their lives to rediscover lost happiness. A psychologist tells us how, after a divorce, she regained the sense of freedom she had as a child through her teenage daughter. We are introduced to a ballet dancer who once shared the limelight with her husband in a famous dance team. Older now and divorced, she has brought meaning back into her life by becoming a ballet teacher. We meet a man who found happiness in a taxicab and on a rugby field once he gave up the daily pressures of operating his small business. These and others who testify in the film show us the rewards of middle age that await those who, unlike our unhappy couple, learn from the crises of middle age to begin again.

Pre-viewing activities will ensure a more successful discussion of *Middle Years*. Students should be encouraged to submit operational definitions and category/sub-category/details definitions of the term "middle age." Have the students determine whether any pattern or common denominators emerge from their definitions. Is it possible to make one universal definition from their replies? Before the film is shown, the students should be given the film's operational definition of the years 22 through 50.

ACTIVITIES FOR THE STUDENT
1. What is the juxtaposition of the fictive couple and the real people meant to show in the film? Is the film's definition of "the middle years" ultimately optimistic or pessimistic?
2. Does your experience with adults corroborate the film's definition? Are there any exceptions to the rule? Should the film's universal pattern be challenged, broadened, or scrapped?

The last three films in this chapter—*Mr. Gimme, L'Adolescence,* and *Les Mistons*—deal with an abstract term in an operational manner. To best appreciate them, or any others that define the term "adolescence," students should first discuss with their teacher the meaning and implications of the term "rite of passage." Once the class understands that all cultures welcome children into adulthood only after they have endured prescribed tests or ordeals, the import of these films will become clear. The model presented below can be used to diagram the experiences of the protagonist in each film before students attempt to explain the filmmaker's operational definition of "adolescence."

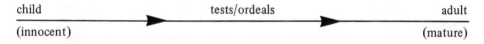

child	tests/ordeals	adult
(innocent)		(mature)

MR. GIMME (Learning Corp. of America: 28 min./color/1979)
This film, a parable about youth, offers a definition of adolescence as a time of total egocentrism. From the moment the main character, Tony, begins hatching get-rich-quick schemes to raise the down payment for a costly set of drums, we can guess what the climax of the story will be. We know because we've lived through this rite of passage already. We, too, have made rash promises and have taken advantage of loved ones to gratify our own desires. We know Tony's schemes will be his downfall; the only question that remains is: Will he learn from his error or will he remain self-centered?

Tony's values are being formed by two role models as the film begins. On the one hand, his father epitomizes the values of the American dream. Each week he drives his cab long hours to support his family and to save money for a medallion that will allow him to operate his own cab and thereby bring a better standard of living to his family. Set against this good example is the image of superheroes and super-stars. The comic books that Tony reads and the posters that cover his walls fan the boy's considerable desire for quick success and acclaim.

After rejecting sensible suggestions from his father and friend that he slowly earn the price of the drum set by working at a part-time job, Tony orders a truckload of greeting cards that he plans to sell door to door. He succeeds initially by playing the high-pressure salesman with relatives and neighbors.

Once the drum set is his, on credit, business fails and eventually the day of reckoning arrives. The drums are repossessed, and his father, who signed the boy's contract with the card company, is fined in court and must use the medallion fund as payment.

After a short sulk, Tony tries to regain his father's trust and affection. He gets a part-time job at a local fruit and vegetable store and, after a week of hard work, presents his paycheck to his father as a first payment on his debt to the medallion fund. His father welcomes him back into the fold and generously offers to split Tony's weekly paycheck with him: half for the medallion fund and half for the drum set fund. The parable ends happily: Tony has learned through his ordeal that sometimes personal desires must be postponed or abandoned for the good of society.

ACTIVITIES FOR THE STUDENT

1. Begin the discussion by diagramming Tony's experiences on the rite of passage model. Name the role models that influence the boy's behavior and the effect they have on his maturation. Capture the film's view of adolescence in an operational or category/subcategory/details definition.

2. Offer your own definition of the central struggles of this time of life. (Students may feel that Tony's problem is not unique to adolescence; perhaps they feel the film offers an adult's definition of adolescence, not one that most teens would accept.)

L'ADOLESCENCE (Macmillan Films: 23 min./b&w/1967)

This film emphasizes the difficulties of adolescence. Its definition might read: adolescence is a rite of passage in which the naive initiate must endure failure and feelings of inadequacy in order to gain the perspective and emotional maturity of adulthood.

Sonia, a 14-year-old ballet student, is shown in contrast to her ballet teacher, Princess Troubetskoy, an 84-year-old woman who was a great ballerina herself and who has taught other great ballet dancers. Throughout the key moments of the film, the camera juxtaposes the youthful, slender Sonia dressed in a leotard against the aged, squat princess dressed in a baggy coat. The comparison of the woman's face and hands with those of the girl also reveals the experience and emotional depth of Troubetskoy and the inexperience and passivity of Sonia.

The scenes of Sonia walking through a loud and garish department store, day-dreaming in chemistry class, and playing with her kitten in her bedroom, all emphasize her incredible vulnerability. Consequently, we are not surprised to see her audition for a position in a ballet company much too early in her career. Nor are we unprepared for the tears that follow her summary dismissal from the audition stage.

Sonia's promise and growing maturity are borne out when the next day we see her bravely resume the rigorous training regimen of Princess Troubetskoy. This time as Sonia imitates her teacher's dance steps to a Chopin sonata, we look for the sorrow that only experience can bring to the adult artist's expression. Through these experiences comes this definition: The self-knowledge and emotional maturity of adulthood can only be gained by suffering through personal failures.

ACTIVITIES FOR THE STUDENT

1. Begin by diagramming Sonia's experiences on the rite of passage model. Why does the filmmaker choose to show Sonia alone so often and in such settings as her bedroom, the chemistry class, the department store? Next, determine the film's view of adolescence in an operational or category/subcategory/details definition.

LES MISTONS (Pyramid Films: 18 min./b&w/1957)

This film offers a fond and funny portrayal of adolescence that emphasizes the sexual awakening boys go through during this period of life. Its definition might read: adolescence is the time in a boy's life when, preoccupied with sexuality, he acts out aggressively to express indirectly his desire.

François Truffaut's five brats attach themselves to Bernadet, an attractive young woman who lives in their village. They follow her as she cycles through the countryside and spy on her as she swims. Eventually, "because they cannot possess her, they decide to hate her." Their campaign is made easier because at this point Bernadet begins to date a young man named Gerard. The boys shadow the couple at a deserted sports stadium and whistle and clown from a safe distance while the two kiss. They announce in graffiti all over the village that the couple is engaged. They cause a scene from their lookout at the back of a movie theater when the couple tries to steal a kiss. Finally, they harass the two in the woods where they have gone to be alone.

The tone and mood of the film are determined largely by the narrator, who describes the boys' actions and motives. The narrator understands because he was one of the boys himself and now looks back with the perspective of an adult in wonder and amusement at his own cruelty and exaggerated behavior. The narrator's voice is sentimental and somewhat sad. He professes to be astonished at the boldness and cruelty of his childhood behavior, but there is also nostalgia in the speaker's voice, a wistful desire to relive the simpler times of youth. The comic tone, which eventually wins out, is created by the preposterous behavior of the boys and by their exaggerated perceptions of what sex must be like. Truffaut also adds two slapstick comedy touches to keep the tone light. At one point, the brats tease a man watering the ground with a hose. He turns it on the boys and the whole sequence is filmed in fast motion. Earlier in the film, when Gerard stops a stranger on the street to ask for a light for his cigarette, the man—who has huge white bulging eyes—screams that he never, never gives anyone a light. These absurdities contribute to the filmmaker's bemused attitude toward the film's action.

The film ends on a tragic note, but one that goes right over the boys' heads. Gerard, who has gone off on a mountaineering trip at the end of the summer, leaving Bernadet behind, dies in a climbing accident. The boys scarcely acknowledge the tragedy, showing us that the full implications of sex as well as death will not fully be understood by them for several years to come.

ACTIVITIES FOR THE STUDENT
1. Begin by diagramming the boys' experiences on the rite of passage model. (The students should discover that this initiation, unlike those in the previous two films, remains incomplete. The boys have experienced the confusion of sexual attraction but, because they are still too young, they simply act out and rough-house rather than suffer, experiment, and grow into adults.)
2. Capture the film's definition of male adolescence by focusing on its view of a young boy's growing sexual awareness. Do so in either an operational or category/subcategory/details definition.
3. After discussion about the narrator's tone, decide if the film offers a sentimental adult's definition of adolescence. If so, how should it be modified?
4. Students who have seen all three films can write an extended definition of adolescence which combines all three viewpoints.

5. Students can write their own extended definition of adolescence that begins by raising and dismissing several adult definitions of adolescence held by school authorities, police departments, insurance companies, etc. (the negation strategy), before launching into its own viewpoint.

FOLLOW-UP ACTIVITIES

1. Several full-length works can be used to summarize and to test the definition skills taught in this chapter. Books written about foreign cultures work well because they spend a considerable time defining. We have used four works for this purpose: *Walkabout* (New York: Belmont Tower, 1971), by James Vance Marshall, which defines the life of Aborigines; *Siddhartha* (New York: New Directions, 1957), by Hermann Hesse, which defines the various castes of India; "The Strong Breed" in *Collected Plays 1* (London: Oxford University Press, 1973), by Wole Soyinka, and *Things Fall Apart* (Greenwich, CT: Fawcett Crest, 1959), by Chinua Achebe, both of which define life in tribal Africa. Each work also centers on a rite of passage for the hero. *Walkabout* will serve as an example of what can be done with each work. During discussion of this novel, students can be asked to define Aborigine words used by the author in the text. Words such as "dingoes," "worwora," "garsha," and "karathara" are used by the author in such a way that their meaning can be determined by the student. Extended definitions of cultural traditions, such as the "burial platform," are also given in the book. As the students proceed, they should be encouraged to keep track of the many aspects or categories of the Aborigine experience that Marshall explores. When they have finished reading, each should complete an extended definition of "Aborigine" based on the book. Categories such as "religion," "courtship," "taboos," and "language" can be used to organize such an essay.

Comparison

There has been a steady rise in the incidence of cancer and heart disease in the United States over the last few decades. Faced with this problem, many scientists have gone to the laboratory for answers. Others have tried a different route. They have looked closely at other cultures whose rates for these diseases are lower than those in the United States. Through comparisons, they hope to unveil the reasons for the discrepancy. These scientists have discovered, among other things, that people who do not eat as much meat as Americans have a lower risk of heart attacks, and that those who have a diet rich in fruits, vegetables, and roughage have a lower incidence of certain types of cancer.

Comparison is an invaluable thinking and study skill that can be used by students and scientists alike to identify similarities and differences, to uncover theories and assertions, and to persuade and educate an audience. Comparisons are made by people every day, but, like breathing, they are unconscious acts. Shoppers use them to solve budgetary problems, to determine the superiority of one product over another, to satisfy individual tastes. Advertisers use them to persuade customers to buy what they are selling. Students use them to evaluate teachers.

The problem for students is to structure a comparison essay effectively so that the message or purpose is conveyed. The first step is to gather information about the items to be compared. This information can and should include facts and statistics, as well as observations, anecdotes, testimonials, opinions, and historical accounts.

Totally unrelated information should not be compared. It would be useless to look at the height of buildings in London in relation to the population in New York. Categories must be identified and each piece of information placed in an appropriate one (*see* "Categories and Classification," page 11). This can be done on a chart such as the following, which deals with three imaginary economy cars.

CATEGORIES

	Price	Miles Per Gallon	Standard Features
Ford Piker	$4,450	35 city/ 45 highway	2 door, standard shift, blackwall tires, 4-cylinder engine.
GM's Decency	$5,795	26 city/ 35 highway	2 door, standard shift, blackwall tires, 4-cylinder engine, power brakes.
Chrysler Potempkin	$7,095	22 city/ 29 highway	4 door, automatic shift, whitewall tires, 6-cylinder engine, power brakes, power steering, AM/FM radio, plush carpeting.

CATEGORIES

	Options	Observations by Previous Owners	Insurance Cost
Ford Piker	AM radio, power brakes.	"Car in repair shop constantly." "No good after 40,000 miles."	$475.50
GM's Decency	AM/FM radio, whitewall tires, air conditioning, automatic shift.	"No repair problems first five years." "Still running well after 80,000 miles."	$599.99
Chrysler Potempkin	none	"After four years car was traded in for $3,500." "After six months miles per gallon dropped appreciably."	$750.50

From such a chart, the student writer can develop assertions for an essay. Assuming that the above has been compiled for a consumer essay, the chartmaker could point out that though the Piker seems the cheapest, it actually contains hidden costs (probable repairs, a lack of durability that will affect longevity) which may not make it the wisest buy. The writer might also note that initial high cost, rapid drop in mileage per gallon, a relatively high insurance premium, and rapid depreciation make the Potempkin an economy car only at Chrysler's insistence.

Once students have learned to gather and arrange information into categories and to develop assertions from them, the essay must be organized. Of the many structures commonly used in essays of comparison, the writer should select the paragraph model for simple comparisons and the essay model for more complex ones. Both are explained below.

The Paragraph must begin with an assertion or topic sentence. The proof follows in a category-by-category discussion.

The Essay must begin with a topic paragraph that identifies subjects to be compared, the assertions, and the categories of the comparison. Each of the succeeding paragraphs will deal with a single category and present the appropriate information for both items being compared. The summary recapitulates the assertions and may conclude with a question or some new observation about the comparison the author wishes the reader to ponder.

Other structural decisions must be made. It should be determined whether the comparison will be *balanced*. Such a comparison offers roughly the same amount of information and spends roughly the same amount of space on each of its subjects, as opposed to one that is *unbalanced*. If students have a *slant* or *bias* (if they seek to praise or condemn one subject more than the other), they may find the unbalanced comparison better suited to their purpose. If the essay is to be *unbiased* (if subjects are to be compared without a value judgment being offered), a balanced approach is probably a necessity.

PRE-FILM ACTIVITIES

1. On the day before or the day of a major boxing match, some newspapers list important statistics (height, weight, reach, etc.) on the fighters in a chart sometimes known as the "Tale of the Tape." Have the student look up the statistics for a famous fight of the past (Leonard-Duran, 1980; Leonard-Hearns, 1981; Ali-Holmes, 1981; etc.) and come up with assertions about the fight. What advantages and disadvantages does each fighter have? What strategy should each adopt? What light did the data shed on the eventual outcome of the fight? Explain these findings in a paragraph.

2. As a result of recent changes in the law, companies can now compare their products with those of competitors. The problem with such commercials is that they often compare categories that are not valid. A commercial may say, for example, that drug A has 750 milligrams of a painkiller while drug B has only 500. What it does not discuss is the relative strength of the two ingredients; the painkiller in drug B may actually be stronger than that in drug A, thereby obviating the comparison. Unless the ingredients are the same, the comparison can be misleading. Companies have also been known to use imaginary categories, such as "kissability" to compare toothpastes. Have the student draw up charts for the information in several such commercials, present the charts to the class,

and discuss whether the comparisons are valid. Put these charts into a comparison essay.

3.   *Consumer Reports* is devoted almost totally to the art of comparison. Have the student read an article from the magazine, identify its categories, and list the author's assertions. Then have the student research three television or stereo models, and prepare a final comparison and evaluation essay modeled on *Consumer Reports*.

The films *Two Cities* and *Two Factories* offer excellent examples of comparisons that are *both* slanted and balanced. Each favors one of its subjects (though neither directly states which) but spends the same amount of time on them. As with any comparison concerned with differences, each starts with the similarities, then dismisses them. From then on, the films abound with striking contrasts in a category-by-category comparison.

TWO CITIES: LONDON AND NEW YORK (Learning Corp. of America: 23 min./color/1973)

New York and London have the same language, have almost equal populations, and are both centers of commerce and culture, but this film would have us believe that there is little else about them that is similar. Through facts and observations presented by citizens and the narrator and through a musical score that is harsh for the scenes of one city, but gentle for those of the other, the film makes clear its preference between the two. *Two Cities* explores the categories of public housing, the police, transportation, and entertainment to defend its bias.

The profiles of London and New York offer a striking visual contrast. New York jolts the eye with its imposing skyline. Buildings are being erected everywhere, many of them for public housing. Such housing is generally too expensive for the poor. The lower-middle-class families stay only until they can afford something better. A housewife takes us into her multi-story, city-owned apartment complex. It is a monolithic structure of brick and cement with a concrete playground in front. The woman is afraid of encountering strangers on the elevator; there have been robberies at knife point in the building. She takes pride in her comfortable, clean, modern apartment, but must keep two extra locks on the door and constantly look out her window to make certain that her children, playing several stories below, are safe. London is a city of few tall buildings; its profile is serene, its landscape dotted with many parks. Ninety percent of the housing is public, consisting mainly of two- and three-story flats in which the inhabitants will probably live the rest of their lives. London's Director of Housing tells us that most of the people want a little house and a garden. The city's Lansbury Estates provides just that. A housewife puttering in her garden explains that the Estates' neighborhood is almost crime free and that the neighbors watch out for the welfare of each other. A planner who has worked for both cities says that Londoners have always expected "their God, their church, and their government to control the shape of their city." In New York, he asserts, "the individual has always controlled his own land." The result in New York is haphazard and often pointless growth.

Police work reflects the widely differing attitudes of the people in the two cities. In London, Constable Lee mingles casually with shoppers in an outdoor market. In seven years, he says, he has never drawn his truncheon. The citizens respect the police who respond with a friendly, personal touch. A New York policeman says that he would never work without his gun. He feels that New York society, unlike that of

London, is inherently violent and that much of that violence is directed against authority. He does, however, enjoy his role, that of a diplomat, social worker, and guidance counselor combined. The last scene shows him and his partner drawing their guns to apprehend a criminal.

Transportation in New York demonstrates the neglect of government and the hostility of the people; in London, it shows the sane, orderly intervention of city administration. New York subways are dark and dirty; they are breeding grounds for crime. Public transportation vehicles are covered with graffiti, evidencing a disrespect for city property. A cab driver, who seems harried, hustles his cab along crowded city streets. He explains that he enjoys his job because of the variety of people he meets and the pay, but that he does not enjoy the "nutcakes" he encounters; he has been robbed twice. Many years ago, London city leaders chose not to widen the streets as a way to discourage automobile use. Thus, Londoners opt for a subway that is clean, efficient, and almost crime free. An affable, neatly dressed cab driver steers his cab down London's uncluttered lanes. He insists that the city's streets are perfectly safe and expresses dismay about the stories he has heard of crime in "the States."

The theater industries in the two cities differ diametrically in their attitudes toward social class and profits. London performances are priced to attract all audiences; New York's are affordable only for the well-off. The result is the opposite of what you would expect. A British actor explains that most of the city's 75 to 85 theaters are now offering performances, even though gallery seats are sold for as little as one dollar. He enjoys London because it is one of the world's centers of theater and because its audiences are a cross-section of society. An American actress says that there are more opportunities for her in New York than anywhere else in the country, but that those opportunities are dwindling. Of 35 theaters on Broadway, only 17 are putting on productions. She laments that tickets are too expensive for most people. In the land of democracy, it would seem, art is available only to the rich, and plays are geared to a "sink or swim," "feast or famine" philosophy. At the film's end, the actress studies *Variety* for job opportunities, while the Britisher memorizes a script.

The state of the two theater industries is indicative of the dissimilar conditions of the two cities as shown in the film. London is concerned with the welfare of the entire community; New York has created a jungle in which survival and success are left entirely to the individual. Clearly, the film is slanted in attitude toward London, despite the work's balance in structure. The film explains the dissimilarities of the two cities by positing that each is an expression of its people's beliefs: individualism and freedom in the United States, trust and cooperation in Britain. It would be interesting to travel to the two cities to learn if those values still prevail.

TWO FACTORIES: JAPANESE AND AMERICAN (Learning Corp. of America: 22 min./color/1974)

Matsushita Electric in Japan and Sylvania in the United States employ vast labor forces, exist to make profits, produce the same types of products, use similar materials, and are part of major industrial complexes. Beyond these details, they have little in common. Using facts and observations from people in both firms, *Two Factories* compares the differing attitudes of the workers, the management, and the unions. Along the way, it also uncovers some fundamental dissimilarities between the two countries that may play key roles in determining their respective futures. The film makes it obvious that Japan's is brighter.

Workers in Japan, the film shows, take a greater pride in their jobs and their company than their American counterparts. A Japanese girl says that she comes to work early to prepare herself emotionally; an American woman says she arrives at Sylvania a few minutes early to get a good parking space. A day at Matsushita begins with the reading of the company creed ("national service through industry, fairness, harmony and cooperation, struggle for betterment," etc.) and the singing of the company song. At Sylvania, workers start by punching the time clock, an assurance that everyone is on time. The Japanese girl says she finds much of the meaning of her life in her job, while the American woman insists that most of the girls at Sylvania work for extra money or to pay for their homes.

Sylvania's management feels that, for laborers to do their job, a distance between employers and employees must be maintained; Matsushita uses the opposite approach. A Sylvania manager says that it is his task "to get the situation so people can do their work and make decisions." He oversees production from afar as employees chat amiably and perform their jobs. Sylvania provides a bowling league and picnics for laborers, but Americans would not want too many after-hours activities. He asserts: "People want to run their own lives." At home, he is able to forget the factory while playing basketball and gardening. A section manager at Matsushita says that employees think of the company as a family. He is "the older brother," and the president is "the father." He leans over a woman to assist her while in the background his people are silently working. After hours, he is the manager of a company-sponsored athletic team. At home, he is able to "recharge my energy source . . . like a machine," but is often visited there by employees with personal or work-related problems.

Unlike unions in America, those in Japan cooperate with management. The relationship between the two is seen as analogous to that between a husband and a wife. Matsushita's president asserts that, after a 20% raise in each of the last six years, workers make as much money as West Germans and may soon be earning the equivalent of American salaries. He lists the many benefits at Matsushita: low-rent apartments, low-interest housing mortgages, country clubs, company hospitals, etc. Workers receive a yearly share in Matsushita's profits. The implication is that labor unions have worked together with management to achieve these advances. Laborers in the United States view their unions as "defenders, advocates, and bargaining agents." A vice-president at Sylvania, however, wonders about this role. He complains that the world has caught up with American industry and that unions must now work more closely with management. He does not despair of the American system: industry in the United States is free to act, experiment, and innovate. But he does imply that unions bear much of the responsibility for industry's recent decline.

That such a remark is made by a member of management is one of the many (and perhaps the most obvious) instances of slanting in the film. But it is difficult to criticize the filmmaker for his bias. He does show some of the less desirable aspects of Japanese industry (such as the regimentation of clothes and behavior), and he has to cope with a truth: America's industrial leadership is threatened now by Japan's progress. With such a truth, it would be hard not to slant in favor of the Japanese.

FROM COURTSHIP TO MARRIAGE (National Film Board of Canada: 60 min./ b&w/1961)

Dealing with specific situations from Sicily, Iran, Canada, and India, customs and practices of courtship in four cultures are compared. Moderator George Burwash and his guests, Doctor Frank Jones (Chairman of the Department of Sociology at McMaster University) and Donica d'Hondt (actress, TV commentator, and panelist), focus on the economic and social backgrounds of the communities involved, the role of the families in courtship, and the restrictions placed on the couples. A simple comparison structure is employed: each culture is dealt with in separate segments (filmic paragraphs) consisting of scenes from the actual courtship. Similarities and differences are discussed by the panelists at the end of each sequence. Throughout, *From Courtship to Marriage* provides a lesson in balanced and unbiased comparison.

The courtship of Teresa and Carlo in a poor Sicilian town is inhibited by economic factors. After an old woman determines that Teresa is interested in Carlo, chaperoned Sunday meetings in public between the two are allowed. Soon, the families dicker over marriage arrangements. They must decide where the two will live and must provide furnishings and other household items. The poverty of the families, parental caution, or Carlo's military service obligation all could delay the engagement for years. When these obstacles have been surmounted, a simple engagement party is held at one of the family households. There, Carlo presents the ring, which may represent years of his savings and which symbolizes his respect for Teresa and her family. The marriage will have to wait, however, until the necessary household objects have been accumulated. Meanwhile, the couple will continue to meet in public and with a chaperon.

The courtship of the girl Rubadi and the boy Hassan takes place in modern, middle-class Tehran (Iran), but nevertheless adheres to old customs. Hassan's mother meets with Rubadi's father to suggest the engagement (at this point, Hassan and Rubadi have seen each other but have not spoken). The mother praises her son, but the man questions to see if he is a good worker and a devout Muslim. She observes Rubadi and decides that she is suitable for her son. Once the girl's father approves the match, the wheels of courtship are set in motion. Some time later, Rubadi's uncle secretly evaluates Hassan at his place of work and reports his findings. Next, the couple is introduced to each other. Rubadi's father sanctions the engagement at that time with the words, "I hope you both grow old together." The two may meet from then on, but only with a chaperon. Hassan's mother (she is a widow) must supply furnishings and household items; Rubadi's father *may* make a monetary gift on the wedding day, which will probably occur a few months later.

Courtship in middle-class Richmond Hill (Canada) places few overt restrictions on Jane and Doug, but in reality they cope with as many behavioral guidelines as the film's other couples. The two are allowed to meet unchaperoned, but middle-class Canadian values insist they limit sexual contact. Their relationship is conducted in an objective, businesslike manner. Recently graduated from high school, the two have been saving money, and Doug is trying for a "serious" job at a bank (at an annual salary of $2,000.00). After he gets the job, the couple calculates that their savings will be adequate for marriage by the next November. Later, Doug presents Jane with the engagement ring in the town's park. Letting their parents know is a minor formality. Parents have little actual control over the marriage, though it is assumed they have been educating their children to choose their partners wisely. The couple receives gifts at parties and showers. The marriage will take place, as planned, in November.

In India, a young man and woman choose each other, but their mothers decide whether or not they marry. Romani (the girl) and Balaan (the boy) live in a poor town in Southeast India. They run into each other at the factory where he works, but can do no more than exchange glances. Balaan's mother sends her brother to meet Romani's parents to determine whether the girl is free of deformity. On her brother's report, the woman will prevent or allow the marriage. With her approval, Balaan makes his only formal visit to Romani. The girl's mother assesses him and consents to the union. A village astrologer then casts a horoscope to see if the marriage will be auspicious. He could stop the engagement, but sanctions it with the tying of a ceremonial knot. Until the wedding, however, contact between Romani and Balaan is limited to exchanged glances when they meet in the town.

After each segment, the moderators compare the various customs. Donica d'Hondt is surprised by many of the practices in Sicily, Iran, and India (as most students will be by Canada's at the time of the film). Her value judgments allow Dr. Jones to stress that one courtship code is not really any better than another. Each is simply appropriate to the beliefs, lifestyles, and economics of the given culture. *From Courtship to Marriage* reminds us that comparisons can simply be used to identify similarities and differences without passing judgment.

LOOK BEFORE YOU EAT (Churchill Films: 22 min./color/1979)

"The more the diet of a country approximates that of the United States," nutritionist Dr. D. Mark Hegsted says, "the more heart disease, cancer of certain types, diabetes, hypertension, and obesity all increase." With an unbalanced comparison that has a definite slant, *Look Before You Eat* proves his point. To promote a healthy diet of natural foods, it uses facts, statistics, and testimonials that show the dangers of processed or "junk" foods. It examines the insidious techniques used to promote such foods, their ingredients, and their deleterious effects. Most of the stage is given over to the villain. So little time is spent on healthy food that the audience will, for the most part, have to discover its components on their own.

Advertising is chiefly responsible for the shift over the past couple of decades in American eating habits. Nutritionist Dr. Joan Gussow points out that there was no conflict between what a person should and did eat in the past; a family simply ate the natural fare on its table. Food companies, however, have tried to make the public forget how to prepare their meals and leave the processing up to them. At the time of the film, a pound of potatoes sold for $0.12, an equal weight of potato chips for $1.92. To reap large profits, a corporation has only to invent a novel combination of foods, put the product in an attractive package, give it a clever name, and advertise heavily to generate sales. How can natural foods compete? Everyone is familiar with the taste and appearance of an apple. Fruit companies can hardly increase sales or consumer interest with clever advertising or packaging.

Unlike natural foods, processed foods may contain chemical additives and ingredients that provide extra calories *sans* nutrition. A potato contains no fat, a potato chip 65% fat. Chips may also have salt, dextrose, hydrogenated cotton seed oil, and mono- and di-glycerides. A particular breakfast food named for its vitamins, the film points out, has more sugar per serving than a bowl of candy. Fresh produce contains no salt; canned vegetables contain a great amount. One can only wonder what is in dehydrated ice cream. The film need say little about natural foods in comparison. They, by definition, contain no chemical additives or added ingredients.

The film offers its strongest comparison when it shows the harmful effects of the added ingredients in processed foods. Salt, sugar, and fat—the most notorious additions in junk food—endanger the consumer's health. Sugar can cause diabetes and obesity. Salt contributes to hypertension, itself a source of heart attacks and strokes. Saturated fats—excessive in fast-food fare—clog arteries and lead to heart attacks. Dr. Gussow even suggests that Americans cut down on such fatty natural foods as beef and pork. "Other cultures have existed without meat," she says, "and have developed interesting foods." She cites, among others, the bean, rice, and corn mixture favored by Mexicans. An experiment in the District of Columbia schools shows how this difficult task of changing a diet can be accomplished. Students were asked to substitute their normal diet with natural foods. After three weeks, they testify that they feel better and have more energy. Some even insist they will make a conscious effort to cut down on junk foods.

Though it is not a balanced comparison, the film succeeds. When it comes to health, viewers will often respond more readily to "fatherly" warnings than to carefully balanced arguments. *Look Before You Eat* startles, though recent media concern with dietary problems makes some of the film's revelations less arresting now than when it was first made. How can one argue with a work that clearly has its audience's best interests at heart? The lesson is clear: When the facts are startling and not controversial, balance can be sacrificed without risking audience sympathy.

BATTLE OF CULLODEN (Time-Life: 72 min./b&w/1967)

On April 16, 1746, the Highland Scots and an English army engaged in the last battle fought on British soil. Using interviews with actors playing the roles of the historical combatants and an intrusive camera which forces them to react to its presence, *Battle of Culloden* gives the audience the feeling that it is present at the battle. A "you are there" narrator offers background information and leads the film through events chronologically. Hidden within the details, however, are implied categories (*see* "Categories and Classification," page 11) that force the viewer into making comparisons. Through juxtaposition, the film focuses on the leaders of the two armies, on the societies each represents, and on the contrasting styles of warfare to reveal a clash of cultures orchestrated by the powerful.

There is little to choose between the two leaders, Charles Edward Stuart and William Augustus. "Bonnie Prince Charles," a Catholic and part Scot, has rallied the Highlanders in an effort to unseat England's Protestant, German-born king, George II. An alcoholic dandy in powdered curls, Charles possesses only limited military experience: two days' attendance at a siege when he was 13. He has demoted his brilliant military commander, Lord George Murray, who was responsible for two earlier Highland victories during which British forces fled in a "panic-stricken rout." He ignores Lord Murray's complaints that the flat, treeless battlefield—the Culloden moor—leaves the army vulnerable to superior British cannon and to outflanking. He is not worried that most of his food and ammunition is still at Inverness and that his men are tired, hungry, rebellious, and dispirited. He tells the camera that "only those who are afraid can doubt my victory" and that his army will win because "God is on our side." Pitted against him is his cousin, William Augustus, the Duke of Cumberland, third son of George II, and commander-in-chief of England's army in Scotland. Like Charles, he is effete and aristocratic, but instead of a faith in God and the righteousness of his cause, he relies on a three-to-one superiority in numbers, a rigid disciplining of his men, and a sound battle plan. Before he leaves Scotland, Cumberland will have made his mark in military history for the excessive brutality of his command. He, however, has no more experience than his cousin; Culloden was to be his only victory. The film captures the similarities and differences of the two men in two often repeated images: each man on horseback safely behind his ranks—Charles in panic struggling to see through the haze of cannon fire, Cumberland's cold face breaking into a cruel smile as his maneuvers succeed.

Behind the battle itself are two aristocratic, oppressive social structures. The Highland commoners have been pressed into service by the ruthless clan system, a feudal hierarchy in which a chieftain and his senior officers use people as "human rent." Each Highlander must follow his overlord into battle in exchange for the use of the land he farms. Those who refuse have their cattle stolen and their homes burned. But not everyone has responded to the clan call to battle. In the British reserves are thousands of Highland Scots. The Campbells, for instance, have joined

Cumberland to settle a feud with the MacDonalds who are with Charles. Angus Ian Campbell is with the Duke because his wife was murdered by the MacDonalds. James Chisolm and his brother, Robert, are fighting on opposite sides. By implication, the film analyzes the British social system to show that it is no less ruthless and unfair. The Duke receives £15,000 a year while his privates, forced into service to save a German, Protestant king from his Catholic enemy, earn sixpence a day. Cumberland's harsh rule is imposed by well-paid lieutenants described as a "fraternity where the least pretension to learning, to propriety, to common morals would endanger the owner to be cashiered." It is they who administer the whippings for violations of Cumberland's discipline. The Duke's army is a microcosm of British society, a bastion of the same oppressions and brutalities that have led the Highland Scots to civil war.

If the societies are similar in structure, the battle itself reflects the profound differences that are at the heart of the struggle. Highland Scotland is medieval in its war making, while the British forces are modern. Charles' only strategy is to hold ranks and to draw the British to attack him. This will render British cannon useless and put the emphasis on hand-to-hand combat, at which his men are superior. The Duke has no intention of obliging. Cumberland's round shot, three-pound balls of iron, silence the few Highland cannons and cut down hundreds of Scots before Charles gives the order to advance. When they do attack, British cannon fire grape shot, filled with musket balls and jagged iron, cutting down still more. A British bayonet maneuver renders Highland swords useless and drives the Scots back across the moor where they have been outflanked. Charles, who has made no plans for either battle or retreat, flees for his life. The entire fight lasts little more than an hour. On the moor, 1,200 Scots lie wounded or dead; only 50 British soldiers have fallen. The battle is a testimony to the power of cannon, bayonet, and military strategy; against them, Scottish swords and medieval valor have meant nothing.

The aftermath is further testimony to the cold efficiency of the British military. Any Highlander found on the moor or on the road to Inverness is butchered, whether or not he had anything to do with the battle. Prisoners are refused food and medical attention to make certain the mortality rate is high. Over the next several months, British patrols murder many of the families they find hiding in the Highlands. The rest are exiled to factories in England or to Canada and Australia. Legislation in Parliament makes illegal Highland garb, songs, and language. Charles himself escapes to Europe, taking with him the funds that were donated to fight his cause.

Battle of Culloden is not a neatly arranged, category-by-category comparison. The film is primarily a historical study. The viewer must work hard to glean the comparisons implied by the juxtapositions of Charles and Cumberland, the two societies, and the two techniques of warfare. In this sense, the film is an accurate reflection of reality where comparisons are the product of human reflection rather than of nature's ordering. The film shows how comparisons can be intermingled into the overall fabric of a work to offer insight while not violating realism.

ACTIVITIES FOR THE STUDENT
1. *Battle of Culloden* casts its two central characters, Prince Charles and the Duke of Cumberland, as villains. The film's comparison of the two is complex, revealing both similarities and differences. Identify those similarities and differences and all the reasons the film gives for condemning each man.

FOLLOW-UP ACTIVITIES
1. Compare popular leisure activities of two different seasons. Your essay should show how the activities are adapted to fit the opportunities and restrictions of

temperature, atmospheric conditions, amount of daylight, etc. Your essay may simply inform your reader or indicate your preference for one season over the other.

2. Compare Middle School to High School to show which, in your opinion, is better. Be sure to identify categories (courses, extracurricular activities, rules, etc.) that serve as the bases for the comparison. Your essay should do more than simply identify similarities and differences; you should show how each supports your overall contention.

3. Examine art books of two painters (Rembrandt and Van Gogh, for example). In an essay that identifies categories, compare the two artists to inform your readers about their similarities and differences. Your categories may include themes, subject matter, predominant colors and shades, etc. (The introduction in the books will tell you what to look for in the work of each painter. Additional research may help you to understand the works.)

4. Compare in an essay the TV programs offered on a given night. You may observe the three major networks, a VHF station and a UHF station, or an educational one and a network one. Determine categories, such as types of shows, amount of commercials, and type of audience for each show. Discuss the strategies for capturing the intended audience. As it is impossible to watch two or three channels at once, your research will have to be conducted for two or three weeks. Use the *TV Guide* and television reviews in newspapers and magazines to add expert testimony. Your essay may simply inform the audience on the similarities and differences or may attempt to persuade them that one station's "lineup" is superior.

5. Compare in an essay the girls' and boys' sports programs in your school. Either
   a. discuss the similarities and differences in the way one sport is played by the two sexes, or
   b. discuss the school's attitude toward each program, concerning yourself with such issues as the amount of money spent, the popularity of each program with the student body, the facilities, etc.

Chronology

As a device for organizing information or structuring an essay, chronology has great potential for providing insight and perspective. When, for example, it is realized that Shakespeare and Cervantes wrote at the same time and were soon followed by Milton and Molière, one senses the magnificence of their era, the late sixteenth and early seventeenth centuries. Further investigation may help to identify some of the factors that produced such giants in one period of time: the wealth in Europe from the New World, the rise of cities, the expansion of the merchant class, a growth in leisure time, and a concomitant preoccupation with the arts.

In addition to uncovering hidden cause-and-effect relationships, chronology can reveal changes in development, separate key moments from ordinary ones, show ironies, etc. Time sequencing of biographical data, for example, can lead to the understanding of a man—his major drives and influences. A series of photographs from the different stages of a person's life can illustrate periods of happiness and sorrow, success and failure, frustration and fulfillment. They allow one to note the impact of time's burdens on the personality etched in the lines of the face, the curve of the posture, the changing features of the body.

But there are dangers in the use of chronology. A simple listing of facts in time sequence is no great feat. The child who insists on recounting everything that happened during the day with a series of clauses that open with "and then I ..." will no doubt evoke smiles from parents, but an adult who employs this technique will soon exhaust an audience's patience. A successful chronology must contain only those facts that are pertinent to the author's point and lead to understanding for the reader. Attempting to include everything from a time span will be no more illuminating than a child's all-encompassing summary of the day's events.

An illustration will help. Assume one wishes to use chronology to study the reason for language change. Begin by collecting facts and arranging them on a time line.

Old English (450-1100)	Anglo-Saxon Invasions (5th and 6th centuries)	Anglo-Saxon provides basis for English. Most English common words are Anglo-Saxon in origin.
	Introduction of Christianity (6th and 7th centuries)	Monks add religious, scientific, and scholarly terms. They introduce ideas from the European continent and transcribe Saxon and Celtic legends into Latin.
	Viking Invasions (8th through 10th centuries)	Vikings add place names and fighting and sailing terms to English.
	Norman Invasion (1066)	Norman French introduce terms for foods, spices, and finery into English. They suppress the Saxon tongue and make French the official language for government, law, and commerce.
Middle English (1100-1500)	Writings of the Scottish poet Dunbar (14th century)	Dunbar writes popular ballads in Scottish dialect.
	Writings of Chaucer (14th century)	Chaucer proves that English can sustain great poetry. His influence causes other writers to eschew Latin and French in favor of English.
	Invention of the Printing Press (15th century)	The printing press makes books available to more people. It advances literacy and helps to standardize spelling, punctuation, and rules of grammar. It also makes new words available to the public.

Modern English (1500 to the present)	Writings of Shakespeare (16th and 17th centuries)	Shakespeare adds quotes and allusions to the language, and he brings many new foreign terms to English. The names of many of his characters become a part of English literary tradition.
	King James Bible (17th century)	The Bible adds quotes and allusions to the language. This edition makes the Bible available to more people because it is written in English.
	Johnson's *Dictionary* (18th century)	The *Dictionary* standardizes spelling and provides a reference for word meanings. It paves the way for more exhaustive dictionaries that follow.

To serve as a basis for an effective essay, the above chronology would have to contain a great deal more information, but it will be adequate as it stands to demonstrate the technique's usefulness. First, it has provided a second opportunity for the elimination of irrelevant data. While the Celtic and Roman invasions were no doubt included during data gathering, they were not placed in the time sequence because they occurred before Old English was spoken in Britain. Second, the chronology has organized the facts.

A careful examination of the chronology will identify cause-and-effect relationships not perceived before and raise questions for further consideration. The researcher might note, for example, that the effect of the Norman Conquest on English was extreme. Such an invasion would probably not produce the same results today. While the Japanese adopted some American expressions and customs after World War II, their language did not go into hiding (as in a sense Anglo-Saxon did after 1066), their writers did not "convert" to English, and their language remained the norm for business, law, and commerce. Perhaps the printing press has made language capable of enduring an invader's tongue. Conversely, the printed word now affects language the way invasions once did; literature adds quotes, allusions, and new words, radically altering over time the way people speak and write. The researcher might observe that the Norman invasion was the last on British soil. Additional research may reveal that Norman military strength made the island secure or that the Christianization of Scandinavia "tamed" the Vikings. This close scrutiny of the chronology should also lead to a final editing of the facts. The poet Dunbar will probably be excluded from the essay because he, unlike Chaucer, did not write in the London dialect that would eventually become Modern English. The researcher now has collected, organized, and analyzed the information. Now the essay can be written.

The temptation when the student begins writing is to present the information in the order in which he or she organized it, chronologically, but a strict chronological essay runs the risk of being monotonous and predictable. The student should at least consider other structural options. In an essay on the history of the English language, the student could, for example, present information and assertions in the order of their importance, beginning with the influence of the Norman Conquest on the language. Or the writer might decide on a category-by-category structure, starting with the military influence, then going into the literary and technological ones. The essay could even limit itself to the three most important language changes, such as the introduction of new terms by Christianity, the Vikings, and the Normans, the standardizations brought about by the printing press and Johnson's *Dictionary*, and the elevation in the status of English brought about by Chaucer.

If the author decides a chronological structure is best, he or she will need to embellish the work to provide relief from the strict time sequencing of facts. Anecdotes, definitions of key terms, background information, and humor will bring life to the structure. (The essay could, for example, explain that Dr. Johnson's dictionary shows the author's prejudices. In one definition, he defines "oats" as a grain that in England is eaten by horses, but in Scotland, by the people.) Puns, comparisons, asides, and metaphors also can serve to make chronological information compelling. (The essay may note, for instance, that Shakespeare's plays have loosed a tempest of quotes and allusions on the language and filled the reservoirs of literature with themes and characters.) Subchronologies within the overall time sequence may also be used to explore key points further. (A paragraph or two on Chaucer's literary career will illuminate his success with Middle English while his competitors continued to labor in French and Latin.)

Through the use of film, students will be able to gain a sense of when time sequencing is appropriate for their work. Biographies, histories, and scientific works still use chronology because they are essentially time studies. *Evolution* and *The Sea behind the Dunes* are scientific chronologies; each, however, adds embellishments to stress insights and to gain appeal—the former with humor, the latter with artistic camera work and narration. Because it can provide an uncluttered background for facts, time sequencing is often effective when the subject itself is inherently dramatic. *Heartbeat of a Volcano* monitors the building pressures under the surface of Mount Kilauea, until it erupts. The events themselves are so tension-filled as to require little more than a bald chronology (the simple presentation of data without embellishments). Conversely, when the ideas are complex and the facts numerous, this uncomplicated structure allows the writer to spend more time on content. *Icarus Montgolfier Wright* uses three stories (two historical, one mythical) to unveil the philosophy and psychology of the quest to master the heavens. It is essentially a poetic work whose logic requires a great deal of viewer reflection. *Italian American* demonstrates that chronology can be employed for part of a work. While the opening of the film is loosely organized to establish the contentious characters of its two subjects, the Scorseses, the second half details their memories in time sequence to show the strength of their bond of old-world Italian traditions.

No writer can ignore chronology altogether, regardless of the form chosen. Even with a work of fiction that begins *in medias res* and employs frequent flashbacks and flashforwards, the reader must be able to reassemble events as they occurred. The author who fails to consider chronology at some point is ignoring a valuable tool and courting confusion in the audience.

HEARTBEAT OF A VOLCANO (Encyclopaedia Britannica: 20 min./color/ 1970)

Chronology is often the correct approach when dealing with science. Strict time sequencing helps the audience to assimilate a great deal of information and to identify causes and effects. When the subject is also inherently dramatic, chronology is all the more appropriate. *Heartbeat of a Volcano* is a case in point. Its presentation of scientific data is a bald chronology, a simple ordering of facts without embellishment. Even the narrator makes no attempt to convey emotion. He hardly needs to. Because the audience knows where the film is headed, they are riveted as the film follows Mount Kilauea (a volcano on the island of Hawaii) from its first tremors to the final explosion and reveals the workings of a volcano. The audience is rewarded as spectacular shots of the eruption provide a breathtaking experience.

The film's purpose is to educate. As such, it pays a reverence to the facts, presenting them in order of occurrence and in abundance. When frequent quakes follow four days after an initial eruption of Kilaueau, scientists go to its slopes for a closer look. Later, the volcano inflates, and hot gases and steam pour from vents in its surface. The caldera, the cone-shaped summit of a volcano, expands. Three days later there is increased lava activity. Pressure builds, and lava overflows the vents, but subsides after 15 minutes. The mountain is preparing for its blast. Soon, spatter cones spit lava all along the surface. The ground shakes with heavy tremors; the swelling of the mountain is too great to contain the pressure within.

The drama, unimpeded by anticipatory remarks or flights of poetic awe, comes to climax. Kilauea erupts violently for five hours. The fountain, the spray of lava that is shot into the sky, reaches 200 to 300 meters in height. Smaller vents open in order to release the inner pressure that is too great even for the caldera to displace. The cascade, the distance the lava falls from the height of the fountain to the ground, is around 500 meters, taller than the Empire State Building. After nine hours, the fountain begins to subside, and the lava later flows back into the vents. The volcano dies and a scene of immense turmoil grows still.

The camera need do no more than record the events; the narrator only has to keep the viewer informed with the necessary facts. The mountain—an inscrutable presence—does all the work. Kilauea's periodic ritual is captured by objective scientists. Their tilt triangles, geodimeter, geomodera, and seismometer (all of which are defined) record the data. The script carefully describes the volcano's parts and slowly reveals the chain of causes and effects that leads to the eruption. A great deal of information is presented painlessly, thanks to the filmmaker's insistence on strict time sequencing and his willingness to let the facts speak for themselves. When facts alone are enough to stimulate emotions, chronology and the restraint of a good filmmaker are all that are needed.

ACTIVITIES FOR THE STUDENT
1. The film is loaded with scientific terms. The following is a list of some of the most important ones.

caldera	harmonic tremor
vents	tilt triangle
spatter cone	geodimeter
fountain	geomodera
cascade	seismometer

In order to facilitate discussion of the film, define the words as soon as the film ends.

THE SEA BEHIND THE DUNES (Time-Life: 57 min./color/1981)
The Sea behind the Dunes employs chronology in perhaps its most appropriate setting: the study of nature and time. The film follows the complex yearly cycle of life in Pleasant Bay (Cape Cod, Massachusetts), 11 miles of barrier beach, salt marshes, and bay. It uses time sequencing to show the workings of cause and effect in nature (*see* "Cause and Effect," page 62) and to document seasonal change. The film also

demonstrates that chronology can simplify an involved topic, organize details, and provide a clear structure that allows for considerable verbal and visual embellishments, which give the work energy and appeal.

The complex chain of nature's causes and effects is a yearly cycle in Pleasant Bay. That chain depends on the spartani grass, which provides 8,000 tons of food yearly for the area's fauna. In March, when the film begins, the grass lies dormant and will remain so until May; the bay seems quiet and almost devoid of life. During March and April, the previous autumn's dead grass is harvested by recycling specialists like the tiny creatures called marsh shrimp. Their feeding attracts the minnows who bring in the larger fish. The alewives, which are fish, return from the sea to lay eggs in the freshwater ponds where they were themselves spawned; gulls flock to the stream to feed on them. In the spring, when the spartani grass begins to grow again, the once near-barren bay abounds with hundreds of species. The sea fills with plankton, whose abundance attracts larger marine life for feeding. As the waters warm during summer and food supplies further increase, more creatures are drawn in to breed. The terns lay their eggs on the barrier beach, and terrapins crawl overland for two days to hide their eggs in the sand. In September, life begins to decline. The terns prepare for southern migration; the alewife young make for the sea; the just-hatched terrapins crawl overland for the ocean. The winter follows with its stillness. Insect eggs lie dormant; minnows and crabs bury themselves in the sand. The ecology of the bay is a cycle of "life, death, and life again."

Within the yearly spin of seasons, the cycle of the moon and tides reveals the bay's ecology in even greater detail. When the tide recedes, the fiddler crab, which has gills that double as lungs, emerges to feed; when the tide rises, the grass sea cucumber forages for bits of decomposed spartani. During the conjunction of the full moon and high tide the exchange of food between the bay and the sea and the activity of animal life is greatest. The female horseshoe crab releases her scent, which draws the males on the concurrence of the highest tide of June and one of the longest days of the year. The eggs that she leaves in the sand will develop according to the tides and the phases of the moon.

Nature's complex cycles function with the precision of a Swiss watch. The film's chronological format organizes the details of the bay's life to make this precision apparent. The simplicity of the format also allows the filmmaker to add poetic touches. The camera lingers on Pleasant Bay's most exciting and beautiful creatures: the relentless hunting of the spider and the praying mantis, the frenzied feeding of the young terns by their parents, the delicate development of the moon jellyfish polyp into a mature adult, the intricate forms of the plankton and the minute pipefish. To augment the camera work, the narrator employs rhetorical devices such as metaphor and personification. Pleasant Bay is described as a "food factory" and an "incubator," the moon jellyfish as a "fluid bell." The changeable autumn weather is "a rogue," the praying mantis a "hunter of stealth and patience." The narrator does not reach for anger or drama with his voice, but rather deemphasizes the brutality through his understanding calm: the creatures are all struggling for survival, the victors must be viewed as triumphant heroes, the defeated are to be sympathized with.

Throughout, chronology provides structure and insight. Even the shape of Pleasant Bay follows cyclical laws. The land is constantly being carved by the sea. For all the changes in shape over the years, the coastline now looks almost exactly as it did around a century ago. In ancient times, the Greeks scanned the heavens to find poetry in harmoniously spinning planets, stars, and constellations. *The Sea behind the Dunes* looks closer to home for a similar beauty, an earthly music of the spheres.

———————

ICARUS MONTGOLFIER WRIGHT (Pyramid Films: 23 min./color/1962)

When a work's content is complex, chronology offers a basic structure that allows one to focus on theme and meaning. Made several years before the actual event, *Icarus Montgolfier Wright* (based on Ray Bradbury's short story) is a fantasy about man's first flight to the moon. Providing structural simplicity and historical perspective, the chronology blends the stories of Icarus' wings, Montgolfier's hot-air balloon, and the Wright brothers' airplane into an astronaut's dream sequence. In the process, poetic narration and symbolic animation illuminate the philosophical and psychological significance of the quest in outer space.

Astronaut Jedediah Prentiss, feeling alone and doubting his worthiness, suffers a fitful sleep on the night before the first moonflight. A voice haunts his dreams. It charges that his name is not grand enough for the deed he is about to perform. It then recounts the three stories in a continuous chronology. The filmmaker assumes that his audience knows the tales; the dream voice offers only the barest details of plot and character. The next morning, the astronaut assumes the name of Icarus Montgolfier Wright. No longer oppressed by the coming challenge, he confidently recounts his 3,000-year history to a reporter.

The narration is rich with puns, metaphor, personification, and hyperbole. "Thee sun or my son, the heat of the one, the fever of the other, could melt these wings," the mythic Daedalus says to Icarus, his child, a subconscious projection of man's obsession to master the heavens. Montgolfier says "I was right" as his balloon soars and the film shifts to the Wright brothers. The space rocket is later called "a combustible dream" that "speaks for three billion men." The animation is redolent with symbolism. The fierce sun above Icarus and the lightning and storm clouds that imperil Montgolfier's balloon represent nature at its most threatening. The swirling wind and sea of the Icarus story blend into the streaming heat that lifts Montgolfier's balloon. The motifs of sea and sky are repeated in the Wright brothers' tale, though the motifs are more tame, ready to be conquered by human invention. Prentiss is merely one representative of humankind's inner drive to master nature, a drive that unites all in the Nietzschean pursuit of knowledge and power. When the astronaut boards the rocket, his burden has been lifted. He is not alone.

The danger and drama of the first moonflight are not important here. Even the actual stories of Icarus, Montgolfier, and the Wright brothers take on a secondary importance. Details from each are sketchy; the film leaves out, among other things, the reason Icarus and Daedalus had to take to the air, and the doubts, struggles, and failures of Montgolfier and the Wright brothers prior to their historic achievements. The filmmaker's chronology includes only those details that contribute to the central issue in the film: his message, the astronaut's awareness. That awareness is both a philosophical and psychological one. Complex ideas cannot always be explored through involved plots and structures. When an author wants to rivet the audience's attention to ideas, images, and words, chronology provides a background of simplicity against which imagination and intellect can play. The work produced may not exhaust the viewers' emotions, but it should engage their minds.

ACTIVITIES FOR THE STUDENT

1. The film is rich with verbal devices (metaphors, puns, personifications, hyperboles, etc.) and with vivid images. Each deals with some aspect of the attempt to fly. Select an image and a verbal device from each of the three stories and fill in charts in your notebook modeled after those below. (The teacher will fill in the quotes in the second chart.)

Story	Image	Aspects of Flight
Icarus	The sun melts the wings.	The gods represented by the forces of nature are hostile to man's attempts to fly.
Montgolfier		
Wright Brothers		

Story	Quote	Verbal Device	Aspects of Flight
Icarus	"Thee sun or my son, the heat of the one, the fever of the other could melt these wings."	pun and metaphor	Man's desire to fly is reckless, potentially self-destructive.
Montgolfier			
Wright Brothers			

EVOLUTION (Learning Corp. of America: 11 min./color/1971)

Chronology is particularly useful for the study of any type of development. When dealing with Darwin's theory, time sequencing is perhaps the only possible structure, but evolution has been explored so frequently that one risks being redundant. The animated film *Evolution* is more than a chronological study. The filmmaker is aware that his audience is familiar with the theory. Thus, he reduces evolution to two or three steps and adds comic touches and irony to provide new insight.

There is nothing innately funny about evolution, as any dinosaur would surely assert. To find humor in it, one would think, requires a powerful leap of the imagination, which is exactly what the filmmaker has done. Following the evolutionary order of single- to multi-celled marine organisms, small to large fish, amphibious animals to warm-blooded mammals, man to those machines that allow man to become a super-man, he provides creatures that are comic parodies of the familiar forms. One fish, for example, has a propeller on its tail for locomotion. These grotesque shapes in the various stages of evolution are motivated by the same drives that Darwin identified. But, while Darwin's organisms are driven by the instincts for sex and survival to maintain life, those in the film are spurred on to absurdity. When the first amphibian flees the water to escape a predator, it hangs near the edge, panting. Soon this creature realizes that it is lonely and howls at the moon out of the longing for a mate. Like Darwin's work, the film shows that only the strongest survive, but this natural selection, nature's groping in the dark, is cruel and ridiculous. Among the varieties of creatures with bizarre forms of locomotion is one with square wheels. It falls when it tries to move, a definite candidate for natural liquidation: a blithely indifferent father squashes with his foot the unfit infant. "Give the poor thing a break," the viewer, no doubt, wants to say. The apes invent machines that are modeled after the peculiarities of earlier creatures on the evolutionary chain: one of the machines, for example, employs the fish propeller mentioned above. The machines culminate in war devices and vehicles for travel in outer space.

The filmmaker assumes that the viewer already understands evolution; the film can hardly be used to teach the theory. Except for the primate, the filmmaker deals with his creatures in only the most cursory manner, refusing to slow the chronology with well-worn details. Eliminating most of the detail from Darwin's chronology, he includes only those aspects of the theory (such as natural selection and the role of the instincts) that will allow him to explore its humor and absurdity. What he offers is wit, not science. Life is shown as a frantic diner whose stools are occupied by patrons so rapacious and frightening as to be laughable. Organisms survive in spite of their awkwardness and foolishness. The force that shaped them is almost an insult to the principle of trial and error. The viewer is ready to accept the world of the cartoon as earth because the jokes are mere exaggerations of life in our world. But the final joke, alas, is on the viewer. The film's planet is not his. One of the primates hurtles in a spaceship for a different planet, one with continent shapes that are ours. When he lands, the inhabitants speak in English. In our world humankind is no more than a hungry and egotistical master of a private evolution. Competing and superior life systems may one day feed on it. Almost as an afterthought, the last scene shows a giant bird devouring earth in one bite. Garnished with a fresh approach, the old chronologies are tasty morsels.

ITALIAN AMERICAN (Macmillan Films: 26 min./color/1974)

The strength of chronology is its potential for providing insight into events: their causes, their meaning, their significance. The weakness can be its structural rigidity; facts arranged one after the other according to time can lose their edge if the author is not careful. To be successful, a chronology must employ striking and significant details that draw attention away from the structure and lead to awareness in the audience. It is all the better if the details can be presented in an informal ambience. *Italian American* traces the history of Italian immigrants in the United States through the experiences of one family. Director Martin Scorsese records the reminiscences of his parents, Katie and Charlie. At first, they discuss their family background and Italian heritage in random details and generalities. No attempt is made to organize their remarks in a chronology. As if they are unaware of the camera's presence, the two spend more time arguing than giving information and seem to reveal more about their relationship than about Italians in general. This changes when Katie talks about her own parents and Scorsese, the interviewer, insists on a strict time sequencing of facts. Eventually, the couple emerges as a product of their Italian heritage. The film thus manages through the informality of conversation to suggest a chronology that provides insight and clarity.

The first half of *Italian American* is jarring, disconcerting. The Scorseses are an enigmatic couple. Katie is emotional, warm, and romantic, but gets annoyed when her husband, Charlie, is less than responsive to her affection. He is detached, argumentative, and plays on her feelings with irony and sarcasm, challenging her when, in his opinion, she allows sentimentality to cloud the truth. They have been married for years, but they bicker frequently and trade barbs mercilessly. Their disputes leave the viewer wondering about their marriage. Katie scolds her husband for sitting far away from her on the other end of the couch; begrudgingly and half-heartedly he moves a little closer to her. Charlie complains that his wife is "putting on airs" for the camera, trying to behave like an actress. When they argue about the tomato sauce she is preparing for a meal, Katie asks, "Do you want me to admit that your mother taught me to cook?" Her husband teases her by saying, "It has been known that a man is a better cook than a woman." He, however, does not prepare the food because "When I come home from work, that's it." To her remark that they don't talk anymore, Charlie pleadingly asks the camera, "What do you say to a woman you've known for 40 years?" The two argue about the wine Katie's father used to make, she insisting that he crushed the grapes with his feet, her husband that the man used a machine. After Charlie says that bars opened in their neighborhood as soon as the Irish moved in, his wife flees to the kitchen, so disgusted is she by what she construes as his racial slur.

This view of the Scorseses changes radically when they begin to give significant details of the past in a near-perfect chronology. Martin Scorsese asks his mother to "start at the beginning" when she discusses her own parents. She tells of their romantic courtship (begun when Katie's mother first saw, from her balcony in Sicily, the handsome blue-uniformed soldier on horseback), their first years in the United States (where they and 12 others shared a three-room apartment), and their many weeks apart when he traveled to find work. Katie's father enjoyed teasing his children; once he shaved off his handlebar moustache so that they would not recognize him when he returned from a week's labor away from home. He complained loudly after his daughters removed an old, worn picture of him from the living room wall so their boyfriends wouldn't have to see it. Later, when he died, however, the girls distributed copies of the picture to relatives so that they would not forget him. Charlie stops teasing his wife at this point and lends anecdotes to support her story. The two adopt complementary roles, she the romantic storyteller, he the chronicler of precise details. As he helps her recall the past, his affection for her parents emerges. Katie tells of the fig trees her mother hated, one of which her husband fell from when he was old. The mother cursed them hoping that they would die. When Katie recalls that they never bloomed again after her mother's death that winter, Charlie's face grows serious and sad.

On balance, Charlie and Katie Scorsese reflect their Italian-American heritage. Their relationship—as shown in the film's first half—with its arguing and teasing, affection and humor, epitomizes the Italian-American temperament and traditions. As with her parents' marriage, Katie is the heart and warmth of that relationship, Charlie, its wit and cool. *Italian American* demonstrates in its second half how chronology can be effectively employed: in an environment that is informal and as enigmatic as humans themselves are.

ACTIVITIES FOR THE STUDENT

1. The sections of a person's life can be divided into categories such as childhood, adolescence, young adulthood, middle age, old age. Using these as category headings, construct a chart for the couple and insert in the proper places the information given about them. Indicate what the filmmaker is trying to say about the lives of his parents. Discuss why he provided little or no information for certain categories.

FOLLOW-UP ACTIVITIES

1. In a humorous essay, discuss the key occurrences of the previous year as experienced by you, your family, or your school, and indicate whether it was a good or a bad year. Your writing may be structured chronologically, or according to the importance of each event. Whichever structure you choose, make sure your essay is clear enough that the reader can follow the time sequence.

2. Research a historical incident, such as Pearl Harbor, the battle of the Alamo, or the 1929 stock market crash, and write a "you are there" account. You may, for example, imagine that you are a participant in the event or that you have "behind-the-scenes" information on some of the key participants. As with any "you are there" account, your work must be structured chronologically, using time designations to indicate the precise hour (or even the precise minute) in which your scenes occur. You do not have to record, however, every detail or moment from your research. Include only those events that add to the tension of your narration.

3. Imagine that the following is the concluding event in a mystery story:

> The man reached into the case and pulled out a diamond
> ring. The woman behind him smiled.

Using the flashback technique, and beginning with this conclusion, tell a story in chronological order that leads up to this moment.

4. Chronology can be invaluable for note taking, especially if a writer is covering an event in progress. An essay based on such notes will need, however, to do more than just summarize what happened in chronological order. Occurrences often should be presented in the order of their importance, once the trivial events have been discarded. Cover one of the following:

   a. an awards banquet
   b. a guest lecture or a speech
   c. a school committee or a town council meeting
   d. a sporting event
   e. a television awards show

   Submit an outline of events as they occurred with an essay that presents only the key facts in order of importance.

5. Recall an anecdote based on a common occurrence such as your road test for a driver's license, your first day at work, a field trip with your class, etc. Since most people have had the same experience, you will have to strive to make your anecdote interesting and meaningful. Use techniques of embellishment (description, puns, humor, dialogue, metaphors, name calling, etc.) to make the chronology of details lively and significant.

Process

A September 1982 issue of the *New York Times Book Review* lists six "how to" books among the 15 most popular trade paperbacks in the country. If one subtracts the four Garfield the cat books, more than half the best-seller list is devoted to process writers, that is, to writers who excel at telling others in colorful, step-by-step fashion "how to" apply beauty aides, behave like an MBA (without attending business school), find a job, control their weight, achieve "personhood," and make love.

While these authors may be forgotten as soon as Americans abandon the "how to" craze, the demand for skillful process writers will endure. In technical fields, such writers are needed to compose assembly manuals and promotional literature—especially for computers—that make mechanical operations clear and simple for laypersons. More than one large firm hires instructors to teach executives to write clear and concise memos. In routine expository writing, it is often necessary for a writer to pause and explain how something is done. The September 13, 1982, issue of the *New Yorker*, for example, contains an article on geology by John McPhee that opens with a brief summary of how the crust of the eastern United States was formed, according to the theory of plate tectonics. Even Shakespeare, in *Hamlet*, had his young hero tell the traveling actors how to perform their play so that it would embarrass and enrage Claudius. The fact is that process writing is not an easy or trivial skill, but one that is called upon often.

"How to" writing should succeed on two levels: technical clarity and style. For the first, the writer must: 1) carefully consider what the audience needs to know, 2) plan the correct ordering of steps within the process, and 3) determine which key terms will need defining. These abilities come only with practice. Beginning with the simplest process writing—giving directions—the teacher might ask students to write out directions from the school to their houses for someone unfamiliar with the town. Remind students to include occasional landmarks (a church, a gas station, a tall hedge, etc.) for the reader to follow as well as street names and approximate distances. Next, have students explain in a few paragraphs how to perform one relatively simple task required in a sport or hobby they know well. Examples could be how to place kick, to thread a sewing machine, to remove and replace a spark plug, to braid someone's hair. Make certain that all jargon terms used within the sport or hobby are defined. After this, have students prepare oral reports in which they use props to explain a more complex process, such as reading the handicap form at a race track before choosing a horse to bet on, applying a splint to a broken leg, building a bench press, throwing a clay pot. Here, as in other exercises, students should be evaluated by the teacher and students on the degree of clarity they achieve.

Once students have learned to be sensitive to their audience, to define terms briefly, and to organize the presentation of their processes, they should move on to longer process essays where style is as important as clarity and the goal is to create interest, as well as to explain. By now, students will know that process writing can be tedious and exacting work. The danger, of course, is that occasionally the writer's boredom and annoyance will be conveyed to the reader. With a little work and creative planning, the writer can learn to convey enthusiasm for the process being explained.

The five films in this chapter were chosen because they have technical clarity and a winning style. Unlike mundane training films that show cooks how to make an omelet or soldiers how to march in formation, but that ignore their audiences' need for suspense, warmth, and beauty, these five films inform and intrigue. Although students may not be able to imitate them exactly in their own process writing, the films show the possibilities of the art form. The makers of *Problem Solvers* show four different professionals using the same process (the scientific method) in their line of work. The filmmakers bring this old process to life by showing the different ways it can be used. In *Solo* suspense is added to process when an expert mountain climber is shown risking his life on a dangerous climb. *Log House* adds warmth and humor to process by focusing on an eccentric carpenter and mason named Lionel Belisle. *Glass* combines editorial and process composition to assert that hand-blown glass is far superior to mass-produced glass. And *Metamorphosis* broadens our understanding and appreciation of nature's processes by drawing a parallel between a caterpillar transforming into a butterfly and a young girl turning into a woman.

A number of the films emphasize style to the point that they intentionally neglect to give the names of the tools or operations being shown. To aid the teacher, we have researched these subjects and provide these names in the film summaries. In one case, diagrams are included to make a carpentry process shown in the film clear to the reader. Teachers may wish to photocopy all or part of these summaries to show students what must be added to convey the film's information in print. Or teachers may ask students to research the names of the tools and processes shown in the film, as we did.

By the end of the unit, the student will approach future process assignments, even the odd process paragraph called for in a longer work, knowing the pitfalls and the possibilities of the art form. If the student has learned these process lessons, that odd paragraph will sparkle like the rest of a polished work instead of becoming the one dull spot in an otherwise glowing piece.

METAMORPHOSIS (Texture Films, Inc.: 10 min./color/1977)

Metamorphosis shows, in an unusual and dramatic way, the transformation of a tiny larva into a beautiful Viceroy butterfly. Unlike many scientific documentaries, this film eschews narration and the laboratory setting in favor of a more personal touch. We watch a young girl monitor the metamorphosis, viewing it for the first time in her own home as part of her ongoing investigation of nature's wonders. Along the way, we learn how to build a device for monitoring the final stages of the caterpillar's transformation.

The young girl lives near a lush field alive with small animals and insects. The camera briefly focuses on a spider, a frog, and some bees; in the background we hear birds singing. A stroll, which we assume is only one of many, takes the child to a weeping willow tree where she collects branches that hold several tiny, wormlike larvae which she apparently recognizes as the early insect form of the majestic Viceroy butterfly.

One glance around her bedroom shows us that the child is an avid natural experimenter. Every windowsill holds a different variety of plant: an ivy plant, a potato plant, even a terrarium in a jar. After a quick inspection of these prized possessions, what appears to be her first experiment with insects begins.

Inside a large jar she places the long willow branches that hold the larvae. Cheesecloth is draped over the top of the jar. Inside the habitat, the larvae grow into brightly colored caterpillars whose hairy spines quiver and twist as they feed voraciously on leaves inside the jar.

Soon, the caterpillars begin to encase themselves in silky, gooey cocoons that protect them during the pupal or inactive stage of their development. The young scientist oversees each stage of the metamorphosis, jotting down observations in a notebook. Once the cocoons are fully formed, she transfers one to a homemade gadget which will apprise her of the exact moment the adult butterfly begins to emerge from the cocoon.

This device, which she labels "Alarm System For Metamorphosis," is made by nailing a bare, Y-shaped tree branch to a board so that one flange of the branch rests about six inches above the board. A store-bought alarm is then secured to the board with screws. Next, two wires are connected to a large dry cell battery and run to the upper branch where they are coiled around it so that the stripped copper tips of each dangle close together just short of actually touching. One cocoon is then attached to the upper branch between the two wires so that, should the adult butterfly begin to wriggle free of its cocoon, this jiggling motion will cause the tips of the wires to touch and thus set off the alarm.

When the bell sounds, we and the young girl watch the dramatic emergence of the Viceroy butterfly. In closeup photography, we see the jet black antennae appear, followed by the kicking legs and then the orange and black wings which, still damp and crumpled, hang like flaccid, empty balloons. Soon the butterfly's wings dry and assume the delicacy and beauty of a Japanese silkscreen, and the girl, after wetting her finger in a sugar water solution, entices her new charge onto her fingertip. From there, the butterfly rides back outside into the field where it is set free to fly about on its own.

At the film's close, we are left with the impression that the girl was cast in the movie for a reason. She seems to identify with the caterpillar's metamorphosis because she, too, is about to make a similar transformation into womanhood. Through this parallel, we begin to appreciate metamorphosis as a process that all species in nature—plants, insects, animals, and humans—share in common.

PROBLEM SOLVERS (Churchill Films: 20 min./color/1974)

The scientific method—formulate a question, collect data, develop a theory, test it, and draw conclusions—is explored in this film as a process one should use to solve problems. Four problem solvers are shown at work: a furniture designer, an inventor of a device for the legally blind, an astronomy student, and a truck mechanic. All adhere to this time-honored approach, although two—the designer and the inventor—add to the process trial and error, creativity, and intuition. All believe that problem solving is difficult, yet rewarding, and insist that random guessing and impulsiveness are not enough; to solve a problem, you need a process.

The astronomy student and the truck mechanic follow the scientific method to the letter. The stargazer's work is abstract and often inconclusive. She hopes to determine the relationship between a star's chromosphere—an incandescent, transparent layer of gas around a star—and its age. Working with a university professor who serves as her advisor, she collects data using a giant telescope and a spectrum. With the telescope she monitors the heavens, taking pictures of selected stars from 9 p.m. until dawn. The spectrum is used to break starlight into its chemical elements. Large amounts of data culled from both instruments sometimes confuse her. Often she must think all day before discovering a pattern of meaningful observation from her information. Her ultimate goal is to publish a verified astronomical theory of her own. A little closer to earth, the truck mechanic uses the same process. To analyze each malfunctioning truck brought to him, he runs it on his dynamometer, a device that simulates for the engine the same load that it would pull going down the highway at various speeds. If listening to the sound of the engine does not indicate to him where the problem lies, he develops a list of areas to check. This is not mere guessing, he says, but an informed search based on many years of experience. By investigating each hunch or theory successively, the mechanic finds the engine's problem and fixes the truck. Curiosity is what motivates his problem solving, he says. When a solution is found, he feels satisfied.

The children's furniture designer and the inventor add a little mysticism to the scientific method. The first, who sets out to develop a new combination bed and couch, relies heavily on freewheeling trial and error, and intuition. He begins by sketching hundreds of furniture designs until a suitable one emerges. When this happens, he uses a wood cylinder the diameter of a storm drain pipe and a series of foam-rubber cylinders the size of baseball bats to build a mock-up. Following the chosen design first, he then improvises on it, always looking for the right combination that will best suit a child's sleeping and leisure habits. Once the prototype is finished, new problems inevitably emerge during its mass production. These "bugs" are also worked out in a trial-and-error fashion. Experimenting directly with materials, the designer says, allows theories to be quickly tested and rejected so that new and unforeseen possibilities can arise. Over the years, he has found that to engage successfully in this type of problem solving, he needs supreme confidence in his own abilities and intuition. Like the designer, the inventor ventures into the unknown to find solutions. He has just created a device that allows the legally blind to read and to write. To invent useful creations like this, he says, one must put oneself in the position of the person who will use it—either literally or in one's imagination. Unlike the first two problem solvers, he says that having a good idea is something one does not wholly plan. He begins by immersing himself in the problem the invention must solve. In this instance that was easy because he, too, is legally blind. Eventually, during the immersion phase an idea suggests itself, and this must be modified through persistent trial and error. Only then, he says, "something may happen in the mental processes so that things just come together." For problem solving in his line of work, the inventor offers two tips. First, you must be motivated by a feeling that what you are doing is really worthwhile. Second, you must not get too specialized in any one field. Otherwise, you may lose the broad outlook in both the sciences and the arts necessary to make the intuitive connections that lead to creative problem solving.

What this film shows, apart from good problem solving in action, is that a process is a guide, not a straight jacket. Process writing should make it clear to the reader that the steps offered are a general format that the individual should tinker with until it becomes his or her own.

GLASS (McGraw-Hill Contemporary Films: 11 min./color/1958)

This film combines process and opinion. It shows us how glass is hand blown by craftsmen and mass produced by machines. Although both processes are shown in detail, the amount of time devoted to glassmaking by hand and the type of music played during this segment of the film clearly show that the old-fashioned way is favored by the filmmaker.

Beer bottles and jars, as the film shows, are often made on high-speed assembly lines where machines do almost all the work. In staccato steps, various mechanical arms, air guns, and stamps turn out functional glass objects at an incredible rate. The men employed to watch the machine for malfunctions are all but superfluous. One scene shows an employee pick up a newly formed jar with tongs and touch it to his just-rolled cigarette for a light. This is meant to illustrate the worker's casual attitude toward the product he helps create. At another point, a mechanical arm that is lifting and transporting newly formed beer bottles grabs the top of one and snaps it off at the neck. The bottom of the bottle, which is left behind, creates a roadblock, and those bottles that follow crash to the floor, one at a time, until an attendant rushes in, shoves the congestion of bottles to the floor, and clears the line. During this scene, and others within the automated factory, dissonant music is played.

The footage of glassblowing is a study in contrast. It shows us seven glassblowers who make pitchers, wine glasses, figurines, and candelabra. While the camera carefully explores each step of the process, it focuses our attention on the individual style and grace of each craftsman. We watch them nimbly manipulate their blowpipes and fashion exquisite glass objects with the various tongs and tools of their trade. Even the glass drippings that fall from the molten blobs the men pull from the furnace leave a shiny spider's web that runs from the oven's door to the floor. The music played as we watch the glassblowers work—soft clarinet and piano jazz—seems to emphasize their artistry.

During these sequences, we are given a close look at the process of glassblowing. To begin, a small blob of glass from a blazing furnace is spun onto the end of a long, thin and hollow metal pipe. A short puff of air is then blown into the other end of the pipe to inflate the blob to a size commensurate with the shape of the desired object. Constantly twirling the pipe between his fingers, the artisan lowers the glass-bearing end of the pipe into a metal mold which can be opened and shut to enclose the glass while it is still held on the end of the blowing pipe. An assistant opens and closes the mold while the glassmaker continually blows into the other end of his pipe. The craftsman then removes the thinner and clearer glass bulb, examines it for imperfections, and trims or smooths away any excess edges with a tool that resembles metal shears.

A number of tools are used to embellish and refine the bulb of clear glass into its final shape. Sometimes, the still-cooling glass is further shaped by applying a fire-retardant cloth to it. The blower presses the cloth to the glass with one hand while he twirls the blowing pipe with the other. Tongs coated with a fire-retardant material and a metal spatula-shaped tool are also used to straighten and texture the glass while it is cooling. The bulb can be elongated by swinging the blowing pipe back and forth through the air. The metal tongs can also be pressed on either side of the bulb to squeeze it into a thin "neck." Features such as handles or stems can be added to the bulb of glass by affixing strips of red-hot glass and stretching them to the appropriate size with a pair of tongs. When each glass product is finished, it is gently disconnected from the pipe by an assistant and carried off with tongs or lightly gripped between two rods.

The film closes with a series of quick cuts back and forth between the craftsmen and the driving assembly line. The implication by this time is obvious: glassblowing is a time-honored art that must be preserved if beautiful glass objects are of any value to us; assembly-line glassmaking may be fine for functional glass products, but the price of relegating human beings to the role of unskilled automatons may be high.

_____

SOLO (Pyramid Films: 15 min./color/1972)

This film documents a one-day trek up and down a very large, snow-capped mountain by a solitary, expert climber. The photography is so lush and inventive and the climber so invigorated by his experience that even though this sport obviously demands a good deal of expensive equipment, know-how, supreme physical fitness, and tremendous courage, we feel mad enough to follow in the climber's footsteps. The filmmaker so moves us because he elevates process to an art. He shows the various rock- and mountain-climbing techniques by focusing on a Promethean figure who challenges fate in a story closely resembling an ancient myth.

As the film opens, we see the young, athletic climber—who wears only a red woolen cap, a white shirt, knickers, wool socks, climbing boots, and a knapsack—hiking through the foothills of a mountain range just as a full moon sinks and morning begins. A wolf is heard howling. The climber proceeds past a stream that, at some points, breaks into wild, cascading rapids. Soon, he is walking above the timberline and along a sheer rock ledge that passes a plummeting waterfall which feeds the stream far below. To hoist himself up a very steep rock face, he hammers pitons—small metal spikes fitted at one end with an eye or ring—into small cracks he finds in the wall. To these, he attaches karabiners, which are oblong, steel rings that snap into the eye of a piton. The karabiners hold a rope which in turn is attached to a harness worn by the climber. As the athlete begins to insert one particular piton into a small hole, he hears, then coaxes out of hiding, a tiny frog which he wraps in a piece of paper and inserts in his breast pocket. The next scene shows the entire rock face from a great distance as we hear what sounds like yodeling. The camera's lens zooms closer and we see a tiny dot swinging back and forth in a pendulum motion across the rock wall. When the climber finally emerges, we see that he is swinging at great speed back and forth across the rock face at the end of his rope which is secured high above him. As he runs from side to side of the wall, he occasionally pushes off with his feet and spins in circles at the end of his rope. This move, somewhat wildly executed here, is called a pendulum. Other rock climbing maneuvers he uses as he moves on include "jamming" and "climbing a chimney." To complete the first, he drives or wedges his hands into a crevice or crack in the rock to pull himself up a steep incline. In the second procedure, he moves up a narrow cleft between two giant rock slabs, as one would shinny up the inside of a chimney.

The first of two climaxes in the film—a brush with death—soon follows. The climber finds himself below an overhanging rock ledge that juts out away from the mountain wall about 15 feet. To overcome this obstacle, he drives pitons into the bottom surface of the ledge, attaches karabiners to them, and suspends a harness from the karabiners. With both feet in the harness, he begins to inch along the bottom surface of the overhang, moving the harness forward each time he inserts another piton and karabiner. Suddenly, one piton he has just hammered in falls out and plummets down and out of sight ringing at each bounce. A tense moment later, the next to last piton he inserted lets go and he falls. Luckily, though the harness gave way, the other pitons and his rope hold so that, apart from a bloody nose received when he crashed against the mountain, the climber is able to proceed. He regains his foothold by swinging back and forth at the end of his rope suspended beneath the ledge (the pendulum maneuver).

The second climax of the film occurs when he is forced to execute a lay-back to reach the very peak of the mountain. The summit is a large overhanging boulder that sits atop a rock wall where the climber is stopped. To perform the lay-back, the mountaineer leans away from the wall, grabs the edge of the overhanging boulder, which he obviously cannot see, and momentarily hangs, suspended full length from his outstretched arms. Then with a tremendous effort, he swings one leg to the side and up over the edge of the boulder. From this vantage point he launches himself onto the summit. Here, consistent with his courageous nature, he stands, arms extended, while the snow and wind howl and he rocks back and forth perilously close to falling or being blown from the peak.

The denouement shows the mountaineer literally running and somersaulting pell-mell down the ice cap, happy to have achieved his goal. He leaps across chasms and rappels down the rock faces. (To rappel, one uses a double rope passed under one thigh and over the opposite shoulder. By gripping and releasing the rope and bouncing his feet against the rock wall, he descends.) In no time at all, the climber is running and leaping through the foothills again where he finally splashes to a halt in a quiet pool of the stream. Here he releases the frog which swims off briefly only to return to the climber's hand. Soon, however, it ventures off on a solo of its own, and at the film's close the camera pans across the entire mountain range aglow now in the orange flush of sundown.

Solo does more than inform, it inspires. It is proof positive that process writing, like process films, can be more than plodding, unimaginative, and objective exercises. With it, the writer can teach processes and define specialized equipment and convey a love of the field at the same time.

LOG HOUSE (Bullfrong Films: 27.30 min./color/1979)

This film does more than show us how to build a log house; it inspires us to emulate a whole way of life, a life in the country where peace of mind can be found in the traditional values of independence, artistry, hard work, and a close-knit family. Lionel Belisle, an elderly and affable carpenter, assisted by three men from another family, builds a log cabin from trees felled in the forests of Morin Heights, Quebec. Watching Belisle work, we gain considerable knowledge about the many processes needed to build a log cabin and considerable respect for his skill and ingenuity. By the time the four men have finished—they hold a small square dance inside their new dwelling as snow falls outside—we feel tempted to pull up stakes from the city, town, or suburb where we live to build our own log cabin deep in the forest.

When the film begins, it is autumn and Belisle is selecting from the forest those trees that are long and thick enough to be cut by chain saw for the log house. Throughout the film the few words spoken are in French. We, like the three apprentices, learn by watching Belisle work. Like all good teachers, he loves his work. He sings, clowns around in front of the camera, and teases his protégés as they haltingly follow his instructions.

Each tree, about one foot in diameter, is felled and stripped of its branches with a single-bladed ax that has a hammerhead opposite the blade. Belisle measures each log to a uniform length using a branch as his yardstick, then cuts it with the chain saw. These logs are dragged one at a time by horse and stacked up off the ground in a clearing. Two logs function as the base across which the timber is piled. The logs are then left to age until winter, when Belisle and his helpers transport them via horse-drawn sled to the vicinity of the cabin site where they are again stacked in the same fashion and allowed to age until early spring. During these early stages and throughout the building, a peavey, a tool with a long wooden handle that grips with a metal point and a hinged hook at the other end, is used by the men to handle the logs.

Once the ground thaws, the foundation is built. A hole is dug and a plywood rectangular frame is constructed and placed down in the hole about two feet inside the dirt walls. Between the wood and the edge of the hole, Belisle erects a stone foundation which is approximately a foot thick. Cement is used to bind the rocks his assistants carry from the forest. The wooden rectangle, up against which he stacks the foundation, keeps the rock wall straight and square.

The logs are then dragged to the foundation and stacked atop each wall, one at a time, so that their ends overlap at the corners. Each log is notched so that it fits snugly over the one it crosses. To do this, Belisle secures each newly hoisted log over the one it will cross with a gadget that resembles a large staple. It measures about one foot across and has two sharp points. One end of the staple is hammered into the top log and the other into the bottom log at the corner of the foundation (*see* figure 1, page 60). Belisle then measures with a small twig the amount of space showing between the two logs and draws, with a red marker, a crescent this height into the top log (*see* figure 2). The staple is removed, the top log rolled over, the staple is replaced, and the crescent chopped out with the chain saw and ax. The saw is used to cut several vertical slices into the crescent, then the ax is used to knock out these chips (*see* figures 3 and 4). The staple is once more removed, the top log is rolled over again, and with a bang it clamps tightly onto the log beneath it, leaving only a small space between the two (*see* figure 5). In this fashion, the four walls rise. To hold each log in place, a piece of bristly felt resembling woven horsehair is put between each crescent and the log below it, and foot-long nails are driven through each log into the one beneath it at several points along its length.

A steeply sloped roof is begun by notching, in several places, the top logs of the walls on two sides of the house. New logs are then placed in the notches so that their other ends rest on a cross-beam log nailed in earlier, which forms the peak of the house. These ceiling logs are then secured at both ends, and sheets of plywood are nailed down over the roof of logs to form a smooth surface. Next, two-by-fours are nailed into the plywood at three-foot intervals, and strips of wooly insulation are unrolled to fill each resulting trough (*see* figure 6). A second layer of plywood is then added to this and wooden shingles called shakes nailed on the top of that. To complete the roof, the builder shellacs the shakes with a sealant.

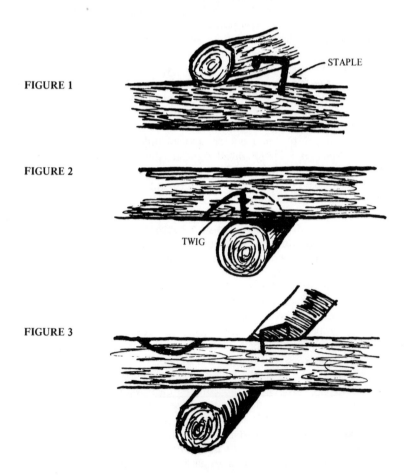

FIGURE 1   STAPLE

FIGURE 2   TWIG

FIGURE 3

FIGURE 4

FIGURE 5

FIGURE 6

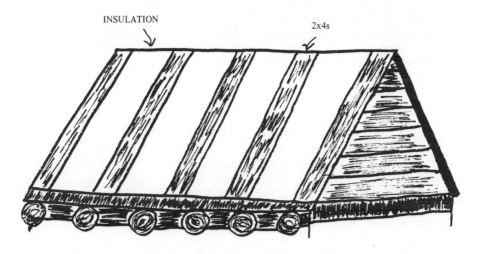

Drawings by Margaret Dineen.

Rectangular holes in the walls for windows and doors are created with a flick of the chain saw, and prefabricated window and door frames are hammered into place after the top and bottom log of each hole is leveled off with an ax. Belisle next constructs a beautiful stone and cement fireplace whose chimney begins at the foundation and rises to just above the peak of the house. Inside this stone shell, the carpenter and mason install a heatalator unit, the prefabricated metal guts of the fireplace. In what will be the kitchen, Belisle fashions shelves and a wooden frame that will support a prefabricated sink and counter. Using a caulk gun, an assistant applies caulk to the spaces between each log and door or window frame for added insulation.

At the end of the film, when we see the family and friends of Belisle dancing inside the new cabin as he plays the fiddle, we share the builder's sense of satisfaction. *Log House* succeeds where other process films have failed because it focuses on Belisle to convey its technical information and because it does so with enthusiasm for the lifestyle of those who do this kind of work. By personalizing the processes of cabin building, without unduly romanticizing or exaggerating its rewards, the filmmakers show that warmth, humor, and depth can be conveyed through process without sacrificing clarity.

FOLLOW-UP ACTIVITIES

1. In a sense, each of the films is a "field of interest" essay in which the enthusiast tells the audience how to do something he or she loves doing. Students can do this, too, by taking a field of interest they participate in—cross-country skiing, jogging, gourmet cooking, car customizing, etc.—and trying to "hook" others on it. Introductions to these process essays of three to five pages must really "talk up" the field, explaining to the reader what it has meant to the writer's life, how long the writer has been a fanatic, what the field can do for others, and what kind of person would most enjoy it. Within the body of the essay, the student should explain how to perform the three to five most basic operations that any beginner should know right away. Such paragraphs could even offer some inside information known only to an aficionado, such as how to buy the best or most inexpensive equipment, where to find the best playing field, what to wear, or how to maintain one's equipment. Finally, in the conclusion of the essay, the student should offer the beginner encouragement, explain how long it will take to get good in the field, tell where to find books that will explain more advanced techniques, and add any last-minute tips the reader should keep in mind. Throughout the essay, the student must work hard to spice up the writing with a wide variety of transition words (*see* "Refining the Message," page 198) and even throw in a joke or two.

Cause and Effect

Cause-and-effect reasoning is a skill that takes a short time to learn but a lifetime to use well. Many of us, in fact, never manage to apply dispassionately the straightforward and simple logic of cause and effect to the important decisions we make in our own lives. Even a novice, however, can greatly improve the quality of his or her thinking and writing by learning to use cause-and-effect reasoning to organize and to follow through on his or her ideas.

Approached for the first time, cause and effect is easier understood and practiced when aspects of chronology (*see* "Chronology," page 42) also are introduced. For the sake of simplicity, cause-and-effect reasoning can be divided into three common patterns (or relationships) that correspond to past, present, and future time. Pattern 1 is forward looking. In it the thinker begins with a current condition and asks what the future effect(s) of that condition will be. In other words, he or she predicts the future based on an existing situation.

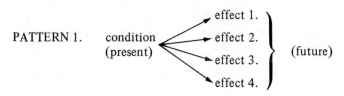

PATTERN 1.   condition (present)   →   effect 1. / effect 2. / effect 3. / effect 4.   (future)

Pattern 2 is backward looking. In it the thinker begins with a current effect and asks what the past condition(s) were that led to it. In other words, he or she reconstructs the past based on an existing situation.

PATTERN 2.   (past)   condition 1. / condition 2. / condition 3. / condition 4. → effect (present)

Pattern 3 is both forward and backward looking. In it the thinker begins at any one point along a chain of events and asks what the past conditions were that led to that one event *and* what the future effects of that event will be. In other words, like a domino player, the thinker picks any one of a long line of dominoes and looks backward to discover what caused the domino in question to fall *and* looks forward to discover what will happen after the domino in question has fallen.

PATTERN 3. ...condition ⟶ effect (condition) ⟶ effect (condition) ⟶
⟶ effect (condition) ⟶ effect (condition) ⟶ effect...

Even though it is not easy to find a passage in which a writer uses only one of these cause-and-effect patterns at a time, it is essential that students examine and analyze at least a few undiluted selections before graduating to longer selections where several of the patterns are used simultaneously. Students should identify the pattern at work in each of the selections that follow, then use the diagram to outline the steps in the author's argument. After each passage, hypothetical samples will be used to reinforce the students' understanding of each pattern.

In 1965, Isaac Asimov, scientist and science fiction writer, used pattern 1 to predict what our world would be like in 1990. Asimov believed that the United States and the world would witness many changes by 1990 because of the then current population explosion. An analysis of Asimov's short essay, "The World of 1990" (in *Is Anyone There?* [New York: Doubleday and Co., 1965]), might look something like this (*see* page 64):

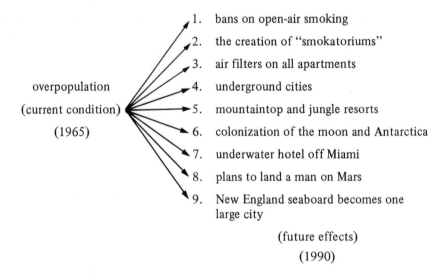

overpopulation

(current condition)

(1965)

1. bans on open-air smoking

2. the creation of "smokatoriums"

3. air filters on all apartments

4. underground cities

5. mountaintop and jungle resorts

6. colonization of the moon and Antarctica

7. underwater hotel off Miami

8. plans to land a man on Mars

9. New England seaboard becomes one large city

(future effects)

(1990)

Hypothetical examples of pattern 1 are offered below. If examples more topical and relevant to the students' school and community can be substituted, all the better.

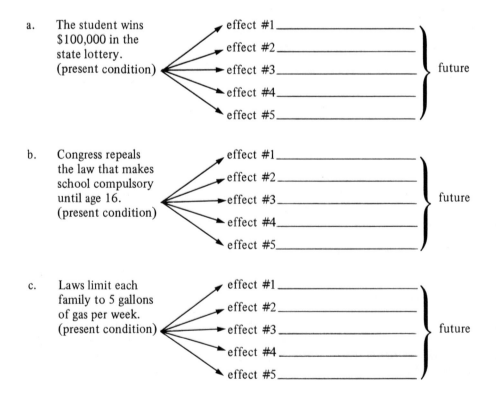

a. The student wins $100,000 in the state lottery. (present condition)

effect #1_____

effect #2_____

effect #3_____

effect #4_____

effect #5_____

future

b. Congress repeals the law that makes school compulsory until age 16. (present condition)

effect #1_____

effect #2_____

effect #3_____

effect #4_____

effect #5_____

future

c. Laws limit each family to 5 gallons of gas per week. (present condition)

effect #1_____

effect #2_____

effect #3_____

effect #4_____

effect #5_____

future

In 1962, a boxer named Benny Paret was killed in the ring. In the twelfth round, he was punched repeatedly in the head, went down, was counted out, and was pronounced dead a week later. A number of official investigations into the tragedy followed. Unsatisfied that these had uncovered the real cause of the fighter's death, Norman Cousins, writing in the *Saturday Review* (May 5, 1962), claimed that Paret had died simply because the human skull cannot protect the fragile brain from continual pounding. Cousins' short article, which uses pattern 2, can be analyzed in the following way. (The Cousins selection was originally used to teach cause and effect in *Concept and Statement* [Glenview, IL: Scott, Foresman, 1974], pp. 223-29).

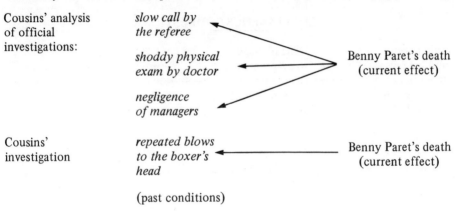

Cousins' analysis of official investigations:

slow call by the referee

shoddy physical exam by doctor → Benny Paret's death (current effect)

negligence of managers

Cousins' investigation

repeated blows to the boxer's head ← Benny Paret's death (current effect)

(past conditions)

Some hypothetic practice examples of pattern 2 are printed below.

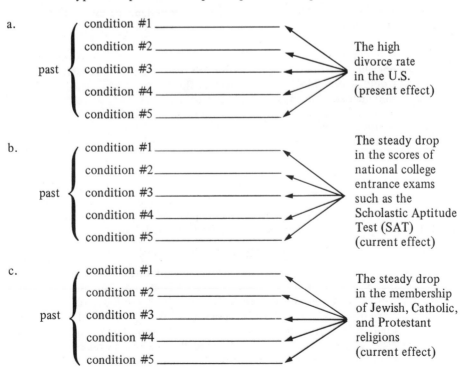

a.

past { condition #1 _____ → condition #2 _____ → condition #3 _____ → condition #4 _____ → condition #5 _____ →

The high divorce rate in the U.S. (present effect)

b.

past { condition #1 _____ → condition #2 _____ → condition #3 _____ → condition #4 _____ → condition #5 _____ →

The steady drop in the scores of national college entrance exams such as the Scholastic Aptitude Test (SAT) (current effect)

c.

past { condition #1 _____ → condition #2 _____ → condition #3 _____ → condition #4 _____ → condition #5 _____ →

The steady drop in the membership of Jewish, Catholic, and Protestant religions (current effect)

The clearest examples of pattern 3 often are found in scientific and historical texts. One passage from each discipline is reprinted and analyzed below. The first comes from *Firemanship*, a pamphlet in the Boy Scouts of America Merit Badge Series ([Irving, TX: Boy Scouts of America, 1981 printing of 1968 revision], p. 23), and is diagrammed here according to the pattern. The series explains how a household fire can begin from "spontaneous combustion." It may surprise students to see that once the initial condition exists—"a pile of oily polishing rags" left in a closet—a chain reaction of effects and causes can result, leading to the final effect, a major household fire.

SPONTANEOUS COMBUSTION

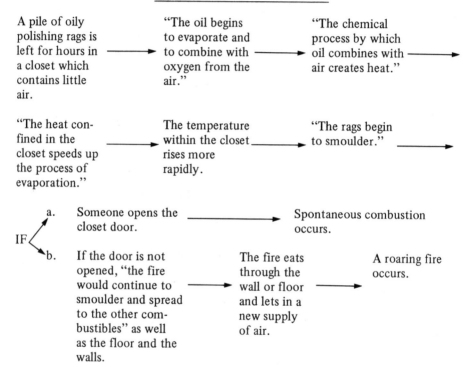

The second passage, drawn from a history textbook (T. Harry Williams, Richard N. Current, and Frank Freidel, *A History of the United States to 1877*, 2nd ed. [New York: Alfred A. Knopf, 1964], pp. 242-43), describes the series of events that led up to the Industrial Revolution in the United States.

THE INDUSTRIAL REVOLUTION

In part, the new technology came from England, where the Industrial Revolution was beginning at the time the American Revolution occurred. The essence of the Industrial Revolution was simply this: more rapidly and extensively than ever before power-driven machines were taking the place of hand-operated tools. To tend the machines, workers were brought together in factories or mills located at the sources of power. New factory towns arose, with a new class of dependent laborers and another of millowners or industrial capitalists. The factory system was adapted most readily to the manufacture of cotton thread and cloth. . . . Water, wind, and animal power continued to be used but began to be supplemented and replaced by steam. Especially was this true after the appearance of James Watt's steam engine (patented in 1769) . . . .

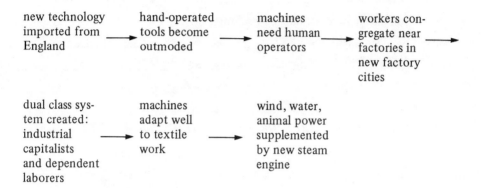

new technology imported from England → hand-operated tools become outmoded → machines need human operators → workers congregate near factories in new factory cities →

dual class system created: industrial capitalists and dependent laborers → machines adapt well to textile work → wind, water, animal power supplemented by new steam engine

PRE-FILM ACTIVITIES

One caution about cause-and-effect reasoning: it is easy to misuse. Before the final written activity of the lesson, students should come to appreciate how easy it is to create spurious cause-and-effect relationships in which the connections they make in pattern 1, 2, or 3 are either tenuous, hyperbolic, or downright false.

1. What better area is there to observe cause-and-effect reasoning gone astray than advertising? The students should look for ads in magazines that have a text in addition to a picture. They should analyze the chains of effect using pattern 3, and be careful to note implied as well as stated causes and effects. The students could note, for example, that an ad for a house-cleaning product might show a woman who not only gets a cleaner house (stated), but also receives attention and praise from husband, friends, or neighbors (implied). Once the students have finished, they should describe how cause-and-effect reasoning has been misused by the advertisers and state what each advertiser hoped to gain through the ad.

2. Finally, students should complete a cause-and-effect assignment that calls for the use of patterns 1 and 2. Have them write an essay that includes: a) a cause-and-effect evaluation of an administrative step that has been taken in the past at their school to reduce one of the following school problems: vandalism, truancy, tardiness, or unexcused absences; b) a discussion of the three chief causes of the school problem they have chosen; c) a presentation of a new and original approach to the problem; and d) a prediction of how that new approach will work on the student body. Before writing the essay, each student should submit an outline containing four cause-and-effect diagrams and a single paragraph describing their proposed solution to the problem. A model of this outline is given on page 68.

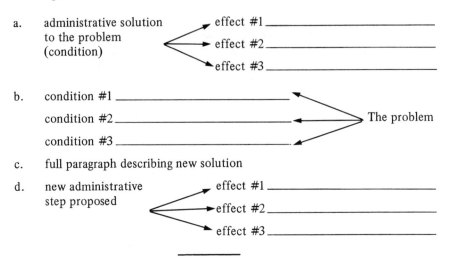

a. administrative solution
    to the problem
    (condition)

    effect #1 _____
    effect #2 _____
    effect #3 _____

b. condition #1 _____

    condition #2 _____   The problem

    condition #3 _____

c. full paragraph describing new solution

d. new administrative
    step proposed

    effect #1 _____
    effect #2 _____
    effect #3 _____

YOUR CREDIT IS GOOD, UNFORTUNATELY (Pyramid Films: 10 min./ color/1976)

Your Credit Is Good, Unfortunately is a parable about credit told twice over: first in a worst-case scenario, then in a best-case scenario. The first time through, the heroes, a young couple named Gilbert and Gloria Gully, make a number of mistakes that lead them into debt. On the instant replay, the Gullys avoid the allure of luxurious possessions and live happily within their means. The moral also is given twice: "Don't go in hock today for what you can buy tomorrow," and "Raindrops can fall on anybody's head, but don't be your own rainmaker."

The story, which is told by the narrator while the young couple act it out, is about people who act rashly without considering the consequences. In take number one, the Gullys discover one evening that their refrigerator is broken. This small tragedy sends them out to dinner and then to shop for a new one. Offered both a small model, like the one they owned, and a larger, deluxe model, the Gullys choose the latter, opting to buy it on a weekly installment plan. Falling prey to a clever salesman even further, the couple purchase, on credit, a washer, dryer, and convertible sofa, which are all on sale. When the two sign the credit contract, they neglect to put a line through a blank space at the bottom. Later, when the goods are delivered, they are charged $22.00 for delivery, (the salesman added a sentence about delivery after they left the store), and the Gullys are forced to surrender their grocery money. Three months pass and the two are swamped with bills, which in turn cause tension and fights between them. Finally, since they are unable to pay their debts, the store repossesses their new refrigerator, sofa, washer, and dryer.

Given a second chance by the lenient narrator, the Gullys proceed more wisely. This time they settle on the small refrigerator and pass up the salesman's glittery offers. This time they have the salesman fill in the blank at the bottom of the credit contract with a promise of free delivery and installment. And, this time, even though Gloria's job is cut back unexpectedly to three days a week soon after their purchase, the Gullys, who now have a little money put aside for a rainy day, keep their new appliance, remain safely out of debt, and avoid the arguments that money problems caused earlier.

To convey its moral, the film relies heavily on the third cause-and-effect pattern: chain of events. In the first scenario, the couple's opening mistake leads them step by step into greater and greater problems until they are on the brink of poverty and divorce. In the second scenario, the Gullys' initial good sense and restraint keep them solvent, even when Gloria's salary is cut back. The message is inescapably plain at the end of the chains: credit is neither something to be afraid of, nor something to be abused. For those in the know, credit is good, fortunately.

THE FAMILY THAT DWELT APART (Learning Corp. of America: 8 min./ color/1973)

The Family That Dwelt Apart is a down-Maine tall tale about the mess a few do-gooders and city folk can make of a country boy's simple and happy life. Exaggeration and the deadpan voice of author and narrator E. B. White contribute to the film's black humor. Although White's voice expresses no sympathy for the Pruitts, the story's victims, the real butts of the satire are the prying do-gooders and media people who do not know when to leave well enough alone.

The members of the Pruitt family lead a solitary existence in their dwelling on a small island off the coast of Maine. Subsisting on canned foods and pressed duck, the clan enjoys a simple life, summer and winter. According to the narrator, "they like the island and live there from choice." One severe winter, the bay freezes and the Pruitts are marooned. They hardly notice, however, because they go ashore only occasionally to collect their mail, "which is entirely second class." Soon, a busybody on the mainland realizes the Pruitts are stranded out there and sounds the alarm. This touches off a zany and unlikely sequence of events that leads inexorably to the death of all but one of the Pruitts and a score of others. As soon as the chief of police is notified, he calls the army and the press. The army dispatches three bombers which, much to the Pruitts' surprise, drop dried foods on the island. Taking matters into his own hands, the police chief, who has heard a false rumor that one of the Pruitt sons has acute appendicitis, calls for a dogsled team to be sent via plane from New Hampshire. Meanwhile, he dispatches a squad of troopers to the rescue across the frozen bay. They fall through the ice and die. Ice that forms on the wings of the plane carrying the dogsled is solid, though, and this, plus the dog bone that gets lodged in the plane's control stick, sends the craft down, killing all men and animals on board. Not, however, before another dog bone falls out of the falling plane and strikes the head of a boy walking through Stamford, Connecticut. He is killed instantly. A helicopter chartered by a news service then lands on the island to inform Mr. Pruitt that his eldest son is ill. In spite of his protests to the contrary, the boy is removed and operated on in Maryland. Meanwhile, another plane containing a surgeon, two nurses, and a radio reporter lands on the island. The second son is operated on for appendicitis while the reporter gives a blow-by-blow account on the air. The operation is a success, but the boy eats a piece of dried fruit too soon after surgery and dies. When the oldest son recovers and returns to the island by boat in the summer, he finds the house burned to the ground and the family dead. It turns out that the house caught fire when a flare, dropped from one of the departing planes, landed on the porch. The family, desperate for shelter, moved into an emergency shed thrown up by the radio announcer. There they survived until Mr. Pruitt and the family drank from a bottle containing a 10% solution of carbolic acid which they mistook for alcohol. After burying the members of his family, the boy heads for the mainland where he will begin a new life alone.

To achieve humor, E. B. White hyper-exaggerates cause-and-effect pattern 3, chain of events. Once the initial alarm over the Pruitts is sounded, a monolithic line of dominoes falls, each piece more tragic than the last, without a moment's reprieve. Apart from making fun of cause and effect itself, White's joke underscores some painful truths. Careless rumors can snowball until they become outrageous lies. Do-gooders have been known to interfere and to impose remedies that are far more destructive than the ills they were meant to eliminate. And colossal misunderstandings between groups of people with different values (black versus white, country versus city, communist versus capitalist) can result when mole-hill-sized misunderstandings go unchecked.

Snowbound, Friend or Foe, and *The Shopping Bag Lady* all feature teenagers as main characters. Each protagonist suffers through a painful ordeal that causes him or her to shed some of the egocentrism of youth. Initiations used in values clarification films such as these rely heavily on cause-and-effect relationships. As the heroes come to see the inappropriateness of their selfish behavior, they generally adopt a broader, more mature perspective on life.

SNOWBOUND (Learning Corp. of America: 33 min./ color/1977)

Tony and his girlfriend Jeanine possess three qualities most treasured by high school students: good looks, popularity, and wealth. As the two argue at a skating rink at the beginning of *Snowbound* over when they will leave to attend a party, it is clear that both are spoiled, inconsiderate, and stubborn. Cindy, a short, pudgy, and unfashionably dressed teen, gets caught in the middle of their argument as Tony uses her to make Jeanine jealous. In a moment of pique, he declines to take his girlfriend to the party at all, and offers, instead, to drive Cindy, whose bus is late, to a nearby town where she is to meet her grandmother. (Jeanine, meanwhile, calls another boyfriend for a ride.) Cindy accepts the ride, though she clearly understands the lack of sincerity behind the offer.

When Tony, Cindy, and her dog arrive at the turnpike entrance in his Volkswagen, they are barred from entry because a blizzard is raging and he does not have snow tires. Playing the bravura role to the hilt, he suggests they circumvent the turnpike by taking a road through the state park, despite indications that the weather is worsening. Once on their way, Cindy begs him to turn around when it is obvious they have become lost on the remote forest road. He ignores her, however, and soon they skid off the road and crash into a tree. Tony blames Cindy for the accident, saying she grabbed the steering wheel, though when she did so the car was already skidding out of control. In his rage he calls her "fatso" and says she's "weird." She fires back by calling him a "goon."

During the next few days, Tony consistently makes poor decisions about strategies they should adopt to survive, and it becomes obvious that Cindy has the cooler head under pressure, the greater courage, and a more ready intelligence. Tony suggests they wait during the first day for a snowplow to come by. Cindy doubts one will, and eventually she is proven correct. Cindy collects wood while Tony searches the area. She lights a fire by touching some damp matches she has to the car's cigarette lighter. When he returns from the search, Tony does not tell Cindy he has discovered the road they skidded off is closed for the winter and therefore will not be plowed. His motive is not a chivalrous regard for the weaker sex, but his own fear of facing up to the facts. The two rely for sustenance on a few Oreo cookies Cindy has at the bottom of her bag, although at one point Tony shares some canned dog food with Cindy's pet. That night a pack of wild dogs attacks the car. Tony panics, though the two are both relatively safe inside. Cindy cleverly thinks to honk the car's horn to scare them off. Next morning the two leave the car, despite Tony's reluctance to do so. Toward the end of the day, they spot a snowmobile rider in the distance, but they fail to attract his attention. Overanxious to flag the snowmobiler, Tony falls down a steep embankment and hurts his leg. Cindy claims it is only sprained; Tony insists it is broken. Cindy helps him as they move on, acting as a brace for him to lean on. The two find an abandoned shack where they spend the night warmed by another makeshift fire. Here the two have their first real conversation as equals when they exchange anecdotes about their past. Tony confesses to having let down a friend who tried to confide in him while dying in the hospital. Cindy says her mother died a few years ago and explains that she is writing in her diary a fond farewell to her father, who, though gruff with her sometimes, must have found it hard "to bring up a weirdo like me." In an effort to cheer her up, Tony tells her that maybe she is not so weird after all. Suddenly, the pack of wild dogs that threatened them earlier returns and Cindy's little dog runs outside after them. She pursues carrying a fiery stick, but is too late; her pet has been killed. Next morning she is stonily quiet as she prepares a splint and walking stick for Tony's leg. He complains his foot is too sore and refuses to move, saying melodramatically that their whole predicament is his fault and asking to be left alone to die. Cindy demands he stop feeling sorry for himself and asks that he help for a change. She calls him gutless and leaves. He eventually follows her and late that night the two find themselves back at the car. They have wandered full circle. All is not lost, however, as they see that rescuers have discovered the car and have gone off to find them. Soon a helicopter passes overhead and thinking quickly, Cindy sets the car on fire and they are spotted and rescued.

A number of cause-and-effect strands make this film work. On a simple level, Tony's decision to give Cindy a ride and rashly to risk the mountain road (effects), are caused by: his attempt to pay Jeanine back, his lack of consideration for others' feelings (i.e., Cindy's), and a belief that he must live up to his "big man on campus" image. On a subtler level, Cindy's strength of character in adversity (effect) and Tony's weakness and tendency to panic (effect) can be explained by the very different conditions of their backgrounds. Cindy has learned how to survive as a social outcast and a child without a mother. She has a poor self-image, but has learned how to fight for the little attention she gets and to fend off unfair attacks. Tony, on the other hand, has led a charmed life. He normally gets everything he wants, even when he is inconsiderate, and the only response he has learned to denial is a temper tantrum. By the end of the film, both Cindy and Tony have grown (effects). When Cindy appears at the hospital, she looks better kept and more self-assured. Jeanine, also there to visit, immediately tries to exclude Cindy by giving Tony a kiss and by starting a private conversation. Cindy does not do a slow burn when she is snubbed by Jeanine, nor does she blame herself for the event. Rather, she feels proud she has acted more maturely. Tony, too, has learned. He no longer acts as if Cindy is just another awestruck member of his fan club, but treats her as an equal and a friend. He brushes the cruel and petty Jeanine aside as well as he can and begs Cindy to stay, showing us that he no longer values himself above all else in life.

––––––––

FRIEND OR FOE (Learning Corp. of America: 26 min./color/1975)

The character lineup in *Friend or Foe* reminds one of the setup commonly used in old cartoons to show the lead character's momentary moral dilemmas: a good angel is shown perched on one of his shoulders, a bad angel on the other. Here the young protagonist, Jim, finds himself caught between a kindly older woman named Else and a juvenile delinquent named Johnny. Eventually the young hero learns by way of this dilemma that he must choose his friends carefully, even if this means accepting loneliness for a time.

Jim's family moves to an unfamiliar section of London when his father is transferred. Having no friends, the boy is eager to fall in with Johnny, the first young tough he meets. Johnny rides an expensive new Honda motorcycle which he bought on credit and can barely afford. Jim works part-time for a firm that does painting and light construction. One day Jim meets Else while delivering to her his firm's estimate on the cost of redecorating her apartment. Once there, Jim notices solid silver cups and plates that Else's husband, now dead, won as a fisherman. (Earlier, to impress Johnny, Jim said he would keep his eye out for capers that would result in a little spare cash.) Else is somewhat taken aback by the price estimate, but she agrees to think it over and invites Jim back. Jim presents the following plan to Johnny later: Else will visit her sister in southern England while the work is being done. She will give Jim the spare key to her apartment so he and the other workmen can get in. Jim and Johnny will let themselves in after hours and steal the cups and plates. On Jim's next visit, the plans are dashed when Else says the estimate is too high and puts off the work. Desperate not to let Johnny down, Jim steals the spare key while Else's back is turned. She is busy in the kitchen preparing food for the boy because she feels guilty about declining the redecoration.

Over cake and tea, the two strike it off when they discover they are both suffering from loneliness. He is shy and new to the area; she is stuck in an impersonal, high-rise apartment building. Touched by the boy's predicament, Else takes him on a shopping junket. Jim enjoys the older woman, but feels ashamed when her comments unwittingly remind him of the planned heist and his friendship with Johnny. When Else sees Jim admiring her husband's trophies just before the two leave, she says, "I couldn't sell them. There are some things worth more than money, you know." Later she compliments Jim saying, "You're a nice young lad, not like some of these modern tearabouts." While shopping in an open-air market, Else, acting on a whim, buys Jim a sporty cloth cap. When he tries to protest she says, "You can't take it (money) with you. You can't even keep it while you're here." On the way back to the apartment, Else reminisces aloud about her first boyfriend who was "flash" but "a rotter" who broke her heart. "He taught me," she says, "you can't be too careful when you choose your friends. It's better to have no friends and be lonely; only don't pick the wrong friends." By the time he bids Else farewell, Jim has decided to forget about the heist, but Johnny, who is desperate for his next bike payment, won't let him. In a scuffle Johnny steals the key to Else's apartment. Johnny is forced to delay the robbery, however, until Else's planned vacation. In the meantime, Jim works extra hours for his boss to earn 20 pounds. We assume he wants the money for Johnny's payment so they can call the robbery off. Johnny declines the gift, though, and Jim reluctantly joins the break-in plot. The two let themselves into the apartment only to discover Else is still there. She screams for help and in what appears at first to be an unbelievable coincidence, Jim's mates from work arrive with ladders and drop cloths and begin to work. They don't realize what is happening when Jim throws Johnny out of the apartment. We understand that Jim earned the extra money so Else could afford the redecoration. Still somewhat confused about what has just transpired, Else is quieted by Jim, who explains that the other boy was only someone who "used to be a friend of mine."

Jim's momentary slip into dishonesty and his recovery of good sense can be analyzed in two cause-and-effect diagrams. His initial loneliness and need for acceptance led to the following: attraction to Johnny, reckless boasting about get-rich-quick schemes, the robbery plan, and the stealing of Else's key. Jim's decision to change his mind stems from: the kindness Else shows him, the guilt caused by her casual remarks, and Johnny's refusal of the money. While the film may oversimplify the difficulty of life's many dilemmas, the truth of this scenario, for anyone who has ever been lonely, is hard to deny.

THE SHOPPING BAG LADY (Learning Corp. of America: 21 min./color/1975)

In *The Shopping Bag Lady*, a young girl learns to appreciate her own grandmother after a series of unexpected encounters with a street person in New York City. As is often the case in life, an outside, unrelated experience sheds light on a long-standing problem at home.

As the film opens, Emily's behavior is influenced heavily by a cruel and petty friend, Lucy. On the way home from school, Emily and Lucy accidentally bump into an old bag lady. The somewhat eccentric woman, named Annie, yells at the girls, calling them "disrespectful." The next day when the girls spy Annie on a park bench in Central Park, Lucy leads them in an attack on the old woman's possessions. They trample her bags by marching over them. Annie strikes back, hitting one of the girls on the leg. Later Emily realizes that she has dropped the puppet she made in art class. She returns to the park, but searches in vain. Unknown to her, Annie discovered the doll, fell in love with it, and returned to the cardboard hovel beneath the park bridge where she lives.

The next day, still searching for her doll, Emily comes upon Annie, who is giving the doll a dramatic reading of *Alice in Wonderland*. Emily watches from a distance for a while, then walks over without speaking and takes her doll back. On the following morning, Emily and Lucy arrive at the park to give Lucy's younger brother a ride on the carousel. Annie happens to be there too, enjoying the colorful, whirling horses and the music. While the girls gossip, the boy wanders over to Annie, and the two begin talking. He points to his favorite horse on the ride and she takes him to the side of the carousel to show him hers. Looking frantically for her brother, Lucy spots him with Annie and calls for the police. She accuses the old woman of trying to kidnap the boy and, bending to peer pressure, Emily supports her friend's story. Annie is taken first into custody and then to a hospital for the infirm and homeless. Feeling guilty and ashamed, Emily takes Annie's bags, which were left behind, home intending to return them when she finds out where the old woman has been taken.

That night in her bedroom, Emily happens to look through the bags and discovers they contain scrapbooks of pictures and old letters that identify the shopping bag lady as Miss Annie Lewis, a beautiful child who later married and became an actress. Emily is moved deeply by the pictures, especially those taken when Annie was Emily's age. The young girl puts herself in Annie's place and feels compassion for her. The next day she returns Annie's property to her at the hospital where the broken woman rests in a bed surrounded by other castaways from the streets of New York. Emily also gives the doll to Annie and as the girl leaves, the old woman immediately begins talking with it as if it were her long-lost child. On the way home through the park, Emily meets her grandmother who shares a bedroom with her at home. Until now the two have not had an easy relationship, but thanks to Emily's experiences with Annie, the teenager is now ready to listen and understand. The two appreciate each other for the first time.

Insightful human truths, not readily apparent at first, emerge when this film's cause-and-effect strands are examined. Emily's initial cruelty to Annie (effect) is clearly caused by Lucy's bad influence and perhaps by the harsh environment of Manhattan, home of many frightening castaways. Looking deeper, though, a third cause is apparent. When Emily mistreats Annie she is having trouble with her grandmother with whom she must share a room. Perhaps the pent-up irritation that she is not allowed to express directly at home is taken out on the shopping bag lady.

Looking at Emily's eventual reconciliation with her grandmother (effect), a number of causes are possible here, too—some complex, some simple. Emily feels guilty (cause) for allowing the old woman to be wrongfully arrested and for taking the doll back when Annie so clearly needed it more than she. On a deeper level, by looking through the scrapbook, Emily begins to identify with the old woman (cause), seeing beyond her scruffy appearance to a human being who was an attractive teen, like herself, and who suffered an undisclosed tragedy that reduced her to her present state. Finally, it is possible that Emily recognizes her petty attitude toward her grandmother reflected in exaggerated fashion when Lucy turns the old woman in (cause).

HENRY FORD'S AMERICA (National Film Board of Canada: 57 min./color/ 1977)

As the title suggests, this film is both biography and social history. It offers a profile of the Ford men and the company they built, and it examines the tremendous impact the auto industry has had upon the United States. Because it combines biography and social history, the film presents a wealth of cause-and-effect relationships. We see the reasons Henry I, who was a humanistic genius as a young man, became a bungling tyrant as an old man. We learn why Edsel I (Henry's son) succumbed to the ruthless pressures of the business world, while his son, Henry II, thrived in it. Each rise and fall in the fortunes of the Ford Company is shown and analyzed. On a larger scale, the fantastic changes in the values, culture, industry, trade unions, consumer protection movement, demography, and environment of the United States in the twentieth century are surveyed. These cause-and-effect links are not presented as definitive statements or as dogma, however. Rather, they are given by the narrator in an offhand manner in the nature of probes that suggest connections. By choosing the speculative approach, the filmmakers have prevented this film from becoming dated in the years since its release. If anything, the film's role in a cause-and-effect unit has been enhanced. Anyone who has followed newspaper accounts about the current fate of Detroit, its foreign competitors, and the Chrysler Corporation will find it easy and rewarding to complete the picture Henry Ford's America has begun to sketch.

Henry I profoundly influenced the country when, early in the 1900s, he gave it the Model T and the moving assembly line. According to the narrator, the new car "was cheap, durable, and easy to fix, and precisely right for a restless, migrant population trying to fill up a huge and undeveloped country." The cost-efficient assembly line put "the toy of the European rich" into the hands of the "American masses" and "made Americans free to move." What effect did these two inventions have upon other industries? upon the American values of individuality and adventure? upon life in small towns across the country? The film does not say; by moving quickly on in a pell-mell fashion, it leaves the door open for student speculation and research.

By 1927, 15 million Americans owned Model Ts, but soon General Motors (GM) invaded Ford's territory. The narrator explains: "Henry Ford offered a single model and if you wanted any color but black, you had to paint it yourself." GM, on the other hand, offered the public "chrome, color, comfort, and power," in an expanded line of more luxurious, though less durable, cars. GM reasoned correctly that Americans "only wanted a car to run until they could afford something better," and Ford's customers, perhaps unwisely, jumped to GM. Soon, GM and then Chrysler outdistanced the Ford Company.

Up until this point in his career, Henry I was considered the emancipator of the working man. He introduced the guaranteed wage and built the La Rouge Plant, which employed 90,000 men and was considered a model of safety and beauty. Then the

Depression struck, and this, coupled with the decline of the Model T, caused something to snap inside Henry I. Frustrated by the banking community, he turned anti-Semitic. Angered by union organizers who began to leaflet his plant, he introduced brutal union-busting tactics that led to a strike of 50,000 workers. Eventually, his company in ruins, Henry I was convinced by his wife to retire. Ownership of Ford passed to his 27-year-old grandson, Henry II. (Edsel I, Henry I's son, literally died trying to curb his father's despotism.)

Despite his youth and inexperience, Henry II turned his grandfather's company around in short order. He fired his father's stool pigeons, army of goons, and cutthroat, ineffective executives who were paralyzing the firm, and hired a new breed of leaders that included Lee Iacocca. Soon, the Ford Company was the home of 450,000 employees and, thanks in part to Iacocca's Mustang, Ford became number two behind GM.

Although the film continues to scrutinize the influence Henry II had on Ford and on the auto industry, it broadens its lens at this point to consider the effect the auto had on the nation. In the late 1950s and early 1960s, Ford introduced the Edsel and GM unveiled the Corvair. The first became a laughingstock, the second made consumer advocate Ralph Nader's name a household word and launched his movement. Eventually, Nader and others turned Washington's agencies and lawmakers against the auto industry. The narrator credits the car with promoting the sexual revolution and the freedom and mischief of American teenagers. The jalopy, not to mention the rumble seat, became popular places of private misconduct. The car's horn became a mating call. The "chariots of love" also became vehicles for self-advertisement. Teens are shown parading down Van Nuys Boulevard in Los Angeles by the thousands to show off their customized cars.

Soon, the film's narrator becomes the moderator of a point-counterpoint battle over the nature of the automobile's impact on the country. A few examples follow. Sign-carrying protest marchers are shown demanding that GM stop making autos in Chile. They claim the manufacturer's presence there condones an oppressive regime. Washington politicians demand that the automakers help solve the energy problem by producing fuel-efficient cars. The industry, in turn, complains that creating newly designed cars takes time. A Gallup poll shows that car dealers—both new and used— are distrusted more than all other businesspeople. Henry II counters by pointing to his good relationship with labor; he says he has humanized the assembly line as much as possible, and that he has introduced innovative labor policies and pioneered equal opportunity for blacks. The automakers are then blamed for creating the "ruptured wasteland of Detroit" that, because of upper class flight to the suburbs, has become a slum of "poor, confused migrants drawn to Detroit by the promise of big money." Henry II points to Renaissance Center, a high-rise cluster of office buildings he built to draw businesses and homeowners back into the city's core.

Henry Ford's America comes to an appropriately ironic and ambiguous close: a minister explains why he conducts his services in an old drive-in movie complex. Now the pastor of the biggest drive-in church in the world, he has come to realize that parishioners prefer the privacy and convenience of the auto over a house of God. The product of Henry I's idealistic dreams has been reduced to a sideshow curiosity.

The film sets up cause and effect sequences that follow pattern 3. Analysis indicates how unexpected outside forces (shown in brackets, page 76) twice influence the fate of the family and the company.

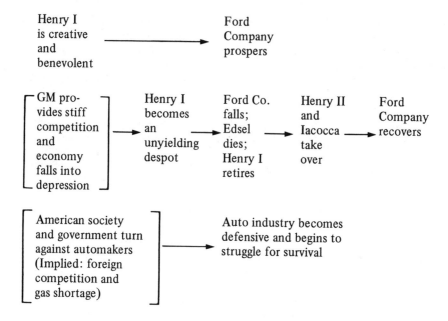

A further breakdown of the film with patterns 1 and 2 makes each wrinkle of the slow decline and eventual recovery clear.

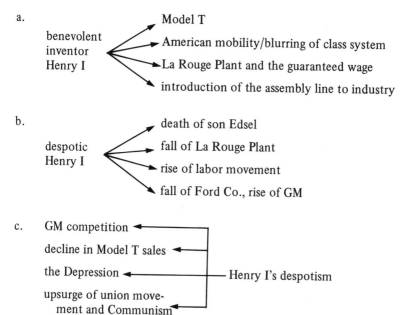

d.

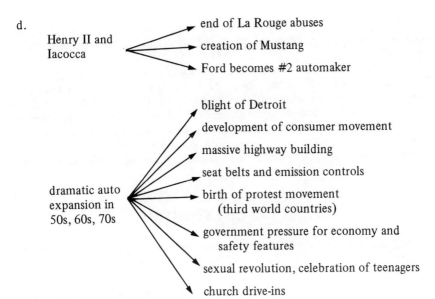

Henry II and Iacocca
- end of La Rouge abuses
- creation of Mustang
- Ford becomes #2 automaker

dramatic auto expansion in 50s, 60s, 70s
- blight of Detroit
- development of consumer movement
- massive highway building
- seat belts and emission controls
- birth of protest movement (third world countries)
- government pressure for economy and safety features
- sexual revolution, celebration of teenagers
- church drive-ins

FOLLOW-UP ACTIVITIES

1. The advent of various teenage fads has caused many adults to worry that their children are being led down the road to immorality and corruption. Examples that come immediately to mind are pool halls, rock 'n' roll, pinball machines, and—most recently—electronic video games. In most cases, adults overreacted and predicted (using pattern 1) that these teenage rages would cause a wide variety of social ills. Choose one of the fads mentioned above, or one of your own choosing, and research in magazines and newspapers the predictions made by adults when one of these fads was the rage. Then choose one of the following writing assignments:

   a. Summarize your cause-and-effect findings, then determine what your research shows about teen fads and the reactions they engender in adults.

   b. Summarize your cause-and-effect research and separate those adult predictions that were reasonable from those that were unfounded.

   c. Summarize your cause-and-effect research on two past fads—rock 'n' roll and pool halls—and use this information to evaluate adult reaction to a recent teen fad such as video games.

2. Analyze a friendship—preferably a friendship you know well, but from a distance—that has broken up. Using pattern 2, sort out the reasons the relationship failed. End with a comment about what the problems of this friendship indicate about all relationships

3. Letters to the editor written in the pique of the moment often rely on poorly drawn or false cause-and-effect reasoning. Choose three such letters from your local newspaper and point out the faults in each and indicate what can be done with the cause-and-effect reasoning to shore up the writers' arguments.

4. How have computers affected and how will they continue to affect our lives? To answer this question you will need research and your imagination. First, become familiar with the ways computers have already changed our lives by browsing through computer books and magazines in your library or by visiting local firms that rely heavily upon computers. Then, based on what you know,

predict the future (pattern 1). Do you see computers adding to the quality of life, or diminishing it, or both? How will the average citizen perceive these changes?

5. Newspapers continually look for the "local angle" or the way a national or international event will affect cities and towns like yours. Recent examples would be the Reagan administration budget cuts, the Middle East conflict, the European antinuclear weapons movement, the John Hinkley trial, Supreme Court decisions on busing, prayer in public schools, etc. Determine what effects one or two of these issues are having on your community. To research this question, interview local officials and people in your neighborhood to collect their responses.

TECHNIQUES OF EXPOSITION

A topic has been chosen. The topic sentence or assertion has been determined. From that moment, the student faces a blank piece of paper and the business of exposition, that is, explaining, expanding, analyzing, describing. Key questions must be answered. What kind of proof is needed? How much supporting data is necessary to prove the point? What would be the best way to expand and to structure the material?

Perhaps the starting point for the student should be the structure; different topics call for different formats as the films in this chapter show. The goal is to have as many structures at one's disposal as possible. Thus, *The Cooking of France* shows how to prepare a complete dinner, so the filmmaker must record the process necessary to achieve the goal (*see* "Process," page 53). *Spivey's Corner* explores the folkloric phenomenon of "hollerin'" and therefore offers definitions (*see* "Definition," page 20) and categories (*see* "Categories and Classification," page 11). *Ancient Games* gives information about the original Greek pentathlon, analyzing each event in the order in which it occurred in the competition (*see* "Chronology," page 42). *Tops* visually juxtaposes every form of the toy from around the world (*see* "Comparison," page 32). *Castles of Clay* documents how the termite mound becomes a home for many animals, and how the flight of termites to start a new colony becomes a time of feeding for various predators (*see* "Cause and Effect," page 62).

Other overall structures should be considered. A deductive approach starts with an assertion or observation, then shows the steps that lead to the formation of it. An inductive approach, the obverse, starts with the evidence for a problem and works toward a solution. Probably the easiest way to set up an inductive structure is to begin with a question. The film *Aging* uses this technique. The topic is the question, "What is it like to be old?" The film first gives negative aspects of being old (and offers rebuttals for each). It then discusses two successful ways of dealing with old age, continues with a category breakdown of various types of old people, and concludes by asserting that the later years can be very rewarding. Sometimes narrative structures normally found outside of essay writing offer the best exposition of the topic. *The Flight of the Gossamer Condor* tells the true account of Paul MacCready's successful attempt to win the Kremer prize for human-powered flight. The heroic aspects of such an undertaking are heightened by the quest structure. As in fiction, tension is needed, so the filmmaker supplies an opposing force in the form of some students in Tokyo, Japan, who have built a plane they believe will win the prize. To emphasize the suspense of the race against time, the film uses a diary or journal format.

Many ways of presenting information within a structure exist. Generally, we rely too heavily on facts and examples as the only kinds of proof that can be used, but the good writer should be aware of the following techniques:

1. *Description.*
   Description is found in a number of types of nonfiction writing. In the travel piece or the fashion report, the author can lead the reader through description to formulate an unstated assertion such as, "Yes, I want to visit that place," or "I want to buy that article of clothing." In a profile, description can do the same thing. The details the writer stresses in the verbal portrait force us both to "see" the subject and to develop an attitude toward him or her. For example, so many illustrations of the daily victories of an armless woman in *A Day in the Life of Bonnie Consolo* are given that we are forced to say, "That is one courageous, well-adjusted woman." (Please note that the overall structure is inductive.)

2. *Anecdote.*
   An anecdote is an informal way of giving variety or punch, as well as warmth and clarity, to the proof. An economically told story or incident can be used to illustrate a point or to add color, and is often amusing. Although an anecdote usually will be personal, it can also be a paraphrased account of another's experience.

3. *Quotation.*
   If we have not personally experienced an event, we must rely on the findings of others. Usually we paraphrase such information, but sometimes we find wit, imagery, or emotional comments that will contribute to the effectiveness of our own writing. Truly distinctive direct quotations are best. Nothing is more boring in a paper than to encounter a series of quotes that have no punch to them. The borrower should always explain what the significance of the quote is.

4. *Allusion.*
   In writing, allusion is a quick reference to a famous artistic work or historical event. Although it does not prove anything, an allusion can make the style of writing more interesting or profound. The connotations of the reference can increase the reader's perceptions of the point being made. An allusion also lends credibility to an essay by associating its point with respected writers and thinkers from the past.

5. *Figure of Speech.*
   Like the allusion, the use of metaphor is not a proof, but a rhetorical device, a means of improving style. At times, however, a fresh metaphor can make an opinion or observation clearer or more powerful.

6. *Aside.*
   An aside is any additional comment, a bit of tangential information, that we insert in the exposition. It is not a proving device, but it is a way to give those prized nuggets of information that are charming, bizarre, or even other-worldly, information that contributes further insight into the subject.

Ideally, an essay guides the reader through a carefully planned exhibit of information that will convince the observer that the tour was worthwhile. The films that follow use a variety of techniques that can be helpful to future tour guides.

TOPS (Encyclopaedia Britannica: 8 min./color/1968)

This brief but stylish film shows a number of different types of tops starting, spinning, wobbling, then coming to a stop. That's it. Through the rapid juxtaposition of the various tops, we are able to make comparisons. There is no narration, and exposition is through repetition and example, yet we see all there is to see about the subject—in fact, we see more than we "know."

The film structures itself to coincide with the different stages of the toy's operation. Within each phase are variations. Some tops are started by pulling a rope wound around the base, others by plungers. Some seem motionless in full spin, some move across a surface. A tiny one even flips over to continue spinning on the other end. We are given ample evidence of the way the top goes into procession.

Repetition in exposition has the same value it does in music—one has a chance to discover more in the material. The size of tops ranges from the very large (a ballerina) to the very small (jacks and even a thumb tack). Variations on the gyroscope shape include a shallow cup, a Saturn with rings, and a top shaped like an angel. Top design is colorful and artistic. The toy seems to be universal (we see children with tops from a number of cultures), to be used in a number of games (a player spins a top into a circle to knock other tops, coins, or objects out), and to have a variety of features (notches on the side allow the top to hum; some are constructed to have an incredibly long spinning time). Not bad for a small obconic toy.

This film provides good incentive for the young writer, showing that even a children's toy can be the subject of an essay. The writer, however, must do more than just show the material, as this film does. He or she can use repetition, but also must place the information in categories, explain differences, form generalizations, and draw conclusions. To sum it up: the writer must show *and* tell.

A DAY IN THE LIFE OF BONNIE CONSOLO (Arthur Barr Productions: 16.30 min./color/1975)

Although this profile does not contain a directly stated topic sentence, the implied assertion is clear: Bonnie Consolo, born without arms, has successfully compensated for her handicap and is leading a happy, productive life. Within a few minutes, most of us will be convinced of the truth of the assertion, but for the skeptic, details are accumulated to show that Consolo can indeed cope with the normal problems facing a housewife and mother. Just how much evidence is needed to prove an assertion? Any proof should contain at least three pieces of evidence. In this film, there are 25 visual details plus Consolo's verbal comments. We are made to accept what we would have thought impossible. The young essayist would do well to aim for such thoroughness.

As the film follows Bonnie Consolo through a "typical" day, we see her functioning as a normal person in ordinary activities. In each instance, she uses her feet as if they were hands. She cooks (cutting apples with a paring knife between her toes, emptying a large pot of water into the sink, kneading sourdough bread, then putting it in a pan), shops (picking out fruit, weighing it, then placing it in a paper bag with her feet; writing out a check at the cash register), drives a car (opening the door, turning on the radio, driving off), deals with her children (cutting her son's hair with scissors and comb, tying her younger boy's sneaker laces, attending a school function), and performs daily rituals (applying face makeup, taking care of plants, washing dishes, answering the phone). The evidence is overwhelming.

During these activities, Consolo provides a steady stream of commentary that reveals her personality and amazing adjustment. The doctor told her parents it would be better if she did not live, and she adds with a justifiable pride in her voice, "I made it." She would never have had children if there were a chance of their being born with her condition because it would "not be right to put others through what I went through . . . ." At the same time, she admits there is "nothing I can't do" and "I don't feel I'm any different than anyone else." For her, the greatest compliment is given when someone forgets she is armless and hands her a cup of coffee. She jokes about the way some react to her ("To heck with it, people are going to stare at me . . ."), but shows contempt for the grocery store manager who asked her not to shop in his store any more ("I could have sued . . . but let it go . . .").

This is more than just a profile. We are hit with so much detail that we inductively reach the conclusion the filmmaker wants us to draw. A different point of view is given to show there is no distortion to the evidence, that this is not camera trickery: the film interviews a neighbor who corroborates what we have seen and heard. The filmmaker, like any good writer, attacks our incredulity with an abundance of proof. By the end, no one in the audience could possibly disagree.

SPIVEY'S CORNER (Perspective Films: 16.50 min./color/1978)

If the student is asked to prepare a report based on observation and interviews, as opposed to one based on print research, *Spivey's Corner* offers the correct techniques of exposition to use. The filmaker does not impose preconceived concepts on the folkloric phenomenon called "hollerin'," but has "informants" in a small North Carolina community give definitions, categories, examples, and anecdotes. There is also repetition, a necessary technique when the essayist uses field research to show that the definitions and classification are more than the whims of the individual.

Hollerin' is defined at the outset by Leonard, a 73-year-old native of Spivey's Corner, who tells us that it was a way the farmers had of keeping in touch with their neighbors, all of whom lived a distance away. Stressing the functions of a holler, he classifies the information callers give as:

    a.   saying good morning
    b.   coming home from work
    c.   calling for help
    d.   wanting to borrow
    e.   meeting at a specific place

Other informants corroborate the categories. Before the film ends, three more possible functions have been added:

    f.   calling for water
    g.   calling for dogs
    h.   expressing feelings through songs (such as "When My Blue Moon Turns to Gold")

To illustrate the phenomenon, the film records over 15 examples of hollerin'. Some are from the yearly Hollerin' Contest at Spivey's Corner, some from nameless informants, but all the examples are the best available. As a matter of fact, the informants carefully give us their credentials, such as 80-year-old Mr. Jackson, who tells us he was the first champion of the contest in 1969.

The informal atmosphere and the sense of authenticity are maintained by the use of anecdotes—reminiscences about hollerin' situations. Mr. Jackson recounts how he won out over his brother in the competition: he hollered the melody of "What a Friend I Had in Jesus," a song that impressed the judges—who happened to be preachers. A nameless old man tells us about going on the "Mike Douglas Show" with his family to demonstrate hollerin'. Leonard says he invented a holler to say hello to a riverboat passing by.

This film is a model on how to communicate in print. In the first few minutes, there is a definition of the term, and a discussion of its functions. Through repetition, we see that the inhabitants of Spivey's Corner share a "universal" definition and agree on category terms. A number of examples prove that hollerin' is a genuine folkloric entity. The anecdotes give us further insight into the phenomenon, and add humor and warmth to the essay.

AGING (CRM Educational Films: 22 min./color/1973)

This film demonstrates some of the exposition techniques that are possible in a research paper on a general subject. Through a question, the narrator introduces the topic: "What is it like to be old?" Filmmaker Peter Jordan uses statistics, theories, and generalizations from the research of experts and adds interviews of a number of old people. Through this inductive structure, Jordan reaches the conclusion that aging can be a happy, productive experience and not something to be feared.

In this film, statistics help to disprove negative stereotypes about being old. For example, the belief that "the aged are sick and dependent" is disproven by a survey that revealed only 5% of the old were in institutions, whereas 95% maintained their own households. Again, the complaint that "retirement is bad—the aged sicken from feelings of idleness and worthlessness" was not an attitude of three-quarters of those polled.

Gerontologists have formed two theories about lifestyles and eight generalizations about typical personalities of the aged. The Activity Theory proposes that to age successfully, one should keep active physically and socially. What an individual wants does not change after middle age. The theory is illustrated through people at Leisure World in Laguna Hills, California, square dancing, horseback riding, and singing. The Disengagement Theory posits that the elderly need to withdraw socially and psychologically from their environment. Old age is a separate period of life with new needs. The example is an old man who goes out for a walk, feeds the pigeons, does some shopping, then returns home. The filmmaker reaches the conclusion, however, that both theories are too extreme. The individual will determine the way of life that best suits his or her personality. Based on a number of interviews of old people, scientists have made generalizations about personality. The researchers have decided there are eight types: Reorganizer, Holding-on, Disengaged, Constricted, Apathetic, Succorance Seeker, Disorganized, and Focused. The filmmaker offers an example of each of the first three types, but only lists the negative personalities.

Jordan's interviews with old people contribute a great deal toward the formation of his conclusion. At the beginning of the film we meet 84-year-old Harry Baker, a charming and articulate man who happily reminisces about his life. Later on, Marion Fox, Frank Schaeffer, and John Ehrle exhibit the same characteristics. All four would be nice people to know. With their interests and enthusiasms, they serve as proof that old age can still be productive.

The student should note one final thing. Jordan did his research, cited some authorities, presented some findings, but also interacted with his material. He interprets and comments on what he uses, coming up with his own conclusions. His approach is a clear model for this type of essay.

FLIGHT OF THE GOSSAMER CONDOR (Churchill Films: 27 min./color/1978)

Using a diary or journal format, this superior film records Paul MacCready's quest to accomplish a heretofore unattained goal: the winning of the Kremer Prize (offered by the Royal Aereonautical Society, London) of £50,000 for constructing a human-powered airplane that can fly a figure eight and clear two 16-foot markers a half-mile apart. In chronological order, the film follows the metamorphosis of the clumsy glider into the streamlined *Condor* that can make a complete left turn, a complete right turn, and achieve the desired height. Tension mounts during the year of hard work, over 400 test flights, frustrating setbacks, and many design modifications. Unexpected competition from Japan makes the quest even more suspenseful. On August 23, 1977, Brian Allen pedals the *Condor* through the course to win the prize. If young writers were able to use exposition techniques the way this film does, they also could be prize winners.

If nothing else, the film shows how to make a diary or journal approach effective. Not all days or events are noted; summary statements are frequently made ("one-half year of hard work, persistence, and inventiveness beginning to pay off" or "late night sessions become more frequent"), and information is recorded only when it offers a significant change or an example of the problems MacCready has to overcome. Thus, we are told that son Tyler is replaced as the engine pedaler by bike racer Greg Miller, who is later replaced by Allen. We are not buried in data or in trivia; the film does not dawdle. The climactic point has emphasis ("Dawn, August 23, 1977," the narrator dramatically intones at the start of the first successful trial run) and enough time spent on it to warrant the buildup (we can enjoy the moment we have been waiting for, the first complete flight).

To keep the chronology of the quest exciting, the film builds tension. First, we learn that some students in Tokyo, Japan, have built a plane called *The Stork* out of balsa wood and handmade paper. Although this human-powered plane is never mentioned again (we assume it was unsuccessful in doing the figure eight), it serves as a challenge to MacCready. Second, we witness a few *Condor* crashes that look extremely painful for the pedalling pilot. There are enough bad accidents to make us unsure of the future of each attempted trial flight.

Finally, *The Flight* has a good concluding "paragraph." It is short but effective. We are told *The Gossamer Condor* now hangs in the Smithsonian Institute between the Wright Brothers' plane and the *Apollo II* moon capsule. This has truly been a quest as exciting as that of Wright and Armstrong.

THE COOKING OF FRANCE: AN ALPINE MENU (Screenscope, Inc.: 25 min./ color/1978)

One of the most common uses for process writing (*see* "Process," page 53) is the directions for preparing food. The recipe must be clear: there should be an accurate listing of ingredients, and the techniques of preparation should be in an efficient sequence, detailed but not wordy. This mouth-watering film shows French chef André Revest in the kitchen at his Inn of the Flowering Hearth, preparing a gourmet meal of fresh trout stuffed with almond paste, tomatoes à la Provençale, potato gratin dauphinois, lamb chops and la neige à la liqueur Chartreuse. In addition, asides give a unique flavor to the exposition.

We watch the preparation of each dish except the mushrooms saute Provençale. Each process is visually clear with verbal commentary by Revest and a narrator to ensure comprehension. There are explanations for some of the cooking techniques (to keep the fish moist, the heads and tails are not removed; most of the fat of the lamb chop is removed to avoid a strong taste), and demonstrations of terms that in print can be difficult for the novice to interpret (such as the word "fold"). The best compliment that could be paid any cooking film applies here: the audience could probably recreate the meal with success because the directions are so clear.

Thanks to asides on cooking philosophy, the audience can even improve as cooks. Revest tells us the two secrets of great cooking he learned from his grandfather: "Always buy fresh. Always buy what is in season." Careful shopping is necessary (one should have a good relationship with a butcher and be able to explain exactly what one wants). Revest further explains that "good cooks do not measure things exactly . . . it is an intuition . . . ." If the butter is unsalted, the cook has better control over seasoning. Good cooking takes time and should appeal to more than just taste.

Other asides tell us more about the food peculiar to the region. We learn about the nearby monastery that produces the liqueur Green Chartreuse, an ingredient that is part of the dessert. We are shown that the Dauphiné potato ("firm and tasty") is farmed on nearby mountain slopes. There is information about the aged cheeses that Revest serves. The asides are relevant because they contribute local color as well as information on cooking.

THE ANCIENT GAMES (Xerox Films: 28 min./color/1972)

The subject is a reasonable research project, the ancient Greek pentathlon. The student's challenge is to make the material vivid. This film shows two ways of doing so: comparison of the present to the past, and the inclusion of relevant classical sayings, quotations, and allusions to contribute information that is unusual, often shocking, and sometimes funny. These techniques help to give Erich Segal's script a distinctly original quality.

The comparison between the past and the present holds the film together. Two present-day decathlon champions, Bill Toomey and Rafer Johnson, reenact the competitions of the 195-yard dash, the discus throw, the broad jump, the javelin throw, and wrestling, using the ancient rules and equipment. The enactment of the games owes something to the "you are there" approach of TV and radio over 20 years ago, a technique that students might find difficult to imitate. There is more to the comparison, however. The modern athletes chat about the difficulty of the events, kid each other, and muse about the life of the ancient athlete. Toomey and Johnson have awkward moments as they try to adjust to the old way of doing things, but they do seem to be caught up by the challenge. These are not rehearsed stunt men, but two genuine superstars trying to win the famous laurel. Their competitiveness brings excitement to the film.

The classical sayings, quotations, and allusions bring the past to life. As a race starts, we hear the words of Herodotus: "he who is left at the start will win no crown." A quotation by Pindar is made at the end of the film: "We're creatures of a day . . . When bright victory comes, a beam of light illumines men and life is good . . . ." Telemachus killed his opponent in the wrestling matches and set up a marker announcing that "Telemachus is very sorry." Anatiphon the Sophist tells about the boy picking up the javelin from the field only to be speared by a careless contestant. We learn that Phalus of Crotuna set a broad jump record in 478 B.C. of 55 feet, but broke both his legs in doing it. An allusion is made to the discus throw of Odysseus by which the observers knew he was an epic hero. This type of information rivets the attention through its violence or unusualness.

There is power in any writing that compares the mores and ways of solving problems of ancient times to those used now. Toomey makes a false start in the dash, and we learn that the ancient judges whipped such offenders. The men performed nude and the rules barred women, on pain of death, from the stadium. At first we are shocked, then reminded of our own strange ways of doing things, such as a player spiking a football after a touchdown.

CASTLES OF CLAY (Benchmark Films: 55 min./color/1978)

It might not seem possible, but Alan Root has made an unforgettable film on the subject of termites. Yes, termites. The movie explores the structure, habits, and life cycle of termite society as well as the effects of the termite on the surrounding environment. The techniques of exposition are so skillful that by the end of the film, we feel a definite empathy for the tiny creatures. Root accomplishes this in many ways. He organizes an incredible amount of information into two cause-and-effect sequences. For a climax in the second part, he even has a thrilling battle between a snake and a monitor lizard, a sequence that is actually an aside. He uses figures of speech in his explication to clarify points and to add emotion and humor. These techniques make the script as memorable as the photography.

There are four distinct sequences: 1) an analysis of a termite colony and description of the interior of a mound; 2) a look at the animals that use the mound as a shelter (with the tolerance of the termites); 3) the documentation of the yearly flight of the alates (a special caste of termite that will be the future queen and king of a new colony) and the start of a new mound; and 4) the techniques of predators ranging from insect to human in obtaining termites as food. Cause and effect connects the first two and the final two sections. We learn, for example, in the first section how the workers keep the interior of the mound at 85°F. through an air-conditioning system: the many tunnels and air vents allow cool air to enter at the base and warm air to leave near the top, and the workers spread water on the walls to reduce heat. In the second section we find that various small animals like the comforts of the tunnels, such as dwarf mongooses, a monitor lizard, jackal pups, elephant shrews, and the assassin bug. As these various beings clog up tunnels, the termites have to form new ones to keep the air conditioning working (note, the effect becomes a cause producing a new effect). In the second cause-and-effect sequence, the relationship between termite and "others" is not congenial, but deadly.

Through an aside, Root creates a climax to the material in the second section. Near the end of a "typical" day that shows the various animals who make use of the mound, some baby dwarf mongooses have ringside seats to a battle to the death between a five-foot monitor lizard and a spitting cobra. The fight, which the lizard wins, is violent, vivid, and unforgettable, but it also has little to do with the mounds or the termites. It does show the dangers of survival in nature, however.

Whenever there is a density of information, Root introduces figurative language. In the first part, for example, we learn that the builders of the "fortress" mounds (metaphor) have a strict caste system (metaphor). Two percent of the population are major or minor soldiers (metaphor), sterile females with massive heads. Workers (metaphor), also in major and minor categories and also sterile, gather food and build. At the "heart of the colony" (metaphor), is the royal cell where the queen with her four-inch body lays her 30,000 eggs a day, lives with her normal-sized king and receives food from her workers. She is in "prison for life" (metaphor). In another section of the mound is the nursery area (metaphor) where, after three weeks, the termites hatch into "delicate miniature(s) in spun glass" (metaphor). The workers keep these tiny ones fed and "the termite baby begs for food as appealingly as any puppy" (simile). To help digest the cellulose in the grass and wood they eat, the termites raise a crop of mushrooms (metaphor) in the mound; the enzyme in their "hanging gardens" (metaphor) helps to break down the cellulose. For the most part, these images compare the termite world to human institutions and behavior, "humanizing" this near relative of the cockroach, and causing us to feel empathy for the tiny being when danger threatens.

The final quarter of the film is extremely emotive thanks to such metaphors. Once a year, a new caste of termite is born, the alate (winged one). They are "fairy-tale princes and princesses" (metaphor) who fly off to start new colonies. The predators for the alates include foxes, birds, lizards, ants, grasshoppers, and humans (tribes "own" mounds and eat the alates both raw and roasted). Scene after scene shows alates being devoured. Back at the mound, an aardvark tears the "heart" (metaphor) out of a nest, leaving the queen exposed to an invasion of army ants (metaphor). We watch the "battle to the death" between termites and ants "in open combat" (metaphor). There is so much sympathy for the termites by this point in the film that the queen's death is tragic.

The student should note that the images never appear at the expense of the facts. We learn a great deal about the termite, but we are also able to enjoy the way in which the author presents this information. In fact, he has a sense of humor that he reveals in his metaphors. The pangolin or scaly anteater is called a "clockwork artichoke." The workers taking care of the queen are compared to a ground crew dealing with a "half-inflated airship." Because of the "air-conditioning system" of the termite mound, there is an "army of uninvited guests" that like to live in the cool air shafts. Young dwarf mongooses, who number among the uninvited, are called "squatter pups." The images give a definite zest to the writing, a zest that students should try to achieve.

FOLLOW-UP ACTIVITIES

1. Often experiences, people, or objects that appeared threatening when we were children (such as the annual shot we received from the doctor, the local police officer, or the woods behind our house) no longer seem so when we are grown. Our fear or respect may strike us as comical from our adult perspective. Select a childhood "bête noire," and in an essay describe it from your point of view at the time. Offer asides that reveal the ridiculousness of your original attitude interspersed with the description. Conclude with a paragraph that shows your feeling about the subject today.

2. What does your high school student body do on a Saturday night? Interview several schoolmates, and in an essay survey the activities for an average Saturday night. Make sure you cover as wide a range of groups as possible (kids from each of the grades, athletes, scholars, etc.). This assignment will provide you with the opportunity to use direct quotes and anecdotes from those interviewed.

3. Listed below are a few proverbs. Choose one from the list (or choose one you know already), and explore the meaning of the proverb in an essay. You should be able to offer examples, anecdotes, and direct quotations in the exposition. A few proverbs:

    Chinese

    "It's hard to dismount from a tiger."

    "Let your children taste a little cold and a little hunger."

    "A liar is an egg in midair."

    Gypsy

    "Do not try to jump over your own shadow."

    "Don't scratch where it doesn't itch."

Norwegian

"The acorn doesn't fall far from the tree."

4. Choose someone with an interesting profession and "shadow" him or her for a full day. Then interview the person to determine the subject's background, views, and values. In your written profile, juxtapose paragraphs on the person's job with ones on his or her personality and background. The paragraphs on the job should be arranged chronologically (i.e., 9 a.m., 11 a.m., 3 p.m., etc.) and the biographical paragraphs should be introduced to explain why the person works as he or she does.

5. Write an extended definition of your school class. Consider its strengths, its weaknesses, the quirks that set it off from others. To structure the essay, determine three to five categories that will be developed in the definition, such as the class' school spirit, cohesiveness, values, cliques, etc.

II

SENDER–MESSAGE–RECEIVER RELATIONSHIPS

Communication takes place when a sender, for some reason, conveys a message to a receiver. Through the information in the message, the sender intends to change the behavior of the audience even if the change is nothing more than having the audience pay attention. There is a better chance of success in this cause if the author considers the problems inherent in the communication process. If the originator of the message makes the wrong assumptions about the values of the audience or adopts the wrong tone of voice, the receivers will block the message. The following chart sums up the aspects of the communication process of which the sender should be aware:

SENDER - - - - - - - - - - - -► **MESSAGE** - - - - - - - - - - - -► **RECEIVER**

1. Purpose: What is the effect the Sender wants the message to have on the Receiver?	1. Assertion 2. Attention-Getting Devices	Assumptions about the Receiver: Age? Occupation? Social class?
2. Voice: What is the appropriate attitude needed to create this effect?	3. Persuasion Techniques 4. Sign Models	Ethnic group? Beliefs? Place of residence?
3. Persona: What is the appropriate role or personality for the Sender to assume?		Interests? Sensitivities? Knowledge about the message?

The following sections will approach the aspects of communication by first considering the audience assumptions, attention-getting devices, and assertions, then the voice of the sender with a separate discussion of irony, and finally persona. Sections "Persuasion," "Signs," and "A Sign Model: Biography" discuss aspects of the message itself. The student will have opportunity to analyze the full range of the communication process and to experiment in writing for a variety of audiences. Too often, the student writes only for an audience of one, the teacher.

Attention-Getting Devices,
Assertions, and Audience Assumptions

A student walking through his high school on the way to class stops suddenly to read a campaign poster put up by someone running for student council president. Although this student walked by many other posters without so much as a glance, something in this one caught his eye. Across the top of it, in foot-high letters, is the word "SEX." Below this, in much smaller letters, the script continues: "Now that I've got your attention, I'd like your vote. My name is Alex Bryant and in the three years I've been a student at Central High . . . ." That's as far as the reader gets. Emitting a sign of disgust, he continues to make his way toward class.

What makes one attention-getting device work and another fail? Certainly Bryant had the right idea. He knew what would turn his audience's head, but he lost out when he used a device that had nothing to do with the rest of his message. By doing so, he made the reader feel he had been tricked rather than entertained in a meaningful way. Attention getters should complement the tone and theme of what follows; otherwise, the writer has wrongfully misled the audience and is going to have a difficult time bridging, with a suitable transition, the gap between that opening device and the text of the message.

Four quick examples from *Christian Science Monitor* articles published between July 20 and July 22, 1982, will show how attention-getting devices (or leads) can establish the tone and content of what follows, leave the door open for a reasonable transition, and still be entertaining enough to snap the reader to attention.

Just before Vice-President George Bush took the podium, a congressional aide edged over to the press corps and asked a question that put in perspective President Reagan's July 19 rally in support of a constitutional amendment to balance the budget. *(anecdote lead)*

"Is Channel 39 here?" he asked quietly. "Congressman [Duncan] Hunter wants to know."

The rally, conducted on the west steps of the Capitol in sweltering heat, was a carefully crafted media event intended to pressure Congress by going over its head to the voters, a tactic used with devastating effect to help pass last year's tax and budget cuts. *(transition)*

—New England ed., July 20, 1982, p. 1

By beginning the piece with such an anecdote, the author presages a fairly serious and somewhat cynical discussion of White House politics. The second example uses a kicker lead, or one that quickly jolts the reader with an outrageous, incongruous, or unexpected remark (somewhat like Bryant's "SEX" poster did).

Mickey Mouse is about to get some new neighbors. *(kicker lead)*

There's Dreamfinder and his helper Figment, a dragon, of sorts. Then there's Bonnie Appetit, a walking, talking version of Benjamin Franklin, and even some singing Italian waiters.

> You can meet them here any time after Oct. 1,   *(transition)*
> when Disney World opens its $800 million show-
> case known as Epcot Center . . . .
>
> —New England ed., July 21, 1982, p. 3

The topic here, the new Epcot Center amusement park built next to Disney World, gets the kind of opener it deserves: one that is playful yet germane to the topic. The third example uses a symbol for its attention-getting device.

> Five stories high and filled with aging belt-
> driven machines, an idle New Bedford, Mass., tool   *(symbol lead)*
> and die plant is fast becoming a national symbol
> of labor militancy.
> The reason: Striking members of the United
> Electrical Workers Union (UE) claim their employer
> hasn't invested enough money in the plant to keep
> it competitive with others in the industry. They   *(transition)*
> want not only a wage increase and job-protection
> guarantees but also a commitment that the plant be
> modernized.
>
> —New England ed., July 22, 1982, p. 9

The symbol is ominous and labor-related, so it fairly and interestingly anticipates the topic of the piece—labor militancy. The final lead uses a question and an allusion to a famous television show.

>   *(question &*
> Would Ozzie and Harriet have lived like this?   *allusion lead)*
> It looks like a stylish new California house
> from the street—nice, but standard fare. It isn't.
> In fact it is a trial balloon for a concept foreign   *(transition)*
> to classically suburban tracts.
>
> —New England ed., July 20, 1982, p. 6

The concept the writer goes on to discuss, a new trend in multi-family housing units, is a fad (from California, no less), so it warrants a light-hearted opener. Ozzie and Harriet once represented the epitome of middle-class suburban values, so they are appropriate judges of the suitability of such a new housing option.

Unlike these polished and resourceful writers, students often see no option to the standard "start right in" opening when they put pen to paper. To break this habit, the teacher should bring in samples (from magazines, newspapers, or essays) that employ one or more of these 12 standard attention-getting devices:

a.   narrative (the piece begins with a careful description of a scene almost as a short story would)

b.   old saying (either used exactly as it is commonly heard or doctored by the writer to reflect the article's theme and tone)

c.   question (or a series of questions, or a question-and-answer combination)

d.   anecdote

e.   metaphor, conceit, or symbol

f.   quote (or paraphrased quote)

g.   hypothetical situation

h.   cause-and-effect relationship

     i.   contrast or irony

     j.   comparison (especially between the past and the present)

     k.   kicker

     l.   survey (a quick listing of several examples that illustrate the writer's point).

Once students become familiar with these devices, they should be asked to find examples of each. In this manner (and with a well-stocked copier), each member of the class can eventually build a large collection of opening paragraphs. Then, depending on how much time the teacher wishes to devote to this skill, students can flip through this file of attention-getting samples looking for an appropriate model to imitate when they begin subsequent writing assignments. If this route is taken, the teacher will also have to spend time discussing transitions from the attention-getting device to the main idea. This is best accomplished by studying how professional writers make the bridge between their openers and texts and by examining in class the more successful transitions used by student writers in their own writing (*see* "Appropriateness of Structure, Details, and Transitions," page 215).

If young writers are to get sufficient practice using opening devices and transitions, teachers may have to increase the number of free themes they assign; that is, ones for which the student is allowed to select a topic, limit it, and develop a personal assertion about it. As teachers we often, and with good reason, heavily emphasize literary criticism or report essays in which students either summarize what they have read or prove they know a book's theme, tone, genre, etc. The openings of these essays are often highly conventional and stylized and as such offer no practice with attention-getting devices. Further, because the students have been given an assertion or asked to answer one of the teacher's essay questions, they have little, if any, emotional commitment to the point they are trying to prove.

When the student is encouraged to select a topic, he or she might settle on something like "football," or "school," or "rock 'n' roll"—all of which are too large to develop fully in an essay. Young writers should therefore be encouraged to whittle topics down to an aspect or subcategory (*see* the activities in "Categories and Classification," page 11) that can be completely explored in a two- or three-page essay. Once this is done, they each need an assertion. This can be thought of as the verb phrase that complements the noun in a sentence. If the topic is "study halls," for instance, the assertion (or verb phrase) might be "should be optional for all students." Because students often express opinions that they and their friends feel are obvious ("School stinks." "This band is great."), they may not be accustomed to thinking about how to prove their opinions. The proof, like the attention-getting device, should be taught as a conscious strategy, a way to manipulate the thinking of the audience. (*See* "Persuasion," page 134.)

To form such a strategy, the writer obviously needs to know who the audience is. Sensitivity to one's audience can be fostered in a number of ways. Students should be encouraged to consider: 1) what their readers already know about the topic, 2) how their audience will first react to their assertion, and 3) what prejudices the audience holds that may interfere with conveying the assertion. Before the teacher introduces the films in this chapter, students should discuss hypothetical writing situations.

PRE-FILM ACTIVITIES

1.   Pretend that you are the public relations person for the McDonald's restaurant chain and are involved in the following scenario. The McDonald's Corporation wishes to build a new store on a vacant lot that borders the playing fields behind the local high school. This site is also adjacent to a closely-knit and politically

active neighborhood of single-family homes. You, as the public relations person, have been asked to write a series of letters to residents and local officials who live or work in the area to convince them that such a restaurant will be in their best interests. You have five different audiences on your correspondence list: the student council at the high school, the high school principal, the local neighborhood association, the police chief, and the Chamber of Commerce. The students should prepare in their notebooks a "profile" of each audience, listing what each knows and does not know about McDonald's, how they are likely to react to such a proposal or assertion, and which of their prejudices may come into play during such a discussion. Finally, the students should list what McDonald's could reasonably promise each group and what kind of proof should be used with each group: statistics, testimonials from officials in nearby towns, etc. (If the McDonald's restaurant does not prove a provocative subject for the students, a flea market, pinball arcade, dance hall, bar, or other such establishment could easily be substituted in the scenario.)

2. Several written samples can be introduced to increase further students' sensitivity to audience and to reinforce points already made about assertion and proof strategies. For several years now, Mobil Oil Company has periodically run a series of advertisements on the editorial pages of the country's larger daily newspapers. These "ads" look very much like editorials in that their text is long, unsigned, unaccompanied by pictures, and usually refers to no specific product. In them, the company's writers editorialize about the direction our country and government should take in developing energy. Obviously, the pieces are self-serving and seek to correct or promote certain prejudices or opinions Americans hold about energy in general and oil companies in particular. As such, these short writing samples are a great resource in the classroom. Teachers can ask the students to determine each ad's assertion, audience assumptions, and method of proof. (The ads can be copied from newspapers found in the library or obtained directly from Mobil Oil headquarters in New York.)

3. An unusual short story, "Dear Bill, Remember Me," in a collection by the same name (by Norma Fox Mazer [New York: Dell, 1976]) is also useful. Composed solely of letters, the story presents Kathy Kalman, a 15-year-old girl who is trying to write a letter to Bill, an older boy whom she had a crush on when he was dating her older sister several years ago. The story shows us the 14 letters Kathy begins then discards before she finally drafts the fifteenth, the one she will send. While reading the rejected letters, we learn all about Bill, Kathy, and her older sister. Some of Kathy's unsuccessful letters make assertions that are too self-revelatory, others are too blunt. Each, however, can be analyzed to reveal what Kathy assumes about her audience, Bill, and what her assertions reveal about herself.

4. Another dramatic example that shows the importance of knowing one's audience involves writer Nick Phillips, who once worked for *Boston* magazine (*see* August 1978 issue). He planned to write a number of satirical character sketches of famous Boston personalities. They would appear in a series, one per issue of the magazine. His first, on Cardinal Humberto Madeiros, was his last. Although the sketch was very humorous, it also deeply offended many of the magazine's readers who considered their prelate to be above any sort of criticism, but especially that of the sarcastic Phillips. The writer was fired and the series discontinued, but, once they are told that the magazine's audience is largely Catholic, the students will guess this outcome upon reading the piece

themselves. In fact, they will probably scratch their heads and wonder how any writer could have made such an assertion and used such a poor strategy.

NOISE POLLUTION (Learning Corp. of America: 18 min./color/1972)

This film opens with an attention-getting device that introduces its scientific topic, establishes its light tone, and assures its restless student audience that this will be an offbeat and entertaining educational film, unlike many they have had to endure before. The device that achieves these ends in the first few moments of the film is comic juxtaposition (the equivalent of a kicker or comparison lead). When the first images of the film appear, most high school audiences will groan. A teenage symphonic orchestra, formally dressed, is seen and heard tuning up for a performance. After a pause, their conductor enters, bows before an appreciative audience, then launches his orchestra into the familiar opening four chords that are repeated at the start of Beethoven's Fifth Symphony. Suddenly, in place of the fourth chord, we see and hear not the orchestra, but a jackhammer pounding a city street. This sudden intrusion is brief; just long enough to take the place of the orchestra's fourth chord. The group continues playing. The four well-known chords are repeated, but this time, in place of the fourth chord we see and hear a motorcycle revving up. The orchestra continues until the fourth chord is again superseded, this time by a jet taking off at an airport. The credits of the film then appear and we find ourselves into the body of the film. The attention-getting device suggests the film will be informal and geared to the student (notice the choice of a student, rather than adult, professional orchestra), and will not be dogmatic or overly technical as it might be if geared to the scientific community. As the film unfolds, we discover its assertion: although the difference between sound and noise is actually a personal and subjective decision, people can qualify and control the effects of noise pollution on the environment if they begin to understand and to appreciate the fundamental nature of sound. Assuming that the students, like most adults, know little about the basics of sound, but have little patience for scientific detail, the film delivers its information in a brief and informal show-and-tell format that incorporates only the simplified results of complex tests and studies.

The filmmakers assume the students only want to gain a passing knowledge of the nature of sound, just enough to make some informed choices about noise pollution. The narrator defines the terms "sound wave," "frequency," and "decibel" and concretizes their meaning for the students by showing how a tuning fork in water produces similar waves, and by allowing us to watch the different wavelengths a telephone, a fog horn, a motorcycle, and a rock band make on an oscilloscope. Showing students a plastic model of the human ear, the narrator gives a very cursory explanation of how the ear receives sound, then indicates the different decibel levels that the ear can tolerate comfortably without protection or short-term hearing loss. Much of the recent increase in noise pollution is blamed on the advent of technology, and the narrator gives students the dramatic results, but not the complex methodologies and statistics, of experiments with lab animals and of studies conducted in Europe. The viewers learn that extended noise pollution as suffered by factory workers and city dwellers can lead to mental disorders, heart disease, even tooth decay. Students are told that even though attempts to limit sound in cities have failed, city planners and politicians can take scientific findings into consideration when building for the future. Simple diagrams show how wind direction and air temperature can, for instance, make life noisy for neighborhoods that border a factory on one side, but not on the other.

All the studies explored in *Noise Pollution* fall within the film's stated topic and support its premise. Simple definitions of "sound" and "noise" are given. The ways in which they are transmitted through the air and received by the ear are explored. The levels of sound and noise are shown, both those that are safe and those that are harmful to humans. Although the outlook for meaningful reduction of noise pollution is bleak, the narrator offers some hope for the future if politicians and city planners consider the science of sound.

THE FEMININE MISTAKE (Pyramid Films: 25 min./color/1977)

The Feminine Mistake is a calculated and persuasive attempt to make women—especially young women—quit smoking. Everything from the title—an ironic pun on the term "feminine mystique"— to the overall structure of the film is used to shock and frighten its audience into quitting. The authors of the film, who assume they are dealing primarily with young women who have been thoroughly brainwashed by their culture to believe that smoking is relatively safe and desirable, repeatedly show how everything young women value can be destroyed by cigarette smoke. By steadfastly sticking to its assertion, by cleverly combining positive and negative reinforcement techniques, and by using an attention-getting device that surveys typical, everyday women, the filmmakers show an acute understanding of the young women in their audience and an ability to reach them.

The attention-getting device works because it provides testimony from ordinary young women, not finger-wagging doctors or psychologists in white lab coats. As the film opens we see four women smoking (the survey lead): a pregnant woman, a black and a white high school student, and a young businesswoman. The first three will be featured in the body of the film, but at this point the narrator appears, introducing the film's topic and assertion. She has been carefully chosen to appeal to the audience. She is attractive, young, and smiling. Dressed in a white, cotton sun dress and barefooted, she addresses her audience informally as an understanding older sister might discuss a confidential matter. From where she sits on a retaining wall in a sunny backyard, she holds a pack of cigarettes and reads the warning on its side. It pitifully understates the dangers of smoking, she says. She rattles off some startling statistics. Equality of the sexes, she says, has apparently come to include equality of self-destruction, too. Anticipating the attitude of her audience, she adds, "If you think you've heard it all before, we have some startling surprises for you." Having stated the obvious—smoking is dangerous—she gives the audience the benefit of the doubt; "How much smoking is dangerous?" she asks. Rather than answer, she allows the body of the film to begin.

The film's assault on the smoking habit is many faceted and well-balanced. It begins with several healthy female smokers who are shocked to discover what smoking is doing to their lungs, blood circulation, complexions, and unborn babies. A few quit smoking immediately when they are given the bad news by physicians. The first subject, a heavy smoker of 17 years, is shown in a sophisticated laboratory test that just one cigarette makes her lungs work 15% harder to breathe, raises her blood pressure by 20 points, and doubles the carbon monoxide level in her blood. Even the small blood vessels of her hands are shown to constrict dramatically after one cigarette. Next, a California doctor shows that smoking causes a woman's (and a man's) skin to wrinkle heavily at a young age. The leathery visages of three middle-aged women attest to the accuracy of this finding. Subsequently, we watch on an oscilloscope the pulse of an unborn fetus that beats normally until its mother lights a cigarette, whereupon the unformed infant's pulse actually stops, temporarily. Then the filmmakers play their emotional trump card by introducing Mary Brown, a dreadfully emaciated, terminally ill lung cancer patient, who tells how smoking has put an end to her life. A photo shows that early in her 43rd year, Mary was a vibrant, attractive, and somewhat chubby housewife. As the camera focuses in on her now, less than a year later, the transformation cigarette-induced lung cancer has worked on her is striking. Although still attractive, she now weighs only 88 pounds. Lying on a couch at home, she tells us how she still cannot believe that she—a light smoker—was struck down so young. The image of her sunken cheeks and temples, her broomstick arms, and her bald head is hard to forget. Pathetically, she says that after treatment she is finally feeling healthy again; six days later she died.

Having hit its skeptical audience with horror, the film then uses positive reinforcement to nail home its anti-smoking assertion. The success stories of people who have quit smoking at a relatively young age, who have escaped the fate of Mary Brown, are shown. At JFK High School, a "kick the habit" campaign has been so successful among students that some carry the anti-smoking message down to the junior high level. After meeting some resistance—"It's our choice," one of the junior high students says defiantly—the high school students find success by introducing an older woman who suffered cancer of the throat and who addresses the youngsters in a froggy, artificial voice that underlines the risks of smoking. Next, the film shows a session of a stop-smoking encounter group of adults organized by the American Cancer Society. Here, many, with the help of a trained instructor and each other, have quit the habit. Finally, a group of girls at JFK High School, some of whom were subjects in *The Feminine Mistake*, are seen watching the just-completed film. The film is not unrealistically hopeful: after the private screening many, but not all of them pledge that they, too, will quit.

The makers of *The Feminine Mistake* succeed with their young and middle-aged female audience because they have done their homework. They know what their viewers have already heard about smoking and the moralistic terms in which they have heard it discussed. The writers therefore come at their target audience with a wide variety of fresh and dramatic facts that show how cigarette smoke threatens most of what they value in life. By emphasizing the horrible and the hopeful, and by casting a young, attractive, and nonsmoking fellow female as the narrator, the filmmakers drive home their assertion.

MOONWALK (Learning Corp. of America: 40 min./color/1976)

About halfway through *Moonwalk*, a history of the first manned landing on the moon, several Americans are heard questioning the value of the space race. Essentially, they complain that it is a waste of money, and the challenge the size of NASA's budget at a time when so many social programs are being cut. Although this group of disgruntled Americans is allowed only a moment of protest in this otherwise laudatory film, it is safe to say that *Moonwalk* was made with them in mind. The film's very purpose, in fact, seems to be to dramatize and to glorify the *Apollo 11* moon flight in order to advocate the continuation of the space program. The filmmakers seem to reason that if they can reach the naysayers represented in the film and those who may have become uninterested in the space program in the years since the public euphoria over the first moonwalk of 1969, then perhaps the space effort will remain an American priority. Using stunning photography of the *Apollo 11* mission and footage of ebullient spectators of that flight the world over, the filmmakers show how space exploration can bring beauty and wonder to our daily lives and glory to our nation. By drawing a comparison between the mounting of the *Apollo* flight and the building of Stonehenge in the film's attention-getting device, the authors suggest that the space race can be seen as the culmination of humankind's ancient efforts to understand the universe and the human role in it.

Moonwalk's opening compares the *Apollo 11* mission and Stonehenge to suggest that both grew out of a noble and historic desire to reach out beyond earthly limits, to explore the unknown. While showing Stonehenge at dawn during the peak of its beauty and mystery, the narrator asks in a serious, philosophical tone that dominates the film, "Was it a magic circle, an observatory, a temple?" What, he asks, made its builders drag huge stones immense distances to build Stonehenge? Immediately, the treads of a huge tank appear; then as the camera pulls back, we see the treads are attached to the huge, slow-moving machine that is transporting an *Apollo* rocket from its bay to the launch pad at Cape Kennedy in Florida in preparation for its 1969 launch. The implication of the juxtaposition is clear: both Stonehenge and *Apollo* were superhuman efforts. Later, when Neal Armstrong delivers from the surface of the moon his "one small step . . ." speech, he becomes the mythic hero whose brave deed unites us all in pride and stirs us on to higher and higher personal achievements. Later still, a scientist is shown studying a fragment of a moon rock enlarged by a microscope in a laboratory. As the fragment is enlarged dramatically to show us the mysterious threads and pockets of its hidden surface, the narrator asks, "will man find the source of all life in his space explorations?" Placed as it is in such a grand, mythic tradition with such high humanitarian aspirations, the *Apollo* program seems unreproachable. Who could question the size of NASA's budget?

Perhaps even more impressive to the skeptic is the resplendent footage of the *Apollo* launch. Although the narrator explains clearly and simply the incredible size and sophistication of the rocket, the artful and glossy photography of the takeoff wows us more. Cameras placed below, alongside, and above the rocket capture the impressive spectacle of the launch far better than the networks that filmed the early space probes for television did. Cameras on tracking jets follow the projectile as it races up through the atmosphere. Shedding its stages one by one in fiery halos that all but obscure it from view, the giant rocket becomes a dwarfed dot streaking from view into space.

Great pains are taken to maintain the drama of the flight after takeoff. The filmmakers play up the danger of the mission and strive to make the astronauts into men we can both identify with and look up to. By focusing on the risks as well as the fun of the astronauts' mission and by showing the ecstatic reaction of spectators on earth, the film shows how the enjoyment of life on earth is increased by the space race. The day-by-day, minute-by-minute, hold-your-breath chronology leading to the launch continues during the flight. With the difficulty and risk of each step into the unknown, the tension builds. When the astronauts approach reentry into the earth's atmosphere, for example, the narrator explains that if their speed is not precisely correct, they will either burn up or bounce off the earth's atmosphere and back into space, never to return. The narrator shows people on street corners around the world glued to storefront televisions. Five hundred million people, we are proudly told, watched the historic event on TV, and millions more listened to it on the radio. Back home, the hero-astronauts are shown riding in cars through cheering crowds and a white-out of ticker tape.

Moonwalk is a clever piece of propaganda. By focusing on the proudest moment of the space race, by comparing *Apollo* with Stonehenge, by courting us with elegant launch photography, and by recreating for us the suspense and heroism of the astronauts' maiden voyage to the moon, the film makes any criticism of NASA's current and future space probes sound mean-spirited, irrelevant, and downright unpatriotic.

WHAT IS POETRY? (BFA: 9 min./color/1963)

As teachers of English, we are always searching for the clearest, most undiluted print examples of dramatic irony, or imagery, or conflict, or any other literary device we wish to introduce to our students. In no area is this search more desperate or more important than in poetry. Here we bend over backwards to find "easy" poems, knowing we will need them to counter our students' prejudices against the art form. We dig up all the action-packed lyrics we can find—poems that describe everyday events, use vivid images and simple figures, flow clearly from specific observations to general commentary, and employ colloquial or easily accessible diction. In a way, we misrepresent poetry by avoiding its beautiful gray areas at first to concentrate on black-and-white examples of such elements as metaphor, allusion, and image patterning. Only after we have convinced our skeptical or insecure students that poetry is not an intentionally confusing way of saying something simple, and have shown them that easily-tapped poems do exist, do we dare lead them into the mainstream of the poetic tradition.

The film *What Is Poetry?* understands that students generally believe that all poetry describes contrived events with esoteric or flowery language. Therefore, the film takes an everyday occurrence—a car crash—and compares the way a newspaper story and Karl Shapiro's poem "Autowreck" describe it. In this nonthreatening, start-from-scratch manner, the filmmakers assert that poetic language is unusual because its goals are different from those of everyday language. They convey this message through a simple comparison and a catchy attention-getting device.

The attention getter (again, the equivalent here of a kicker lead) grabs the students because it introduces a scene they never would have expected to find in a poem or in a film entitled *What Is Poetry?* As the film opens, an ambulance, its red light flashing, arrives at the scene of a grisly accident. Solemnly, the narrator reads a brief newspaper account of the tragedy. Although the teacher will realize that the story (and the accident) is fictitious, the authors make it appear real by showing the authentic-looking newspaper article and by inventing the names of two victims— one who died, one who was critically injured. In Shapiro's poem, which the newspaper account copies, no names are mentioned. These details and others have been added to catch the students up in the tragic mood of the moment.

The narrator's tone and the film's format may also surprise the students. The speaker does not lecture; his voice is matter-of-fact and his approach is to inquire. He outlines the simple plan of the movie—a comparison of journalistic and poetic accounts of the accident. The newspaper report gives all the essentials: what, when, where, and to whom. Notice, the narrator says, that this account is factual and objective; it neither expresses the feelings of the writer nor interprets the significance of the tragedy. Then the narrator reads "Autowreck," and the students watch the scenario unfold on the screen, line by line. An ambulance arrives; its attendants lift the two victims aboard on stretchers; a crowd of curious onlookers gathers; a policeman washes away the blood that has spilled on the pavement. The last stanza of the poem contains Shapiro's philosophic questioning of the event. Then, the narrator reviews the results of the comparison. A news story, he says, is objective, impersonal, and unemotional; a poem, on the other hand, is subjective, personal, and highly emotional. Highlights of the event are replayed, and the speaker describes the features of poetic language: impressive elements of the event are isolated and examined closely; image-evoking words and phrases are used to make us see and feel the event as the onlookers and the poet did.

Many of the intricate figures and images of the poem become clear during the film's visual presentation. For example, the red ambulance light is described in the poem as "a ruby flare/Pulsing out red light like an artery." Although this metaphor and simile combination would be too complex for most novice poetry readers to unravel, when it is heard while watching the spinning light atop the vehicle, its meaning and emotional impact are clear. Similarly, when Shapiro describes the paradoxical revulsion and attraction the onlookers feel toward the scene, it is imperative that the students see the uneasy smiles and grimaces of the crowd in the film to appreciate fully the lines of poetry. Finally, when Shapiro launches into a philosophic discussion of the nature of death in the last stanza: "Already old, the question Who shall die?/Becomes unspoken Who is innocent? . . .," the filmmakers add a few details to the scene (not mentioned by Shapiro) to put the students in an appropriate state of mind. Inside the overturned and totalled auto the camera focuses on a panda bear doll. How did that get there? the students are made to wonder. Was there a small boy or girl in the car? Was the young child injured or killed? How tragic that one so young should be maimed or killed. Outside the vehicle, the wandering camera spots a broken pair of glasses lying away from the car on the roadway. Seeing one of the victims' eyeglasses and hearing the poet's lines, the students will ponder the sudden, cruel, and random violence of the crash and of death itself.

Perhaps the greatest success of the film is that once it has been viewed, the teacher can hand out a copy of the poem and share it with the students again. Chances are that on reading it aloud or to themselves, the students will experience the joy of reading imagery and figures that are clear and vivid to them. Also, it is likely they will feel glad to understand such a "difficult" poem. In short, by anticipating the negative attitude and inexperience most students bring to poetry, by finding an action-packed lyric, by comparing poetry with journalism, and by allowing students to watch the scene that the poem describes, the makers of *What Is Poetry?* actually give the students the feeling that they are beginning to understand poetry after all.

THE GREAT SOCIETY (Pyramid Films: 3 min./color/1966)

The Great Society tells us that despite all the high ideals our country is supposed to represent—equality, democracy, and the American Dream—the United States is really noted for, and defined by, the snazzy line of products its companies produce and its people crave. Only during the 1960s when anti-materialism and anti-American sentiments ran high would such a film have been popular, and it is exactly this counter-culture mindset that the filmmaker plays toward. He makes his assertion by ironically juxtaposing "The Battle Hymn of the Republic" with shot after shot of well-known household products. The message—for those who understand irony and juxtaposition—is that America is the land of the consumer. To grab the viewers' attention, the filmmaker begins without an introduction of any kind, thereby forcing the audience to determine for itself what is going on.

As the film opens, determining what is going on seems easy. The title and the familiar "Battle Hymn" suggest that this will be a patriotic profile of America. Almost immediately, however, the visual images sharply contradict this first impression, and we begin to suspect that this juxtaposition is ironic. This suspicion claims our attention as we scan the various products, looking for a clue in their names, colors, and ordering to reveal the filmmaker's intention. What, we wonder, is the connection among the film's title (a reference to LBJ's idealistic social programs), "The Battle Hymn of the Republic," and these familiar American-made products? What could mundane products like Coke, Campbell's soup, Skippy peanut butter, and Yoo-Hoo soft drink have to do with America's proud heritage and the great society? The answer, of course, is very little, as the viewer who believes that America is not so great after all will attest.

Most of the products briefly glimpsed are simply common household goods that most Americans would readily recognize. They include: Sun-Maid raisins, Cheer laundry detergent, Tums antacids, Spam, a Mary Jane candy bar, Mott's apple juice, Fab detergent, Dentyne chewing gum, a Baby Ruth candy bar, etc. The simple presentation of these many well-known, brand-name goods eventually leads the viewer to realize that these items are probably as familiar to us as the Stars and Stripes, and maybe even more familiar than the lyrics of another patriotic song, the national anthem.

Some of the products seem to have been chosen because their packaging and brand names show how American advertising has trivialized aspects of our heritage. Arm and Hammer Baking Soda, for example, has coopted the mighty forearm and hammer of the labor movement; Cream of Wheat has assimilated the black chef; Argo Corn Starch, the American Indian's corn goddess; Quaker Oats, the Quaker minister; Bulgar cut tobacco, the soldier of World War I; Uncle Sam cereal, the name of America's symbolic leader; and Union Leader Smoking Tobacco, the name of labor again.

A number of products seem to have been selected because their names embody America's well-known and exalted self-image. Products such as the Jolly Green Giant wax beans, Tip Top bread, Mr. Big, Action bleach, Planet facial tissue, Mr. Clean, and True cigarettes, all parody America's image as the world's protector, the honest and strong defender of the little guy. The ironic tone of the film makes us question the accuracy of such a view.

Other products suggest that America has always been the land favoring the wealthy, not the little guy, and that the United States is headed for a fall. Evidence of the former view can be found in such product names as: Royal Prince Yams, Rex Paste (pictured in a red, white, and blue package), Rex dog food, Nestle's $100,000 Candy Bar, the Hollywood candy bar, and Swish (meaning effeminate or fashionable) Dish Wash. Products that imply America is falling apart include: Rescue, SOS, and Slip O'Way. Perhaps the baldest statement of the filmmaker's criticism of America is given in the closing sequence of the film, when a package of Liberty Tobacco is shown, then a box of Niagra Instant Laundry Starch which is pushed over on its face by a human hand. Such a close suggests that the coercion of Wall Street may even be endangering the time-honored American tradition of liberty.

This reading of *The Great Society* is probably close to the typical one it received with its intended audience during the 1960s. How it would be interpreted today is another matter. Back then, when this view of America and middle-class consumerism was common, the filmmaker knew he had little convincing to do; therefore, he simply set up an ironic juxtaposition which confirmed the audience's hefty distrust of mainstream American values. Although the film's assertion was no doubt seen as fairly light-hearted and comical then, viewers today may be offended. Chances are that the film's irony, which would have been immediately apparent to a crowd in the sixties, would not even be perceived by some viewers today, or if understood, not nearly so well received.

FOLLOW-UP ACTIVITIES

1. Get a copy of the magazine section from any Sunday *New York Times*. Read the first two or three paragraphs of each article and determine the attention-getting device used by the author in each. Based on the type of device used by each writer and its tone (solemn, humorous, ironic, etc.), predict what the topic and purpose of the entire article will be.

2. Examine two copies of any nationally distributed magazine to determine who its editors are trying to reach. Prepare a brief profile of the magazine's average reader, including gender, age, political beliefs, most important values, income, and level of education. Base this profile on observations you have made about the articles, columns, advertisements, pictures/illustrations, and writers included in the magazine. The bulk of your proof should come from a close consideration of what each writer in the two issues assumes about his or her audience.

3. Mystery writers often carve out a very specific and loyal following of readers who identify in one way or another with their main character—the detective. These readers follow the private eye's exploits because they enjoy his or her social status, physical and mental prowess, detection skills, values, virtues, and vices. Read two popular mystery novels that follow the work of two very different detectives. Then describe briefly the average reader who would admire this type of main character. Your brief profiles should include a description of the reader's most important values.

4. Imagine that your favorite teacher has been dismissed because of a cutback in staff. Write a letter of recommendation to a potential employer (outside education) outlining the teacher's strengths and the reasons he or she should be hired. Remember to consider your audience. Employers are busy and often snowed under by job inquiries, so yours must stand out and be convincing. Prepare a realistic assertion and include concrete evidence of the teacher's skills and personality. You need not adopt any role or voice other than that of the sincere, helpful, and loyal student.

5. Read one of the following essay collections. Then write a review of the work for your classmates outlining the writer's ideas and methods. In your analysis, concentrate on the assertions, audience assumptions, and attention-getting devices of two representative essays.

    A Collection of Essays, by George Orwell (New York: Harcourt Brace Jovanovich, 1953).

    Essays of E. B. White (New York: Harper & Row, 1977).

    The World of Farley Mowat (Boston, MA: Little, Brown, 1980).

    Slouching Towards Bethlehem, by Joan Didion (New York: Dell, 1968).

Voice

Communications—whether spoken or written—adopt a tone of voice: a sound that is a reflection of the sender's attitude toward the subject matter and audience. In a speaking situation, tones of voice—excited, annoyed, solemn—are easy to identify because the sender's gestures, facial expressions, and behavior tip the receiver off. In writing situations, however, the only clue to the sender's attitude is the symbols he or she has left behind, and "tone of voice" is much harder to determine. Diction, language choices, syntax, the types of argument or persuasion, and the amount of information supplied all become important. The obvious implication for teachers is that students should learn "tone of voice" (hereafter referred to as "voice") first by observing speaking situations, then by studying written situations. Film—an audio-visual medium—gives the teacher the perfect starting point.

Attitude toward subject matter is easier to perceive than attitude toward audience. The former is relatively tangible, the latter much more evasive. Consequently, attitude toward subject matter is considered first in this section, attitude toward audience is examined second.

Two antonym pairs can be used to describe the full range of attitudes a speaker or writer can have toward a subject. Broadly speaking, a sender's attitude can be classified as either "serious" or "humorous" and as either "emotional" or "objective." Once we place the sender's attitude on one end or the other of these two spectra, the more specific work of identifying the exact voice(s) is easier. The following list of voice labels can be used to pinpoint voice:

Voice: Attitude toward Material

foreboding	angry	naive
cynical	indifferent	flippant
sentimental	solemn	gentle
amazed	contented	whimsical
enthusiastic	frazzled	skeptical
critical	sarcastic	disbelieving
concerned	happy	mocking
sad	resigned	melodramatic
outraged	wise-cracking	disappointed
light-hearted	compassionate	scholarly

To determine the other aspect of voice—attitude of the sender toward audience—another grid establishing broad possibilities is helpful. Does the sender feel "superior," "inferior," or "equal" to the audience? The chart below indicates this range of possible relationships.

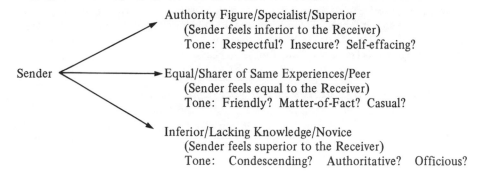

Sender

Authority Figure/Specialist/Superior
(Sender feels inferior to the Receiver)
Tone: Respectful? Insecure? Self-effacing?

Equal/Sharer of Same Experiences/Peer
(Sender feels equal to the Receiver)
Tone: Friendly? Matter-of-Fact? Casual?

Inferior/Lacking Knowledge/Novice
(Sender feels superior to the Receiver)
Tone: Condescending? Authoritative? Officious?

Again, once the sender's attitude toward the audience is broadly determined, a list of specific labels will help pinpoint the exact voice.

Voice: Attitude toward Audience

self-conscious	condescending	insecure
shrill	snobbish	matter-of-fact
self-mocking	bewildered	authoritative
confident	affectionate	self-effacing
brash	ashamed	casual
reticent	respectful	nervous
self-righteous	pleading	"know-it-all"
superior	friendly	officious

Of the five films in this section, two—*The Plow That Broke the Plains* and *The Magic Rolling Board*—concentrate on the attitude of the sender toward subject matter. The tragic scenario of *The Plow* makes it obvious that the speaker's voice is both "serious" and "emotional." The speaker's formal diction and dark, figurative language, and the images of the needless destruction of the plains and its people, lead the viewer to the more specific voice labels of "melodramatic," "solemn," and "outraged." *Magic Rolling Board*, a film about skateboarding enthusiasts, is quite obviously "emotional" and "humorous." A closer look at the film's stunts and at the narrator's bouncy, slang-filled monologue will lead the audience to such voice labels as "enthusiastic" and "light-hearted."

For studying the attitude of the sender toward his or her audience, *I Think I Got the Job*, *Trader Vic*, and *Dinosaur* are ideal. The two characters who are interviewed by the same prospective employer in *I Think I Got the Job* use diametrically opposed voices. One boy is respectful, insecure, and self-effacing because he knows he is dealing with his superior. The other is friendly, matter-of-fact, and casual because he mistakenly believes he is talking with an equal. In *Dinosaur*, a boy giving an oral report in class adopts two voices—one that fails with his audience and another that succeeds. At first, the young speaker sounds like a "know-it-all" who condescends to his classmates as he talks about dinosaurs. Later, to avoid total disaster, the speaker adopts a casual tone of voice, one more appropriate to an audience of his peers. The used car salesperson in *Trader Vic* is the most complicated character of all. Speaking to his used-car customers, whom he treats as his equals and even his betters, he sounds self-effacing, friendly, and matter-of-fact. But speaking about his customers to the film's audience, the real voice of Trader Vic emerges—one that is condescending and authoritative, the voice of a con man.

The activities following the five films will provide an opportunity for students to learn to perceive tone in writing situations. The teacher should concentrate first on simple exercises, such as reading passages aloud to exaggerate the sound of tone, then on having the students study newspapers and magazines, and finally, on extended reading assignments (*see also* "Tone," page 232).

THE PLOW THAT BROKE THE PLAINS (National Audiovisual Center: 25 min./
   b&w/1936)

The Plow recounts the history of the development and destruction of the plains states in the late nineteenth and early twentieth centuries up to the Great Depression. It shows how those seemingly endless and virgin fields used solely for the grazing of cattle were destroyed by the overzealous use of technology. Bankers and farm owners conspired to drive the cattle owners off and to consolidate the plains into huge farms that became food-producing enterprises. To keep up with the growing demand for food throughout the United States and with their own need for cash to extend their businesses and to pay loans, the farmers introduced gas-powered threshers and combines, stripped the land of its mineral wealth, and left a dust bowl. As the film ends, the impoverished families gather their scant possessions and head west for jobs, abandoning fields now choked with dust.

This sad story is told through three different voices: melodramatic, solemn, and outraged. The students can determine the various devices used to create these tones of voice, and they can observe the ways in which pictures and sounds—in this case both the musical score and the narrator's voice—can work together to produce a dramatic effect. The script observes the most formal of grammatical rules (parallel structure is obvious throughout the film), employs rhetorical devices (the repetition of key phrases, dramatic pauses, alliteration, metaphor, symbol), and uses emotive diction. As the narrator recites these highly structured and literary lines, the filmmaker shows the audience a series of dramatic and emotional scenes (a dust storm sweeping across the plains; plows, threshers, and combines gouging the earth in a frenzy; poor farmers heading west in defeat) and employs visual metaphors (the comparison of a tractor to an army tank to show that the farmers waged a kind of destructive war on the land) and symbols (rusted and abandoned tractors and plows; farmhouses nearly engulfed by dust; cracked and dried earth) to blend the images and words of the movie into a coherent whole. Finally, the background music runs the gamut of emotions from serenity (in the early, Edenic years of the cattle ranchers), to a frenzied excitement (during the height of the technological development of the plains), to sorrowful (during the dust bowl years of the Depression).

In addition to this exploration of tone, the students can be asked to consider the intended audience of the film. The complex language devices and the shifting tones suggest an educated audience, and the inveighing against the financial establishment in the United States points to a liberal, perhaps socialistic, audience. Here the teacher can show the significance of the time in which the film was made: in 1936, American politics was dominated by the liberalism of Franklin Delano Roosevelt, whose programs as president sought to conserve the country's natural resources, to place strict controls on the actions of America's conservative financial institutions, and to rescue the common person from the evils of the Great Depression.

ACTIVITIES FOR THE STUDENT

The following questions can focus student discussion on the objectives:

1. The language of the narrator is highly formalized in that it uses devices not normally employed in common or informal speech. Why does the author use such alliterative phrases as "plow at your peril"? How does this help to achieve the effect he is striving for? Why does he repeat the phrase "high winds and sun"? What is the narrator's purpose in using such stylized language? What do these phrases, and others like them, tell us about the audience for which the film was intended?

2. Several visual metaphors force the viewer to respond to the film emotionally and imaginatively. For instance, very early in the film, the plow (the first one that we see) is compared to a knife. Many other metaphors are created through the juxtaposition of scenes. Indicate, in the space provided, what each item in the following list is being compared to through the device of juxtaposition:

   a. farming   a. _____

   b. plowing   b. _____

   c. tractors   c. _____

   Make a list of the visual metaphors in the movie. How do these metaphors help to convey emotion? In what ways do they add to the impact of the narrator's words and his tone of voice? What type of audience would not be responsive to the use of these metaphors? What audience would be? Explain your answers.

3. The filmmaker uses music to augment the effect of tone of voice and the visual images. Describe the emotion conveyed by the music in each of the following sections of the film:

   a. the cattle grazing scenes

   b. the threshing and harvesting scenes

   c. the dust storm scene

   d. the migration of the farmers scene

In each case, explain how the music contributes to the overall effect, helps convey the filmaker's ideas and attitudes, persuades us to accept his beliefs.

MAGIC ROLLING BOARD (Pyramid Films: 15 min./color/1976)

As its title suggests, this film shows the remarkable stunts accomplished by skateboard enthusiasts on the West Coast, and the ways the skateboard had influenced the lives of California's young people at the time the film was made. Some devotees specialize in events like the downhill slalom or the downhill race; the film shows one rider setting a downhill skateboard record of 50 mph. Others practice jumps and spins for competition, while some merely have fun skateboarding around their empty swimming pools or through the town's storm drain pipes. The film has its humorous moments, too. It shows a rooster and then a dog wearing sunglasses riding on a skateboard. One eccentric male rider dresses up in white tie and tails to perform among the crowds on a boardwalk. Another wears the uniform of a test pilot and straps what looks like a hydrofoil on his back.

Whether silly or serious, however, the film's narrator glorifies the skateboard and convinces us of its many advantages. The students can be led to hear the enthusiasm and lightheartedness in his voice. He speaks to us in idiomatic English peppered with current clichés, slang, and the occasional pun. He suggests he is one of us— young, fad-conscious, and ready for fun. A variety of film techniques augment these tones of voice to further the film's propaganda. The skateboard is often filmed from the ground up so that it seems to soar. Gimmicks such as slow motion, fast motion, and the fish-eye camera lens make the toy seem supernatural, if not surreal. The choice of settings—beachfronts, sunsets, etc.—convinces us of the skateboard's grandeur and romance. The exclusive use of young, attractive, blond teens ties the toy to youth and even to wholesomeness. Finally, the rock 'n' roll music keeps our feet tapping and our attention focused on the energy and excitement associated with the skateboard.

ACTIVITIES FOR THE STUDENT

1. Listen to the narrator's voice and choice of words. Is his diction formal or colloquial? Point out examples of slang, clichés, and puns in his speech. What does this use of language tell us about the speaker's age, background, and values?
2. Choose three labels that describe the tones of voice in the film. Be sure that these labels are consistent with what you think the narrator's attitude toward the skateboard is. What reasons would he advance for participation in the sport?
3. What type of camera angles are used to film the skateboard and its riders? What other camera gimmicks are used to show the skateboard in action? Do these tricks reinforce the narrator's attitude toward the sport? Specify.

JOB INTERVIEW: I GUESS I GOT THE JOB (McGraw-Hill Contemporary Films: 13 min./color/1975)

Two teenage roommates apply for the same airline job. Tony is reticent and self-conscious during his interview; Roger is brash and over-confident. Back home, while the two await the results of the interviews, Tony is convinced by Roger that he failed to adopt a winning personality with the interviewer. Moments later, however, Tony gets a call asking him to report for work the next day.

The film demonstrates that all speech and writing occasions require the sender to consider audience expectations before choosing an appropriate tone of voice. Roger's friendly, matter-of-fact, and casual voices, which might have been effective with his friends, offend the interviewer. Tony's respectful, insecure, and self-effacing voices, which probably would have puzzled his friends, convince the interviewer that he will be an honest and reliable worker.

Through the film, the students can learn that an important goal is to have control over a wide range of tones of voice. Only then will the sender be able to reach all types of audiences and sell them ideas, or, as in Tony's case, the sender himself.

ACTIVITIES FOR THE STUDENT

1. Before discussing the film, or perhaps even before seeing it, consider these questions:
    a. What personality traits should all job applicants try to project in a letter of application or interview?
    b. What are some appropriate tones of voice to use with a prospective employer?
    c. What topics of conversation would be inappropriate to bring up in an interview?
    d. What type of language (formal or informal) should be used in an interview?
2. Use the following chart to describe what happened in the film:

TONY		ROGER
	behavior exhibited	
	tone of voice used	
	personality traits revealed	

3. Using the sender-message-receiver chart (*see* introduction to "Sender—Message—Receiver Relationships," page 88), describe the reason for Tony's success and Roger's failure in the film.

TRADER VIC'S USED CARS (Encyclopaedia Britannica: 10 min./color/1975)
Trader Vic is a documentary about a used car salesperson. The main character is a master manipulator who knows his audience well: the film shows him working his customers, conning them and cajoling them with his warm personality. At the same time, he confides in us, the film's audience, through asides.

Realizing that his customers are of lower class and poorly educated, Trader Vic establishes an informal, nonthreatening environment: his staff is casually dressed; his office is a converted gas station. He develops trust in his customers by making fun of the very cars he sells and by granting them credit without checking their ability to pay. His voice is friendly, matter-of-fact, and self-effacing.

But while he is dealing with his customers, he is also enjoying a laugh with us at his customers' expense. His voice as revealed to us is condescending and authoritative. Through the asides and voice-overs, he tells us that he mails rusty pennies to every fourth trade-in customer, pretending that his staff found them in the back seat when they cleaned the car. The customer usually returns with a neighbor, so impressed is he with Vic's honesty. In the neighbor, of course, Trader Vic has what he is after—a new customer.

Through accurate audience assumptions (*see* "Attention-Getting Devices, Assertions, and Audience Assumptions," page 89) and well-chosen tones of voice, Trader Vic creates trust and loyalty in his audience. In this successful sender—message—receiver relationship, the students can see how one's choice of words and the sound with which they are delivered affect the receiver's perception. Vic proves that it is not the message that is important so much as the way in which it is delivered.

This movie is complicated by the fact that the filmmaker includes a second sender—message—receiver relationship. While we watch Trader Vic sell cars, we hear him talking directly to us in speeches that his customers on the lot obviously have not heard. Indeed, it is easy to see that if they had, they would never trust Trader Vic again.

ACTIVITIES FOR THE STUDENT

1. Answer the following questions concerning the two sender—message—receiver relationships of *Trader Vic.*
   a. What tone(s) of voice does Trader Vic use with his customers on the car lot?
   b. What tone(s) of voice does he use when he is talking directly to the film audience?
   c. What overall image does Trader Vic develop in the film audience's eyes?
   d. What is his overall image in the community from which his customers come?

DINOSAUR (Pyramid Films: 14 min./color/1980)

A grammar school student gives an oral report on the dinosaur to his inattentive, rowdy classmates. At the onset, Philip presents facts in a dry, scholarly voice and loses his audience. It is only when he changes tack that he captures the kids and pleases his teacher. *Dinosaur* is an uproarious film that gives a great deal of scientific information and much pleasure with its humor, but it is also a lesson in the selection of an appropriate voice. It is not the students who are out of synch with the situation; the audience cannot be blamed for an honest reaction to a speaker. It is Philip (as well as his teacher) who has made the mistake.

Paper airplanes fly and students wisecrack as their teacher announces that Philip will report on dinosaurs. Her voice alternates from shrill to condescending, and she manages only partially to control her charges. Philip steps into the breach with the logical assumption that he, because he knows his material, is superior to his listeners. "The word 'dinosaur' means 'terrible lizard,'" he opens in a voice heard most often from the lectern in *The Paper Chase.*

Logical assumptions are usually irrelevant, however, in the often illogical elementary school classroom. As Philip goes on, the kids take off on his statements to hurl comic insults at each other. When he describes a dinosaur whose brain was so small it needed a "sort of helper" brain in its back, a classmate quips to another, "You ought to get one of those, Richard." Neither Philip nor his audience is seen in this animated film. Instead, comic depictions of Philip's data (a herbivore, for example, wears a bib and holds utensils at a table filled with vegetables) are shown, as if projected on the blackboard, to reflect the attitude of the class to the report. Philip lectures on a dinosaur noted for its armor-plated skin. "That looks like Margaret's mother," someone yells.

When Philip finally gets angry, he drops the dry, scholarly tone for an informal, enthusiastic one. The name of the *Tyrannosaurus rex*, he says, "means the 'tyrant lizard king,' and when he talked everybody listened." The wisecracking diminishes, Philip talks as if to equals, and he gains a measure of revenge on his tormentors. The once-comic dinosaurs are suddenly ferocious jungle killers as he frightens the imaginations of his classmates. One of the dinosaur depictions grows larger, as if it will step out of the blackboard to lunch on the kids. Philip says above their screams, "Wow, man, nobody messed with them." He concludes by imagining how they would have behaved toward such a creature. "You don't speak," he says, "you just be quiet as a mouse and hope he doesn't stomp on you."

Philip, ever the precocious one, has outfoxed his friends. His voluntary and clever change of voice produces an involuntary change in his friends. They switch from wisecracking troublemakers to attentive listeners. Only the teacher undergoes no transformation. Just as she failed to analyze correctly her audience in the beginning, she takes over the class with her usual condescending tone. But Philip, using Machiavelli's prescription for handling the unruly masses, has subdued the class. Philip savors his triumph. A classmate asks him if it isn't sad that the dinosaur is extinct. He answers, with his original scholarliness: "It isn't sad; it's nature's way, for after the dinosaur died, the mammal had the chance to develop. And mammals have a superior brain, if I do say so myself." Having learned his lesson, he has a right to be arrogant.

ACTIVITIES FOR THE STUDENT
1. After viewing the film, fill in the following chart. Note that the voice changes for many of the characters.

	Tones of Voice Used	Personality Traits Revealed
Teacher		
Philip		
Other Students		

FOLLOW-UP ACTIVITIES
1. The following activities will test your ability to detect an author's attitude toward the subject matter.
   a. On the day after the Academy or Grammy Awards show, newspapers review the proceedings. Though a journalist will devote a good deal of space to telling what happened and who won the awards, his or her attitude toward the stars and the show will also reveal itself. Did the writer

find the proceedings exciting? Is the show just another news event? Does he or she feel that it is given too much hoopla, that it is no more than a triviality? Find two articles on the same awards show. Compare in an essay two reviewers' voices (attitudes towards the program).

b.   Cut out a reasonably short news story from your local paper. Rewrite the article by changing the objective tone of voice to a subjective one. For instance, you may adopt a humorous, mocking, or sad voice, but be sure to include the same facts used by the original author.

c.   Read an essay collection by a popular writer such as John McPhee, Thomas Wolfe, or Gilbert Highet. As you read the selections, make a list of the various subjects and the author's voice for each. Then analyze in detail the attitude toward the subject matter in your favorite one. You should discuss specific sentences to show how the writer achieved that voice.

2.   The following activities will test your ability to determine an author's attitude toward the audience.

a.   Read Winston Churchill's famous "Dunkirk" speech. (It is readily available in the library.) Speaking both to Parliament and over the radio to the entire populace, Churchill delivered the speech at the lowest point in the war for the British, just after its army had been driven off the European continent by the Nazis. Analyze the speaker's attitudes toward his audience and the reasons he adopted those attitudes.

b.   Select two articles from your high school newspaper, one that covers an event and one that is primarily filled with gossip. Discuss in an essay how the attitudes toward the audience differ in each case and whether or not you feel the voices are appropriate.

c.   Read a regularly appearing newspaper or magazine column (such as "Talk of the Town" in *The New Yorker*) over several issues. In an essay, generalize on the most prevalent attitudes toward the audience, using quotes to demonstrate your points.

Irony

A substitute teacher, Mr. Engels, takes over Ms. French's science class in January when she goes out on a maternity leave. The first day after the switch Mr. Engels begins class by calling roll. All goes well until two students correct his pronunciation of their names. (He has told them to do this if he makes a mistake.) Gerry Comollo (Cŏm-ŏl'-lō) says he is called Gerry (Cŭm'-ĕllō) and Richard Viglione (Vĭg'-lĭŏn) insists his is pronounced Richard (Vĭl-yō'-nāy). The teacher thanks them for the information, looks up to see several students smiling, and smiles back from where he sits at the front of the room. To get off on the right foot, Mr. Engels decides to conduct a simple experiment to prove that containers can be filled with liquid beyond their capacity. To illustrate this law, he fills a beaker with water until the fluid hovers above the rim, then takes out a piece of cardboard. "When I place the cardboard on top of the filled beaker and turn it over," he says, "the excess water above the lip will form a seal between the beaker and the cardboard and hold the water inside when I turn the container upside down." At first, the experiment works, but then the cardboard slowly begins to slide sideways and down comes a torrent of water, soaking Mr. Engels' desk, tie, and rank book. When the teacher finally restores order to the classroom, the period is almost over, so he has the students read chapter seven quietly and answer the study questions at its conclusion. When the bell rings and most of the students have mercifully filed out, Gerry Comollo stops by Mr. Engels' desk and says, "That was great, Mr. Engels, much more educational than anything Ms. French ever did. I'm glad you're here and she's gone. Welcome aboard." Comollo shakes the teacher's hand, then exits. From further down the hall the teacher hears an explosion of laughter.

What would life be like without irony? A lot easier for substitute teachers, perhaps, but certainly less entertaining for the rest of us. What happened to Mr. Engels could, of course, happen to anyone who is the sole outsider of a close-knit group. In fact, one of the fundamental goals of irony is to draw those who "get it" into an in-group and exclude all others. When Comollo and Viglione played their name game, they were using dramatic irony; that is, they were creating a circumstance where one character—the teacher—knew less than everyone else—the students. When Mr. Engels performed his ill-fated experiment, he unwittingly created situational irony—the audience was lead to expect one outcome and its opposite occurred. And finally, when Comollo came up to console Mr. Engels, he was using sarcasm, one form of verbal irony which occurs when the speaker says one thing but really means something else.

The teacher may well ask why irony should be taught when students like Viglione and Comollo already use it so effectively. The reasons are several. First, most classes usually contain only a few students who are well-versed in the three ironies discussed here, and even their powers are often limited to slapstick humor and broad sarcasm. Rarely can a high school student decode the subtleties of irony used in print or film as competently as those used in everyday speech. By the same token, even fewer can use these three ironies to good effect in their own writing. Although a student's rudimentary understanding of dramatic irony (making a gesture at the teacher when his back is turned), verbal irony (being sarcastic with a friend), and situational irony (laughing when someone says watch this card trick and then fails to pull it off) should be drawn upon, the real challenge is to bolster this basic understanding and to refine and extend it to the study of the novel and essay.

PRE-FILM ACTIVITIES
1. The study of history uncovers countless ironies of situation that become apparent to us in hindsight. Students should have no trouble recalling some from their own courses. Certainly it is ironic that England's Prime Minister Neville Chamberlain initially received praise for having appeased Adolph Hitler with small concessions on the Continent. Similarly, it is ironic that King Henry VIII's frantic search for a male heir produced only one son, who died before having children, and one of England's greatest queens.
2. Television's situation comedies abound in situational ironies. Once several examples from current sitcoms have been discussed in class, the students should write a one- to three-sentence *TV Guide*-type summary of a favorite show that points out the program's central irony. A summary of an *All in the Family* episode could be: "The Bunker household is thrown into disarray when Archie's best friend, Joe, asks him to be his best man. Archie is all smiles until he realizes that his buddy's bride-to-be is a black woman." (Situational irony.)
3. Many sitcoms feature one or more naive characters who either seriously misuse the language or simply do not get what is obviously going on around them. Such examples of dramatic irony—Archie's hilarious prejudices and malapropisms, Edith's naive remarks—should be jotted down by students at home and presented for discussion in class.

4. Greeting cards often achieve their effects by setting up an expectation in the picture and words on the cover of the card that is shattered or contradicted by the punch line inside. Verbal irony (especially puns) is also commonly used to give the cards a slight sexual connotation. Examples of both these greeting card conventions should be analyzed by students.
5. Comic strips, magazine advertisements, and letters to the editor in newspapers also contain examples of these three ironies. These should be analyzed in short paragraphs or discussed in brief oral reports.

The films that follow provide an excellent introduction to the functions the three ironies can serve in art, and the techniques used by artists to produce them. By and large, the films chosen are satires that will appeal to students because they are opinionated and often brash. Through them students will realize that by learning to decode irony they will better appreciate any work of art's theme, tone, and beauty. For the teacher's convenience, the chart below briefly outlines the type(s) of irony used by each and the functions the device is meant to serve. Bill Cosby, the narrator of *Black History: Lost, Stolen or Strayed*, uses verbal irony to persuade white liberals that their efforts against racism, which one generally regarded as adequate, actually fall short of what is needed by the country's oppressed black people. As such, it is a goad to do better. *Doubletalk* uses dramatic irony to reveal the insincerity and unkindnesses of four people caught in an awkward social situation. The result is a cynical and humorous satire on dating and the social graces. *Worshipping* employs situational irony to satirize gently those in the United States who elevate car customizing to a personal religion. By its conclusion the viewer has been given a unique understanding of a not-so-common hobby. The makers of *Beauty Knows No Pain* use situational irony to deliver a scathing satire of the Rangerettes (a color guard dance team) and their values. Through this device, the insidiousness of the Rangerettes and their leader is exposed in the hope that the audience will oppose institutions like it that promote and instill derogatory views of women. In *Bach to Bach*, the medium is dramatic irony and the message is a humorous "put-down" of two pretentious and pseudo-intellectual characters. We may not be as phoney as they, the film indicates, but we all have a little of them in us. The verbal irony of Mel Brooks in *The Critic* cuts both ways, poking fun at needlessly esoteric works of art and at those Philistines who dismiss all modern art as garbage.

FUNCTIONS AND TYPES OF IRONY

		Black History	Double-talk	Worshipping	Beauty Knows...	Bach to Bach	The Critic
functions	inspires the viewer to action	X			X		
	reveals character		X		X	X	X
	uncovers an unusual point about something familiar	X		X	X		
	makes fun of a human foible or institution (satire)		X	X	X	X	X
types of irony	dramatic irony		X			X	
	situational irony			X	X		
	verbal irony	X					X

BLACK HISTORY: LOST, STOLEN OR STRAYED (BFA: 53 min./color/1968)

Black History: Lost, Stolen or Strayed, a film about racism against blacks in the United States, is carefully aimed at educated, liberal, white viewers. It tells them that despite the gains blacks made by 1968, the year the film was released, reforms must continue if real equality is the goal. Using verbal irony and a semi-militant, black-power persona (*see* "Persona," page 122), narrator Bill Cosby attempts to produce guilt about past American injustices to motivate the viewers to fight even harder against racism. Knowing full well how sheepish many whites felt during the reform-minded 1960s about the country's chauvinistic past, Cosby mounts an aggressive assault on the United States' shabby human rights record. (Cosby also provides the blacks in the audience with a strong and proud Afro-American role model.) He lambasts standard American history books that still ignore famous black figures and denigrate the proud heritage of black slaves. Cosby compares the drawings of black and white grade school children to show how racism has damaged the personalities of black youngsters. During the bulk of the film, the actor takes us on a tour through Hollywood's archives to show film and newsreel clips that luridly document the vicious black stereotypes created and enjoyed by white Americans. The film then shows us pathetic examples of blacks trying to find acceptance as middle-class Negroes, and closes with a stop at a storefront school where a black man tries to prepare black preschool children for the prejudice they will encounter in Philadelphia's public school system. Both the film's conclusion and its opening focus on young school children. In this way, Cosby holds out the innocent and as yet undamaged inheritors of America's future like lambs on the chopping block and asks his audience with a consistent verbal irony—"Need they be destroyed, too?"

When the film begins, Bill Cosby addresses the audience from inside an integrated grade school classroom where young children, following the lead of their black teacher, have just finished singing a song about Charlie Brown. In the background, on the room's walls, the children's art work is displayed. When the song stops, the children resume their work and Cosby speaks to the camera. Soon, it becomes apparent that this setting, this narrator, even the Charlie Brown song, have been chosen to establish in the audience a sense of urgency and concern. First of all, Cosby, the normally warm and gentle comedian, is not being funny. This, by itself, is startling. Quite the contrary, in fact, his tone is serious, sarcastic, and ironic. Today, he will talk about racism, not Fat Albert. Second, the integrated classroom with a black teacher is not held up as a grand achievement of liberal reforms; rather, it is seen as only a small victory over racism which cannot be allowed to mask the racial hatred and confusion that Cosby says still eats away at all Americans. Third, and somewhat less obviously, Charlie Brown is used as a symbol of the black child and adult who is constantly persecuted and belittled by his peers. Finally, Cosby picks up the school children's drawings which depict famous black men in history who for one reason or another—and here is the film's theme—were "Lost, Stolen, or Strayed" out of white men and women's U.S. history books.

Cosby's opening remarks about an all-but-unknown black man, Norbert Rillieux (pictured in a child's drawing) who revolutionized the sugar refining industry, establish the ironic tone and semi-militant persona he will use throughout the film to make whites feel guilty about America's racist ways. In that sequence he says:

> Now, what's the whitest thing you know? Sugar. Noninte-
> grated, nonblack, sweet sugar. But you see, there is a black
> man in your sugar. His name is Norbert Rillieux. In 1846

> he invented a vacuum pan that revolutionized the sugar
> refining industry. You have to dig to find that fact. I mean,
> it's not much history, but it's still history.

Even though there is some humor in Cosby's remarks, it is grim humor, and the impression that lasts is that whiteness or at least the historical obsession for "pure whiteness" is being mocked. This feeling is achieved through verbal irony: the words "nonintegrated," "nonblack," and "sweet" are sarcastic. And when Cosby says, "it's not much history," he is using understatement. Sugar, he says, is thought to be pure white, but it isn't. Rillieux is no George Washington, but he is not a nobody either. Cosby's semi-militant, we're-not-going-to-take-it-anymore persona is also evident in other remarks. Holding up a picture showing white men trying to wash the color out of a black man named York who helped Lewis and Clark explore the West, Cosby says: "They're trying to wash the black out of York. That's what you might call historically significant because a lot of people think we ought to wash white, but we ain't gonna." Using rhetorical questions, he remarks, "There were 5,000 black cowboys in Texas who never made it to the Hollywood westerns. Did you know that? Huh?" And, "How about the North Pole? Snow white? Well, the first man there was black." Cosby says, "Napoleon said 'history' is the fable agreed upon. And the fable agreed to up until now is white on white." The speaker's sarcastic expressions— "snow white" and "white on white"—establish an aggressive, almost militant persona. Later, while introducing clips from D. W. Griffith's film classic "Birth of a Nation," which Cosby attacks for its racism, he says, "Cat named D. W. Griffith produced it and he knew how." When the clip shows the birth of the KKK, Cosby defines it sarcastically as "that great white all-American organization." And, finally, describing one of the many film versions of *Uncle Tom's Cabin*, Cosby says, "By 1903, Uncle Tom is just white man's idea of a good nigger. You might say he was what H. Rap Brown ain't." To say that Uncle Tom and H. Rap Brown are dissimilar is to use obvious understatement.

Cosby's verbal irony is constant throughout the film. Representative examples include: "And what about Teddy Roosevelt's charge up San Juan Hill? [Rhetorical question.] Four black regiments went up the hill right beside Teddy. They didn't get lost going up the hill, they got lost in the history books." (Notice that Cosby makes his point here by choosing the euphemism or understatement "lost" instead of the harsher "censored" or "banished" from the history books.) Reading selections from a 1942 edition of a history book written by two Pulitzer Prize winning professors, Cosby says, "'As for Sambo . . .'" Then he looks up at the audience and says, "Sambo? Professor Cumminger?" (Rhetorical question.) In an effort to show that natives of Africa had sophisticated cultures before they were stolen by white slave traders, Cosby shows art works by Picasso, Klee, and Modigliani that borrowed heavily from African works. Note how his discussion makes use of invective and sarcasm: "Here's a sculpture by an unknown African artist. Here's what Paul Klee took from it. Here's a painting by an unknown African artist. And Pablo Picasso liked what he saw. Here's a painting by an unknown African artist. Modigliani swiped it, or was influenced by it, or whatever polite word you want to use for it." Cosby's sarcasm and use of simile are also caustic. He describes Shirley Temple's attitude toward her black slaves in clips from old movies this way: "She was good to them and they were good to her. Sort of a master-pet relationship."

Cosby's ironic script, with its sarcasm, rhetorical questions, invective, similes, understatement, and wide variety of references, suggests the film was made for a primarily white, liberal, and educated audience. The way Cosby alludes to Napoleon, Lewis and Clark, Bat Masterson, Jesse James, Billy the Kid, Teddy Roosevelt, Admiral

Perry, and *Uncle Tom's Cabin*, when he discusses the children's drawings, shows he clearly assumes the audience knows its history and to some extent its literature. On the other hand, by carefully explaining each obscure black historical figure, he assumes the audience is not familiar with them, but thinks it should be and is therefore willing to listen. By saying, at one point, that "most people think that if we [blacks] get enough education and enough jobs, everything's going to take care of itself," Cosby describes the majority of his audience as concerned white citizens who have favored affirmative action and integration, and who now probably hope racism is on the decline in the United States. Cosby knows that this audience remembers the race riots that swept the country and that they deplored and feared them. Cosby's confidence in his audience's willingness to listen is further evident when he lashes out at popular TV shows such as "Our Gang" and "Amos and Andy," and film stars such as Shirley Temple and Sidney Poitier. Cosby knows his audience 1) believes racism is widespread and 2) thinks no vested interest should interfere with its eradication. So confident is he of his audience's sympathy with his cause that at one point Cosby says sarcastically, "This is a lot of fun, isn't it?" Earlier, while talking about an unknown black heart surgeon, he said, "What about your heart? Can we get there?" One does not ask a rhetorical question like this if one is uncertain of how the audience will reply.

DOUBLETALK (Learning Corp. of America: 9 min./color/1977)

Few filmmakers would be willing to limit themselves to a plot that contains so little action. The entire scenario of *Doubletalk* can be summarized as follows. A young man named David arrives at Karen Peterson's house to take her out on their first date. While waiting for her to appear downstairs, he speaks for the first time with her parents. When Karen arrives, the two depart for the beach. Nothing could sound less significant or dramatic: There is no apparent conflict, problem, character development, resolution, or theme. Yet by adding to this simple script the device of dramatic irony, the filmmaker takes a few nondescript moments and transforms them into a sometimes humorous, sometimes cynical social commentary. Quite simply, the filmmaker allows us to listen in on the dialogues that take place among these individuals *and* on the thoughts that simultaneously pass through their minds. By allowing us to hear interior monologues that reveal each character's secret motivations, fears, and prejudices, the filmmaker puts us in the position of knowing more than the characters do about what is actually taking place. In the process, we are given a good laugh and a somewhat cynical view of the nature of dating, communications, and human relations in general.

In part, the dramatic irony of these conversations reveals the insecurity ("Will I be accepted as I am?") and the insincerity ("Did I make a good first impression?") that accompany all first meetings, and that normally transform them into stilted affairs. When David approaches Karen's house for the first time, he feels intimidated because the Petersons appear to be much wealthier than his family is. He also fantasizes about midnight swims with Karen in the family's pool. "This could be all right," we hear him think. So preoccupied is he with a combination of fear and lust that when Mrs. Peterson arrives at the door, he almost forgets the family surname. The pressure of the moment causes David first to flatter Mrs. Peterson excessively, then to bring up obvious and mundane topics of conversation. "I can see where Karen gets her good looks," he says to the attractive mother. "Oh, brother," she thinks, "get this kid a shovel." He tries again: "I see you play tennis." (She is dressed in tennis whites.) "No, I bake bread in this outfit," she thinks, although she says, "Yes, and you?" David pretends to enjoy tennis although he really hates it. He then feigns appreciation of an Oriental statue that sits on an end table beside their couch. She graciously accepts the compliment of the statue, saying, "My husband's fond of Oriental art," but thinks, "and Oriental women like that rotten little Japanese secretary." When David comments on the beauty of their home, the gracious and modest hostess replies in kind, but thinks, "Being poor (only several years ago) was awful." Prejudice and personal problems clearly have a deleterious effect on the conversations at this first meeting.

After Mrs. Peterson has excused herself (actually fled) to find Karen, David and Mr. Peterson meet. The mutual suspicions and the prejudice of their thoughts keep the conversation tense and labored. One look at the way the other is dressed has David thinking Mr. Peterson is a "golf nut," and Mr. Peterson believing David is a "beach boy." Asked if he wants a drink, David is suspicious that the father is trying to determine whether or not he is a lush. When David accepts it, the father thinks to himself "the boy must smoke pot, too." When Mr. Peterson asks David if he's related to a well-known realtor in town, David's insecurity about his family's status (his father owns a dry cleaning store) causes him to assume the man wants to know his social class. The father discovers that the boy has just finished a psychology degree. He calls psychology "an interesting field," but thinks, "What the hell good is it?" Peterson wonders quietly if the Scotch he and David now drink has been watered down. Is his wife "hitting the bottle?" he wonders. His interior mulling over this question shows up on his face as a look of thoughtfulness and worry. Even the relatively safe topic of sports does not work well between the two. When David says he does not follow football, the father wonders if "the kid is a faggot." The way Mr. Peterson talks about the good old days of football, David would never know the man still feels bad that as a third stringer, he never saw action.

When Karen finally arrives, the din created by the combination of everyone's words and thoughts is deafening for the audience, and it makes us understand how first meetings such as these can be so fraught with tension and discomfort. Both the father and David comment on how good Karen looks in her slacks and halter top, but the youth thinks, "What an amazing body!" and Mr. Peterson thinks, "She's just asking for trouble dressing like that—she's practically naked." Karen, meanwhile, is worrying about the pimple on her forehead and whether it is completely covered or not. Sensing that the Petersons already think he is a wolf out to prey on their daughter, David says the two plan to see a movie, thus hiding his real plan to head for the beach. Karen wonders why David has made this switch, but says nothing, so preoccupied is she with monitoring the painfully embarrassing remarks of her parents. Each time one of them cautions the couple about driving safely and being in on time, she groans internally, "Oh, Daddy," or "Mother!" Finally David pretends that they are late for the movie, and they leave. Just outside the door, he begins to explain about the ruse, but Karen seems more anxious to head for the beach. "Fantastic," David thinks. He is a wolf!

The steady use of dramatic irony in *Doubletalk* transforms an essentially undramatic few moments into rich melodrama. At first, we laugh at the foursome because we recognize ourselves in their discomfort and insincerity. We may even learn something about the complex nature of communication, especially why exchanges that take place between strangers are rarely successful. Eventually, however, the tone of the film becomes more serious and cynical. We begin to lose sympathy with the four characters because they are so underhanded and distrustful. The parents seem cruel to each other and needlessly unhappy in marriage. Why, we wonder, has the intimacy of years together not eased the tension and insincerity of daily conversation between them? The young adults also seem unusually self-centered and inconsiderate.

They allow the prejudices of their generation to block any meaningful or compassion-ate conversation with the adults. Finally, we see the intended significance of the pun in the title of the film. On the one hand, the dramatic irony gives us a "doubletalk" in that we hear each person's thoughts and speech simultaneously. On the other hand, we wonder if the filmmaker is not making a fairly cynical comment on the way our own petty, self-concerns destroy communication.

WORSHIPPING (Creative Film Society: 8 min./color/1976)

The opening of *Worshipping* is very effective, but somewhat misleading. Pit crews and admirers help the drivers of drag race cars make last-minute preparations before they thunder down the long, thin straightaways at incredible speed in vehicles whose front wheels jump sky-high at the moment of takeoff. In addition to the roar of their engines, we hear the driving guitar work of the rock group The Byrds playing the song "Eight Miles High." At this point, we feel a sense of wonder and admiration for the racers, but soon the tone of the film changes. Though there is no narration, the filmmaker, through his choice of songs, setting, title, and interview subject, encourages us to laugh at these people who put cars at the centers of their lives. This gradual reversal in tone, or dramatic irony, is achieved largely through comparison. The filmmaker compares the subjects' car hobby—which we would, obviously, regard as secular—to a religious ritual. The absurdity of the comparison, which makes the hobbyists and their fans act in ways so contrary to twentieth century behavior (dra-matic irony), allows us to feel superior to these people who appear freakish and oddly out of step with their time. We do not hate them, however; we just smile at their fanaticism and at the notion that a hobby can fulfill such a vital role in anyone's life.

A simple listing of some of the film's song titles suggests the maker will compare car customizing—as these people engage in it—to a personal religion. They are "Eight Miles High," "Angel Baby," "Alleluiah," and "Earth Angel." Even without the further reinforcement of the film's title, *Worshipping*, the comparison would be firmly estab-lished, but the filmmaker achieves additional humor by piling on even more references to it. After the dramatic opening, the film's setting shifts to a convention hall where car enthusiasts apply last-minute touches to their customized Corvette Stingrays, Model T's, Roadsters, and assorted 1950s classics. While the owners prepare their babies for display, the camera concentrates on the exteriors of the customized autos, whose metallic pink, gold, lime green, and chrome surfaces reflect in dazzling brilliance the bright light of the hall. The owners appear as penitents, kneeling before their private altars, which must be polished even though they are already spotless or sur-rounded at the wheel base by a border of cotton wool. One suppliant is even shown holding a string of beads (a reference to a rosary) which he will use to adorn his car. A few of the cars are mounted on rotating daises. As if these touches were not enough, at the end of the film the camera slowly crosses a room that contains at the other end a long table stacked with the gleaming trophies that will be awarded to the winners of the show. Under bright lights, the image clearly resembles a candlelit altar in a church. When the spectators arrive for the opening of the show, they, too, appear to take this religion seriously, even to the point of dressing up as if they were still living in the fifties era of the Fonz and "Happy Days" when a man defined himself by the speed of his wheels and the looks of his babe in the front seat next to him. It has already been observed that few, if any, of the customized cars are modern. Most of them serve for their owners as homages to the vintage days of Detroit. The spectators also share this reactionary love of the past. The men slick their hair back in "duck tails" and the women swirl theirs onto the tops of their heads in foot-high beehive hairdos. We, the outsiders, look at all this reverence for automobiles and for a bygone era and wonder why.

Finally, the filmmaker adds to the soundtrack the voice of one of the chosen few, who explains the reasons for his worshipping. "I wanted something that would draw attention," the car owner says. "I've always wanted something to drive down the street, so people would look." Speaking so earnestly about something that has been shown to be so comical, the subject sounds like a member of a superstitious cult from a bygone era.

Using a carefully controlled, if somewhat overused, comparison, the maker of *Worshipping* takes an ironic and humorous look at the hobby of car customizing. Using situational irony, he shows the hobbyists dedicating their lives and taking their identities from what were originally production line automobiles. Although the irony is far from cynical, the filmmaker, in assuming that we will not be offended by the religious imagery, probably also assumes that we think it "uncool" to take anything, even religion, all that seriously.

BEAUTY KNOWS NO PAIN (Benchmark Films: 25 min./color/1971)

The makers of *Beauty Knows No Pain* assume their audience finds sexism offensive and has no trouble decoding irony. On the surface, the film is a profile of the Kilgore Rangerettes (a color guard or dance team that performs at halftime during professional football games) and of their instructor, Betsy Nelson. Its real intent, however, is to outrage the audience by portraying the organization and its leader as a villainous symbol of all institutions that reinforce and perpetuate negative female sex-role stereotypes. Nelson and the Rangerette organization are shown as indoctrinators who brainwash young girls to believe they should be passive, dependent, and sexually attractive, even to the point of masochism, to please others. The critical and snide tone of the film is achieved through situational irony. Snippets of interviews with Nelson and a few of the Rangerettes are used as the film's only narration. Their comments give us the group's philosophy. The filmmaker then systematically undermines each Rangerette tenet by showing us scenes from a two-week Rangerette training program of new candidates that contradict these professed goals. In interviews they tell us, for instance, that Rangerettes are trained to be individuals, but the camera shows the girls being drilled to conform utterly to the uniformity of the Rangerette dance line. This type of situational irony is used repeatedly to make the organization and its leader appear hypocritical and insidious.

The opening and closing of the film are good examples of the maker's critical and ironic tones. As the film begins, we hear "The Battle Hymn of the Republic," a song that stirs in us patriotic feelings and suggests that a performance is underway. At first, the visual seems to complement the music. We see Rangerettes marching in formation along the lines of a football field, twirling poles that hold oversized flags of red, white, and blue. Then we notice that some of the girls have curlers in their hair—a situational irony that is humorous and uncomplimentary. Eventually, we realize that the girls are merely practicing in an empty football stadium, but the effect remains. The close of the film coincides with the last day of the girls' two-week tryout for the Rangerettes. The camera focuses in on an empty room with a portable chalk board facing away from us. Again, we hear "The Battle Hymn of the Republic." Suddenly, a bell rings and the candidates come rushing into the room and up to the blackboard. The camera is poised behind and above it so we can see the girls' faces when they scan the board to find out if they have been selected as Rangerettes. Those who have been scream, cry, jump into the air and into each others' arms. Soon, however, we see one girl who looks in vain for her number on the blackboard. Her somewhat chubby and homely face freezes as if she had suddenly been taken ill; her stare shows desperation. Twice she turns away, then glances back to see if she is mistaken. Finally, to hide her feelings, she hugs one girl who has made it, then walks off to be alone. At the same time, we hear Nelson's voice predicting what the selection day will be like for the girls. "When we finally post the numbers," we hear her say, "there will be great emotion. It will be one of the most vivid memories the girls will ever have." While we hear her speak, we cannot help but feel that Nelson is callous and unsympathetic. How, we think, can she call the pain of this homely girl "great"? Only a woman who has never experienced this girl's sense of failure and shame could talk with pride about how vivid her memory will be. The juxtaposition of Nelson's remarks, the tragedy of the scene, and "The Battle Hymn of the Republic" create in us a revulsion for Nelson, the Rangerettes, and the Southern Belle tradition this group seems to embrace.

The remainder of the film capitalizes on similar ironies of situation. Just as the two-week Rangerette tryout begins, we hear Nelson say she instills specific values in her girls. They will be lovely, poised young ladies, dependable, and morally sound, she says. They will get along with society so long as it does not curb their individuality. While we listen to Nelson deliver this speech, we watch her bark at the girls through a bullhorn and see them march toward the camera in two parallel lines repeating the exact same flick of the head. Where, we wonder, is their individuality? Later, we watch the Rangerettes, who are dressed in their red, white, and blue uniforms replete with cowboy boots and hats, posing for their team picture. The location Nelson has chosen requires that half the girls stand with their left legs pressed against a sticker bush. This hardship, she says, should not diminish their bright smiles, however, because, as she tells them, "Beauty knows no pain." Is the teaching of this kind of masochism moral? We wonder. Is it a sign of morality or individuality when one of the Rangerettes tells us with a giggle how beautiful they look in their uniforms even though their belts, which must be tightened two inches smaller than their waist sizes, leave a few welts? Do we feel that Nelson should be entrusted with the girls' training when she informs us that "when they [the girls] come off the [football] field, they've smiled so much . . . it's hard to get their faces back into normal positions again"?

Perhaps the most ironic moment in the film occurs when Nelson tells the young candidates that the Rangerettes who help in the tryout are their "big sisters." By this we assume Nelson means they will help and guide the younger girls through their auditions. Nothing could be further from the truth. The camera shows the "big sisters" do nothing but berate and chide their charges. Two scenes epitomize the older girls' cruelty. One of their duties is to give the candidates "the treatment." This consists of forcing them to perform idiotic pantomimes in the college cafeteria where the other Kilgore College students watch. The "big sisters" clearly enjoy carrying out this hazing ritual; some of them look quite sadistic as they force the younger girls to roll around on the cafeteria floor in peculiar gyrations. The "big sister" who earlier giggled about the pain the Rangerette belts cause, makes a remark indicating that she is not sadistic, but merely brainwashed by the Rangerette philosophy. Describing the hazing, she says, "We weren't used to the treatment we were given by the sophomores, but now that I'm a sophomore I understand why this treatment is necessary."

We may look in vain for signs of poise, individuality, and big sisterhood among these Rangerettes, but the filmmaker does not leave us looking for someone to blame for their lack of compassion. In a scene that captures the filmmaker's view of Nelson better than any other, we see the teacher leaning over a balcony that sits high above a gym floor where the candidates stand. Nelson, in trying to teach the girls the count of a dance step, screams, "One, two, three, four, five, six, seven, eight," and punctuates each number with a slash of her arm through the air. Poised as she is above the aspirants, Nelson is the image of Hitler or Mussolini. In her we see the source of sadism and hypocrisy in the Rangerette organization and the masochism and the passivity of the candidates. Then, as the camera pulls back slightly, we see a huge sign that has been mounted just below the balcony. "Smile," it reads. This final situational irony of a screaming Hitler saying smile does not make us laugh; it makes us shake our heads at Nelson's phenomenal lack of self-knowledge.

BACH TO BACH (McGraw-Hill Contemporary Films: 6 min./color/1966)

The title *Bach to Bach*, a pun on the phrase "back to back," aptly describes the position in which the film's two characters find themselves in the morning after meeting for the first time in a bar. We hear, but do not see, a man and a woman talking from bed while Bach's *Goldberg Variations* plays on the stereo and the camera circles the room to show us its contents and furnishings. Understandably, having just met, the couple's conversation is somewhat formal and exploratory—they seek out areas of common interest, and they try to impress one another. However, Elaine May and Mike Nichols, whose voices we hear, so exaggerate this process that soon we are laughing at these silly characters. In the course of their conversation, the two drop the names of philosophers and classical composers to establish their intellectualism; they discuss the dreadful bourgeois upbringings they escaped to confirm their own sensitivity and taste; they even talk about the woman's role in society and the difficulty of maintaining relationships today to show how enlightened their sensibilities are. While this goes on, we laugh at their affectations and at their apparent lack of self-knowledge. Most of all, though, we enjoy listening to how hard they work to make it clear that persons of their caliber certainly do not just engage in a sordid or typical one-night stand. The filmmaker creates the humorous dramatic irony of the sequence by focusing the camera on several artifacts in the room that, through juxtaposition, make the conversation even more ludicrous, and by pacing the entire conversation so it actually suggests the seduction scene that surely took place the night before.

Almost every line of the couple's dialogue reveals to us their self-serving motives. To establish how artistic and intellectual they are, the two discuss (or at least casually mention) Bach, Bartok, Adler, and Nietzsche. Talking of Bach, she says the composer instills his music with "a mathematical certainty that's almost sensual." He agrees, saying the music has "an order, a finality . . . finally." At one point during the Bach *Variations* he points out, somewhat mystically as far as we are concerned, "the amazing comment" of the music. She in turn extols the music's "social insight." He continues: "A whole world opened for me when I discovered Nietzsche, when I read *Thus Spake Zarathustra*." She agrees passionately, implying that she was similarly moved. To show how he developed sensitivity against all odds, the man tells the woman how as a child he had to sneak into his room to listen to Bach, so little was there for him in his bourgeois family. Not to be outdone, she describes her ordinary, middle-class family, where "there was proximity, but no relating." The two demonstrate they are fashionably aware of the important issues by discussing the "incredibly ambivalent role of women." They even reveal just the right amount of neuroticism in their personalities in this exchange: SHE: "I have my problems in relating, but I think I can work through them." HE: "A relationship is so difficult, to try to get a dynamic approach to it, so there are no absolutes necessary."

To make the dialogue sound even more absurd, to further establish the personality of the male, to sketch out the proceedings of the night before, the camera circles the room. In it (we assume it is the male's room), we see artifacts that conform to the man's self-image. A stained-glass window, a carved wooden sculpture, a statuette, the music, prints by Picasso, Matisse, Lautrec, a few highbrow magazines chosen to establish his taste and culture, a candle stuck in a wine bottle, two goldfish, a pair of blue sneakers, and a Charlie Chaplin poster all reveal just the correct amount of Bohemianism. A plate of cheese and apples, a half-empty bottle of wine, and pieces of clothing scattered over the furniture and floor all conspire to tell the tale of the night before. Finally, the inquisitive and mischievous camera intermittently makes fun of the couple's conversations by absurdly juxtaposing objects in the room with their remarks. When the woman reveals that she has "a great many difficulties to resolve," the camera spots a long, standing nude in a print whose arm reaches out into the darkness. But when the man answers supportively, "and I think you are resolving them," the camera shows a photo containing a solitary man standing sheepishly beneath the only tree in the middle of a vast, empty plain. As the two discuss the "ambivalent role of women," we look at a comic poster of Buster Keaton imitating an armless Greek statue of a woman clad in a white robe. When the two babble on about the difficulty of relationships, the camera focuses on one of the goldfish as its mouth repeatedly opens and shuts. Finally, to mimic the back and forth rhythm of the dialogue on the greatness of Nietzsche, the camera jumps back and forth between a woman in a painting and the man's blue sneakers.

The film further mocks the couple by showing them try to cloak their one-night stand in the euphemistic garb of "a relationship." We see through this effort as we did the others; the consistent dramatic irony makes us laugh, or at least smile. By making these two characters so transparently foolish, yet so much like ourselves, the filmmakers create a satire that makes us laugh, yet squirm in our seats a little, too.

THE CRITIC (Learning Corp. of America: 4 min./color/1963)

Even a filmgoer with a tin ear for tone will know this film is ironic as soon as he hears the exaggeratedly Jewish voice of Mel Brooks. Playing in *The Critic* the role of a 71-year-old man who has just paid $2.00 to see a French movie, the Brooks character is heard making wisecracks from his seat in the audience about a series of abstract shapes that are appearing on the screen both we and the audience he sits in are watching. (We never see Brooks' character or those in the audience who shush him.) Although Brooks' loudmouthed criticisms of the film ("What the hell is this?") are obviously meant to be hyperbolic, the very nature of the verbal irony changes as the film develops. At first, we dismiss Brooks as an insensitive and boorish Philistine. He complains that the abstract images do not mean anything and that the film is not worth the $2.00 he paid. Eventually, however, his comments, especially his choice of words, remind us of the outrage we may have felt (though we might not have had the nerve to say so) when we encountered art that was difficult or esoteric or damningly over our heads. The character's remarks at this point subtly attack those who falsely claim to hold the sole key to art's locked and exalted tabernacle. Soon it becomes clear that despite its modest length and simplicity, this film has achieved one of the highest goals of satire—to make fun of everyone in the audience without sparing any in-group the rod. The Philistine and the artiste are both slain by this little David. The viewer who may consider himself enlightened will smugly patronize the Brooks character until he suddenly realizes he is the butt of the humor, too. The Babbits in the audience will also squirm under Brooks' parody of them.

The film Brooks watches shows a series of abstract images that infuriate him. The images appear in a wide variety of shapes, ranging in number from few to many, and we hear the Brooks character either complain or speculate what the images are supposed to resemble. When a small dot moves toward and then inside a larger circle, the character says, "This must be birth." When he sees two asterisk-shaped images appear and move toward one another, he says, "Looks like a bug. Yes, two things in love. Could this be the sex life of two things?" At intervals the character gets truly frustrated. Feeling he has been duped, he calls out, "What's this? . . . Usher!" or "This is cute; this is cute; this is nice. What the hell is it? . . . It's garbage, that's what it is." Periodically, members of the audience try to silence him, saying: "Shhh" and "Hey, could you shut up?" And, at this point in the film, despite our laughter at the character's comments, that's exactly what we wish he'd do.

Brooks' comments soon become more astute, however, as they take on the uncomfortably familiar ring of legitimate criticisms made against teachers, artists, and art critics. At a loss to understand what he sees, the character mumbles, "Must be some kind of symbolism." This, of course, is exactly what the literati sometimes say to justify art that is inaccessible to the common viewer. After thinking he has spotted a "cock-a-roach" and "a pair of lips," the character begins to overread every image in an attempt to understand it. He discovers sexual significance that is not there. "See," he says, "even if they don't want to, they get dirty." Overreading and seeing sexual references everywhere are, of course, two common complaints against English teachers and critics. Finally, the character asks, in his exaggerated way, a fairly reasonable question of modern art: "Why does he [the abstract filmmaker] waste his time like that? He could drive a truck, make a shoe, do something constructive." In short, if art serves no useful function for the public, what good is it?

As the title of *The Critic* suggests, the Brooks character satirizes both the yahoo and the lover of modern art. The film's verbal irony is two-sided: Brooks' voice parodies the uninformed complaints of the boor, but also attacks needlessly esoteric artists and the snobbish in-group who celebrate them. The Brooks character does this by exaggerating the crudeness of the first and by echoing the affected "readings" of the second.

FOLLOW-UP ACTIVITIES

1. As the film *Doubletalk* indicates, many social situations create their own dramatic irony when a sharp contrast develops between what we say or show to the outside world and what we are actually thinking and feeling. Make use of such dramatic irony to complete one of the following writing assignments.

   a. Imagine you are being disciplined in the vice-principal's office for a minor transgression of a school rule. The administrator first overreacts to the severity of your crime, then uses a multitude of silly platitudes to straighten you out. You must sit there and play the penitent, of course, but your thoughts are filled with clever retorts to each scolding remark. The vice-principal, though he may be skeptical of your penitence (after all, he has your record in front of him), is to accept graciously your compliance. Write two interspersed dialogues. One will record the conversation in the office, the other the remarks in both minds. (Place the two imagined monologues in parentheses.) Your goal is to compose a humorous and satiric commentary on such incidents without slipping into cynicism.

   b. Envision a graduation ceremony where you are reading the senior speech. It, of course, contains the usual platitudes everyone expects to hear— "we've all worked hard to reach this day," "we are this country's future leaders," "tomorrow we will go our separate ways," etc. Inside your mind you hear the speech you would rather be giving, one that deals with real issues without glossing over controversy or tells what you really think about graduation. Intersperse the real speech with editorial asides in parentheses. Your objective is to write a humorous and satiric commentary on graduation without adopting a cynical tone.

2. Newspaper comic strips often make use of the three ironies. Collect clippings of your favorite cartoonist's work and determine how he or she uses irony to create humor. Present your findings to the class in an oral report which will make them want to follow the comic strip as well.

3. Photographers, especially those who work for newspapers, often look for incongruous or poignant juxtapositions in the real world. Captured on film, these unusual contrasts elicit a strong reaction from readers. For example, pictures of a veteran soldier carrying an infant refugee, or well-dressed secretaries walking to work in track shoes, or young toughs smoking cigarettes on a subway just under the no smoking sign, or business executives wearing Walkman headsets, all capture situational ironies. Sometimes they make us sad, sometimes they make us laugh, sometimes they give us pause to think about everyday occurrences that we take for granted. Collect such photographs or take your own and describe in a paragraph the effect each situational irony is intended to have on the viewer. Then make some of your own by combining parts of photographs or magazine pictures into a composite.

4. Collect flyers and advertisements put out by candidates running for political office. Study them to determine common characteristics, such as pictures of the candidate with his or her family, self-serving biographical sketches, glowing political promises, mudslinging innuendos about opponents, etc. Then write a parody of such ads and flyers using the device of overstatement. The objective of your verbal irony is to make fun of the excesses and borderline dishonesty of these communications.

5. Listen to a comedy album put out by a well-known comedian. Determine how irony contributes to the performer's humor. Does he or she primarily use verbal, dramatic, or situational irony? What devices (puns, overstatement, incongruous juxtapositions, etc.) does the comedian rely on most in his or her routines? Play selections from the record for your class and analyze some of the best examples of irony.

Persona

Like most elements of art, persona (the role assumed by a real or fictional character) is drawn from life itself. The student who openly defies a teacher has adopted the persona of the "rebel." When stopped by a police officer for speeding, a person may play the "penitent" or if unwise (or an intimate of local politicos), may put on the persona of the "disputant." In each case the person is playing the role he or she deems necessary. The choice may be a conscious effort to manipulate others (as at a job interview, when most of us are the "perfect employee"—confident, efficient, organized, agreeable), or it may be natural (as at church, when truly religious people are "devout believers"). People will don the *masks* (step into the roles) that best suit their intentions. Psychologists tell us that people are always wearing masks, changing from one persona to another to adapt to circumstances and to survive with a minimal amount of psychic bloodshed.

A writer must also survive. The good writer has access to a variety of personae; the trick is to find the correct one for each writing situation. The author of an article on relativity for a scientific journal wants to impress other scientists with his or her understanding of physics. Persona in this case establishes the writer's credentials, his or her right to be taken seriously by men and women of the profession. Playing the humorist by interspersing Einsteinian equations with comic asides will not allow the message to be well received. The distinguished audience will attend to a message in its own field only if it is sent by an "authority" or, at the very least, by an "analytical observer" whose voice is detached, measured, and rational.

Persona, then, creates the proper relationship between the message sender and the receiver. Just as a man must be a "father" to his child, a "husband" to his wife, and a "co-worker" to fellow employees, the writer must let each audience know who he or she "is." A person uses behavior, voice, and gestures to accomplish a task. A writer has word choice, writing style, sentence structure, organization—in short, all the tools of language. Writing for laypeople, the same author on relativity may well decide on the masks of the "humorist" and the "teacher." Like Carl Sagan, an author in such a situation must try to popularize complex theories. The uninitiated do not want to be intimidated, do not want to feel that the essay is over their heads. Comic remarks, just as they do in the classroom, calm anxiety and illustrate difficult points simplistically. Short paragraphs, quick sentences, and well-defined terms instruct and stimulate, rather than overwhelm. The scientific writer becomes a benevolent "Merlin," not the sadistic, abstruse "Morgan le Fey." Persona, then, is the image, the impression of the author that is created in the reader's mind. If it is the correct one for the audience and the situation, communication is enhanced.

The relationship between persona and message is critical. Only the naive would believe that an author can clinch a point on the strength of argument alone. Persona is a part of the author's logic. John Hersey's *Hiroshima* is a good example. Writing in 1946 at the height of postwar euphoria in the United States, Hersey sensed that his readers would be skeptical about his message: that the use of the first atomic bomb was not only immoral, but also prophetic of a calamitous future. The author does not argue directly, as he might to a receptive audience, but lets his readers reach their own conclusions. Hersey distances himself from his subject (he writes in the third person; at no point does he become a part of the narrative), adopts the detached persona of the "investigative reporter," and lets the nuclear horrors of the Japanese city speak for themselves. "These are just the facts," Hersey is saying, "not the ravings of a prophet of doom. Make of them what you will." His message, which would sound mild or timid now, could have seemed radical, more like science fiction than truth, had he sermonized. The restraint of the persona is part of Hersey's strategy for the book. Michael Lenehan, in his article "The Quality of the Instrument" (*The Atlantic*, Vol. 250, No. 2, [August 1982], pp. 32-58), also includes the mask in his strategy. The article follows the building of a Steinway piano from the cutting of the wood to the final tuning. Lenehan recognizes that his topic might be dry to most readers, so he plays the "humanist" and the "music lover." In addition to piano making, he covers the controversial acquisition of the Steinway Company by CBS, which hopes to automate some of the plant's operations. By making himself a part of the narrative and interacting with the craftspeople, Lenehan is able to show the great care they take in the process (it takes nearly a year to build one piano), their uniquely unscientific skills (most work is done by eye or ear), and their humanizing eccentricities (one secretly autographs every piano he works on). Lenehan and the workers develop an attachment to the piano (which they name the "Atlantic Piano"); they root for it when pianist André-Michel Schub chooses a Steinway for a concert. In a concluding scene, Lenehan takes one of the craftspeople to the first performance of the instrument and then backstage to meet the artist. The warmth of the author's personae, the "humanist" and the "music lover," transforms the piano from a simple example of Steinway expertise to a symbol of hand craftsmanship everywhere. The reader feels sympathy for the workers and regrets that an old tradition is dying.

Picking out a writer's persona from a written passage is not an exact science. Unlike the chemist who will determine the precise components of a solution, the student will not always be able to decide on an author's exact roles. Often, one or two masks will not account for all of the sentences. Sensitivity to persona is sharpened by discussion in which opposing viewpoints are considered. Is Swift the "misanthrope" or the "social critic" in "A Modest Proposal"? No doubt he is both. A line-by-line analysis will reveal which remarks show a discouraging hatred of mankind and which cry out (hopefully) for social reform.

Persona is easiest to recognize in fictional characters. Unlike an author who is a shadowy presence behind a work, a character is palpable; his or her actions, attitudes, and behavior are out front. Simple observations will help narrow the range of persona choices. Is the character well educated? Does he or she speak the King's English? Or does he or she rely on slang and vulgarity? Is he or she outgoing, somber, restrained? Falstaff, from Shakespeare's *Henry IV* plays, is rich with personae (if not money). His primary deeds are his robberies and his connivings to get on the good side of the prince. But his remarks make one wonder if he is more interested in fun than in material gain. More than by manipulativeness, he is characterized by his cowardice and the wit he uses to cover up his follies. His speeches indicate that he has thought deeply about his debauchery. The society whose rules he breaks is not virtuous. Justice is not just, he thinks, but is the whim of the mighty. The people are farm animals for the wealthy aristocrats and fodder for Mars. Righteous living is drudgery. To Falstaff, life is meant for the high-spirited libertine. It is a brief feast on which he gorges. Despite the depth of his ideas, Falstaff's voice is farcical and his diction informal, even crude (indeed, he speaks in prose while most of the other characters talk in verse). From such observations, the class should determine that he plays the "thief," the "roisterer," and the "common-man philosopher."

In fiction and nonfiction the narrator can provide insight into the author's persona, especially when the roles of the two differ. The narrator may be the mask the author hides behind, but when the narrator's views are clearly in error or when the narrator's perspective is limited, he or she and the author are not one. The aforementioned "A Modest Proposal" is one of the most famous examples. Swift's speaker uses formal diction and logic to discuss the economics of roasting the children of the poor (not to mention the delicacy of their taste). Clearly, his ideas are absurd, his formal word choice, educated speech, and complex sentence structure unsuited to the barbarity of his proposal. The author is ridiculing the narrator and the British upper class he represents. Behind the "aristocratic fool" of a narrator is Swift, the "satirist," "misanthrope," and "social critic."

The subject of persona encourages imaginativeness and freedom of interpretation. Persona is, like beauty, sometimes "in the eyes of the beholder." All actors realize this. A performer will try to put something of him- or herself into an old character, will give Falstaff a slightly different persona (or personae) than is customary. Wild guesses must be guarded against, however. In classroom analysis, students may hurl at the teacher totally irrelevant labels, hoping to catch a big fish with an idle cast. Before discussion of a work, the teacher should decide on a range of roles, while keeping an open mind for the student who may see something he or she has missed.

PRE-FILM ACTIVITIES

1. The following is a list of possible personae. It is not exhaustive, so the student should be encouraged to add to it. The list can be used until the class is able to recognize an author's roles on its own. The teacher should discuss unfamiliar terms and offer examples of each persona label from reading done earlier in the year, from movies, and from TV shows. At this point, the teacher must stress that a persona, because it describes a role, is always a noun, though adjectives can be used to qualify it. Like a person's name, it is a label. The voice (*see* "Voice," page 100), the sound of a character's speech, is usually described with an adjective. Voice is one of the critical factors in producing a clear persona.

the disputant
the radical
the conservative
the moderate
the outsider
the art critic
the psychologist
the social critic
the cosmopolitan man
  (or woman)
the country boy (or girl)
the common man (or woman)
the scientist
the confessor
the penitent
the child
the innocent
the devil's advocate
the muckraker
the investigative reporter
the idealist
the humanitarian
the optimist
the observer
the layperson
the authority
the historian
the friend
the bad boy (or girl)
the rebel
the doomsayer
the connoisseur
the defender of the little guy
the devout believer
the adventurer
the explorer
the fanatic
the family man (or woman)
the traditional man (or woman)

the roisterer
the teacher
the salesperson
the philosopher
the misanthrope
the underdog
the loser
the fool
the humorist
the artist
the radical artist
the common man (or common
  woman) artist
the music lover
the enthusiast
the malcontent
the minority of one
the Northerner
the Southerner
the cowboy (or girl)
the patriot
the foreigner
the convert
the wise old man (or woman)
the protestor
the flower child
the spokesperson for a
  generation
the last sane person
the eccentric
the fan
the soul searcher
the prophet
the storyteller
the city dweller
the aristocrat
the victim of society
the feminist
the nature lover

the common man (or common woman) philosopher	the self-made man (or woman)
the nonconformist	the thief

2. Using the list above, the students could analyze the personae of characters in TV situation comedies, newscasts, and cartoons. Students can make a list of the important actions, gestures, and mannerisms that prove their labels are accurate. They can make observations on the character's remarks, his or her tones of voice and diction.

3. The next step is to analyze the personae of the more complex characters from short stories, novels, and dramas that have been read in class. Have the student construct a single paragraph in which he or she labels one persona of a favorite character and from memory offers proof.

The following films will give the students a chance to determine personae. Of them, *Magic Machines* has a single character who is also the narrator. The filmmaker and the character have the same personae. *The Fable of He and She* has a narrator whose mask differs from that of the characters, but is the same as that of the film-maker. *Fireworks* and *Pinter People* are character studies in which filmmaker and subject have contrasting roles. *Men of Bronze* has a three-tiered structure, with characters, narrator, and filmmaker having different, but complementary, roles. The teacher can use the blackboard to record and narrow student observations on the films. The students should defend their persona choices, and disagreement and debate should be encouraged. When this process has been completed, the students will be ready for post-unit activities, which require them to determine or create personae on their own.

MAGIC MACHINES–AND OTHER TRICKS (Learning Corp. of America: 14 min./color/1970)

Robert Gilbert, a 25-year-old sculptor, discusses his art, his beliefs, and himself in this 1969 Academy Award winning film. He constructs his metal sculptures from junk and objects found mostly in the desert, where he goes to get close to nature. His creations, the magic machines, look something like hallucinations or distorted dream images and are intended to protest social ills and to appeal to the love of fantasy. Their maker adopts the personae of the spokesperson for a generation, the radical artist, and the flower child.

The sculptor's diction marks him as a spokesperson for the hippie movement of the late 1960s. This diction combines childhood speech with drug slang and inflammatory political clichés. He describes his sculpture as a "happy thing . . . a joyful, laughter machinery." "Goofing" is his term for the street scenes he puts on to jolt passersby from their political slumber; "The Stash" is his name for his favorite creation. He divides American society into "us" (the hippies) and "them" (America's power elite), whom he also calls "management" to connote manipulativeness and ruthless capitalism. Gilbert's diction does not bridge the gap between generations but galvanizes the young who agree with him.

His machines portray his role as the radical artist. His junk creations symbolize his rejection of American materialism. Things (and people) are not to be valued solely for their economic usefulness. His machines condemn the ills of capitalism and the establishment. "The Groper"–metal bars, cogs, wheels, and ornamental grating made to look like an ugly, oversized swan–attacks the evil of grasping for power and possessions; "June 23rd," the evils of war and the police state that suppresses the peace movement. If his dungarees and work shirt cast him as the proletarian Bolshevik, he is actually a soft Trotskyite. His fantasy works, such as "The Little Black Knight" (modeled after the "Knight of Fantasy" in *Alice in Wonderland*), are not only a rejection of Middle America's reality, but also a mind-expanding leap into an "Oz" more childlike than political. Like other radical artists, he plays the Pied Piper, who wants to save the innocents and get rid of the rats.

Unlike the Hamlin hero, however, he is both piper and child (in this case flower child) when he expounds his philosophy. "I've seen where the grownups are at," he says. "I don't want to be there." Of his sculpture "The Rape of the Flower" he explains, "The machine [American technology] really is raping the young or the [hippie] movement or nature . . . I think I was what [the establishment] labeled a flower child. Still am, I guess." Man's innate goodness, he feels, has been stifled by status-seeking and materialism. The magical vision of the pre-adolescent—non-violent, loving, imaginative, and unencapsulated—is "where it's at." But recovering one's childhood fantasy (which Gilbert says is "realer than most of the reality") is like reaching for the brass ring, and only those who are willing to ride the merry-go-round can attain it. "There is this magic show," Gilbert says. "Some people live in the magic show; some people are the magic show; some people wonder what magic is; others know." Gilbert offers his own method for escaping adult hang-ups: a Rousseauian return to nature. The film concludes with him atop a dune, a silhouetted image against the evening sun. The flower child, the feral philosopher, the innocent deified, he transcends the morass of adult society.

THE FABLE OF HE AND SHE (Learning Corp. of America: 11 min./color/ 1974)

"Once, long ago there was a land called Barelmel," the narrator says. "Wonderful birds and beasts lived there—the savage chapachuck, the fierce mushmu, and the wild melachuck. There were two kinds of people—the hardybars (male) and mushemels (female)." Thus begins the tale of how a simple society endures a catastrophe, discovers the sexism of its traditional family roles, and changes them. When a storm and earthquake split the island in half, separating the hardybars and mushemels, neither group is prepared to perform all the tasks necessary for survival. By the time the island is magically rejoined, everyone has learned the lesson: a person's role should not be determined by sex. This parody of a fable is told by a narrator who wears the masks of the humorist and the feminist. The hardybars and the mushemels have, respectively, the personae of the traditional man and woman, each blended with that of a child. Only Hebar (a hardybar) and Shemel (a mushemel) break the expected mold; they are nonconformists who, with their unique outlooks, rally the others and save the day.

The comic diction and mock melodrama of the narrator's voice tip off his role as the humorist. The holiday on which the hardybars and mushemels go to separate halves of the island for games he calls "Ompa Day"; the storm which eventually rejoins the island he labels a "reverse-a-quake." All of the specialized terms for the imaginary world are childlike and silly, a constant reminder that the film is a fable. The absurdity established by the diction is reinforced by the melodramatic narration. When the narrator announces the storm on Ompa Day by saying, "Suddenly, in the midst of the festivities disaster struck," the audience feels no tension but rather laughs. Even the fable's obvious moral at the end is delivered with enough intended heavy-handedness to make one smile. "The people wanted Hebar and Shemel [the heroes] to be remembered forever," the narrator says, "so from then on they called all hardybars 'he' and all mushemels 'she,' and so they are still called in Barelemel . . . and a few other places." This and a host of other explicit parallels to the real world reveal the underlying seriousness of the narrator's feminist mask. It is as if he is using his humor to point at the childish characters and say, "Look what ludicrous things rigid sexual roles make of us!"

At the film's onset, the hardybars and mushemels are nothing if not silly. Each is firmly fixed in the traditional roles of men and women, though their simple language, their emotionalism, and their tendency to panic cast them as children. The hardybars hunt and build the houses; the mushemels clean, cook, and tend the infants. When Hebar, the nonconformist, says that he would rather paint and beautify homes than build them and hunt, he is mocked. Shemel suffers the same fate when she says she prefers to hunt and build. Yet it is Hebar who quiets the male infants and calms the hysterical hardybars when the storm separates them from their mates. He talks them into learning how to cook and take care of themselves. It is Shemel who silences the wailing mushemels and talks them into building shelters and hunting, even though they feel paralyzed without the hardybars. When the island is united, the traditional sex-roles are abandoned. Each hardybar and mushemel can be what he or she wants to be.

The transparent masks and the inoffensive content of the film make *The Fable of He and She* the gentlest possible introduction to persona. The story demonstrates the least controversial principle of feminism: people should be what they want to be. Hardly anyone would disagree. The hardybars and mushemels—animated clay figures not unlike Winnie the Pooh—think, talk, and act like children. Their follies, like those of the pre-adolescent, do not rouse one to anger, but rather to bemusement. How could we hold their misdeeds against them? After all, they are modeled after the typical adult image. They could hardly behave any differently.

FIREWORKS (Serious Business Company: 8 min./color/1979)

At first glance, it would seem that the putting on of a fireworks display is child's play, that people involved are unskilled laborers. The film *Fireworks* disagrees. In interviewing pyrotechnician John Sinclair and capturing one of his performances, the film shows the intricacies of his job and its gratifications. Sinclair becomes as interesting as his displays and, by the end, just as complex. Armed with the facts of his profession and an almost missionary zeal, he has the personae of the authority, the artist, and the enthusiast. By the conclusion of the film, a grand finale of 300 exploding shells, the audience is ready to embrace his creed. Few would feel that his devotion is misplaced.

Sinclair's extensive knowledge of fireworks makes him the authority. With a calm, measured technician's voice he describes the composition of a firework: the lift charge and the tightly packed mix of burst charge and pyrotechnic composition (such as stars). He directs the workers as they dig holes and firmly set the pipes, called mortars, in the ground for the evening's show. The grand finale requires the greatest care. Each of the fuses for the 300 shells, he explains, must be tied to a quick match, a paper fuse filled with gunpowder which, when lit, will set off all the fireworks in six to ten seconds.

There is more than a touch of the artist in the man. As the film opens, he gives us the exotic sounding names of some Chinese fireworks, such as "Red Rose with a Green Heart," "Sparkling Like Pink Lights," and "Purple-Laced Flowers." (The screen is dark at this point, forcing the audience to concentrate on the labels.) Sinclair seems to be saying that the Chinese felt a reverence for the fireworks; even their names had to be beautiful. The subject of art is not far from Sinclair's mind. "I think the real art," he says, "may be involved in the pacing and the way you set it [the display] up." Like a good writer or painter, he strives for effects. Thus, he captures the crowd's attention with an opening volley of 15 shells, then uses explosions of 10 shots each to work up to the finale.

Sinclair is as much a devotee of the cult of fireworks as he hopes his audience will be. The pleasure he derives is not solely that of the artist contemplating his masterpiece; like the audience, he derives a "kick" from the show, though his is different, more intense and personal. "The most startling thing," he says, "is that shock wave that comes off the mortar . . . just runs right up your spine. That becomes the quintessential element that makes it a thrill." This is particularly evident during and after the grand finale. As the night sky is emblazoned with color and the ashes of the explosions sprinkle earthward, he and his helpers let out whoops of triumph and cries of exultation. Sinclair, the ultimate enthusiast at this point, surrenders himself to the beauty and energy of his creation. His zeal, conveyed earlier not through his voice but through the depth of his knowledge and the care lavished on his work, now consumes him.

The audience may be incredulous at first: who would make so much of a frivolity such as fireworks? Not many people will entertain this question by the film's end. Sinclair is dedicated to his profession; his skill and enthusiasm as well as the results of his work prove that he is no half-baked "crackpot." The filmmaker seems convinced that Sinclair will win the audience over, just as he does the stadium crowd. There is no interviewer to prod Sinclair with questions or narrator to provide additional information. The camera records the action objectively and lets the expert speak for himself. The filmmaker adopts the simple persona of the observer. Nothing more complex is required.

PINTER PEOPLE (Grove Press Films: 58 min./color/1969)

"I'm not interested in talking about anything," playwright Harold Pinter insists in this film about him and his work. Yet, despite the denial, he *is* interested in talking about a great deal. His remarks about the world, London, his own life, and his art reveal a complex man whose often contradictory personae include the misanthrope, the social critic, the family man, and the common man artist. The film juxtaposes five of his short plays in cartoon form with an interview conducted at the dramatist's home. *Pinter People* reveals a writer who refuses to be pinned down or defined. Like Proteus, the artist jumps from persona to persona and plays games with the interviewer, who persistently holds on in an attempt to reveal Pinter's "real shape." The questioner/filmmaker thus becomes the investigative reporter.

"I find that I do become quite hostile towards people," Pinter says, playing the role of the misanthrope. Dressed in a black pullover shirt and black pants, wearing slippers, and reclining in his lounge chair, he cuts a dark, inscrutable figure. He dismisses his fellow man with a voice that is often coldly superior and mocking, at times casual, only occasionally intense. To find the source of this misanthropy, the filmmaker offers scenes from inner London similar to those of the rough Hackney neighborhood where Pinter grew up. Shabbily dressed working-class people and outright vagabonds wander like spectres amid run-down buildings. Two women laugh crudely at a joke; another makes a spectacle of herself by singing to a crowd while beating on a trash can with drumsticks. Politics among the masses is no less sordid to Pinter. In between such shots as those of a black man arguing on a soapbox for third world rights, a discussion among some youths and an elderly man that almost erupts into a fight, and a man giving a speech to passersby from a stepladder, Pinter's dark quips are spliced: "Who the hell cares? . . . I haven't any idea at all . . . It doesn't mean that much to me really, chat . . . ." The crudity, egotism, and self-rightousness of these street scenes, the filmmaker feels, are grist for the misanthrope's skits. After an old lady at a bus stop spits on the sidewalk, the animation of Pinter's play "Bus Stop" begins. In it, a woman cruelly harasses a gentleman she mistakenly thinks has made an impolite remark to her. Both are in a queue waiting for a bus. From an emotional soapbox, she inveighs against the vulgarity of the times, demands the sympathy of the others in the queue (who ignore her), accuses the man of being a foreigner, and threatens to call the police. Never once does she realize her own vulgarity. Perhaps the memory of actually having witnessed similar displays motivates Pinter when he says, "It's possibly true to say that I'm a member of the human race, I suppose."

But Pinter is not wholly insensitive to human suffering and social injustice. The London of his youth and young manhood was haunted by tough fascists and by police who used their power with a sadistic caprice. Once, he says, he was almost arrested for singing in crowded and noisy Covent Gardens because the "copper" didn't like his looks. "We didn't have ties on, I think," Pinter says. Nothing disturbs him more than class prejudice and social alienation. His play, "The Black and the White," expands on these themes. Two old women meet at a diner late at night. Homeless, they must spend their time riding the all-night busses and avoiding the police. One of them dreads the hour-and-a-half each night during which the diner closes for cleaning. Their alienation from a society that disapproves of them and their poverty disturbs Pinter. The camera takes up this theme by roaming the streets of London. The filmmaker interviews an old man who spends most of his time in a park observing youngsters playing football. He says he has been alone since 1950. Watching the sport is his only diversion. A shrill-voiced woman in a ghetto sings a song whose chorus is:

Why build a wall round a graveyard
when nobody wants to come in?
Why build a wall round a graveyard
when nobody wants to come out?

Pinter senses that such alienation can never be ameliorated by political means. "Political structures and conflicts cause a great deal of suffering in the world, " he says, though he also remarks: "I have no kind of expectation of the world getting any better." In such comments, one can see his discontent with the human condition and his desire for change. Can a confirmed misanthrope also feel the social critic's sympathy for people? Twain and Swift, two noted misanthropes, might in a moment of honesty answer yes.

Pinter is not morbid. When talking about himself, he adopts the persona of the family man, insisting that although a famous author, he is no different from anybody else. He gets his greatest pleasure from being with his family. "I've been married for 12 years," he says, "and we like each other. But you see there's nothing particularly special about the things I like." Scenes in a London park showing a mother playing with her children and people strolling reflect his contentment with family life. To the investigative filmmaker, these shots offer escape from the camera's preoccupation with the darker side of the city, just as Pinter's family may provide psychic escape from cynicism for Pinter. "I feel better year after year," Pinter says, ". . . I'm enjoying life more as I'm getting older." Even thoughts of death do not seem to disturb him. "I think the heart just stops and that's it," he says, ". . . I've no special feelings about dying." This version of Pinter is in striking contrast to the misanthrope and the social critic. Is the audience to accept the persona? It is interesting to note that none of the five cartoons reflects the contented family man.

It is when he is the common artist that Pinter becomes most ironic and hardest to pin down. He disavows all significance to his work and denies that he has any special powers of insight. Even his diction, which is often no more formal than that of the man in the street, defies the stereotype of the highly educated artist. "Just because you're a writer doesn't mean you're any kind of a prophet," he says, refusing to romanticize himself just as he refuses to romanticize in his plays. Though he has been praised for the realism of his characters, he insists, "I don't know any more about people than anyone else does." The man is paradoxically blunt and enigmatic, like so many of his characters. Neither the misanthrope, the social critic, nor the visionary artist, he would convince the audience that writing for him is no different from lathe work for the laborers in his old Hackney neighborhood. But the filmmaker includes just enough of Pinter's remarks to show that even here the artist may be teasing. "I'm aware that I'm in front of a camera," Pinter says, a line which suggests the actor. The quote gains emphasis because it comes out of nowhere. The suggestion is of a mercurial nature, the artist who insists on not taking shape; the personae may be masking, rather than expressing, the inner self. At the core of the common man artist is mystery—does he delight in hiding or does he need to remain secretive? "I'm a lot more constipated than I used to be," he says of his writing, ". . . there are gaps between the sentences now . . . It isn't all that easy . . . tough, tough life." The remark is delivered from his lounge chair as he takes a leisurely puff of his cigarette and smiles the ironic smile of the cat who has swallowed the canary.

MEN OF BRONZE (Films, Inc.: 58 min./color/1977)

Though individuals may share the same experience, the memory of it will often produce different emotions for each. Moreover, the recounting of such an experience can lead to adoption of dissimilar personae. In its study of the 15th Regiment of New York (the first black regiment to fight in World War I), *Men of Bronze* captures the reminiscences of three veterans to demonstrate this point. Frederick Williams, who was wounded in France, plays the role of the bitter victim; Melville Miller, who enlisted at 16 years of age, is the storyteller, the enthusiast, and the optimist. These two men serve to remind the audience of black heroism in World War I and of the racism black soldiers endured. Hamilton Fish, a white officer in the 15th, offers an overview of the regiment's problems; he adopts the personae of the liberal/humanitarian and, paradoxically, the aristocrat. Documentary footage and a factual narrator make vivid the stories of the three.

Williams' memories of the 15th are anything but pleasant. His tone of voice is alternately angry and sorrowful. He tells the audience that when the 15th was first organized it was not provided with an armory or with weapons and ammunition. "Soldiers drilling with [broom] sticks," is his description of the regiment marching in preparation for the war. The racism would only intensify when the 15th was shipped overseas. Once in France, Williams says, the black soldiers were assaulted by the United States Marines, and some were killed. When France was desperately in need of reinforcements, the regiment was assigned to the French army rather than to the American. Despite this unfair discrimination, the blacks fought fiercely for their country and suffered heavy casualties. The battle of the Argonnes Forest was a particularly bitter memory for Williams. "Company C was going up the hill," he says of one incident. ". . . When we started up the hill, most of the men got it." Moments later in a choked voice, he says, "You see, I'm going to tell you [about the battle]. I'm sitting here talking, but I don't like it." Williams did not return with his fellow soldiers for a hero's welcome, the parade up Fifth Avenue on February 21, 1919. Instead, he came later as a casualty on a transport ship. He is the bitter victim; the hurt and anger he expresses are deeply felt.

Speaking with an irrepressible smile, loaded with enough humor and anecdotes to hold an audience for hours, Melville Miller nearly steals the film. Miller's voice is animated and warm even at his most serious moments; he is a raconteur par excellence. As aware of racism as Fred Williams is, he is still able to see the comic as well as the heroic in what happened. Because it fought in the French army, the 15th was, Miller says, "the only individual regiment of all the 48 states to fight under a state flag [New York's], and that's a violation of some sort or other." He claims that the black soldiers of the 15th were responsible for the battle of Argonnes Forest. A quiet area, the forest erupted in battle when inexperienced and nervous black soldiers began shooting at everything that moved. The Germans heard the fire and attacked. With the voice of the enthusiast, Miller talks of the heroics of Needham Roberts and Henry Johnson, black soldiers who fought off 24 Germans at a lookout station. Of Johnson, he says, "He had 21 wounds, but he refused to die." Of the regiment, he says: "We spent 191 days in the front line, and we never lost a foot of ground or a prisoner." He describes the day of the parade up Fifth Avenue as the "most wonderful day of my life . . . that day there was no prejudice in New York City." Earlier in the film, it was he who told of the "crackers" (whites) in North Carolina who prevented the black regiment from training there. It was he who told of the 15th's original assignment to a stevedore unit in France rather than to the front lines. Indeed, he says he encountered more prejudice in the army than he ever had in civilian life and swore "never to serve a day in this man's army." Always the optimist, however, he reenlisted with the outbreak of World War II. The memories of adventure and triumph, of the camaraderie of the regiment, and of the adulation he was accorded both in Europe and in New York were too compelling to resist.

As a white officer in the 15th, Hamilton Fish provides a look at the prejudice in military and civilian politics of the time. His liberal/humanitarian persona was spawned, perhaps, by the unfair treatment he himself experienced. Though he graduated from Harvard with honors and served three years in the New York legislature, he was denied a promotion to captain by a major who did not think him old enough. (Ever the aristocrat, Fish tells the audience that he did not know then that his own great grandfather, Nicholas Fish, was made a major in the Revolutionary War at 18 years of age.) It was this rejection that led him to join the 15th for an instant promotion. He seems to have been surprised by the cruelty and hostility the blacks faced, as if his life in the upper class had shielded him from such realities. There is still disbelief in his voice as he tells of the Alabama regiment that threatened to attack the blacks until a New York unit lent them its guns. His incredulity intensifies as he describes the long fight he waged in Congress after the war to have a monument erected in France to commemorate the heroism of his men. "These boys fought and died just as the white boys did, fighting for their country, and democracy, and freedom," he says with the naiveté of a wounded idealist. "They're entitled to this monument as much as anybody else."

Behind the three speakers is a narrator who lends credibility to their tales with his persona as the reporter. He speaks with a voice that is, for the most part, unemotional and restricted to the facts. He, for example, tells of the difficulties the 15th had in reaching France on the rickety transport ship *Pocahontas*. Rather than editorialize on the assigning of such a dubious vessel for the regiment, he simply reads from the log of Colonel Haywood (white commanding officer of the 15th) for the day on which France was reached: "Landed at Brest. Right side up." He quotes important men of the times, provides explanations of key events, and offers factual commentary for the documentary footage of the war. One senses that his persona, in its objectivity and calm, differs from the filmmaker's, who is the muckraker exposing a historical injustice that reflects on the country's racism today. Both, however, have subordinated themselves to the three principal speakers in the film. The narrator and the filmmaker are the subdued background against which soldiers Williams, Miller, and Fish sparkle.

FOLLOW-UP ACTIVITIES

1. What kind of people are attracted to various card and board games? What type of person gets hooked on "Risk," "Monopoly," "Life," checkers, poker, "Dungeons and Dragons," backgammon, chess, "Clue," etc.? Write a brief "confession" of a "Risk" player or a chess player (or a player of any other game). Project the voice and persona of this fanatic in your writing.

2. In recent years, companies have begun to market posters and even full-length books that describe the physical appearance and persona of different types of people. Examples include: the politician, the preppie, the nerd, the jock, the real man, etc. Do your own description of a common character type in your town or school. Include observations about this type of person's persona and about the way it is conveyed through speech and appearance.

3. Write a declaration of your New Year's resolutions using one of the following personae: the bad boy (or girl), the devil's advocate, the malcontent, the minority of one, the patriot, the doomsayer, or the nature lover. Do not limit yourself to promises; include information about your past life (real or imagined) to show why you feel the way you do.

4. Get hold of a newsletter issued by a school, organization, or business, an inter-office memo, or a church bulletin. Examine it carefully to determine the persona(e) of the author(s). In your written analysis, which should cite specific sentences as proof, decide whether the persona(e) adopted by the writer(s) is (are) appropriate for the communication's intended audience.

5. Read one of the following extended essays and determine the persona of the author. Does the persona employed suit the author's purpose? Express your opinion and cite passages to support it.

> *Hiroshima*, by John Hersey (New York: Bantam, 1946).
>
> *Travels with Charley*, by John Steinbeck (New York: Bantam, 1962).
>
> *Death Be Not Proud*, by John Gunther (New York: Harper & Row, 1949).
>
> *Letter to His Father*, by Franz Kafka (New York: Schocken Books, 1966).
>
> *Notes of a Native Son*, by James Baldwin (Boston, MA: Beacon Press, 1955).
>
> *The Fire Next Time*, by James Baldwin (New York: Dell, 1964).
>
> *Autobiography of Benjamin Franklin*, (New York: Harper & Row, 1956).

PERSUASION STRATEGIES

It can be argued that persuasion is the essence of writing: the sender of a message wishes, in some way, to change the behavior of the audience. The "behavior" to be worked on can be an action, attitude, or opinion. While urging the young to learn the writing techniques that can best bring about a change in others, we also warn them to avoid being the victims of propaganda. The popular use of "propaganda" implies a certain amount of underhandedness and sinister motivation on the part of the message sender. "Persuasion," however, is an art form, an aboveboard argument for a good cause. The connotations of the two words make them easy to differentiate (our side persuades, the enemy produces propaganda), but soon the student learns that the two camps use weapons from a common arsenal. And a well-stocked arsenal it is, thanks to the research of behaviorists, psychologists, rhetoricians, and social analysts. Instead of worrying about the victimization of the student through propaganda, we should be more concerned perhaps that the young intellectual Faust in our class not lose his soul in his experiments in writing: the student should learn to be fair, not dishonest.

No persuasion will take place if the author does not first consider the members of the audience (*see* "Attention-Getting Devices, Assertions, and Audience Assumptions," page 89). Will they immediately be willing to accept the message and to react? How much resistance can be expected? Do they have to be motivated? Too much insistence on a point can backfire. A reader can move in the opposite direction out of annoyance, rejection of the values of the sender, or even the sheer bravura of showing independence. The author must be sensitive to what the audience will tolerate. If the audience is hostile to an argument, there are motivational techniques that can be used as aids in its presentation. The sender can influence through an appeal to:

1. *Fear.*
   Readers will suffer physical, mental, or social horrors if they do not change.
2. *Authority.*
   As in childhood, the reader obeys the demands of a father (or mother) figure, teacher, or respected individual.
3. *Guilt.*
   The audience has been responsible for certain terrible conditions, and it can cleanse itself by changing behavior.
4. *Sympathy.*
   The audience's love, empathy, and sentimentality are the triggers to its acting differently.
5. *Group membership.*
   If the readers accept the argument, they will have the satisfaction of being part of a group, of belonging.
6. *Status.*
   After changing, the reader will be considered a better person, a superior member of the community.

In making the appeal, the sender should avoid lying, hyperbole, distortion, and threat. At no time should the appeal take the place of an idea or concrete detail.

For the message to work, the author needs a suitable structure. The format of an argument can produce as much motivation as any of the appeals—maybe more. The following structures are frequently effective:

1. *Pro-and-con argument.*
   Normally we have at least three parts to an argument—a statement of the problem, the suggested solution, and a conclusion that shows how the problem can be solved. Sometimes the author will give the drawbacks of the chosen approach or will discuss other possible but rejected ways of dealing with the problem. If there is possible hostility on the part of an audience, giving the opposing view (while maintaining emphasis on the side the sender favors) can suggest emotional and intellectual objectivity and help to undermine the opposition by showing that it is not so formidable. A positive approach—presenting the best reasons for one's own point of view—suggests enthusiasm, conviction, and confidence. Arguing on the defensive, however, implies the possibility of some truth in the opposition's views. Explicit conclusions rivet the attention and clarify the point being made.

2. *Satire.*
   Satire is a humorous attack on an issue with the hope that the ridicule will change manners, improve social conditions, or eliminate destructive attitudes. Ideally, the satirist hopes the audience will change its behavior to avoid being the object of others' laughter.

3. *Exemplum.*
   A story, hypothetical or factual, illustrates the point the author wishes to make. For instance, a narrative that shows the achievement of a goal might convince the audience that it can behave in a similar fashion. The film *The Skating Rink* uses a fictional story to make youngsters realize they can overcome handicaps to achieve happiness. The achievement of the music teacher in the true events of *Close Harmony* might inspire others to find meaningful activities that will bring together the very young and the very old.

Within these structures, a range of persuasion devices can be used. Without being dishonest, the sender has to present the details of his or her proof in the best light in order to increase the chances of convincing and thus altering behavior. A long rhetorical tradition has produced many highly effective techniques to make a point. (We will discuss only those found in the films.)

1. *Either/or.*
   We assert that there are only two possible solutions to a problem (whereas in actuality there might be several), and that one solution is totally absurd or destructive.

2. *Straw man.*
   We create an imaginary opponent who is guilty of many crimes for the purpose of tearing him or her to shreds to prove the worth of our value system by comparison.

3. *Minimizing or maximizing.*
   We minimize the problems in our argument, but maximize the problems of the opposition; the technique can also be used to induce someone to join a group (one's problems are lessened as a result; they would have become worse if one had not joined).

4. *Reduction to absurdity.*
   We oversimplify the opposition's point until no one could possibly believe it to be worthwhile.

5. *Shock.*
   We deliberately chose details for their shock value in order to work on the audience's emotions.

6. *Juxtaposition.*
   The immediate contrast of two items, people, beliefs can produce in the audience a value judgment, reaction, or conclusion.

7. *Dramatic irony* (*see* "Irony," page 108).
   The audience knows more than one (or more) of the characters in the work knows; in dramatic irony, we give the audience enough information so it realizes that a quoted remark is inadequate, or carries a meaning of which the speaker is unaware.

8. *Voice of science or reason.*
   We stress statistics, facts, logic, in a manner that suggests authority, detachment, and control.

9. *Card Stacking.*
   We make the argument stronger than it actually is by stressing only data that supports the point and by ignoring any material that might undermine our view.

10. *Stereotyping.*
    We argue in terms of generalizations that contain popular clichés; the audience will accept or reject the argument based on prejudices that are irrelevant.

11. *Presence of a hero.*
    The support of a hero or celebrity is intended to serve as proof that our points are valid.

12. *Testimonials.*
    One person's views or experiences represent those of a group.

13. *Legitimacy.*
    We show that the new idea or activity has been around for a long time and has prestigious origins.

These techniques will constitute a significant part of an author's argument. There are others that require much less pre-planning and are often instantly grating to a sensitive audience because they are so obviously manipulative: *name-calling* (insulting terms are applied to the enemy), *connotation* (the emotional values of words are intended to sway the audience), *glory by association* (the author convinces us of the worth of a cause by associating it with an already established and successful one). These are terms associated with propaganda, not persuasion.

To insist on using a technique that annoys the audience will not accomplish very much. To convince some audiences, the author might have to forgo the use of manipulative devices altogether and rely solely on the good points outweighing the bad, or on the intrinsic worth of the cause.

The films that follow illustrate the various structures, devices, and appeals an author can use to persuade others to change an action, attitude, or opinion, as the chart below shows. Each film has a legitimate cause. The various filmmakers have approached their task with respect for the audience, a thorough awareness of the problem, and creativity. From these models, the student can learn that persuasion is truly an art. (The film *Marketing the Myths*, an excellent introduction to the art of persuasion because it runs the gamut of techniques, is not included in the analysis below.)

TITLE OF FILM	STRUCTURE	DEVICE	APPEAL
A Metric America	Argument	Minimizing & maximizing, Parable	Group membership, Authority, Fear
Child Abuse	Argument	Testimonial	Guilt, Group membership
Soccer, U.S.A.	Argument	Legitimacy, Presence of hero, Glory by association	Group membership, Status
Separate but Equal	Argument	Voice of reason	Guilt
Night and Fog	Argument	Understatement, Shock, Irony, Juxtaposition	Guilt, Fear, Sympathy
Prelude to War	Argument	Either/or, Connotation, Name-calling, Glory by association	Fear, Group membership
For Tomorrow We Shall Diet	Argument	Straw man, Voice of reason, Testimonial	Guilt, Status
Anything You Want to Be	Satire	Reduction to absurdity, Either/or	Sympathy
What Do You Do When You See a Blind Person?	Exemplum	Straw man, Shock	Authority, Group membership
Close Harmony	Exemplum (true story)	Stereotypes	Sympathy
Campaign	Exemplum (true story)	Minimizing & maximizing	Sympathy, Group membership, Status
The Skating Rink	Exemplum (fictional story)	Card stacking, Stereotypes	Sympathy
A Matter of Survival	Exemplum (fictional story)	Either/or Dramatic irony	Fear
The End of One	Exemplum (parable)	Juxtaposition	Fear

MARKETING THE MYTHS (Phoenix Films: 25 min./color/1977)

This film consists of 25 CLIO Award winning television commercials from 1969 to 1976 that are highly entertaining and unusual. These ads also offer splendid illustrations of the various persuasion techniques. Every type of appeal except that to authority is made, and there are clear examples of reduction to absurdity, shock, juxtaposition, dramatic irony, and presence of a hero. Although the TV commercials are brief, the award winners come in a variety of structures.

The fact that there are motivational appeals in ads should come as no surprise to the students. Fear is the basis of both Dr. Scholl's Foot Deodorant (you will offend people by the smell of your feet if you do not do something about it) and Ultra Brite (if your teeth are not clean enough, you will have no sex appeal). Sympathy is elicited in selling electric blankets (we watch cute little chicks hatch, then stagger about in the folds of the blanket) and Bell Telephone (a tearful separation between two friendly families occurs when one moves away). We will feel guilt watching a commercial asking us to cut back on military spending if we do not "Help to Unsell the War" (Uncle Sam has become a glutton because we have allowed him to have most of the financial pie) and if we do not support the AA (we might be one of the nine million "people who need help"). We gain status if we buy the *Wall Street Journal* or wear Jean Shrimpton's perfume. Group membership is attained when we drink Coke (we join the international brotherhood of man singing on that mountaintop) and wear Levi's (no one in town wears drab clothes anymore). Interestingly enough, the only authority figure (a man wearing a business suit and glasses) in any of the ads makes a speech for General Telephone and has eggs, tomatoes, and a cream pie tossed at him (the straw man is sacrificed so General Telephone can say "it's not the same old line"). In one night of normal television watching, students could observe a number of authority figures such as Karl Malden, Joan Fontaine, or Meredith Baxter Birney, but the CLIO judges obviously did not find these pitches original or interesting enough.

A great deal of creativity, however, is exhibited in the argument techniques. The already mentioned foot deodorant and toothpaste ads provide reduction to absurdity when people faint from an odor and when a good-looking woman admits she has no sex life. A Ford commercial that drops a pickup truck out the back of an airplane uses shock, as does a public highway safety message in which fast-moving uncooked eggs painted to look like vehicles collide and smash apart in slow motion. Rapid juxtaposition of scenes from Caribbean life shows that, thanks to Eastern Airlines, we can visit the island to share the exciting experiences. There is situational irony when an old woman out for a walk narrowly misses being killed by a series of accidents without her having any awareness of danger or realizing that "sooner or later you need insurance." Hero Willie Moscone does intricate pool table shots for Schaefer Beer, and a surfing champ drinks Coke because it also is "the real thing."

Structure, of necessity, is uncomplicated, but takes many forms. In a pro-and-con argument, first the shy, then the confident actions of employees lead to the conclusion that 3M Company helps discover talented people. The dinner table scene showing various types of Americans watching the fat, greedy military general gobble down most of our financial pie is satiric. An exemplum is used to sell Old Home Bakery products (a country song tells how a truck driver at a diner during a storm recharges himself by eating the product) and Count Pushkin Vodka (a stunning cartoon depicts a cross-continent train trip in czarist times by aristocrats who celebrate a major event by drinking the product), as well as insurance (an old lady kicks a ball, breaks a window, and learns that we never know when we will need insurance).

Marketing the Myths is a superior introduction to the problems of persuasion. The unquestionable function of an ad is to change audience behavior—to make us buy a particular product. "Madison Avenue" has become a term loaded with negative connotations, but this film shows that some advertisers approach their work with wit, originality, and artistry. Here we meet persuasion with its best foot forward.

A METRIC AMERICA (2nd Edition) (Aims Instructional Media: 17 min./ color/1976)

Why should the United States go metric? The film assumes there is hostility to such a change on the part of its audience of children and covers all bases in its efforts to overcome that resistance. In its structure, this cartoon presents a logical pro-and-con argument that uses the technique of minimizing and maximizing. To be safe, the film delivers the message a second time in a parable. There are also appeals to group membership, authority, and fear to convince the audience that the metric system is superior to the one we currently have.

In the presentation of the pro-and-con argument the filmmaker maximizes the positive aspects of conversion and minimizes the negative. Twice in the film, the narrator indicates that conversion to metrics would save time (we will be dealing with a few simple factors of 10, thus making our arithmetic easier), increase efficiency (standardization of goods allows easier replacement and allows parts manufacturers to reduce the number of different sizes), and increase international trade (the rest of the world is metric, and our products will fit in better if we use the same measurement so that an American nut will fit a Japanese bolt). All three advantages mean more money, less waste. The film recognizes only a few disadvantages (the Post Office will have to call in small scales for weighing letters; hardware manufacturers will have to redesign products, as will tire manufacturers and carton makers). The paucity of negative outcomes is intended to weaken the opposition to change.

To illustrate the reasons for change, the film offers a parable. Two villages trade pastry and fruit punch with each other, but each uses a different measuring system. The Wimples, the pastry village, have a unit of measurement called a "tuttle," named after the mayor. The second village deals in "larkles." Confusion abounds until the two towns learn from a third that standardization of weights and measurement solves the problems, and they all live happily ever after.

Motivational appeals make the change easier to accept. Appealing to group membership, the narrator captures a folksy sound through his Western accent, his casual phrasing ("It's a darn good thing"), and the calculated clearing of his throat before and after reading a quote from a congressional ruling. He is not an egghead intellectual, but one of us regular people. The narrator is careful to describe his audience as sensible, unassuming, democratic, and willing to change behavior if a more efficient way of life comes along. The group membership in which we are being induced to participate does not hold to stupid ideas, either. Far from it. The narrator attacks such folk wisdom as "an inch is the measurement of three barleycorns laid end to end after they have been dried." More appeals follow. Appeal to authority is offered in that both Thomas Jefferson and John Quincy Adams believed in metrics. We are also reminded that the U.S. Army—after Sputnik, that moment in the cold war when Russia supposedly passed us by in technology—started using metrics in weapons, an obvious appeal to the fear that the Russians will overcome us.

Somehow, after all the appeals, we have no choice but to accept the change. After all, no one wants to be a Tuttle.

CHILD ABUSE: CRADLE OF VIOLENCE (J. Glary Mitchell Film Co.: 20 min./ color/1976)

There is no question that *Child Abuse* is a persuasion film. In cooperation with the Parental Stress Service at Oakland, California, the filmmaker wants to change the behavior of those in the audience who have abused their children. The voice of reason is constant throughout, reassuring the audience that change is possible. The structure of the film consists of three parts: the statement of the problem, the techniques of curing the problem, and the results of the cure. Only one argument is given: abusive parents should go through group therapy. The movie opens with the testimonial of a mother sitting with her son at a picnic table explaining to the camera how she had "dug a hole" in Danny's side with a paring knife. At the end of the film, the same mother embraces the youngster and admits, "In the last couple of years . . . I can look at him and tell him I love him . . . I really love him." The moment is powerful, and clinches the message through its before and after contrast: by sharing one's problems with a group, the testimonial says, one's behavior can change; help is just a phone call away.

In the first section, the testimonials reveal the existence of a parental syndrome that leads to violence. Men and women talk of feelings of inadequacy, of frustration, of isolation, and of uniqueness. A mother who never thought of herself as abusive was sure her child wet the training pants "to get at me" and threw the youngster across the bed "to hurt him back." Another parent wanted just to rest, to leave the house for a change, to escape from feelings of claustrophobia. One woman had a "battle of wills" with her child over eating; when the frustration level became intolerable, the parent resorted to violence.

The syndrome can be cured. Through talking things out, the parent can reduce tension and eventually change behavior. Volunteers at the Parental Stress Service who work the phones are all former sufferers of the syndrome. They listen; they suggest. A few group sessions are shown wherein the participants share their fears, openly admit their cruelties, offer each other advice. These sessions provide a catharsis of the abusing parents' guilt as the group gives the parents the strength to change their ways.

An effective way of concluding an argument is to show the positive outcomes of heeding the advice. A parent who has been through group sessions observes that she now can compromise in terms of what she expects from her child. Another woman finds her "kid is human, just like I am." A father adds, "I have to experience his level of reality, be down there with him . . . ." As he says this, we watch him and his child enjoying each other at play.

The movie studiously avoids sensationalizing its content, or using any persuasion "tricks" to sell its message. There are clear appeals to guilt (the parent who has hurt a child should do something about it before something worse happens) and to group membership (there is less pressure on the person guilty of child abuse when he or she joins with others). Anecdotes of violence are given, but not elaborated on, certainly not "acted out." The voice of reason assures us that not only kids, but also parents, need love, companionship, and understanding. The bulk of the argument rests on this vivid contrast of before and after.

SOCCER, U.S.A. (Learning Corp. of America: 25 min./color/1980)

How do you get an American audience to like soccer? This film by Lazlo Hege structures a one-sided argument into four parts. He traces soccer's history in this country (legitimacy), argues that it fits into the American way of life (group membership), interviews a few superstars (presence of heroes), and compares soccer to football (glory by association). Although at times the arguer is on the defensive, the film accomplishes its goal: it makes soccer look quite appealing.

First, a history lesson on soccer in the United States is given to lend legitimacy to the sport. Legitimacy shows this is not just a new kid on the block. Before 1967, soccer was played in this country, we are told, by "ethnic clubs, Englishmen, and other eccentrics." Professional soccer did not start here until 1967. A year later, the North American Soccer League was formed when two leagues stopped squabbling and merged. Since that time enthusiasm for the sport has been building fast, and changes have been made in the game (such as allowing substitutions and end-of-game shoot-outs) to make it even more exciting for American audiences. The hope, voiced repeatedly in the film, is that America in the 1980s will win a World Cup (the equivalent of winning the World Series or Superbowl).

The film argues that soccer is American because it is democratic, an appeal to group membership. To establish the claim, the camera records soccer played by college students, inner-city youths, public school boys, girls, and small children. We feel national pride that this American version of the game is better than Europe's. Popularity is attested to by showing team after team in various school uniforms engaged in the sport.

Heroes help to sell a product and attract group followers. This motivational technique is a significant part of the argument. Julio Mazzei, a coach, observes that there are two periods in American soccer: "before and after Pelé." For a few glorious moments, Pelé juggles a ball with various parts of his body in a demonstration to some young kids in his soccer summer camp. He shows how to keep with a ball, how to change direction quickly, and how to block. His skill is extraordinary. There are interviews with superstars Franz Beckenbauer and Georgia Chinaglia who assure us that America's teams are improving. A young Californian, Ricky Davis, the best North American League Player in 1979, is an example of the new level of excellence in this country. That he started playing at age six serves as an incentive for American young-sters to start and to keep at their training.

Through glory by association the author sells a new idea, suggesting it is similar to a popular or highly-esteemed one. Here the filmmaker argues that professional soccer creates the same level of excitement as football. We watch the beautiful cheer-leaders at a game between the New York Cosmos and the Tulsa Roughnecks. The fans respond wildly and one bare-chested youth even waves his shirt just as football fans do. Later, there are scenes of excited cheerleaders and fans celebrating a win by the Vancouver White Caps. There are video replays of highlights from great games of the past, breathtaking moments that compare favorably to great plays in football.

The fact that Americans have never won the World Cup—the implication is that Americans do not play as well as other nationalities—puts the filmmaker on the defensive enough that he has an authority figure, the Commissioner of the North American Soccer League, tell us that the World Cup will be ours before the end of the 1980s. The film generates enough excitement that the audience will probably want to have tickets for the series.

SEPARATE BUT EQUAL (Encyclopaedia Britannica: 8 min./color/1971)

This short history lesson dealing with the issues of Southern racial segregation from 1877 to 1954 is an example of the type of persuasion most frequently encoun-tered by students. The script uses the argument technique of the voice of reason. The narrator is controlled and unagitated; his is the normal voice of history, the classroom teacher and authority. The audience is not being asked to become involved actively, to become "heated." Given is the fact that segregation is wrong, an assumption that should produce guilt in the person who disagrees. The narrator assumes that the audience is intelligent, will condemn on its own the examples of unfair behavior, and is optimistic about the course of justice. As in the classroom, everything is under control. The sensationalism of violence, abuse, and pain is ignored, and the film makes no use of any emotional argument technique. The familiarity of the approach makes one feel that one is not being persuaded, that the film is not selling any ideas, that it is just presenting facts. But these facts are structured into an argument for moderation and rational detachment, for the acceptance of the fact that change takes a long time to come about, and for the belief that we can remove society's inequities peacefully through the law.

Through drawings, cartoons, and a few photographs, the film emphasizes the role the Supreme Court has played in dealing with racial problems. In 1883, a Court decision paved the way for the "Jim Crow" laws and the Mississippi Plan to keep blacks from voting. The *Plessy* v. *Ferguson* case of 1896 (Plessy was arrested for refusing to leave a seat in an area reserved for white passengers) established the "separate but equal" doctrine. In 1954, Chief Justice Earl Warren wrote the decision of the court concerning *Brown* v. *Board of Education*: "in the field of public education 'separate but equal' has no place." The film concludes that, thanks to such recent Supreme Court decisions, the black American "was at last on the way to receiving his full rights as a citizen of the United States." In the art of persuasion, the favored point often comes last for emphasis. The implied message here is that the way to effect change is through the legal system, that violence is not the way. The structure of the film makes it seem inevitable that the Supreme Court will correct its own errors.

Based on the assumption that the audience is fair-minded, the film makes motivational appeals to guilt. The script starts with an angry voice saying, "Go back to your own section. These seats are for whites only." The basic rudeness and unfairness of the remarks attempt to produce guilt in white viewers, guilt that is increased with the appearance of segregation signs indicating "colored sections." This is also dramatic irony in that the audience understands more than the speaker. Racist cartoons, pictures of Ku Klux Klan members, and information about the ways white legislators seized power contribute even more to our embarrassment at the inhumanity displayed. There is a way of cleansing the guilt for the past, however: we should act according to the dictates of the voices of reason and humanity.

NIGHT AND FOG (McGraw-Hill Contemporary Films: 32 min./color and b&w/1955)

As a camera using color film prowls through the remains of a Nazi concentration camp, the narrator quietly states that words cannot capture the full horror of what went on within. Motion pictures, however, can, especially when using understatement, shock, and irony. In contrast to the sequences in color in the "present" time (the early 1950s), sections of archive film footage of concentration camp life in black and white show partial documentation of what the narrator tries to evoke. Through these juxtapositions, director Alain Resnais makes some disturbing points. We are forced to acknowledge that humans could be this barbaric to each other—and might be again. Yet there is more on Resnais' mind than that: the Nazis appear to be normal, efficient bureaucrats who are merely doing a job. That job happens to be unthinkably evil. Back then, we were tricked by the appearance of these people going about their business; if we are not careful in these comparably peaceful times, we might be the victims. As Resnais puts it, "somewhere the enemy still exists." He directs his message to "those who refuse to look around them, deaf to the endless cry."

To make his major point, Resnais avoids obvious persuasion techniques and emphasizes understatement. The enemy is not depicted as savage, violent, blood-thirsty creatures. There are no shots of actual torture or brutal treatment, only the effects of a job well done, such as the atrocities of surgical experiments, the gas chambers, the uses for the dead bodies. The commandant of the concentration camp is shown in his middle-class home with his family in the act of entertaining guests. Himmler, wearing a business suit, visits the camp and plans with the leaders the most efficient way of getting rid of the dead—the building of a crematorium. Blueprints are studied as if these men were planning the enlargement of a successful business operation. The camps had all the amenities for the people who worked there, includ-ing a zoo in one, a symphony orchestra in another. We are shown the clean, comfort-able room of a capo. The *S.S.* even followed slogans such as "Cleanliness is Health," "Work is Freedom," "To Each His Due," and "A Louse Means Death." We watch brisk, healthy German women reporting to work in the morning. On the surface, these are normal human beings doing their jobs.

But we are also shown the results of their work. There is really no need to verbalize the specifics in this case, because the film's technique of shock will keep the images in the memory. Left to the imagination in the film are the causes that produced emaciated bodies, the frightened, staring eyes, the postures of pain and sickness. The present-tense camera examines a long line of triple-decker bunks, an unpartitioned latrine, the concrete ceiling of a gas chamber torn by fingernails. As in a horror story, the mind recoils from what it might encounter next. The shock tech-nique reaches its climax when we see huge numbers of corpses being pushed into ditches by bulldozers, a hill of women's shorn hair which becomes rolls of cloth, an expanse of bones intended for fertilizer, a number of human skin parchments that have childlike drawings on them.

Various ironic devices force us to think about Resnais' message. The film opens on a peaceful landscape, then the camera sinks to reveal a barbed wire fence. Appear-ance is not reality in this situational irony. In an aside, we are shown the different styles of architecture for a concentration camp, a demonstration that becomes alarm-ing as we realize the number of camps there were. The narrator explains, using dramatic irony, the social order as shown through insignia assigned the victims, a hierarchy that contains no real significance since all—the Night and Fog, Star of David, Red Triangle, Green Triangle—indicate the doomed. The narrator tells us these horrible things in a quiet, low-key voice, then asks evenly, "War nods, but has one eye open . . . Who is on the lookout for our new executioner's arrival?" As a tech-nique, irony can force us to approach the darkness, can jar us into seeing connections. The result is overwhelming.

PRELUDE TO WAR (National Audiovisual Center: 54 min./b&w/1942)

In 1942, the country was at war. The Office of War Information released a film series to give the members of the armed forces "factual information as to the causes, the events leading up to our entry into the war, and the principles for which we are fighting." *Prelude to War*, the first film in that series, presents to the soldiers an either/or argument: they fight and keep freedom, or they do not fight and become members of a slave race. To convince the audience that there is no choice, the film makes powerful use of a wide range of other argument techniques, such as name-calling, glory by association, connotation, and a constant appeal to fear.

The argument technique of either/or helps to explain why Americans are on the march. There are two worlds, the free and the enslaved. We believe in liberty, the four freedoms. The enslaved, in the supreme irony, have given up "their rights as human beings" to three demagogues, Hitler, Mussolini, and the Emperor Hirohito, in order to become "masters" of the world. The film carefully shows that the goal of the Axis Powers is to take over the United States: Admiral Yamamoto was even looking forward to dictating to enslaved Americans from the White House. John Q. Public did not realize modern technology had reduced the two oceans separating us from the enemy. If we do not fight, we are told we will lose our "homes, jobs, books, food, hope for kids, the kids themselves." Is there really any choice? "One hundred seventy years of freedom decrees our answer."

Today, some of the film's persuasion devices make us wince. We encounter name-calling ("ambitious rabble-rouser," "stooges," "buck-toothed pals" are names for Hitler, the other leaders of the Axis, and the Japanese), glory by association (the American ideology is equated to the ideas of Moses, Mohammed, Confucius, and Christ, while the soundtrack plays "Hark! The Herald Angels Sing"), and honorific connotations (the camera shows the flag, the Liberty Bell, the Jefferson Memorial, the Lincoln Memorial, the Declaration of Independence, and the Statue of Liberty to define the American value system). Such obvious attempts to argue emotionally are as suspect as the stereotypes of the German in the film: a person who inherently loves regimentation and harsh discipline.

Appeal to fear is made throughout. For example, we are told 70 million Japanese, 45 million Italians, and 80 million Germans are prepared to "gang up on us" to make us their slaves. (The fact that the Allies had more than twice the population of the Axis countries is not mentioned.) More Germans are on their way: we see, first, a prize being given to the German mother with the most male children, then, an "assembly line" of German babies who are the result of breeding experiments. We are told that these people mean to win, not only by sheer numbers, but also by the development of expensive military equipment. We learn that $80 billion was spent to modernize the German army.

Although we may resist some of the appeals to our fear today, there are sections of this film that are incredibly effective in accomplishing its goal, and one cannot help but admire the artistry of the propagandist. In one sequence, German youths are shown in a classroom singing "Hitler is our Savior . . . who rules a brave new world." Pictures of the young being trained follow, with the comment that these youths are taken from their families to be taught that the "state is the only church." A musical march with cymbals accenting the beat begins as children parade in order past the camera. Soon the boys are young men—and soldiers. The march music gets louder as the masses of bodies increase. We are shown the numbers of troops increasing. The goose step becomes prominent; the camera, now at a distance, looks down on a large, flat surface as the army, with precision, struts across, filling the space. A quote from Hitler is flashed on the screen: "I want to see again in the eyes of youth the gleam of the beast of prey." We are shocked by the blasphemy of the Evil One, we are disturbed by the threat of the large numbers, and we are frightened by the animalistic connotations of the final metaphor. Today's detached audience cannot help but admire the film's powerful arrangement of images.

The fact that sections of the film still work is impressive. How much of the persuasion material now being released on today's favored causes will still be able to grip our attention 40 years hence?

FOR TOMORROW WE SHALL DIET (Churchill Films: 24 min./color/1977)

Do you want to know how to lose weight? Just follow these easy steps: see a doctor, learn something about food and your body's needs, increase your physical activity, and adopt a lifestyle that will continue to keep the weight off after the diet has ended. After a statement of the problem, this film attacks other diet approaches through straw men, then shows the correct way through an exemplum. Our guilt is appealed to throughout. The argument technique is the voice of reason or science, which is reinforced with concrete details, facts, testimonials, and the logic of cause and effect. At the film's conclusion, most viewers will head for a scale.

In its structure, the film presents a problem, briefly indicates the wrong ways to solve the problem, then offers through a long exemplum the "correct" technique. The problem is simple: Americans overeat and must do something about it. The trouble is, they err in the way they approach dieting. The "instant diets," ranging from Stillman's diet to "the grapefruit diet," "don't teach you anything." They work in the short run, we are told, because they are so boring "you end up eating less." The correct way to diet is illustrated by a perky young woman who wants to take some weight off her hips. Her problem is not extreme, so she is someone with whom most can identify. First, she sees a doctor who demands that she set a weight-loss goal and adopt a lifestyle that will maintain good eating habits. By the end of her tale she has lost her weight, and she sums up the lesson of the film: "Food doesn't have power over me; I have power over food."

The movie's appeal to guilt is very effective. At the outset, we encounter a barrage of junk food, TV ads, meals, billboards, and fast-food chains, all culminating with a person standing on a scale. We Americans overeat. The young woman in the exemplum (like the rest of us, according to the film) is self-conscious about her appearance. Later in the film we learn that parents tend to overfeed their babies and that those excess fat cells from childhood last forever. Moreover, parents also use food as a bribe, especially sweets. This creates a psychological problem later on: when we are under stress we pamper ourselves with desserts. Through this cause-and-effect proposition the film puts the guilt first on the parent and then on us for succumbing to infantile needs. The message is that we should grow up and stop our compulsive eating.

The voice of reason, or in this film science, serves as the surrogate parent who demands that we control our irrational behavior. The voice is relentless. Dr. Philip White, Director of the Food and Nutrition Department of the American Medical Association (an authority figure), slaps us with statistics and cause-and-effect relationships. Americans spend $100 to $125 billion on food annually, and another $10 billion getting rid of the effects of that consumption. In the exemplum, we are given a detailed factual lesson on the calorie. Linda Soriano, a nutritionist (another authority figure), suggests that every night we determine the calories and range of nutrients we need, then plan what to eat the next day. This authoritative voice gives us a few dicta for becoming good little dieters: stop such bad habits as sampling the food while cooking it; find friends to form mutual support groups; and do not cheat on the diet, even for a minute. We learn through historical perspective the cause of our calorie problem today: in the early days, our activity at manual work burned those calories away, but now machines save our energy, and fat cells stockpile. The heroine modifies her behavior and loses the weight. Her self-esteem improves. The result: "I feel terrific."

ANYTHING YOU WANT TO BE (New Day Films: 8 min./b&w/1974)

Satire is ridicule with the intent to change behavior, and this film is a solid example. The filmmaker, Lian Brandon, approaches with humor those important moments in a young girl's life when she is being forced to conform to someone else's standards. To attack sexual stereotypes, the film makes an appeal to sympathy and argues through reduction to absurdity and the either/or technique.

We cannot help but feel sympathy even as we laugh at the predicaments in which this typical girl finds herself. The heroine of the film wants to be a "cowboy, fireman, doctor, mommy." Her proud parents give her dolls. So much for that choice. In high school, she runs for class president, but the audience boos her down—only males are presidents. She runs for secretary, uses the same gestures (and presumably the same arguments), and this time wins. The heroine arm-wrestles a boy and wins; he becomes frustrated and distant. She lets him win, and he looks at her appreciatively. To develop her mind, she wants to read books on politics, but is soon reading *The Joy of Cooking* thanks to pressure. Her parents are happy when she receives a marriage band, a baby, and a saucepan. The young woman wants more. When she tries to explore what it means to be a woman, she encounters so many traditional demands that she starts to scream.

The either/or and reduction to absurdity arguments achieve the hyperbole necessary for the satire. No middle road is possible for the heroine. For example, at one point she wants to be a doctor. She walks down the school corridor to the guidance office. When she emerges, she is carrying a bed pan. There is more to nursing than being a drudge, but the bed pan serves to reduce the nurse's duties to a humiliating, unskilled level. Again, to impress her science teacher, she "reads every book he gave me." Suddenly she is pregnant and she explains, "I must have missed a chapter." The extremes of her choices are illustrated at the end by a male voice insisting she be "sexual, sensual, erotic" and a female voice urging her to be "reserved, cool, captivating."

As in any effective satire, there are various butts of the humor attack. Males are challenged on their selfish attitudes and demands. Parents are attacked for having such a limited vision and for setting up so many restraints. Females are not outside the scope of the satire at all: they should demand the right to achieve self-realization and should not accept less. In its eight-minute running time, the film will give the audience as much to ponder as to laugh at.

WHAT DO YOU DO WHEN YOU SEE A BLIND PERSON? (American Foundation for the Blind: 13 min./color/1971)

Phil, the main character of this film, has the wrong ideas about blind people, with whom he does not know how to interact. He is the straw man whose undesirable values or behavior will be torn apart. Within the structure of an exemplum, Phil meets Jim, blind for three years, and learns how to act correctly. The audience gains knowledge as a narrator discusses and corrects Phil's blunders, so that by the end of the film we realize that "if you do know what to do when you see a blind person, life will be easier for him and more interesting for you."

Phil is the perfect straw man in every way. He thinks blind people are "objects of grief and pity" and suspects that the blind are not "normal" human beings. He first meets Jim at a street crossing. Two skits show how Phil handles the situation. In one, he rushes Jim in and around traffic; in the other, he literally carries Jim across the street. The narrator then tells Phil what the correct technique is: talk, let the person take your arm, relax, let him or her know when you approach the curb. In talking to Jim, Phil learns not to shout (Jim is blind, not deaf) and becomes less self-conscious about using words such as "look," "see," "notice," etc. In other words, he learns to be at ease with his new friend. In a restaurant with the blind man, Phil does all the wrong things again. The narrator stops the action, then has Phil start all over. This time he discovers that the "easiest method is the simplest." Let Jim know where the table is, lead him up to the table, put his hand on the back of the chair, let him know which way the chair is facing. Once seated, either explain the location of food by a clock analogy (the blind person is at six o'clock, items are indicated by their relationship to a clock's numbers) or by directly guiding the person's hand. Most important, let the person talk for him- or herself; he or she does not need an interpreter with the waiter. By the end of the meal, Phil has totally learned his lesson.

The film is excellent at making its point. The audience is motivated through appeals to guilt (we all are capable of making the blunders Phil makes—otherwise, there would be no point in the film), to sympathy (we are forced to realize how uncomfortable a blind person must feel at times as a result of our behavior), and to status (we want to be among the sophisticated people who behave correctly, and who do not act gauchely). The film uses the techniques of shock and stereotyping when it shows Phil's initial idea of blind people: Jim wears beggar's clothes and holds a tin cup; after Phil has carried Jim across the street, he pats the blind man on the head. The narrator uses the voice of reason as he talks Phil through normal, daily activities and offers advice on ways to avoid embarrassing moments. Phil, with the audience, eventually realizes he is dealing with another human being and that he should be thoughtful of that human's needs.

CLOSE HARMONY (Learning Corp. of America: 30 min./color/1981)

The close harmony of this film is achieved between the students of the elementary Brooklyn Friends School and the members of the Council Center for Senior Citizens, before and during an intergenerational choral concern. Along with the children in the fourth and fifth grades in Brooklyn, we gain insight into the capabilities of the elderly, surrender a few stereotypes about old age, and learn that such intergenerational activities offer a great deal of enjoyment. The film accomplishes its goals through the structure of an exemplum and an appeal to sympathy. Indeed, few films can match *Close Harmony*'s heartwarming power as it shows the joys of active, sharing and creative living.

The film's message is implied through the exemplum: the true story of how music teacher Arlene Symons bridged the age gap is a model we all can emulate. One day at a senior citizens concert, attended only by other senior citizens, Symons became disturbed at "how very isolated" the elderly people were. She did something about it. She combined her other chorus of school children with her senior citizens. For the first three months, the two groups rehearsed separately. To break down barriers, the children wrote letters to the senior citizens. By the end of their first joint rehearsal, friendships between pen pals from the two choruses had jelled. For the actual concert, there is a mix in the audience of the young, middle-aged (the parents), and old people. As Symons plays the piano, the young singers escort the senior citizens down the aisle to the stage, and soon they all are singing the lyric, "The dearest love in all the world is waiting somewhere for me . . . ."

There is a tremendous appeal to sympathy in this film. One young boy is later asked by his teacher to share his emotions when he discovered his elder pen pal had died; the boy says that he felt sad, then his voice drifts off, a wordless communication that says a great deal. During the sequence in which the two groups meet for the first time, we hear the children sing Kermit the Frog's famous optimistic song, "Some day, we'll find it, the Rainbow Connection, for lovers and dreamers and me . . . ." We are shown that the Rainbow Connection is a possibility as we watch the young and old enjoy each other.

Stereotypes about the old as children-haters, cranks, and dullards are shattered as we get to know some charming old people. A handicapped woman tells us about her harmonica concert with six others ("We were a sensation"). On the day she meets her young correspondents, she gives them knitted hand puppets as gifts. With total excitement, she prepares herself for the concert: "I washed my blouse again, even though it was perfectly clean." Such nervous behavior comes from a person who earlier confided, "I have no inhibitions in singing, I never get nervous . . . ." The woman's enjoyment of life, her sense of humor, and her warmth show us what we are missing if we ignore the old.

CAMPAIGN (Churchill Films: 20 min./color/1973)

Campaign makes three important points through the exemplum of Democrat Cathy O'Neill's run for the state senate in Sacramento, California's 25th District. First, the American ideal of the grass roots candidate challenging the establishment should be emulated. Second, women should be active in politics. Third, we should *all* be politically active. To persuade the audience, the film appeals to sympathy, group membership, and status. In addition, the filmmaker uses the argument technique of minimizing and maximizing, in portraying the nature of political campaigns.

In an appeal to sympathy, O'Neill is presented as the ideal political figure: an underdog. She acknowledges that it will be difficult to unseat republican Robert Stevens; nonetheless, she challenges him. Because she believes in political fair play, she files an injunction against Stevens when she learns he is using $25,000 of state money for his political mailings. Such action, she explains, is unfair to the other candidates and is in fact undemocratic. She estimates the cost of an election to be at least $50,000 and cheerfully observes that while she might not be able to outspend the incumbent, she can, at least, out-organize him. On the phone, she complains that she has endured "innuendos that have no truth or substance." Speaking to her workers while waiting for the returns, O'Neill emphasizes that even if she loses, Senator Stevens will have to be more responsible because the success of her campaign will have scared the hell out of him. Just as her campaign exhibited idealism, in defeat (she loses by less than one percent) she shows total dignity and thus earns our sympathy.

The appeal to group membership is easy to make since a campaign joins people together for a common cause. In her thank-you speech, she refers to those who worked the phones, did precinct walking or doorbell ringing, designed and developed materials, wrote, collected money, gave fund raisers, and took pictures. On election night, the group spends the entire night interpreting statistics, chatting, and waiting. They are clearly reluctant to disband on the morning after the election. O'Neill's campaign workers are energetic, charming, intense, and close-knit; the work and environment look appealing, and the audience cannot help wanting to be part of that excitement.

Because sexism is a problem in the campaign, we come to believe that any woman who can rise above the opposition gains status. O'Neill observes that a good-looking young male lawyer would not be challenged as to his being qualified for the job, but that she is asked the question. In a TV interview she is asked what will happen to her family if she wins. Her answer points out the sexism of the question: the same as with any legislator—whatever nonworking time there is will be spent with the family and children. When asked how much the women's movement had to do with her candidacy, she states that "women with competencies should run for public office." In terms of this film, her comment is almost an exhortation to the audience to live up to its potential.

The film also minimizes the problems and maximizes the advantages in a campaign. The actual issues are completely ignored; her platform is never mentioned. The beginning steps, which are necessary to any campaign, are not documented. There is no indication that O'Neill made any errors. The film maximizes the excitement, fast pace, and drama of the campaign. Even when O'Neill complains of the work, the film's tone is romantic; we sense that not everyone would be able to have the same drive and energy. Through this positive atmosphere, the film encourages the audience to challenge the establishment, to support women in politics, and to join a community of politically active people.

THE SKATING RINK (Learning Corp. of America: 27 min./color/1975)

A favorite device of the sermon is the exemplum, the colorful story that illustrates the spiritual lesson. This adaptation of Mildred Lee's novel posits that a physical disability does not prevent a person from being successful, that a tragic experience can build character, and that in relationships one should try to express one's feelings. The lesson in values clarification is aimed directly at adolescents, and depicts the world of the underdog, a world with which we all can identify. To make its point, the film uses stereotypes, card stacking, and an appeal to sympathy.

The character of Tuck is a stereotype that teenagers can identify with. Like Ashboy, Cinderella's male counterpart in the fairy tale, he is the underdog, and does not deserve the treatment he receives. His two older brothers tease him; his younger sister tattles on him; his father is not easy to please and yells at him a lot. Tuck is gentle, shy, and unsure of himself. He also has talent, but he does not realize it. The audience can learn ways to solve its problems as Tuck struggles with his.

And problems he has. The film appeals to our sympathy by stacking the cards. Tuck lost his mother in a flood in which he himself almost drowned. Since that traumatic experience, he has stuttered. He walks home from school alone, because the kids on the bus "pick on him and call him dummy." His father, a poor farmer, constantly scolds him and gets frustrated at the son's emotional distance. Life is bleak for Tuck until he meets Pete Dagley, a retired professional ice skater who is opening an Ice Palace. Pete teaches Tuck to figure skate, and teams him with his wife, Lily, for a demonstration on the Palace's opening night. The boy is a success and earns $100.00. Even though his father is sarcastic about the skating ("One hundred dollars for prancing around a skating rink with a girl"), Tuck gives him the money to buy the electric stove his stepmother wants so badly. Startled, the father finally opens his heart to his son.

For the young audience, the message of the exemplum is clear: an adolescent needs guidance, and can solve problems if he or she listens to others. The young man learns by taking the advice of two mentors: the skating instructor and his stepmother. The instructor—a substitute father—is kind and generous, but also demanding. He urges Tuck on to realize his skating ability. His stepmother is understanding and gives him the advice that is the point of the story: "There's a lot of things you don't have to talk good to do." Tuck does not give up; he gets back on his feet when he falls down, and eventually solves his problems. If the audience follows Tuck's example, it can also achieve success.

A MATTER OF SURVIVAL (McGraw-Hill Contemporary Films: 26 min./ color/1969)

This exemplum film makes three points: a worker should not trust management, should join a union, and should be wary of company-directed improvements that might help to eliminate a job. The hero, Jerry, in charge of the accounting department of a growing manufacturing company, is asked by his bosses to show Mr. Cooper, a visitor, how the department runs. What Jerry does not know is that Mr. Cooper is a computer specialist. Once the visitor has programmed the computer with the information Jerry has supplied about the various accounting jobs, Jerry's entire staff is fired. The film uses dramatic irony and the either/or technique. Moreover, it appeals to a fear that has been prevalent in our century, the fear that impersonal machines will replace human workers.

In the either/or world of this exemplum, all upper management, "experts," and technological advances are villainous; all laborers are good workers who take pride in what they do and who believe that a boss should be like a parent. The villains are blacker than black. The company calls in an "expert" as a consultant in the transition to computers. Holding a meeting in an upper management office and behind closed doors (Jerry is not present), the "expert" advises that the company prepare the transition in secret. After all, if there is too much notice, the workers might leave before the company has replaced them. The expert also points out that it costs less to fire people than to retrain them or to find them new jobs. The workers, on the other hand, think they are one happy family with Jerry one of the many middle management father figures. Even the malcontent Kirby is a "sweet guy." A man who fled a purge at another company, Betco, argues that a union is the only possible salvation, but the workers reject his plan. They trust Jerry, who convinces them that they would be losing status if they joined: "You don't want to descend to the level of *workers*."

The dramatic irony colors the whole sequence because the film's audience knows more than Jerry does about the actual intentions of management. He does not realize that he has unwittingly made it easier for management to replace his co-workers without notice. Jerry assumes his bosses think highly of him as a "company man," but after the dismissals, they tell him, "I'm only sorry that you couldn't have known earlier . . . ." Obviously they had not trusted Jerry enough to tell even him the truth. Earlier, in still another example of dramatic irony, Jerry encourages a young man to stay with the company, and even offers him a "permanent" job. Actually, there is no job offer thanks to the machines.

Those machines are the basis for the appeal to fear. Jerry has, at the beginning of the film, nightmares of electronic sounds and images, premonitions of things to come. Before the men are fired, Jerry's department is moved down into the basement of the building (the desks and file cabinets are put in narrow corridors that are similar to those in the film version of Kafka's *The Trial*). Like sheep, the members of the department are herded into a room before the final slaughter, the announcement that they have been terminated at the company. Afterward Jerry returns home and breaks down in tears at his front door. The camera jumps further and further away to show that our hero is just one crushed life in a huge urban complex; electronic sounds crash around him.

The issues of the film are not part of the distant past, but ones that still face us. But, instead of persuading through a carefully balanced pro-and-con argument, the filmmakers chose to use the emotional techniques discussed above. In a way, they had no choice. It would be somewhat ironic to use the unemotional techniques of logic and statistics to make a point against computer technology.

THE END OF ONE (Learning Corp. of America: 7 min./color/1970)

Using the technique of juxtaposition without any verbal commentary, filmmaker Paul Kocela has created a brief but artistic film that offers both a parable that warns the audience to be sensitive to ecology and an existential comment on life and death. The film crosscuts between the activities of a flock of noisy sea gulls and the last moments of a dying, solitary gull. The flock hovers over a garbage dump, swoops down to peck at the swill, scatters when a tractor levels the debris, then returns to fight over tidbits in the refuse. The solitary bird staggers toward the water's edge, collapses, twitches, then dies. Before the gull's final convulsion, we see a healthy bird at the water's edge fly up toward the heavens. The tide comes in; the carcass floats off. The sequence suggests that no matter how social one is, each person dies alone. The ecology message is that the deposits of human waste are creating an environment that is destructive to wildlife (and by extension, to human life).

On a philosophical level, the film suggests an existential message through the juxtaposition of images. There seems to be a cause-and-effect relationship between the garbage eating and the death of the bird. An ugly world (the garbage dump) alternating with a painful one (the death throes), suggests the message, "life is ugly, absurdly competitive (we fight for worthless trash), and painful." The concentration on only two images with no "pleasant" scenes is part of the message: we are hopelessly entrapped in this world. Since the scenes shock, we can assume that part of the message is that "we should do something about this." The impact of vivid images might just move an audience to do something. The lack of verbal comment on the juxtaposed scenes gives enough ambiguity to allow for the two messages.

The filmmaker motivates the audience through three appeals. He uses sympathy for the helpless bird (at one point, it uses its beak as a crutch to rise to its feet). We also feel guilt because the garbage dump is large and ugly—we have helped to produce this potentially unhealthy feeding ground for the birds. And we fear that the environment's destruction will ultimately destroy us. Even more frightening is the bird's dying in a way other than the way we would wish for ourselves. Because of the brevity of the film, the issues are not fully explored, but the emotional appeals quickly produce a reaction in the audience.

The images haunt the viewer long after the film is over. If Kocela had carefully spelled out the ecology message, he would have lost one level of the parable. The images force us to face his cynical view of life, a view that works on deeper levels of the audience's behavior.

FOLLOW-UP ACTIVITIES

1. Construct a persuasion piece in which you either defend or attack a person's dropping out of school at age 16. Construct the life of a drop-out as an exemplum.
2. With the intention of correcting behavior, prepare a satire on
    a. the way students spend their afternoons (perhaps focusing on those who watch afternoon TV soaps)
    b. the people who buy only designer clothes
    c. the behavior of cliques
    d. the ostentatious going-steady crowd
3. Take the most significant issue among your peers and present it to an adult group in a pro-and-con argument. In your report, be sure to present the adult's side of the argument.
4. Follow police reports in the newspaper, or make a trip to the police station, or listen to a police scanner to obtain concrete data on local crimes, then prepare a report in which you try to persuade people to take safety precautions around their homes or in their daily behavior. To help motivate the audience, use an appeal to their fear.
5. Using the step-by-step format found in *What Do You Do When You See a Blind Person?*, set up a straw man for showing what not to do on a first date, or how a parent should not treat a child.

SIGNS

Most of us recall with dread our first encounters with symbol (usually in connection with the study of poetry) in high school English classes. We were both terrified and awed by how the teacher derived such a variety of meanings for Shelley's statue in "Ozymandias" or Shakespeare's use of fog in *Macbeth*. Though the teacher's lecture made us aware of the symbol's place in literature and its power, many of us were left bewildered at the prospect of having to pick out symbols on our own and of having to determine their meaning. How were we to know when an author had given an image enough associations and ideas to elevate it to a symbol? What, we wondered, were the rules for coping with such an intimidating device?

Getting students to see that the literary symbol is only one of the many ways to communicate through signs is the first step in giving them control over this mystifying device. Once they realize that the stop light at the end of their street conveys meaning in much the same way as Shelley's statue, even though the latter is more complex, they will begin to see literary symbols in a proper perspective.

Any sign (including those we call symbols) can be analyzed by looking at its signifier and signified. The *signifier* is anything perceived through the senses: a color, a fragrance, a ringing, a sourness. The *signified* is the meaning that the signifier conveys to us. Some examples: a flashing red light is a sign; its signifiers are the color red and the flashing, its signified is to stop completely and to look both ways before proceeding. A skunk's scent is also a sign. Its signifier is the unpleasant smell; it signifies that a skunk has sprayed or been killed nearby. The many bells that ring throughout the school day are signs. A single blast (signifier) tells students to change class in the four (or so) minutes allotted; a double blast may signify that a custodian is wanted; and a louder, high-pitched, and continuous blast may signify that a fire has broken out and that students and personnel must evacuate the building through their assigned exits. (A false alarm pulled by a student can signify the puller's prowess, scorn, or protest.) A sourness (signifier) to some wine drinkers signifies that the wine they are drinking is of poor quality.

All these are, of course, *conventional signs*; that is, ones whose meanings are known and agreed upon by a large group of people. Each is traditional: the signifier and signified have been passed down through the years by the actions of parents, teachers, advertisers, artists, governments, etc. Obviously, these signs do not have to be taught by English teachers. What is important for them to teach, is that all signs work in the same way even though one could encounter many different sign codes in everyday life, some of which are conventional and others personal. Jargon associated with any one of our many professions, for instance, is simply a set of words (often common words or word combinations) that convey specialized or personal meanings (signifieds) within the company. Literature also has a code of conventional signs that one can learn simply by reading a lot and by breaking the code through inference. (English teachers also help.) *Personal signs*, then, are ones that have a special meaning to an individual or to a small group of people. Artists and authors often create personal signs, and these, too, can be learned by continued exposure to the artists' work.

The correct interpretation of a sign is highly dependent on identifying the environment in which it appears. Few signifiers have a single signified. Traffic signs and directionals used to bridge language barriers are good examples. At Disneyland, one might see a *universal sign* (a static sign understood by all people) telling tourists that smoking is not allowed. It would picture a lit cigarette and show a red line superimposed across it. Pictures or exact models of an object are, of course, the simplest of signs. Red universally means stop, and a slash across something is generally under-stood to disallow whatever it covers. On the other hand, a quick browse through the *Oxford English Dictionary* will show how easily signs can accrue new and different meanings. Signs such as the word "nice," which can have many different meanings—coy, fastidious, attentive, agreeable, ignorant, morally upright, refined, wanton, silly—are called *dynamic*. In other words, the signifier can convey a variety of signi-fieds at once. A few examples: A Mohawk haircut (signifier: a strip of closely cropped hair running along the center of the head from the forehead to the nape of the neck and flanked by a shaved scalp) can mean that its wearer is an Indian belonging to a specific tribe. Recently, the same sign has been adopted by punk rockers to stand for allegiance to that subgroup's beliefs and lifestyle. By the same token, the word "bear" or its picture can be a sign for Russia; a football coach named "Bear" Bryant; death, power, and the old order of things in *The Bear* by William Faulkner; forest fire preven-tion (Smokey the Bear); and a weak (or "bearish") stock market. Only the environ-ment in which the sign is used controls its meaning and allows us to infer that meaning correctly. The sign's so-called *environment* is the set of signs that surround it when it is used. The color pink seen on a bundle of blankets (sign 1) held by a priest (sign 2) over a baptismal font (sign 3) in a church (sign 4) where a number of adults are congre-gated (sign 5) would lead an outsider to infer that a newborn baby girl is being christened. The same color seen from a distance on the outside (sign 1) of a can (sign 2) that someone was drinking from (sign 3) would lead many observers to infer that the can contained TAB (even if the product's trade name were not visible). Bright pink cheeks (sign 1) on a student, surrounded by her peers (sign 2), who has just been caught by the group telling a fib (sign 3), probably indicate the girl is embar-rassed. Similarly, students can be made to see that the color white in an Emily Dickin-son poem (sign set = her collected poems) can have one or more meanings, while the same color in Melville's *Moby Dick* (sign set = the entire novel) can have an entirely different meaning or meanings.

Before proceeding further, the teacher may want to review some of the sign concepts introduced so far. The following chart, page 154, can be duplicated and filled in by students. The teacher is encouraged to add other signs for discussion.

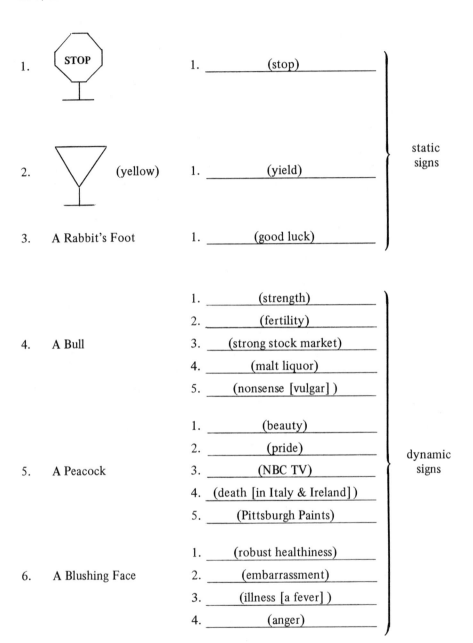

1. STOP   1. _____(stop)_____ ⎫

2. (yellow)   1. _____(yield)_____ ⎬ static signs

3. A Rabbit's Foot   1. _____(good luck)_____ ⎭

4. A Bull
1. _____(strength)_____
2. _____(fertility)_____
3. _(strong stock market)_
4. _____(malt liquor)_____
5. _(nonsense [vulgar])_

5. A Peacock
1. _____(beauty)_____
2. _____(pride)_____
3. _____(NBC TV)_____
4. _(death [in Italy & Ireland])_
5. _(Pittsburgh Paints)_

dynamic signs

6. A Blushing Face
1. _(robust healthiness)_
2. _(embarrassment)_
3. _(illness [a fever])_
4. _____(anger)_____

Some sign sets can best be understood when they are diagrammed on horizontal and vertical lines. The horizontal line of such a grid is called the sign set's *syntagmatic line* and represents the way the signs are arranged and the way they can be arranged in order to make sense or communicate. The vertical line, or the sign set's *paradigmatic line*, shows the range of signs that can be substituted at each point on the syntagmatic line and still make sense. Thus, in the model below, the syntagmatic line shows that in our language an acceptable ordering of signs is article/adjective/noun/verb. Sentences 1, 2, 3, and 4 result from individual paradigmatic sign choices that can be made along the horizontal, syntagmatic line. This syntagmatic line also shows that an adjective must come before, not after, the noun it modifies if that sentence is going to convey meaning to most readers or listeners. (There are exceptions. Lines of poetry often break standard syntagmatic and paradigmatic rules of the language and still convey meaning.) The choices at each point along the paradigmatic line in this example are large but not infinite. For example, in sentence 3, a writer could choose the signs "large" and "round" as paradigmatic options for the adjective slot, but not the sign "cancerous" without seriously jeopardizing the meaning of the sentence. Similarly, "The" is a suitable sign substitute for the article "A" but "An" is not.

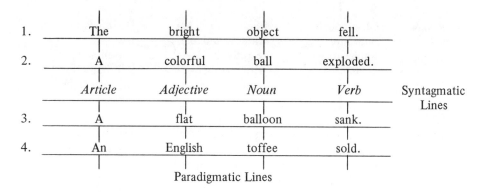

On a much larger scale, a story or an essay can be analyzed on a similar grid. Fundamentally, a story's syntagmatic line can be described as: an Opening, which presents the problem / a Middle, which develops the conflicts caused by the problem / a Conclusion, which resolves those conflicts. Into each of these slots the author can place a wide variety of paradigmatic choices.

One such series of choices was made by mythmakers who long ago told tragic love stories. Eventually, the syntagmatic structure of this story became so rigid it was transformed into a story *archetype* (an archetype is a recurring image, character, or story that triggers instinctual responses). An outline of it is as follows:

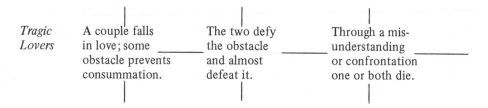

In three well-known examples—*Pyramis and Thisbe*, *Romeo and Juliet*, and *West Side Story*—authors have made paradigmatic choices along the *Tragic Lovers* syntagmatic line. In each case they did so to make the story meaningful to their own times and audiences. A sketch of their paradigmatic choices might look like this:

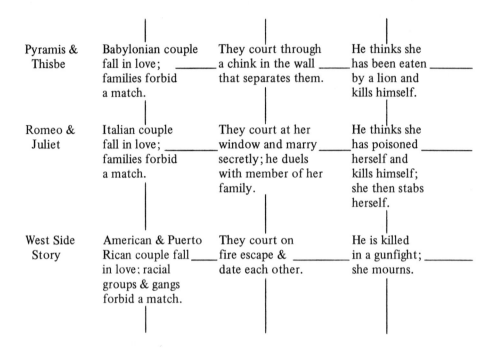

Pyramis & Thisbe	Babylonian couple fall in love; families forbid a match.	They court through a chink in the wall that separates them.	He thinks she has been eaten by a lion and kills himself.
Romeo & Juliet	Italian couple fall in love; families forbid a match.	They court at her window and marry secretly; he duels with member of her family.	He thinks she has poisoned herself and kills himself; she then stabs herself.
West Side Story	American & Puerto Rican couple fall in love; racial groups & gangs forbid a match.	They court on fire escape & date each other.	He is killed in a gunfight; she mourns.

The reader will notice that one paradigmatic change Shakespeare made in the syntagmatic line was to add much more detail than is contained in *Pyramis and Thisbe* and to show more success in the courtship and greater tragedy in the close. The writer of *West Side Story* chose signs consistent with an American, inner-city milieu and broadened the number of people involved in opposing the love to make his own comment on American history and values. All three of the storytellers, however, were bound by the archetype to close with tragedy, even though the means of tragedy and its depth were optional.

Fashion can also be analyzed on such a syntagmatic and paradigmatic grid. The horizontal line, for the male at least, is the headgear/the shirt/the pants/and the footwear. Each of these slots can be filled from numerous paradigmatic options; the wearer of the clothes bases his selections on self-image and the rule of his social group. Thus, a punk rocker might choose a leather jacket and dungarees for a night at his favorite club, while the upper-class gentleman may decide on a top hat and tails for a formal dinner party at the governor's mansion. In the diagram below, notice how much more freedom the punk rocker has in sign options than the formal dresser has. As long as the punk rocker stays within his sign set or chooses a sign from another fashion set to be ironic, he is okay. The formal dresser could never be ironic in his choices, although recently his options have widened to allow for a broader range of colors than just black and, on occasion, a turtleneck.

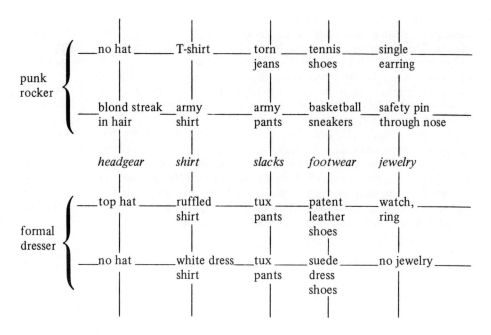

A pair of shoes or a hat can, of course, be chosen by a person for a number of reasons: because they signify his membership in a particular social subgroup, because they indicate his attitude toward the establishment, because they recall an earlier time the person is nostalgic for. In other words, signs serve various functions in communication, whether in clothing or in art.

Three such sign functions will be considered in the films that follow. Signs can: 1) trigger thoughts and emotions in the audience, 2) form a model of something, and 3) alter the behavior of the audience. The American flag and anthem are generally assumed to trigger feelings of patriotism in the viewer. A television advertisement showing an American Indian crying as he overlooks the garbage-strewn, grassy banks of a superhighway is meant to trigger in us guilt for spoiling our environment, especially one we stole from the nature-worshipping Indians. A painting is an obvious sign model of something in nature or the imagination; so is a biography that gives us in words a model of a human being's life. By the same token, it is possible to use a sign or set of signs to form a model of one's world view, theory, or philosophy. A picture series showing a number of apes progressing in size and sophistication until they culminate in a closing picture of a man is a common sign model of Darwin's theory of evolution. A picture of Sisyphus pushing a rock up a hill was once adopted by existentialists as a sign model of their world view. Many of the simplest signs are used to alter our behavior. Most road signs (short of those that merely identify a place, like one that reads "Food & Fuel") seek to make us do something. A skull and crossbones on a bottle of ammonia does, too, as does the more complicated *A Modest Proposal* by Jonathan Swift. His essay (or sign set) was meant to make the British modify their economic and political oppression of the Irish. All satires—cartoons, paintings, films, essays, plays—are meant to end or temper some behavior the artist finds abhorrent or silly.

Of the 15 films that follow, a full 10 rely solely on visual signs to convey their message or to tell their story. Each presents the student with a wealth of signs to discuss. The viewer will find static, dynamic, conventional, and personal signs. In six of the films—*Iran, Street Musique, Les Escargot, Run!, Braverman's Condensed Cream of Beatles*, and *The Olympia Diving Sequence*—the moviemakers use a syntagmatic and paradigmatic grid to arrange through editing the signs they employ. *Iran, The Resurrection of Bronco Billy, Pillar of Wisdom, The Egg*, and *Secrets* deal primarily with the fact that signs change meaning over time. The last three—*Pillar, Egg*, and *Secrets*—show that archetypal signs are reinterpreted continually by each successive generation. *Street Musique, Fantasy, Braverman's Condensed Cream of Beatles*, and *The Olympia Diving Sequence* define an era or genre through its signs. By doing so, they trigger a complex mix of thoughts and emotions in the audience. *Les Escargot, Metropolis*, and *Run!* are out-and-out allegories, or sign models. *Sunday Dinner, Listen to Britain*, and *Star Spangled Banner* use signs to alter the behavior or thinking of the audience. In a sense, each is a persuasive argument.

PILLAR OF WISDOM (National Film Board of Canada: 9 min./color/1970)

In the nineteenth century when anthropology was a young discipline, field and armchair scientists freely used the term "primitive" to describe the tribes they studied. Since then, their modern successors have come to realize that all civilizations are complex and that many of the rites and rituals once thought strictly "primitive" have been an important part of our modern civilizations all along. *Pillar of Wisdom* goes to a Canadian university to show that pole climbing, an ancient rite of passage, is still an important sign to freshmen who wish to gain the respect and acceptance of upper classmen. The film makes it clear that few, if any, of the signs in the ancient pole climbing ritual have changed. In primitive tribes, climbing the pole represents the difficult struggle from boyhood to manhood, or from earth to heaven. At the top, for those young males who make it, the initiates receive the secrets of the tribe, known only to the male adults or elders. A successful struggle also earns the boy the right to sit with the men and participate in their spiritual and martial deliberations.

On the Canadian college campus, by trying to climb the greased pole as a class, the freshmen prove their worth. The upperclassmen who tried the pole in their freshman year taunt the struggling freshmen and pelt them with tomatoes, but the upperclassmen freely accept the frosh as equals if they make it, and the older students look back on their own rites of passage with sentimentality. The freshmen, by undergoing the ordeal, also earn the right to initiate the next year's incoming class. *Pillar of Wisdom* is not a solemn film, however. It achieves humor by satirizing the college administrators who consider themselves the sole wise men who test the students before rewarding them with diplomas. By juxtaposing the soundtrack of a school administrator's clichéd and grave welcoming address to the freshman class with scenes of extravagant college hazing rituals, the filmmaker shows that even though our modern societies try to hide their "primitive" roots in scholarship and bombast, ancient rites of passage are still in place, and the cap at the top of the greased pole is at least as important a sign of adulthood to students as the diploma.

The satiric intent of *Pillar of Wisdom* is evident from the moment the film opens. During the introduction, we hear a ponderous dean tell the freshmen, "You are at a restless stage in your growth to adulthood . . . when the boy becomes a man," but as he is saying this, we see the frosh dressed in yellow and plaid kilts chasing after a greased pig on a football field at halftime, and doing a high-kick Rockettes number in the football stands. When the entire freshman class begins its assault on the greased pole that is surrounded by a soggy mess of axle grease, manure, sludge, sheep blood, old varnish, and urine, the dean is heard saying, "How you cope with this transition into university is up to you"; and "This is a wonderful but turbulent experience"; and "You must adjust to the new tempo or drown in the flood."

Voiceovers of upperclassmen speaking are not meant to be satirical, however. One student says, "If you make it [the pole climb], you're supposed to be all right." Another adds, "Nobody likes it when they're doing it, but nobody forgets it, believe me." A third tries to explain the humiliating ritual this way: "It's like climbing mountains; it doesn't make much sense unless you've done it yourself." The final speaker sounds as if he really believes in the power of the climbing ritual. When this class of freshmen reaches the top after a full day of trying, he says, "We didn't make it our year; these guys are a little smarter, they ought to make pretty good engineers."

Pillar of Wisdom takes a sign—pole climbing—that generally triggers in us thoughts of the "primitive" and shows us that this meaning is too limited. Rites of passage, the film argues, are as important in modern civilizations as in "primitive" ones. To believe otherwise is to have an exaggerated belief of one's own sophistication. To convey this message—to thus persuade us—the film adds to the sign's meaning through juxtaposition. The ancient ritual of pole climbing is set against the sign of "civilization and learning"—the modern college campus. Then the professor's bombastic discussion of the trials and tribulations of school work is juxtaposed with the students' superstitious remarks about hazing rituals. In this manner, the filmmaker redefines the meaning of the ancient sign by carefully controlling the environment in which it appears.

IRAN (Pyramid Films: 18 min./color/1972)

The film *Iran* is tangible proof that signs used by an artist can change dramatically in meaning over time, thus altering the effect a work of art has on us. In 1971, Claude Lelouch made this tribute to Iran, celebrating the beauty of the country and its people and focusing on their ability to retain ancient Eastern traditions while opening the door to modern Western influences. Since that time, however, the sign value of the shah and Iran have changed markedly: Ayatollah Khomeini and the hostages have become the dominant signs of Iran in our minds. Viewed today, Lelouch's film, although still beautiful and powerful, seems naive or ironic. How, we wonder, can anyone seriously suggest that Iran is a model blend of the old and the new, the rich and the poor, the Eastern and the Western?

Lelouch, without the aid of a narrator, portrays Iran as a desert Garden of Eden. Using romantic music in the background, the filmmaker cleverly juxtaposes conventional signs from three pairs of sign systems—new, old; rich, poor; Eastern, Western—to suggest an idyllic unity that perhaps never did exist in Iran. The syntagmatic and paradigmatic lines of the film make his argument convincing, however. On a horizontal line, the film juxtaposes opposite signs. The camera focuses on women dressed in purdah (Eastern), then cuts quickly to women dressed in miniskirts leaving college classes (Western). A gas station attendant, shown removing the nozzle of a gas pump from a car's tank (new) is immediately compared to a camel raising its head from a desert pool where it has been drinking (old). The camera shows peasant boys at play in a desert watering hole (poor), then uniformed prep school boys playing during recess (rich). The syntagmatic structure, simplified here for the purposes of discussion, can be described as: Eastern sign/Western sign; old sign/new sign; poor sign/rich sign. Lelouch spices this approach up by inserting an occasional visual pun or surprise juxtaposition. At one point a peasant touches a match to a kerosene lamp and immediately the camera cuts to a tower of flame rising from a desert oil well.

Further on, the filmmaker focuses on the crystals, gems, and pearls that contribute to a dazzling display of wealth at the shah's royal palace, then cuts to an opened tin of white caviar eggs that look for all the world like pearls.

Lelouch finds many signs of Iran's three dichotomies to vary the structure's syntagmatic line. Examples include: a mosque vs. an oil rig, mud shacks vs. skyscrapers, hookas vs. a television set, a folk dance vs. a military band performance, an ancient desert drinking well vs. a microscope, a whirling dervish vs. a helicopter in flight, and a fisherman hauling in a net vs. the Shah riding a horse around his estate. Lelouch further embellishes this juxtaposition of six sign systems by using a sign motif and by closing with a single summary sign. Throughout, he focuses on the mandala— an Oriental sign of the universe—or its circular shape to underscore unity in diversity. At the film's close, he juxtaposes the faces of young and old, rich and poor, Eastern- and Western-clad Iranians with bas reliefs of human figures on ancient walls of the country's ruins. This device suggests a unity between past and present Iran. He then points the camera five separate times at segments of various ancient wall reliefs that show the hands of two individuals clasped in friendship or cooperation. This sign, repeated in this manner at the close, draws the six sign systems (three dichotomies) together to say that Iran has found richness and strength in its dissimilarities.

Using only conventional signs chosen from the new/old, Western/Eastern, and rich/poor sign sets and arranging them on a syntagmatic line, Lelouch suggests the diversity of Iran. Introducing the mandala as a motif and the handshake in the conclusion, the artist triggers in us thoughts of unity and harmony and feelings of affection for Iran. If the sign value of Iran has now changed in our minds, the filmmaker cannot be blamed, but neither should he be surprised if we view the film *Iran* as a nostalgic glimpse of what once was, or a dreamer's idea of what never was.

THE EGG (National Film Board of Canada: 5 min./color/1973)

Psychologists tell us that certain images attach themselves to the subconscious instincts and become archetypal signs, which, according to Carl Jung, gain a hold on the imagination and surface in our creative and intellectual endeavors. *The Egg* surveys such an image that has recurred throughout history. As an archetype, the egg or sphere has accrued many meanings; the film offers in a rapid montage more than could possibly be understood in one viewing. A dynamic sign, the egg is used in myth, art, architecture, and science. More a tease or a probe than a study, the film uses the image whimsically and impressionistically to stimulate our own interpretations. Why has the egg been so significant to humankind? What do its many appearances say about its underlying meaning? The answers are left totally up to us.

This unnarrated film takes no longer than the time needed to fry an egg. After a cook cracks one open on a hot grill, the animation begins with one of the world's oldest cosmological myths, the universe hatching from an egg. The fertility sign is seen again in the egg-shaped face of the earth mother on an ancient vase. Eggs descend from the sky, like ideas from the cosmos, producing the architecture of Mesopotamia and Egypt (notably the pyramids, which roughly correspond to a half-sphere). The egg is a sign of fertility in the myth of Leda and the swan, in which Leda's children are hatched from shells. The egg's shape is used in the religious mandala design, the geometric sphere, the atom in physics. The image is portrayed humorously at times: for instance, the intellectual is represented as an "egghead."

The very profusion of the sign and the speed with which it appears and disappears lend it mystery. What logic there is in the film is provided by its chronological structure. It proceeds historically from ancient times, revealing the many meanings the egg has accrued over time. It was used as a sign in religion and art in the past and is common in science and art today, showing its fecundity. Surrealistic paintings, art's reaction to the exceptional barbarities of our time, portray the egg as a sign of modern man's predicament. A picture of a grenade—the sphere—is followed by an angry mouth filled with an egg it is about to crush. Images of tyrannical and militaristic government flash onto the screen, the last, the boot of a fascist hovering over several eggs.

Archetypal images are by nature dynamic signs. As our environment, our knowledge, and our societies have changed, our instinctual needs have changed. The imagination that expresses those yearnings reshapes old signs to fit new hopes and fears. Such a process, the film asserts, has made the egg a lasting sign.

THE RESURRECTION OF BRONCO BILLY (University of Southern California: 21 min./sepia and color/1970)

For adolescents, problems occur when their egocentric view of the world conflicts with reality. Growth is stymied when their allegiance to signs with personal significance prevents them from accepting those of the adult world. The hero of *The Resurrection of Bronco Billy* has identified himself with the static signs of the Old Western heroes, even though he is living in a modern city. He is the sign model of the adolescent who refuses to grow up, a Holden Caulfield in cowboy hat and boots. Because he means no harm and is only trying to hide from his own inadequacies, he arouses our pity and affection, but our exasperation as well. Beneath all his troubles, he is a gentle and warm-hearted youth who receives much more abuse than he deserves. We want him to triumph, to rise above his comic-pathetic image. We know, however, that his inability to surrender his romantic illusions dooms him.

Billy's room, a rented attic, is a virtual museum of the Old West as seen through a Hollywood lens. Posters of gunslinging film stars (such as John Wayne and Gary Cooper) fill the walls. After rising from bed, he dons Western boots, a vest, a neckerchief, and a cowboy hat. Outside, his landlady, whose shrill voice has been trying to get him up (he habitually oversleeps), complains about Billy's outfit, even though she herself is dressed in a robe and wears curlers while watering the front lawn. She complains that his rent is overdue, that he spends too much money on Western movies, and that he is not concerned enough about his future. As a sign of the cruel and banal real world, she creates sympathy for Billy, who is a beautiful dreamer. But she also reminds us that the real world must be coped with.

The reasons for Billy's attachment to the past are provided during a visit with Wild Bill Tucker, the only character to show any affection for the boy. Wild Bill knows the Wild West from firsthand experience: he was there at the tailend of that frontier era. Drawings (not film posters) on his wall of a barroom fight, a cowboy being hurled from a bronco, and a hanging reveal the harshness of the period. Tucker, a sign for the Old West as it really was, admits that he was not very good with a gun. He comments that "all cowboys get shot" and then names several who did. But Billy only registers the romance in his tales. A sign for the boy's destructive love for a mythical past is the pocket watch Wild Bill has given him. When Billy realizes that it has stopped and he is late for work, the old man scolds him for forgetting to wind the thing.

Signs change meaning over time, but Billy is too attached to his to perceive the changes. When his boss calls him to his desk to fire him, Billy cuts a comic figure as he approaches with a John Wayne swagger, hoping to intimidate the man. Later at a bar, the boyish looking Billy orders a "redeye," a sign for Western macho behavior. The bartender laughs at the inappropriateness of the antiquated sign and refuses to serve the child-gunfighter. Outside, Billy is beaten up by two toughs, signs for the modern urban non-chivalric realities the boy is in conflict with. The hoods call him a "fag" and steal his wallet and watch. For the rest of the world, the Old West carries its original sign values only in films. When Billy adopts the signs, he is viewed as a "weirdo," someone who is making a spectacle of himself to gain attention. We do not approve of the treatment he gets from the two toughs, but we know from experience that it is realistic.

When a cute girl shows interest in him in a nearby park, Billy demonstrates his inability to understand the signs of the real world. The girl, an art student, asks Billy to pose for a drawing. She is friendly and does not judge him negatively, despite his outfit. He mistakes her interest in him, thinking she has fallen for his rugged, authentic appearance. As she draws, Billy, with newfound confidence, criticizes her picture. He rambles on about the way film stars actually wore their hats and guns, feeling in his adolescent egotism that he is impressing her. Bored with his babbling and not interested in the criticism, she leaves.

We want Billy to learn from the experience. If getting nagged by his landlady, fired from his job, and beaten up are not enough to change him, certainly being put down by the girl is. But this is not the case. The last scene, the only one in color, shows Billy's daydream. To shield himself from this latest brush with the real world, he imagines himself on a horse riding over a hill to the girl. As he pulls her to the back of the steed and they ride off into the sunset, we realize that his love of Wild West has become a compensation for loneliness and lack of self-esteem. Dream has outgunned reality for this Don Quixote of the city sandlots.

SECRETS (Pyramid Films: 13 min./color/1972)

Secrets is a feminist history of woman's struggle to develop an identity free of the stereotypes that have been restrictive and derogatory. As the title suggests, *Secrets* wishes to show that women, like men, are complex and ambiguous; therefore, the analysis of the woman in the film is impressionistic rather than scientific. The film is feminist only in the sense that a woman—here defined as a complex entity of power, goodness, evil, and vulnerability—is shown as a victim of the past. Using the head of a female (a sign of all women) which faces the audience throughout, the filmmaker inundates the viewer with visual and auditory signs. Each visual sign appears either inside the outline of the woman's head, superimposed on it, or around it. Although the signs seem random at first, there is a loose historical structure to them (reinforced by the soundtrack), and in the aggregate, the signs impart to us the impression that, although they have suffered throughout time, women are beginning to reemerge in society as the complex beings nature has always known them to be.

The auditory signs of *Secrets* hold together the visual signs in a historical syntagmatic line. The sounds can be divided into three categories: natural, musical, and human. The sounds of rain, thunder, high winds, birds, and insects are drawn from nature. Several types of music are introduced: rock 'n' roll, folk, jazz, classical, and electronic (or synthesizer music). Although human voices are heard at times, no specific words are intelligible because they are distorted to reduce them to a blur or a primitive growl. Overall, these auditory signs are arranged in a time sequence. At the opening of the film primordial jungle sounds are heard, suggesting the origin of life on earth. Throughout the middle of the film, a variety of music is heard that, because of its harshness and dissonance, suggests a troubled conflict and struggle. At the close of *Secrets*, a quiet and romantic classical selection suggests a peaceful resolution, a coming through the other side of the forest back into daylight.

Visually, the film is more chaotic and random in structure. Its signs, which often repeat with the speed of a strobe light, can be classified for discussion purposes to reveal their meaning. The bulk of the signs shows the dichotomies in the nature and psyche of women. A steady stream of colorful, primitive masks that cover the face suggest woman's savage power and the many personae she has assumed. The wide variety of facial expressions—passive, youthful, elderly, plain, made-up, smiling, screaming, pudgy, gaunt—reinforce her complex personality and range of personae. Several signs indicate the vulnerability of the female. A very small picture of a standing naked girl shown inside the woman's head suggests this aspect of women. A series of crayon drawings that surround and make up the face at times do the same. The woman's sexuality is alluded to by a disturbing image of a man who stands before a dense forest. This Freudian sign appears several times above the woman's face as if it emanated from her thoughts. The religious or spiritual side of the woman is suggested by a cross that appears several times inside the head. The active and vibrant female mind is revealed through two signs drawn from the scientific domain. In one, sound waves originating from the forehead of the figure emanate out in wider and wider circles. In another, the head becomes the nucleus of an atom around which circle the proton and electron.

In a different category altogether are two recurring sign sets that show the woman being analyzed by others. The face of the woman is repeatedly covered by geometric shapes—circles, triangles, squares, etc.—that obscure her features and her identity. The face is further cut up and divided by straight crisscrossing lines. Finally, the face is literally atomized or pulverized into tiny dust particles or its smallest constituent parts. Not surprisingly, the female is shown to suffer. Often the flesh of the face disappears altogether and a skull, the universal sign of death, emerges. In the film's most dramatic sequence, loud and argumentative voices scream (presumably from inside the head of the woman) as thunder claps sound and bloody raindrops pour over her face. Eventually, the unobstructed head—oval-shaped, young, beautiful, passive, and still secret—emerges as the subdued soundtrack signals the end of the analysis and suffering. The woman reemerges, rich in dichotomies and free of restrictive stereotypes.

Secrets is a very ambitious film. It takes the sign "woman," which has been kept static for generations, and makes it dynamic. To achieve this difficult end, the filmmakers take a risk: they approach us not with words but with signs. Subjecting us to an impressionistic whirlwind of visual and auditory signs, they try to alter our thoughts and emotions about women. They demand we concentrate on and participate in *Secrets* and no doubt the film succeeds with those of us who do.

FANTASY (Serious Business Company: 3 min./color/1976)

Fantasy does what a family picture album would do for those familiar with its contents—it jogs the viewer's memory and emotions, recalling the sights, sounds, and feelings of an earlier time. Like the family album, *Fantasy* is not intended for those unfamiliar with its topic: the superhero, horror, and sci-fi comic books popular among children and young people. The film does offer a survey or definition of this specialized art form, but, just as a family album reveals little to the newcomer, *Fantasy* moves too quickly, contains too many allusions, and provides no narrator to explain what the novice would see and hear. Instead, this barrage of visual and auditory signs drawn from the sign set of fantasy comics is intended to recreate in us the violent, creepy, and anything-can-happen atmosphere we entered as youths when we read these comics. The overall effect is cumulative, not specific. Although some of the signs are representational and conventional, and others abstract and personal, all conspire to conjure up the atmosphere of the comics. The syntagmatic line of images—which form, dissolve, and reform in frantic montage—imitates the nightmare illogic of these stories. Even the paradigmatic choice of images is confined to those that make up the sign set of fantasy's darker side. Only a few auditory images defy this rule, and when they occur, we realize that although *Fantasy* is certainly a survey and even a celebration of comic book fantasy, it also may be a parody of the genre's excesses.

The majority of *Fantasy*'s signs recall the creepy and preternatural world of the comics. The film, in fact, is a celebration of the weird. From the very complex sound-track come sounds of a rocket blasting off, of an alien spacecraft hovering, a ray gun firing, a person screaming, a car accelerating, and a storm raging. This is not to say that all the auditory signs are representational. Synthesized and dissonant strains recall the kind of mood music used in horror and outer space thrillers. Of the visual signs that are conventional, we see a coiled snake; a long, winding, luxurious staircase; a line of cyclopses; a shark; a pair of bloodshot eyes; barred windows; and elaborate chandeliers. In addition, we watch a slinky young woman whose pretty human face is transformed into the green visage of a witch, hordes of look-alike clones or monsters that march like lemmings toward the sea, and two Spiderman-like creatures that struggle with each other to gain possession of a barbed lance. Many of the abstract creatures are consistent with those drawn from the comic book sign set because they possess one or more features that we recognize from the real world: crab claws, man-of-war tentacles, a snail's shell, etc. Even the colors and the speed of the animation are signs of the comic book world. Harsh, dayglow purples, greens, oranges, yellows, and blue-greens that color everything suggest the ghoulishness and other-worldliness of the sci-fi, horror, and superhero tales. The abruptness with which the signs come and go and the beat of the frenetic soundtrack also suggest the violence and fast pacing of the comics.

A few well-spaced, less malevolent auditory signs serve occasionally to distance the viewer from the cartoon, pulling us out of our dream and into the observer's role. These sounds—a jungle bird singing out, a herd of cows lowing, and the jingle of a carnival carousel—make us realize that all this mordacity, enmity, and eeriness is humorous and excessive. When a bubble is heard popping at the film's close, we reemerge into the real world of adult concerns, grinning at and nostalgic for the fantasy of the comic books of our youth.

STREET MUSIQUE (Learning Corp. of America: 9 min./color/1972)

Street Musique reminds us how well-suited animation was to artists who embraced or tried to convey the values and philosophy of hippies during the late 1960s and early 1970s. Given its vivid colors, its freeform shapes, and its association with childhood, the cartoon—whether used in films or in psychedelic posters—became a key sign of the imagination, spontaneity, innocence, and drug trips that epitomized the hippie subculture. As if to illustrate this point, the makers of *Street Musique* open and close their film with realistic black-and-white footage, but rely on colorful animation for the bulk or center portion of the film. By using black-and-white scenes of street musicians playing in a Canadian city as a frame for their cartoon, the film-makers suggest that an exuberant performance by street musicians can stimulate the imagination so that it lifts both the player and the passerby above the mundane "hang-ups" of daily life into a fantasy subcreation where all is beautiful, possible, and harmonious.

Once the realistic footage gives way to cartoon, the viewer is shown a string of pleasant images—some recognizable, some wholly abstract—that flow into one another at a speed that matches the tempo of the street music. When the music—played with guitar, mandolin, and French horn—is brisk, one cartoon figure changes rapidly into another, recognizable shapes slide into abstractions, then reemerge into other recognizable forms, etc. For example, a row of houses turns into an abstract beast, which turns into an erupting volcano whose lava blast turns into a sun. A man wearing a hat stands on his head, then melts with a splash into a pool of water inside his hat, which then turns into a bathtub. A man shoots an arrow, which becomes a drop of fluid that lands in an ocean. From this a ship emerges, which becomes first a man and then a mermaid. Many of the "human" and "animal" shapes, if not wholly imaginary, resemble recognizable figures only as much as Picasso's cubist shapes do. Facial features and limbs are not always where they should be, nor are they always drawn to scale. When the music slows, the animated images freeze in place for longer intervals while beautiful, still-life nature scenes take shape, showing sunsets, moonscapes, a tropical landscape, a ship at sea, an island with a cabin on it overlooking a lake.

Although none of the images by themselves—a mermaid, a motorcycle, a naked man, a ship at sea, a dragon, a quiet lake, etc.—are definitive signs of the hippie lifestyle or philosophy, the sign system and the way it is presented are. Arranging the signs along syntagmatic and paradigmatic lines shows why. Normally, signs arranged horizontally like the words in a sentence contain meaning only because they remain discrete. Rules define the different ways they can be arranged horizontally and still convey meaning. For example, these are unacceptable ways of rearranging the sentence "Give me the salt": 1) "Givemethesalt," and 2) "Salt me the give." But in *Street Musique*, there are no syntagmatic rules, and signs are not kept discrete. As one flows into another, the viewer has no idea what will emerge next, and that fact underscores a key precept of the hippie subculture: without risk and spontaneity, life becomes predictable; take a chance, get "unhung-up," and the reaches of imagination are your only limit. A look at the film's paradigmatic line is equally revealing. Normally, the number of paradigmatic options at any point on a syntagmatic line is limited. For instance, in a sentence such as "Big Jim Wright threw the red ball," even though we can select a wide variety of paradigmatic options for "big" (among the adjective group), we cannot choose "green" or "chrome-plated" unless we wish to alter the realism of the sentence. Likewise, we cannot replace "big" with an infinitive such as "to fall" or "to love." In *Street Musique*, however, only images abhorrent to the hippie value system, such as a policeman or a polluting smokestack, can be ruled out. When a human figure in the film shoots an arrow into the air which then becomes a drop of fluid, it could land almost anywhere. As it happens, it falls into the sea and turns into a mermaid, but it could have turned into a balloon and drifted into a field of wheat.

The subcreation that the film produces is wish fulfillment for the hippie subculture. Nature is unspoiled. People and animals, even one man and his few possessions (motorcycle, mandolin), are one. Humans are not limited to one shape. They are no longer confined to land: they can fly and swim underwater indefinitely. Everything is beautiful, spontaneous, harmonious, unique, and free. The Apollonian reason in man has been dethroned, and Dionysian imagination reigns.

THE OLYMPIA DIVING SEQUENCE (Phoenix Films: 4 min./b&w/1936)

The 1936 Olympics were meant by Hitler to be a showcase for his athletes and his philosophy of Aryan supremacy. Though American track stars managed to dim the glory of both, filmmaker Leni Riefenstahl exalted the best of Hitler's Aryans and their Japanese allies in her film *A Festival of Beauty*. One segment, made into *The Olympia Diving Sequence*, shows the graceful precision of those athletes, establishes them as models for Hitler's racial theories, and thus shows them to be godlike heroes. The film contains no narration or other obvious efforts to place itself within a historical context, only a series of dives. Hence, it is a masterwork of communication through visual signs. Making the most effective use of the syntagmatic and paradigmatic aspects of signs, Riefenstahl forces her audience to infer the message: such magnificent Nazi athletes cannot help but achieve their destiny, to conquer the world and master nature.

It is not only the choice of the signs (the athletes), but the syntagmatic ordering of those signs that makes the film a frightening statement of Nazi ideology. That ordering is the steady building from calm control to a peak of frenzy and power, a passage from the Apollonian to the Dionysian, as neat as if it were patterned after Nietzsche's *Birth of Tragedy*. The film proceeds in three stages from male athletes on the lower board to those on the high platform, creating the impression that the skies are being invaded. A sense of mounting power is gained when the camera gradually shifts from showing entire dives—from the approach on the board to the splash in the water—to capturing in rapid fire the men at their zenith only. The clear, sunbathed divers of the beginning give way to soaring silhouettes, dark descendants of Icarus willing to die for the fatherland, German dervishes whirling across the sun at dusk. The facial and body features of these last athletes are indistinguishable; individuality is lost as diver and dive become one and Apollonian reason is overwhelmed by Dionysian fury. The effect is as hypnotic and sinister as Hitler himself.

Historically, the Olympics were designed to glorify all athletes. Riefenstahl's sign choices (from the paradigmatic lines) transform this international contest into a proving ground for Hitler's athletes. She photographs only German and Japanese athletes. Her camera angles are chosen to deify them. Shots from the side of the diving board emphasize the taut musculature of the finely conditioned bodies, human sculptures in the Nazi style. Shots from above stress the heroism of the men who brave the heights in the name of beauty. From below the board, the camera transforms the divers into majestic birds, their arms spread wide like pinions. Through editing, the spin of an athlete at the apogee of his dive is repeated several times; it seems that he will never fall. The descent of another is run backwards; he appears to be climbing from the water to the high platform. Riefenstahl portrays Hitler's athletes as he himself envisioned them, inhumanly and superhumanly defying gravity and, by extension, nature itself. Throughout, only two faces of the crowd are seen, a Japanese girl and a blonde German woman (who may be Riefenstahl herself), both watching in awe. The film is nearly as pure a statement of racial inbreeding as *Mein Kampf*.

Riefenstahl's signs were a model for the concept of Aryan supremacy. Her film is a model for many modern documentary filmmakers who wish to communicate through visual signs. Many critics today have difficulty applauding the film's artistry because of its message. *The Olympia Diving Sequence* is a challenge to those who believe, as Oscar Wilde did, that art is amoral. Despite the film's beauty, informed viewers are restrained in their reactions. How are they to reconcile that beauty with the work's grotesque message?

BRAVERMAN'S CONDENSED CREAM OF BEATLES (Pyramid Films: 15 min./color/1973)

Few people would quibble with the assertion that the Beatles are a sign model for the 1960s. In a rapid-fire montage, this film explains how the group achieved such status, by showing them as heroes almost in a mythical sense. By going through their history in a rough chronology and interspersing it with comparisons to heroes from other periods, *Braverman's* syntagmatic structure captures their meteoric rise, then the tragic fall, a pattern familiar from the legends of King Arthur, Jesus, and Beowulf.

Paradigmatic choices are intended to fill out that structure and recreate the mood of the times. Signs include familiar images (including key personages from the era), a representative sampling of Beatle songs and album covers, paintings and cartoons that simulate key social currents, and film clips that highlight the group's career. These paradigmatic choices place the Beatles at the heart of the sixties and show that, like the above-mentioned figures, they too had their challenges and enemies to slay, victories and defeats. A critic such as Northrup Frye might note that the conforming of the group's career to the age-old, time-tested pattern of the hero myth is why they captured the popular imagination.

The opening animation is of a desert road, perhaps a sign for our own heroless age, on which the four faces appear carved on separate stones, like America's Mt. Rushmore presidents. Then the film begins at the beginning. The first phase of the group's career is idyllic. They are shown as trend setters in clothes and hair style (a photograph of them on barber stools is given) and as wry humorists (to a reporter's question, "Has success changed your life?" one answers simply, "Yes"). They achieve the height of this phase at a Shea Stadium concert during which thousands of fans scream in worship. In the stadium dressing room, a drawing of Ringo's face topped by an olive wreath, like an ancient Greek demigod, is the first hero comparison. Trouble for the group is foreshadowed at a press conference when John cries, "Hey, cool it, man. What's happening here?" In a rapid montage of clips from their films, they crash through a window, spin out of control in a speeding car, and have a practice session broken up by soldiers, while the soundtrack plays the song "Help." Shots of Hollywood western actors, such as the Lone Ranger, portray them as heroes bent on battling evil. Famous movie couples, such as Bogart and Bacall, are compared to the Beatles and their women, a sign that the four are abandoning the adolescent sexuality of their earlier music and becoming mature romantic figures. Lennon's remark that the Beatles "meant more to kids than Jesus did" sparks a banning of their songs on the airwaves and public demonstrations against them. Rather than retreat from controversy, the group protests the Vietnam war and social injustices and calls for consciousness raising through drugs and religious experience. Shots of the pop cultural idols on the "Sergeant Pepper's" album cover portray their increase both in fame and notoriety, and a drawing of Napoleon compares their impact to that of the general in an earlier time of social upheaval. These issues fractured society and the Beatles. In solo concerts, Harrison and Lennon perform for their favored, rather than for group, causes, the former with a benefit for Bangladesh, the latter with a call for consciousness raising, Lennon's "Instant Karma." Battling a personal enemy, Lennon explains in an interview that the United States government, whose people a few years earlier welcomed him as a Beatle with open arms, wants to deport him because he is a peacenik. The chronology concludes with John's remark, at an interview after his victory over the government, that he will always say what he feels, on the war or any issue. The ring is hollow, however. The Beatles have gone from puckish innocents to avenging hero-gods, to common citizens, each with individual concerns and problems.

Paradigmatic choices recall the flavor of that age and just how much the Beatles meant to it. Terms such as "mod," "fab," and "gear," among the many the British rock revolution brought to America, appear on the screen. Famous figures who felt their impact, such as President Nixon and Ed Sullivan, are shown. Early songs like "Can't Buy Me Love" and "Ticket to Ride" represent the changes in music and sexual mores the group helped to bring about. "Eleanor Rigby" is played while surrealistic and impressionistic paintings of solitary people and rushing crowds are seen, each a sign for the alienation and social injustices the Beatles, and the young who followed them, fought against. The faces of the hippies who adopted Beatle hair styles and appearance are juxtaposed with "A Day in a Life," the song that encouraged the young to abandon their social values and expand their minds. The album cover of "Yellow Submarine" and a clip from the cartoon of the same name along with the covers from "Revolver," "Sergeant Pepper's," and "Magical Mystery Tour" reveal a generation's flight from reality into an imaginary world of wild imagery, vivid colors, and hedonism, all a part of the hallucinogenic drug experience. As with heroes throughout history whose tales have inspired imitation, the Beatles were leaders and role models. From their clothes and hair, to their musical style, to their humane values and creativity, they set the tone for millions of young people who created a counter-culture almost in imitation of the four stars.

These are but the most bare sampling of the hundreds of signs in the film. Students will surely be able to identify many that are not noted here. The pattern, no matter which signs are focused on, will always be the same. The Beatles' career parallels those of the heroes for most generations, from innocent beginnings, to bold triumphs, to tragedy and doom. It is always the same, literary and social critics insist, for heroes who serve as a model for their age.

RUN! (Macmillan Films: 16 min./b&w/1962)

The writer of an allegory can use signs to convince an audience to adopt a particular view of life. The signs can form a system that represents an entire philosophy. The allegory *Run!* uses a sign set for the city and a generalized hero to persuade us that modern life makes us an easy prey to evil. The paradigmatic choices of signifiers of the city—a sign itself for the twentieth century world—are drawn exclusively from a nightmarish, Kafkaesque view of reality. The hero, like the setting, is a model. He is pursued by a darkly-dressed villain through the city and is eventually cornered and killed. Because his traits are features of all personalities, he is "Everyman," a sign for all people. The syntagmatic succession of events leads him into the hands of his mysterious enemy and the audience to an ironic ending that explains the triumph of evil in our age.

The burden of conveying the film's view of the city is on the visual and auditory, not linguistic, signs. There is no narration; the soundtrack is composed of dissonant, percussive music, harsh sounds common to the city, and background voices so distorted as to be impossible to decipher. To make the message clear, all sign choices are from the nightmarish set. The emphasis is always on the horrifying. The environment is dehumanizing and alienating; it perverts the soul. An underground plaza is an anarchy of flashing lights against a background as dark as night. Storefront signs ("Speed Wash," "Dance Studio," "$," "24 Hours a Day, 7 Days a Week," etc.) represent the maddening pace, the materialism and greed, and the throb of city sights and sounds that never let up. The streets are jammed with people who are as indifferent to the hero's plight as he is to theirs. A park is filmed to look like a jungle, a sign for the destructiveness and chaos at the core of civilization. In the park's one pastoral section, a beautiful woman reads a romantic magazine whose story titles make "love" seem animalistic. In an amusement park, the disabling effect of modern life is most vivid. A barking carnival hawker, a fire swallower, a midget, and a dancing showgirl represent the bizarre diversions of twentieth century civilization. The roiling, aimless crowds are signs for modern anxiety and hysteria. Viewers are familiar with these signs both from their own experiences and from existential novels (to which this allegory is a first cousin). No effort is made to present the signs in a new light. Their function is to create a psychotic mood and to call to mind the philosophies of the writers who first employed them.

The hero's flight through the city from a man clothed in black is the plot and a sign model for adult life. Dressed in white, this "Everyman" does what we all do: he eats, smokes, reads the newspaper, gets lost in the city's "rat race," and searches for escape. The tension and fear of being pursued are on his face; the gradual disheveling of his clothes is a sign of inner disintegration. By contrast, his enemy remains calm and neat-looking; his identity hidden behind dark glasses, he grows in menace throughout. The evil he represents is the routine of daily life and what it does to the psyche. That routine drives the hero down a dead-end alley and then over rooftops where the crumbling buildings and a church steeple are signs for the spiritual emptiness of life's chase. When he tries to eat a meal "on the run," the hero crashes into a telephone pole. Thoughtlessly, he knocks over a blind man selling pencils and later steps on a little girl's doll, becoming in his hysteria evil himself. At the amusement park, an excruciating pursuit of pleasure is his method for coping with the routine of the chase. He stuffs himself with food and takes a spin on a ride that leaves him nauseous.

Syntagmatically, the chase focuses on the conflict of hero and villain, good and evil, and thus leaves the audience totally unprepared for the ending. "Everyman" has gone from crowded streets to the city park to an amusement park, first to get away from, then to numb himself to the villain's presence. When everything fails, he ends up on a beach, a sign for nature and the origin of life. Disrobed now but for his pants, he backs away from the enemy toward a third man in a plaid shirt who is digging a grave. The hero is pushed into that grave. The enemy removes his dark glasses, and he and the gravedigger smile sadistically. It is then that "Everyman" and the audience realize who the two are: as if in a mirror, the hero sees his face in theirs. He covers himself with sand and dies. The chase has reduced this loner to suicide.

The city, depicted in signs of the macabre, is the source of evil. Its chaos and fast pace transform man into a careening video blip. Amid this hysteria, the dark emotions dominate and life itself becomes a disintegrating process. The individual's personality is split at least in two: his good side reduced to impotence; his evil side strong and inescapable. In the end, the film suggests, we dig our own graves rather than cope with twentieth century anxiety.

METROPOLIS (Manbeck Pictures Corp.: 94 min./b&w/1926)

Fritz Lang's silent film *Metropolis* is an indictment of automation and capitalism, which he believed were leading to the dehumanization of life. To convey this theme, the filmmaker shows a world divided into haves and have-nots, the corrupt and the innocent, and reveals what could happen in a world devoid of compassion. To build this allegory or sign model, he has drawn upon Marxist and Biblical signs and historical allusions.

The city of Metropolis is divided according to status and wealth. In a manner resembling the division of the Eloi and Morlocks in H. G. Wells' *Time Machine*, Metropolis' master and wealthy inhabitants live above the workers and their families. High atop the city's gray and uniformly ugly skyscrapers the affluent play in elaborate pleasure gardens. Below the surface, in the workers' city—a dark and steamy world filled with driving machines—the poor families toil and sleep. Below this, in the underground tunnels, the workers secretly meet to commiserate about the injustice of the situation.

Even before each main character is assigned a role in the Christian scenario that follows, his or her inherent goodness or evil is portrayed through signs. The gaunt master of Metropolis, John Frederson, is clad in a dark business suit. His even and harsh stare and lack of emotional expression of any kind, signify his absence of compassion. At one point, he places his hand inside his jacket, a clear reference to the despot Napoleon. His son, on the contrary, is dressed in a white horse-riding outfit, which signifies his innocence (he is unaware that the workers' city exists) and his wealth. The mad scientist, Rotwang, has wild hair, bulging eyes, and crooked splayed fingers, all of which identify him as a madman. Later, when is is shown trying to create a race of robot workers to replace the downtrodden human laborers, Rotwang becomes the equivalent of Frankenstein. Maria, the young woman who consoles the workers and who eventually enlists the son's help against his father, is also dressed in white. Her dress, which resembles Snow White's, is both modest and simple. The robot model of Maria (hereafter referred to as "Maria") is given wild and lascivious gestures, to signify her moral corruption. At different points in the film, Lang visually compares Maria to Cleopatra, and finally shows her being burned at the stake in a hideous parody of Joan of Arc.

The film's action is based on New and Old Testament signs and scenarios. Early in the film, Frederson's son is interrupted in the pleasure garden by Maria, who has with her a group of the workers' poor children. She says to him, "Look, these are your brothers." Her remark, an echo of the Bible's charge that we are our brother's keeper, startles the young man and causes him to investigate the plight of the workers. From this point on, Maria's character is based on the Virgin Mary's. She shapes her new friend's behavior, preparing him to intercede at the conclusion between the workers and Frederson, as Jesus Christ did between his Father and the chosen people on earth. The young man ventures into the workers' city, then into the tunnels. There, the workers, like the Christians hiding in catacombs from the persecuting Romans, are comforted and led by Maria. She tells them the Tower of Babel story, suggesting that Metropolis will eventually be destroyed. Rotwang, the Satanic figure, learns about these meetings, however, and he creates a "Maria" robot to incite the workers, as a false prophet would, to revolt. "Maria" convinces the workers to destroy the power house on the surface of Metropolis, knowing that this will in turn flood the workers' city and drown their children. Maria and the young man fail to stop the flood but rescue the children from the deluge, which in the manner of Noah's ark begins to cleanse Metropolis as it destroys it. The workers then kill "Maria," and the master's son defeats and kills Rotwang. Finally, Maria, true to her role as the Virgin Mary, convinces the young man to forgive his father, who is repentent.

Although somewhat dated and transparent today, Lang's film is still a moving and revealing example of how signs can be used to manipulate the emotions of an audience. Drawing on historical allusions and signs from Marxism and the Bible, the filmmaker creates an allegorical model that acts upon us as a great opera does. We do not accept its melodrama as reality, but it carries us along nonetheless.

LES ESCARGOTS (McGraw-Hill Contemporary Films: 11 min./color/1969)

In general, signs used in an allegory are static—they have only one meaning. Chaucer's Man of Law in *The Canterbury Tales*, for instance, tells the allegory of Constance, who undergoes a series of trials to determine if she can remain faithful to the Lord. As such, she represents the good Christian. *Les Escargots* is an allegory, too, but its signs are dynamic; that is, they lend themselves to a number of different interpretations. Taken as a Biblical parable, *Les Escargots* warns that men and women's corruption and their indifference to one another will periodically lead to the destruction of civilization as it did in Sodom and Gomorrah. Taken as an allegory commenting on the human species, the film shows that humans, contrary to the tenets of Darwinism, are incapable of any real progress because by nature they repeat their errors again and again in meaningless cycles, failing to adapt to the demands of their environment. Seen in the light of Marxism, the film shows that if the inequities of the class system are allowed to continue, societal structures will again be violently overthrown.

These three interpretations, and others that are possible, depend on how the viewer interprets the sign model offered by the film's story. This animated film, silent except for music, opens by showing a series of small globes—each large enough for a human figure to stand atop—that teeter back and forth precariously. Focusing in on one of the globes closely, the camera reveals a poor farmer. His clothes are shabby, he appears old and tired, and his field is sadly unproductive. In an effort to get his wilted lettuce plants to grow, he tries several experiments that run the gamut from plain silly to downright self-destructive. He holds each leaf upright in three separate ways: first by hanging each one over a Y-shaped branch; second, by spiking each with a nail and holding it up with a magnet; third, by tying each leaf to the string of a helium-filled balloon. Finally, in despair, he cries, and his tears, which fall on one of the plants, do the trick; it sits bolt upright and grows. To manufacture sufficient tears to water his acres of lettuce, he holds an onion to his eyes, he reads tragedies, he builds a machine that beats his head with a hammer and kicks his behind with a boot. His crops prosper beyond his wildest hopes. The lettuce plants grow supernaturally large and that night the snails that feed on them also grow into gigantic monsters that first apparently kill the farmer and destroy his house, then proceed to annihilate the nearby city and its inhabitants. When the creatures descend on the city, we see that it is dark and dirty. The music is a slick and sleazy jazz at this point. Many of the city's inhabitants, pictured as small stick figures, die, but the film focuses on the demise of three female characters. The first is shown undressing near her hotel window. She is pictured in a black, low-cut slip and stockings just before a snail grabs her. A little girl is then shown being lured into a snail's shell by the colorful outline of a kitten which the beast creates inside the dark cavern of its shell. Finally, a frantic woman running through the streets with her shirt torn open is trampled by the snails. Eventually, the holocaust complete, the snails, joining together in threes and fours, form strangely beautiful shapes, freeze in place, and die. Just before the snails retreat and die, an old man dressed in black and sitting on a rock in the countryside surveys the damage with a sad and knowing expression. He is not seen again. Immediately, a new, shiny, white city springs up from the rubble of the old one. A farmer, the exact likeness of the last one, forces tears from his eyes to make his field of stunted carrots grow. Suddenly, on the horizon, two preternaturally large and menacing rabbits appear. Apparently, the film's apocalyptic scenario is about to repeat itself.

This scenario may contain a refutation of Darwinism. According to such a reading of the allegory's signs, the farmer and the city dwellers are interdependent members of an ecosystem. If the smaller entity, the farmer, fails, the "higher order" animals in the city also fail. The film shows the species of man at a crucial point in its evolution; the environment no longer yields food as it did in the past; man must adapt. The farmer changes the procedure he uses but it leads to large-scale destruction. Rather than develop a new approach, the species adamantly repeats its mistake. Unlike the dinosaur, man does not become extinct, he just remains stuck in an existential pattern, like Sisyphus. Thus, the species' history is cyclical, not evolutionary.

A second reading of the film as an Old Testament parable makes use of even more of the film's signs. Here we have a farmer who vainly looks to his own ingenuity and not God's help to grow his crops. Of course he fails. Nearby a decadent city filled with loose women also looks to itself—to its own bodily needs—and not to its God. A prophet appears to warn the people, but he is ignored. Eventually, the world is wrathfully destroyed. In the Bible this occurred by fire and flood, here by monstrous snails and rabbits. As in the Old Testament story of Noah's ark, man is allowed a new beginning, but soon strays off the path of morality again.

A Marxist interpretation also sees a close interrelationship between the farmer and the city dweller. They divide themselves into classes—the proletariat and bourgeois respectively—but this division will not prevent the violent overthrow of both. The farmer is the poor and hard-working victim whose labors support the decadence and idleness of the nearby city. For a time, capitalism yields a type of sick prosperity, but eventually the toll taken on the lower class leads to revolution and to the collapse of the system. This cycle will repeat itself until a more fair, Marxist system is put in its place.

Les Escargots evinces the essential workings of allegory. Given a general, almost mythic story line like this one, the film becomes a close model of several opposing world views. In this case, the syntagmatic arrangement and paradigmatic choice of signs allow for an anti-Darwinian, a Biblical, and a Marxist interpretation. Without further clues from the filmmaker, all three argue compellingly for their own primacy.

LISTEN TO BRITAIN (McGraw-Hill Contemporary Films: 19 min./b&w/1942)

Perhaps no event produces such a profusion of signs as does a war. Nations use signs to stir patriotism and to encourage the public to make the necessary sacrifices. *Listen to Britain*, a World War II propaganda film, uses the sign systems of military and civilian life to show a country united for war and to inspire the British to even greater efforts. Further melding these two sign sets is the country's music, a universal sign of civilization joining the military and civilian worlds in harmony. A classic of war propaganda, the film served as a sign for British determination and unity. Leonard Brockington, in a brief foreword, describes the film, saying, "You will hear that [England's] heartbeat blended together in one great symphony of Britain at war . . . the sound of spitfires . . . the clank of machinery and the shunting of trains . . . the war song of a great people, the first notes of the march to victory." From then on, the signs do all the "talking"; the film is a montage of scenes from the nation's daily war routine of work and play with nary a word of narration.

Signs of the military and the civilian worlds demonstrate a blending of the two systems, a condition the film sees as essential for victory. In a ballroom, soldiers and civilians dance together in a spirit of gaiety. Factory workers, just before dawn, assemble an airplane. A businessman, probably on his way to work, walks London's streets with an air-raid helmet dangling from his shoulders. A woman looks fondly at the photograph of a soldier, presumably her son. Meanwhile, an army convoy moves through a hamlet; its people accept the convoy's presence without a fuss. Throughout the film, crowd scenes reveal the easy mingling of soldiers (those of Britain's allies as well as her own) and civilians. The film progresses from one evening to the following noon; the feeling is that of an average wartime day.

Musical signs tie the scenes together. On a train, a guitarist and an accordian player lead Canadian soldiers in the singing of "Home on the Range." Children in a schoolyard dance to a popular song played on a piano. Factory women sing with a radio as they contentedly labor at machines. The audience at a concert of popular singers Flanagan and Allen whistles along with the tune "Sunnyside Lane," a vocal demonstration that the war will not rob the people of their spirit. The film provides the music from England's various social classes. Music, as a common language, becomes a sign for the nation's unity within its social diversity, its democratic spirit, a spirit whose preservation is the real cause in the war against the elitist German tyrant. Finally, Myra Hess (assisted by a soldier who turns the pages of the score) is shown playing a classical concerto at a noontime concert. Despite the worldwide barbarity, the scene tells us, England will maintain her civilized institutions.

The film is a sign model for national harmony and commitment. The closing scene epitomizes the point. As Myra Hess plays, a soldier and a woman in the audience are seen standing in front of a painting of two young children and one of a medieval war scene. Through juxtaposition, the signs suggest all Britain—children and adults, women and men—united in the grand struggle. The piano's sound is blended with the sounds of a tank factory, an iron works, a British battalion marching to its own band, soldiers and civilians enjoying an art exhibit, crowds going about their business, people eating lunch on building steps. A choral reprise of "Rule Britannia" brings the feelings of optimism and patriotism to a peak. Considering the effect the artistry still has on us today, we can only imagine how greatly it must have stirred wartime audiences.

STAR SPANGLED BANNER (Pyramid Films: 6 min./color/1970)

Most anti-war films in the late 1960s and early 1970s tended to polarize America into two groups: the peaceniks and the rest of the country. *Star Spangled Banner* makes no such distinctions. It condemns all those who stayed at home while showing pity for those who were forced to fight. The film's signs seek to arouse guilt in the audience and force it to stop the Vietnam war. A soldier, presumably in Vietnam, is shown rushing with panic through a jungle and then dying after being shot. In a surrealistic sequence, a crowd of Americans looks on with faces registering indifference and even disdain for the "sap" who has honored the responsibility they have ignored. The soundtrack is a grotesque version of the national anthem (played by the rock group The Grass Roots) that emphasizes the scene's horror and the film's cynicism toward America. The soldier embodies one of the lessons of Vietnam: war is unfair; some people, particularly the young, make the ultimate sacrifice, while others remain at home to prosper and enjoy themselves, some even exploiting the anti-war cry for their own ends.

As a sign, the soldier is dynamic, representing several values. Unlike many anti-war films that seek to villainize the military through the sign of the grisly, "gung-ho" veteran, this one portrays the soldier as a young man. His innocence, the first sign value, is depicted by his youthful, fear-ridden face. His scrambling, like a lost child, through the woods shows his inexperience. The soldier's death is made as disturbing as possible: the film shifts to slow motion; no attempt is made to suppress the gore; blood pours from his mouth; a scream in the background signals his pain. His death adds another layer of meaning to the film. Inexplicably, the crowd of American civilian onlookers falls amidst gunfire and exploding bombs, too. The scene evinces the dependence of the United States upon its young. When a nation loses its healthiest and most idealistic members (in this case "idealism" is defined as the naiveté that leads these young men to live up to the country's heritage) it will not endure much longer.

The crowd is a sign for the country's selfishness and moral decay. The people's silliness is emphasized by the balloons one of them holds. While the young soldier is serving his country, they are enjoying themselves back home. A naive and self-righteous hippie couple make love in a field and a tawdrily dressed woman frivolously blows bubbles at the soldier. The crowd has no appreciation of the boy's sacrifice. A peacenik scowls at him, and a "hardhat" stares coldly with an expression that seems to say, "I've got mine, Jack; you take care of yourself." They and America get what they deserve. No social classes are spared. A businessman falls, his attache case opening and papers scattering. A middle-class family man is mowed down as his wife looks on with horror. An old woman, blue-collar workers, and the rest all die. The off-key "Star Spangled Banner," the film's most cynical sign for America, ends with an eerie, mournful drone.

So much sign value is placed on the soldier that there is some ambiguity as to what he represents. It can be argued that his naiveté is foolish. If he had understood the crowd for what it is, he, too, would have avoided serving in the war. Such a view extends the film's cynicism beyond America to the human condition itself. "Once one recognizes that everyone is out for himself," this meaning insists, "patriotism, national anthems, and moral duty become meaningless." But there is no questioning about the film's attitude toward us, the American onlookers. We are selfish and indifferent, as responsible for battlefield deaths as bullets and grenades, no matter what pose we adopt as private citizens.

SUNDAY DINNER (Phoenix Films: 12 min./color/1976)

A conflict between the syntagmatic and paradigmatic aspects of a sign produces an ironic look at an old, and perhaps dying, tradition in the film *Sunday Dinner*. In the past, most American families felt a Sunday feast was an event for staying at home, donning one's best clothes, and forgetting the cares of the work week—a sign of togetherness, sharing, and civilization. The film's opening shots of a Sunday dawn in New York City are at odds with these ideals. The skyscrapers are daunting; among them, humanity is lost, insignificant; the streets are littered with trash. An old woman and man—both vagabonds, social outcasts—travel different routes through Manhattan. She salvages an umbrella from a streetcorner junk pile and collects bread and vegetables from merchants. Her male friend gathers old furniture and appliances in his cart and lovingly provides water for the moth-eaten horse that pulls it. The two characters will meet in south Manhattan and cross the Hudson for a dinner in the style of bygone, happier days, a ritual that—like the odds and ends the couple has collected from street corners—has been largely discarded.

Syntagmatically, their repast conforms to the traditional requirements or structure of the event. The day is Sunday; they eat in their own "home" (a makeshift structure they construct that morning in a field within view of the World Trade Center). The two are suitably attired. Both participate in the preparations: he cooks the beef stroganoff and chills the wine; she sets the table, slices the bread, and makes the salad. A record player furnishes relaxing, old-time music. They chat amiably through the lingering meal. The couple is an image from an American past that valued hearth, home, and family togetherness.

But the choice of signs (the paradigmatic) attached to the structure clashes with audience expectations and proves that Sunday dinner is more a state of mind than just a meal. The couple's feast is a fantasy that works solely because they want it to. Their house is an imaginary one, a sign both of the dying of the tradition and of their determination to keep it alive. The materials (the door, the bathtub, the toilet, etc.) of which it is composed are junk from the man's cart; the walls and ceiling are nonexistent, being only boundaries agreed upon by the couple. The refrigerator is a broken-down discard (the wine is probably muscatel, circa the month in which the film was made). Though the food looks appetizing, it is cooked in dented pots. The furniture is worn and ripped, the record player a hand-cranked model. Her dress and his dinner jacket are from another era, sidewalk trash. The quality of the clothes and household items is, of course, not what matters. Their togetherness and mutual concern make their meal a true Sunday dinner. The skyline looming across the water is the world that is satirized, not the world of the two vagabonds. The city represents a world in which the couple's values are anomalous. The triumph of their fantasy takes place when it rains. The two hoist umbrellas and continue as if their imaginary house had an actual ceiling and walls.

After dinner, the two dismantle and pack up their home and return to New York, where they part. For the next seven days, until they meet again, they will carry within them the sign of their own respectability.

FOLLOW-UP ACTIVITIES

1. If we are what we eat, we also are where we live. Visit a friend's room and analyze his or her personality in terms of the signs in that room. These will include obvious examples such as wall posters, photographs, trophies, books, records, knickknacks, etc. Also to be considered are the arrangement and neatness of the room. Is it overloaded with furniture or sparsely laid out? Is it hard to find the floor for the mess, or meticulously clean? In the final written report, present a representative sample of the signs and show what they indicate about your friend's personality.

2. In 1920, F. Scott Fitzgerald employed a conventional sign of the period—bobbed hair—as the central motif of his story "Bernice Bobs Her Hair" (in *Stories* by Frank G. Jennings and Charles J. Calitri [New York: Harcourt Brace Jovanovich, 1957]). In it, the main character, Bernice, cuts her locks to prove to her peers that she is liberated, chic, and daring. Fitzgerald's story shows that a sign, a simple haircut, can become more important to people than the thing it is supposed to represent, independence. Read the story, then locate magazines from the period, especially *Collier's* and *Ladies Home Journal*, to read about how the controversy over the hairstyle began and eventually ended. Next, interview two or three elders in your community who remember the scandal firsthand. Finally, in an essay, retell the story of this sign explaining the bob's original meaning and subsequent ones. In your conclusion, say what your research shows about signs in general, and in the area of fashion in particular. Also refer briefly to similar sign controversies raging today.

3. Each generation develops its own signs for common phenomena such as wealth and poverty. For example, the 1930s song "Brother Can You Spare a Dime?" contains the signs "dime" and "khaki pants" to represent the destitution of the working poor. Examine at least 10 popular songs from the thirties to determine the common signs that represented poverty and affluence. Then compare these to those signs that represent wealth and poverty for you and your friends.

4. In primitive societies, young men are often put through a rite of passage at adolescence to mark formally the moment they achieve manhood. As these rituals often subject the initiates to dangerous and painful tasks, they were once considered by missionaries and early anthropologists to be the ultimate sign of primitiveness. Now most specialists realize that such rituals are universal signs, common in all societies. Hazing, for example, continues on college campuses across the United States even though it is widely, officially banned. Look up primitive and modern examples of rites of passage in magazines and library books. To these add others you have been subjected to yourself (in scouting, at work, etc.) and those you have heard about. Arrange the key steps of these rituals on separate horizontal or syntagmatic lines. Next, place each outlined ritual on a single piece of paper. Look at them together, and indicate the basic or underlying syntagmatic line of all rites of passage. What does this sign pattern tell you about rites of passage? Why would such a pattern appeal to all people? Present your findings in an essay.

5.　　For many men, the hairdressing salon has replaced the barber shop as the place to get one's hair styled instead of cut. In the process, a set of signs men once associated with haircutting—the striped pole, the smell of shaving lather and hair tonic, the local gossip from the barber—has been replaced by a sign set that includes potted plants, the smell of bubble-gum-scented shampoos, and gossip from the stylist about the latest TV soap opera. Visit a traditional barber shop and a typical salon that caters to men, and do a detailed sign analysis of each. What are the sights, sounds, and smells that make up the conventional sign set of each? What signs did salons adopt to accommodate the change in men's values, and those of society at large? Present your findings in a written report.

A SIGN MODEL: BIOGRAPHY

How is biography a sign model? It is impossible for a writer to show all the moments in a person's life—no matter how much primary or secondary source material there is; not all moments have been recorded. In biography, the author must create a model of the person and try to persuade the audience that it is an accurate reproduction of the actual life. Like the portrait painter, the biographer has tried to catch a likeness, but that likeness comes from a few, selected sittings. As with other signs, the functions of the model are to change behavior, to trigger thoughts and emotions, and to point to the existence of something. This unit will analyze first the aspects of character, then the different ways to structure a life. Although the filmmaker usually has over the writer the advantage of being able to show the actual behavior of a subject at particular moments in time, the filmmaker, like the author, must select, arrange, edit, and interpret the sign model from a welter of material. Whether film or print, the techniques of biographical reconstruction are similar.

Character

The word "character" originally meant a distinctive mark that an engraving tool would make. Today, the word indicates the qualities, either behavioral or mental, that distinguish one person from another. The same word can also indicate moral worth or eccentric behavior. This proliferation of meanings can cause confusion at times, but we generally equate the term with personality. The study of character in biography includes understanding of 1) the problems in delineating personality, 2) the difference between the *static* and *dynamic* character, 3) the techniques for character revelation, and 4) the use and function of character in the character type and the profile.

There are problems for the author trying to indicate distinguishing qualities. Since the author must use recognizable language signs or generalizations to indicate the traits of a specific person, the same signs will apply to other people as well. To assign general personality traits to a person obviously makes the individual far from unique. To help the reader to understand the subject's personality, the author usually places the person into a category, then tries to show the distinguishing marks within the category. The following are a few of the descriptive adjectives that categorize behavior:

BASIC PERSONALITY TYPES

aggressive	loyal	ambitious
confident	uninhibited	cautious
warm	sensitive	talented
anxious	good-natured	religious
emotional	exhibitionistic	passionate

Through brainstorming, the student can add other characteristics to the list.

One of the peculiarities of our language is that we form "either/or" categories. Without middle-of-the-road categories, the author often is forced to place the subject into an extreme role and then modify the description to fit the subject's actual behavior. A glance at some personality antonyms will clarify the problem:

PERSONALITY ANTONYMS

Serious	Happy-Go-Lucky
Submissive	Dominating
Reserved	Outgoing
Lazy	Conscientious
Timid	Courageous
Thick-Skinned	Sensitive
Trusting	Paranoid
Practical	Theoretical
Forthright	Secretive
Controlled	Uncontrolled

The actions of few people in real life remain consistently within one category. Additional adjectives must be added to these absolutes in order to be accurate in summing up any real personality.

In literature, if a character's personality traits are simple, easy to sum up, and unchanging, we call him or her a *static* character. If the traits are complex, difficult to sum up, changing, even enigmatic, the character becomes *dynamic*. These terms are not judgments on either the person or the artist; they are merely descriptive. Since readers prefer that characters "make sense," they demand that fictional personalities be simplified, easily recognizable, stereotyped. In most biographies, the character is just that, a representative of a generalized personality, a social class, or a behavior syndrome. But in a few biographies, the character is more complex and suggests an actual human with moments of confusion, wayward actions, personality contradictions, and changing ideas. The key word here is "suggests." The biographer would have to know the person very well indeed to discover and to map his or her entire personality. Even those authors who have created the most dynamic characters in biography—Boswell's Johnson, Fronde's Carlyle, Lockhart's Scott, and Bell's Woolf—were not able to reveal everything. In fact, later biographers have been more than happy to point out aspects of character these authors ignored in their studies. The point is, *dynamic* might mean "complex," but characterization is always limited.

How does an author reveal personality (other than through category terms)? Traditionally, in biography, character is revealed through:

a. actions or behavior

b. description

    c.   dialogue, conversation, quotations
    d.   ideas, beliefs, attitudes toward life
    e.   the testimony of friends, enemies, and relatives
    f.   the role the subject played in society

In Elizabeth Gaskell's biography *The Life of Charlotte Brontë* (Harmondsworth: Penguin Books, 1975), letters, remembered conversations, diaries, anecdotes, and juvenilia of the famous nineteenth century writer show her interests, opinions, and ideas. Such material is intended to show the "human" or personal side of the subject as well as the public personae, the weaknesses as well as the strengths.

Just as the word has taken on many meanings, so has character had many literary forms and functions. Of importance in biography are the character type and the profile.

CHARACTER TYPE

The character type is a short, satiric portrait of a nonspecific person. It is a deliberate attempt to create a static stereotype. The earliest "characters" are those of Theophrastus (circa 370-287 B.C.). He wrote satirical portraits of unpleasant behavior found in Greek society, such as "Boorishness," "Nastiness," "Petty Pride," "Officiousness," etc. The behavior, of course, was to be avoided by the ideal citizen. The technique would be easy for a student to imitate. The actons reported are specific, and are ones that many people have performed. For instance, "The Class Clown" might be described as:

> one who always finds a way to turn a teacher's explication
> of grammar into an off-color remark.

The compilation of such observations would produce the character type.

In the seventeenth and eighteenth centuries, the character type was popular in England. Since satire, at that time, uniformly ridiculed public behavior in the hope of improving the reader, Samuel Butler, for one, in his book *Characters* (Cleveland, OH: Press of Case Western Reserve University, 1970) would offer such intolerable types as "A Melancholy Man," "A Huffing Courtier," "An Ungrateful Man," "A Bumpkin or Country-Squire," and "An Ambitious Man." The audience was meant to laugh at the excesses of the type, but also to enjoy the skill of the portrait, the cleverness of the phrasing, and the sharpness of its perception. Each sentence was important, and the author polished the phrasing to allow maximum reflection or to create memorable "sayings." Needless to say, the characters were still static. In Robert P. Tristram Coffin and Alexander M. Witherspoon's *Seventeenth-Century Prose and Poetry* (New York: Harcourt Brace Jovanovich, 1946), the student can find examples of "characters" by Sir Thomas Overbury, John Earle, and Thomas Fuller.

The character type is alive and well today in the personality categories of sociology. David Riesman, in *The Lonely Crowd* (New York: Doubleday & Co., 1955), talks about "Tradition-Directed," "Inner-Directed," and "Other-Directed" people. William H. Whyte, Jr., coined the type of *The Organization Man* (New York: Doubleday & Co., 1957). In *The Greening of America* (New York: Random House, 1970), Charles A. Reich identifies three types of consciousness. Theodore Roszak, in *The Making of a Counter Culture* (New York: Doubleday & Co., 1969), describes the tensions between the "Counter Culture" and "The Technocracy." The modern audience seems to have the same relationship to the material of the sociologists as the eighteenth century audience had to character types: from the security of a "normal" group, we laugh at the eccentric behavior of the person who is not cool, or ironic, or self-detached. Rarely does the shoe fit. The modern character type is still static, one-dimensional, and identified by a few quirks or behavior traits.

One should note that the function of the character type has changed. In the eighteenth century, the character type was intended to change behavior and to trigger laughter. In the modern form, the function is simply to point to the existence of something.

PROFILE

The "profile" is a longer sketch that considers the personality, background, and occupation of a single person, who is usually famous. Unlike the character sketch, the profile stresses the outlook of the subject at the time of the interview—if the person is still alive. The writing technique here is different from that of the character type. The writers of profiles assume: 1) that the flavor of the subject's natural verbal expression is interesting in and of itself and is more revelatory of personality than are controlled, edited, or concise statements, and 2) that all remarks have equal value in the analysis of a personality—indeed, banal statements or throw-away lines show the genuine texture of the subject's mind. The author's hope is to show complexity. We should note, however, that too often, the audience merely gains trivial details from a variety of incidents that reveal the same personality traits over and over. Frequently, the author sees the inner-personality of the famous person as a type. Depending on the author, the function of a profile can be to change behavior (an attitude), to trigger an emotion, or to point to the existence of something.

The films selected offer profiles of four different character types: the short-order cook, the folkloric informant, the elderly woman, and the counter-culture artist. In each case, the filmmaker has interpreted personality. In the films, the technique of the profile (the person talks about him- or herself) is supplemented by the other character revelation techniques discussed above.

In the full-length biography, the student should be sensitive to the way the author presents character. Does he or she qualify personality trait terms? Is the character presented as a type—a social class representative, a sociology type, etc.? Is the biographer trying to create a static or dynamic character? The film *Knud* has been included in this section to allow for a close look at character in a longer biography. The same questions should be applied to the 10 films in the "Life Structure" section, page 183.

SPIDER (Films, Inc.: 8 min./color/1972)

At Paul's Diner, somewhere in New Hampshire, is a character type identified by the nickname "Spider," more a phenomenon than a person, a show that has to be seen to believed. This short, short-order cook moves incredibly fast as he chops up lettuce for salads, breaks eggs, throws hamburgers on the grill, makes sandwiches, works the cash register, and even lights cigarettes for customers. Watching him slam the gigantic knife around, one is in dread of seeing fingers being cut off, but that, of course, is part of the show. Although his behavior shows Spider to be conscientious, hard-working, and exhibitionistic, the filmmaker is laughing at this static character who is so excessive at his job.

We have here a work analogous to the eighteenth century character type. Spider represents any worker who takes his or her job too seriously. He is shown to be hyperactive, extroverted at his work, but close-mouthed about his past. The film-maker's questions reveal his cynical attitude toward Spider and his occupation: "Why do you move so fast?" "If you had enough money, would you do this?" "Do you eat your own cooking?" "Mix up your orders often?" etc. Certainly background information is limited. Spider is only asked, "How'd you get the name?" and "Tell us about your boxing days . . . How did you do?" We know nothing about his childhood, education, home life, range of experiences, or interests beyond the job. The questions are asked when Spider is in full flurry, when he does not have a chance to ponder. A fish-eye lens exaggerates his motions as he hops about. The man is, after all, his job.

Behavior reveals personality, but Spider's behavior is definitely limited. He insists he does not consider what he does as work: "If this were work, I wouldn't do it." As the film portrays him, he never stops. He seems to enjoy the fast pace, and still finds time for bravura displays in the preparation of food. He shows pique when a waitress catches his mistake on an order, but for the most part is pleasant and conscientious. As the diner closes down at 2:00 in the morning, the viewer has the distinct impression that the filmmaker has nothing more to say about this man. Indeed, if Spider were given more of a chance to reveal his mind, the joke might have been lost.

THE GIRL WITH THE INCREDIBLE FEELING (Phoenix Films: 39 min./ color/1977)

Elizabeth Swados is a young person with an incredible range of talents. This film, made by her childhood friend Linda Feferman, offers samples of her work as a writer, composer, musician, performer, artist, director, and experimentalist. For all the richness of the artistic segments of this movie, Elizabeth's character is static: she is the talented experimental artist who is good-natured, confident, intense, and outgoing. We learn about her through her works and her behavior.

Elizabeth is not a run-of-the-mill artist. Since she is interested in communication through sound and tone rather than sentence structure and verbal connotation, a second viewing of the film will be revelatory: there is a great deal of control, insight, and wit in her tradition-breaking art. We watch Elizabeth 1) conduct an audience in an original contrapuntal choral work in 1973, 2) perform in a comic skit as a ventriloquist's dummy (arguing about her right to be independent), 3) sing a composition that has bird sounds for lyrics, 4) have a musical "conversation" between her voice (wordless) and a drum, 5) direct a choral reading of the Jabberwock song from *Alice in Wonderland*, 6) perform her own musical setting for a Sylvia Plath poem, and 7) illustrate through line drawings her children's book, *The Girl with the Incredible Feeling*. In addition, a pianist performs Elizabeth's composition about the folkloric character the Trickster, and the La Mama group does her arrangement of the lamentations from Euripides' *The Trojan Women*. There is no question that Elizabeth has a great range of talent.

The film suggests that the private Elizabeth exhibits the same personality traits as the public artist. Home movies show the child Elizabeth performing with her parents, and the adult Elizabeth talking, playing a guitar, and even dancing in place on a bridge. Biographical data is limited: she was born in 1951; her mother died recently; she made a trip to Africa (one that influenced her art); and she wrote in 1975 the book about a girl born with an incredible feeling that she loses for a while, thanks to the pressures of society, but that she eventually finds once again. Perhaps Elizabeth also had some bad times, but the film supplies no information about them, if they existed. Instead, it suggests that she has always been like the public performer—good-natured, confident, intense, and outgoing.

***

AT 99: A PORTRAIT OF LOUISE TANDY MURCH (Doubleday Eccentric Circle: 23 min./color/1975)

Is it possible to be very old, yet still to have an enjoyable, fulfilling life? The answer is "yes," according to this film. Indeed, Louise Tandy Murch, a warm, religious, and good-natured old woman, is an example for us in our own later years. The profile of Murch reveals, through actions, observations, and ideas, a positive but static character.

Murch's philosophy is that "you gotta lift yourself up," and she practices what she preaches. Visiting various homes for the elderly, she entertains by playing the piano and singing upbeat songs. She tries to help other old people "to think right" through the power of positive thinking. Whether having tea with the filmmaker, going shopping, or preparing food, she exhibits good cheer and energy. Her talk is peppered with original short poems that show both her creativity and her zest for life. In her large home in Toronto, Canada (where she is alone, but not lonely), she uses a slant board on which she does yoga exercises every day—even though she has a pin in each hip. Her hope is that at the end she will not have to suffer from a lingering disease.

The profile is not interested in Murch's early years, marriage, relationship with her children, or her normal, daily activities; instead, it presents an impressive personality celebrating with enthusiasm her ninety-ninth birthday among family and friends. The film ends in the late afternoon as Murch contentedly sings a song and plays the piano; the camera pulls back from the window until the entire front of the house can be seen. The sequence captures the purpose of the film: to show a positive view of old age and a fearless attitude toward death.

***

THE AMERICAN CHARACTER: AUNT ARIE (Encyclopaedia Britannica: 18 min./color/1975)

Aunt Arie Carpenter is an 87-year-old woman who knows and practices old customs that are slipping away. As such, she is a one-person repository of the old country traditions. In an ethnographic study like this one, the emphasis is on the way in which the subject does things, and not on his or her personality. As Aunt Arie reveals her lifestyle and as she talks, however, her character moves from the simple "type"—the country woman who still remembers the old ways—to a dynamic character, one who will haunt the imagination long after the film ends.

Aunt Arie's personality is many-faceted. She lives alone in a cabin in the Blue Ridge Mountains of North Carolina, but she enjoys people. Her approach to living, she tells us, is to "learn to make yourself do what you didn't think you could do." The remark is intriguing and suggests there might have been a time when she was not sure she could stand being alone. Her mother would not let her marry anyone, she laughs, so she has acted out her philosophy by learning "not to be lonely" even though "sometimes you feel blue." She is stoical, but her humor has bite. Later, we learn that the happiest time in her life was when her family was living together. Since then, she has especially enjoyed revival meetings and the making of this movie. During such moments, of course, she is not alone. Although she seems to have had a stroke, she still hoes the garden that includes beans and sweet potatoes, cooks on a wood-burning stove, and draws water from the well. She exhibits the quilts she has made, but comments, "Can't work as well as before." There is in her a courageousness, a pride in her ability to remain independent, and a strength that has not diminished in spite of the physical setbacks. Her life has been hard; when she was young, she worked in the fields, except when she had pneumonic fever. She helped to build the house she has lived in for 43 years, and she is not about to leave it. For all her pluck and humor—she can even joke about the snakes that get underfoot when she goes outside—there is still a somber quality in her.

Aunt Arie faces the dark side of life; she accepts the fact that pain is part of existence. Sometimes ironic, sometimes whimsical, she rises above a limiting, demanding environment that she studiously preserves at the same time. The complexity produces a dynamic character and the wish, on the part of the viewer, to know her better. She is rare indeed.

KNUD (McGraw-Hill Contemporary Films: 31 min./b&w/1968)

Knud Rasmussen (1878-1933) is the enigmatic hero who, for all his success, would end his life, this film suggests, in tragic frustration. Blending archive photographs, drawings, and film footage with modern location shots and reenactments—a blend so skillful that it is not easy to differentiate the old from the new—the biographer captures the danger, excitement, and stark beauty of Rasmussen's expeditions to arctic lands, as well as the complexity of his personality. The man's dynamic character is revealed through actions, comments, evaluations by others, and the change of his function in society.

Rasmussen became a Danish national hero as an explorer and ethnographer of the Eskimo, then found that his type of hero was passé as the times changed. In 1912, he started an expedition to Northeast Greenland that corrected an error on the maps of the time: the so-called Peary Straight did not exist. In 1916, he set out to map the northern coast of Greenland and to find evidence of the old migration routes of the Eskimos. The trip back from the Long Fjord proved to be more hazardous than expected: the men were forced to eat their huskies; one man disappeared in the snow; another demanded to be left to die. Rasmussen's greatest expedition was the trip from Greenland to Nome, Alaska, along the northern boundary of Canada to study the culture of the Eskimo groups and to prove his theory that the Greenland Eskimos could have emigrated from Asia. After three years and 23 days, he reached the Pacific. He returned to Denmark a celebrity and received torchlight parades and honorary degrees. When he sailed north again, he found that "everything had changed." Civilization was now encroaching on the wilderness; the "all-around explorer" had given way to the scientists and specialists; the airplane seemed to be replacing the dog sled. The biography ends with Rasmussen sitting by the fire, pensive, thinking back on the glorious days when he had said, "Give me winter, give me dogs, keep the rest yourself."

The character of the hero is elusive. He marries, but within two years is back at the northernmost house in the world, his private trading station at Tula, then off on an expedition. Three years later he returns to his wife in Denmark, then after six months heads north again. What kind of marriage did he have? Why did he marry at all? He seems to enjoy celebrity status, but also enjoys the isolation of the wilderness and Spartan life among the Eskimos. That he thrives on the dangerous challenge is a given. What is not explained is his motivation. The camera reveals a handsome, personable, extroverted man. Why must he keep moving? Why can he not be satisfied with his achievements? By not explaining the enigma, the filmmaker suggests a complex, dynamic human being.

But there is more. Rasmussen's definition of the hero was challenged by the twentieth century. Some viewers might regret that the days of the all-around explorer are over, but the demands of the lifestyle for such a type are shown to be debilitating: Rasmussen's face shows in the later years the ravages of the quest seeker.

FOLLOW-UP ACTIVITIES

1. The "character type" in the past could be on any of the following categories: a job, a social class, a personality malady (such as the Coward, the Fanatic), an age group (such as the Child, the Old Person), or a presentation of a sin or virtue (such as the Good Samaritan, the Proud Person, the Glutton). Each would start with the definition of the type ("An adolescent is one who is . . ."), followed by specific examples of the type's behavior ("The adolescent frequently has trouble concentrating on school work or a job . . ."). Do a character type found in your community. Remember: you are not describing a specific person, but a generalization into which specific people fit (not "my teacher Miss Bright," but "the Good Teacher").

2. In astrology, each sign in the zodiac designates a "character type" that has good and bad qualities. An Aries, for example, thinks quickly, is highly creative, and enjoys challenges, but is also impatient with details, aggressive, and combative. Look up the characteristics of your zodiac sign in a good astrology book (do not use the newspaper) to determine which aspects describe your personality. In your report, indicate whether you fit into the zodiac type, and back up your conclusion with specific descriptions of your behavior.

3. The "profile," unlike the "character type," stresses the personality, views, background, and activities of a particular person. Do a profile of a peer. Write three separate paragraphs: tie traits to the subject's behavior, attitude, role in the family, friendship groups, and the future (for example, does he or she want to be a professional athlete?). The introduction to the profile should indicate the subject's name and sum up his or her personality traits. Try to include some actual remarks made by the subject to show the way his or her mind works.

4. Write a character sketch of an informant who, like Aunt Arie, is familiar with the "old ways." He or she could be a person who has come from a different country or a different culture. Your informant could also be a businessperson who remembers the way things were before computers, electric cash registers, and frozen or canned goods. Make sure you bring out the subject's personality. Have the person indicate his or her opinion about the activities then, in comparison to activities now.

5. One of the assumptions of *The Girl with the Incredible Feeling* is that the artistic work reveals aspects of the creator's personality. Let us assume that connection. Construct a profile of a popular composer from his or her song lyrics. Also use interview information from magazines to support your interpretation of character.

Life Structure

A biography is not life. No one can capture a "life" intact, can give all the facets of a personality, or can catalog all the major and minor moments in an individual existence. Any biography, no matter how exhaustive, is still highly selective. Because the author must edit masses of materials, simplify complex situations to allow for dramatic structure, and interpret that material, biography is a sign model. As with any sign, the biographical model has a purpose; the author has a reason for constructing the model. The biographer's intent, in turn, influences the "slant" of the work or the interpretation of the material, and it obviously sways the author's choice of data and presentation of character. The artistic tradition of biography also determines the pattern or structure the author chooses with which to present the life. In the construction of the sign model, the author must sift through primary and secondary sources for further insight into the subject. The result of the portrait painting can influence countless people. As a sign model, the "life" contains tremendous power.

The author's purpose in writing a biography is extremely important. That purpose will largely dictate the author's selection of the raw materials of the life. The biographer might wish:

a. to change behavior in the reader by showing either behavior to copy (the ideal) or behavior to avoid (the evil or corrupt).

b. to establish group or nationalistic solidarity through the emotions produced by the life of a leader, a sacrificial hero, etc.

c. to satisfy the curiosity of the reader about other people, to fulfill a desire to hear gossip, and in that sense, to entertain.

d. to point to the existence of a contributor to civilization or to a specific culture (the author thinks the audience should learn what that contribution was).

e. to change the opinion of the reader about the subject by offering material hitherto unknown or by reinterpreting information (the audience learns that the historical hero, for instance, acted for selfish reasons).

f. to instruct the audience about a philosophy by having the subject embody it.

These purposes, in turn, influence the way the author constructs character. The personality might be static or dynamic, might be revealed through a number of techniques, but will be appropriate to those intentions. Thus, nationalistic solidarity will not be accomplished if the obituary column stresses the ethical mistakes the hero made or the difficulty coworkers had in dealing with his or her temper tantrums.

The author's purpose determines the slant he or she will use in interpreting the incidents of a life. Slant or bias can be honorific or pejorative or objective, a term that here means "balanced," relatively detached. Specific types of biography can be found under each of these categories:

a. Honorific

   (1). The Hero. The person has a strong goal throughout life that he or she wishes to accomplish; these include the lives of explorers, scientists, national heroes, such as Henry V and Alexander.

   (2). The Saint. The person lives a life of sacrifice, spiritual accomplishment, and good deeds; these are the lives of religious saints, humanists, and defenders of human rights, such as Martin Luther King and Damien the Leper.

b. Pejorative

   (1). The Victim of the Muckraker. The biographer feels the famous person, usually a legend in his or her own time, has been vastly overrated; the author points out the failings, the sordidness, or the ruthlessness of the subject; rock musicians, Hollywood stars, famous politicians, and anyone who has been very popular are eligible.

    (2). The Victim of a Negative Freudian Interpretation. The major output of a person is reduced to a problem of adjustment in infancy or early childhood; somehow, by the time the reader is through, there is a question as to why people consider the subject to be great—considering that the subject is such a neurotic mess.

c. Objective

    (1). The Public Figure. The person's real life is his or her public one; the biographer maintains the famous person's privacy (more or less) by excluding all gossip about his or her personal life while stressing career, accomplishments, and deeds; these are the lives in the encyclopedias and other reference books, obituaries, etc.

    (2). The Product of Environment. The biographer stresses the influence of upbringing, cultural conditions, mentors, ideologies, and historical events on the shaping of the life; this is the approach of Gail Sheehy in *Passages* and of historians.

The chosen slant is the key to the life. Certain facts will be emphasized to justify the interpretation. Paul Ferris, for example, will stress the dishonesty and alcoholism of Dylan Thomas in a biography that muckrakes so well, one wonders who was silly enough to find Thomas a powerful poet. James Boswell shows Johnson as the heroic gladiator taking on physical sickness, poverty, and cruel friends in his efforts to champion literature.

There are societal expectations as to the structure the sign model of a life will take. Literary tradition usually has the life broken into chronological segments. In general, those segments include:

a. Antecedents (Parents and Relatives)
b. Childhood
c. Education. These establish the economic and social status, the early character, the intellectual prowess of the subject, and the quality of his or her upbringing; in many biographies, the childhood reveals in miniature the characteristics of the adult life.
d. Coming of Age. The rite of passage or initiation into adult life includes early experiments in finding a career or purpose, love affairs, and adjustments to living on one's own.
e. Adult Life Drive. The Adult Life Drive can take many forms; it might be a quest, a career, a love affair, an accomplishment, etc.; whatever form it takes, an Antagonistic Force of some sort is established, such as a person, historical situation, or physical debility.
f. Victory over or Defeat by the Antagonistic Force. Unlike the tragic hero of drama, the subject can be triumphant and lead a pleasant life.
g. Old Age
h. Death. Not all subjects reach old age, but there is definitely a fascination in finding out what happened to the power of the individual.

It is possible in some lives that there is more than one Adult Life Drive. Someone like Paul Gauguin could spend half a life on one pursuit, then at middle age decide on a completely different career. To keep the audience interested in the life story, the biographer borrows from fiction and drama the concept of the Antagonistic Force. Life obviously does not occur in such compact units; sometimes villains are not that easy to find, and the events in the life are mundane, yet the author will try to heighten the action and to build to some sort of climax.

In putting together the components of the sign model that represents a person's actual life, the author will encounter both primary and secondary source material. The distinction between the two is obvious, but important. Primary source material is anything that an eye-witness has recorded; it is a first-hand report. Examples are autobiographies, memoirs, diaries, letters, notebooks, "newsreel" films, town-hall records (births, deaths, marriages, property, police records, voting, etc.), verbal anecdotes (by someone still alive who remembers, or those "taped"), newspaper interviews, or any work done by an artist. Many of these items are fragmentary; they offer only a part of the life, a glimpse at the subject's personality or mind, at one moment in time. The mere fact that the material is primary does not make it "true." Indeed, some primary items are either misleading (the person did not remember accurately) or distorting (the tax return for that year, as the government later found, was not quite accurate). Secondary source material is constructed by a non-eye-witness from primary sources; it is the work of someone reconstructing an event that he or she has read about. When we deal with figures from the past, we approach these secondary sources for data and insight, but would not use the same interpretation as the basis of our new work—for then there would be no reason for writing anything at all.

For the student about to write a biography, information-gathering techniques are important. Some reference books are secondary sources (except those that contain information directly from the author) and indicate other writings on the subject, or primary sources. Activities following the films in this unit complement the research skills section (see "Research Skills," page 275).

When watching any biographical film, the student should look for the aspects of the sign model just discussed:

a. characterization
b. purpose
c. slant or interpretation
d. Adult Life Drive and the Antagonistic Force

Such analysis will reveal what meaning the filmmaker finds in the "life." The chart below will give an example of the approach.

Biography Subject	Character	Purpose	Slant	Structure Adult Life Drive; Antagonistic Force
Churchill	Dynamic	Nationalistic solidarity & contribution	Hero	Search for political power; war enemies and opposing political parties
Roosevelt	Static	Nationalistic solidarity & contribution	Hero	Put America on its feet; Republicans
O'Keeffe	Dynamic	Ideal for women artists & contribution	Hero	Be an artist; traditionalists

(Chart continues on following page)

Biography Subject	Character	Purpose	Slant	Structure Adult Life Drive; Antagonistic Force
King	Static	Group solidarity & contribution	Saint	Gain black rights; segregationists
Henry VIII	Dynamic	Entertain & change opinion	Muckraking	Search for marital happiness; 6 wives
Picasso	Static	Contribution, change opinion, & satisfy curiosity	Muckraking & environment	Be an artist; conservative forces
Coleridge	Static	Contribution & change opinion	Negative Freudian	Search for happiness; loneliness & addiction
Cunningham	Static	Contribution	Public figure	Be an artist; male bias
Newton	Static	Contribution	Public figure	Scientific exploration; conservative forces (Hook)
Kafka	Static	Show a belief	Environment	Be a Writer; environment

CHURCHILL—THE MAN (Pyramid Films: 55 min./color/1974)

Director Peter Lambert sees three aspects of Churchill's life: the private family man, the public adventurer and politician, and the writer and orator who enjoyed language. He structures the biography carefully along traditional lines—the family background, childhood, education, adventures in young manhood, life drive for political power, honors culminating a successful career, and death—and in the process creates an honorific, dynamic portrait of a hero. The director's purposes are to establish nationalistic solidarity and to point to the existence of a contributor to English culture. This figure definitely has setbacks, but the vicissitudes he endures only show the strength of his character, that tenacious optimism and indefatigable zest for active involvement.

The family man is documented through the reminiscences of his daughter Sarah as she walks about the country house of Chartwell. Her anecdote about the garden's Rose Wall, built while Churchill was in the political doldrums, culminates with his witty rejoinder to the visitor who observed that the wall is crooked: "Any fool can see what's wrong . . . can you see what's right?" He liked to work with his hands, to fix up the estate, to build a swimming pool, to paint, even to feed birds and animals. He also enjoyed horses; at the Royal Ascott, he won the Churchill Stakes for three-year-olds three times. One gets the distinct impression that he spent a very active leisure time.

The public figure is exhibited through the chronology that composes most of the film. His American mother, Jennie, bore him two months prematurely while at a dance. He went to Harrow, a prestigious boarding school, "the only barren and unhappy period of my life." Things became better at Sandhurst, a military school. He enjoyed adventures in the Army in India and as a war correspondent during the Boer War, wherein he was captured and escaped. He returned to England and entered politics. By the age of 26, he was a member of Parliament; by 36, he had accumulated an impressive list of responsibilities. He took over the Admiralty to reorganize it and became involved in the Naval Air Force. The first setback in his career was after the British humiliation at Gallipoli, an event for which he took full responsibility and lost his political office. Frustrated because he was unable to control events, he utters a revealing quote: "God, for a month of power and a good shorthand writer." Made a Minister of War after the war was over, he served his country in various capacities until 1929, when he was out of office again "in the wilderness." After the defeat of Poland, he was recalled to the Admiralty and eight months later became Prime Minister. When the war in Europe was over, his party failed to get re-elected and "he never understood why." He was Prime Minister again in 1951. On his eightieth birthday, he was honored by both Houses in a ceremony never before conferred upon, as he put it, "a party politician who has not yet retired . . . and may at any time be involved in controversy." Upon his death in 1965, he was granted a full state funeral from Westminster Hall and was buried in the family graveyard at Blenheim.

The most vivid sections of this film deal with Churchill, the man of words. His inscription for a World War I memorial would be rejected, but nevertheless remembered: "In war, resolution; in defeat, defiance; in victory, magnanimity; in peace, good will." We are told he wrote out every speech, then rehearsed the presentation carefully in front of a mirror, and at times memorized the lines. Samples of his eloquence range from the emotional "Lift up your hearts . . . out of the depths of sorrow and of sacrifice will be born again the glory of mankind"; to the quip in his appearance before the United States Congress that if his father, rather than his mother, had been an American, "I might have got here on my own." There are those quotable one-liners such as his comment on Chancellor of the Exchequer Stafford Cripps: "There, but for the grace of God, goes God." The eloquence was there even in such offhand remarks to his children as the chiasmus: "Do what you like but like what you do."

The film ends appropriately by showing Churchill, about to step into a car with his daughter, flashing his famous "V" for victory sign with his fingers. His energy and optimism helped him to achieve success in so many ways. Even the "gray period" in Harrow is somehow overcome since, in his old age, he returned there yearly to join in the school songs. He died wealthy, honored, a praised author, and the national hero of World War II. The film avoids Freudian analysis of Winston's wish for power and offers British historian Taylor's positive appraisal that Churchill accepted too much responsibility for the Gallipoli debacle. This warm homage to the man amply documents his many contributions.

FRANKLIN D. ROOSEVELT: THE NEW DEAL (ACI Films, Inc.: 22 min./ b&w/1974)

Franklin Delano Roosevelt is the static cultural hero of this documentary composed completely of archive newsreel footage. The film's purposes are to establish nationalistic pride and to document a contribution to America. His quest, or Adult Life Drive, is to overcome the sickness of the Depression and to put America back on its feet. The opposition is what the Republicans had wrought. The film starts on March 4, 1933, Roosevelt's first presidential inauguration, the moment when the "curtain [had] rung down on Hoover," who had left America on the brink of total disaster. "A waiting America," we are told, senses the "strength" in the man being sworn in. The film ends when FDR reaches his goal.

The script is not interested in FDR's total life. Antecedents, childhood, education, and young manhood are ignored. Only two facets of his past are explored. We follow the "road to the White House" from his election as the new state senator at Hyde Park in 1913, through the assignment as Assistant Secretary of the Navy and the unsuccessful attempts to be vice-president, to the office of governor in Albany. We also watch his battle against polio. The bulk of the film concentrates on four of the revolutionary measures of the New Deal that brought the country back to health: 1) the Bank Holiday, 2) the Tennessee Valley project, 3) the National Recovery Acts, and 4) Unemployment Insurance and Social Security. FDR is the untiring man of action, the strong "father" of his nation, the skilled speaker capable of both emotional rhetoric and total clarity (we are told he explained the reason for the Bank Holiday and his economic program with such clarity that even the bankers understood it). His revolution is successful; happy days are here again.

There is no attempt to suggest complexity, personal tragedies (other than the polio), or the full range of FDR's mind. The purpose of the film is to show the values of a political ideology and to establish nationalistic pride in the accomplishments of a leader. Although we hear Republican Alf Landon's 1936 accusations of governmental regimentation, the creation of a political machine, and the high cost of government, such criticisms do not have a chance. We are told that every cornerstone of every dam in the Tennessee Valley project has inscribed on it, "Built for and owned by the people of the United States." The National Recovery Act's codes on prices, wages, and hours were imposed to avoid sweat-shop conditions. And in a moment that shows the power of Roosevelt's personality, we hear him counter Landon with blistering sarcasm, saying that the Republicans promise the country a utopia that no one will have to spend a cent to maintain—it will, they proclaim, come about on its own. FDR knew better, we are told, and gave back to the country the simplicity and cleanliness of its original government through his so-called revolutionary measures.

GEORGIA O'KEEFFE (Films, Inc.: 60 min./color/1977)

The purpose of this biography on Georgia O'Keeffe is to offer women an ideal to follow, and to document the work of a major artist. A number of "experts" pay homage—author Herbert Seligman, art critic Barbara Rose, museum curator Daniel Catton Rich, and critic William Fisher—but the pungent observations by O'Keeffe on her own life, friends, and work are what give this biography distinction. At 90, O'Keeffe exhibits intelligence, wit, and the ability to shape an anecdote. Her ironic humor ranges from the whimsical ("People keep asking me why my flowers are so large . . . I answer, why don't you ask me why the rivers are so small?") to the caustic (if people see sexual symbolism in her work, "that's their problem," not hers). She is fond of putting down pretentiousness in criticism. Images simply come to her and she tries to capture them. The famous cattle skulls are not a symbol of death, she insists, but a shape she likes. She painted big flowers to make people see them, she explains. Yet, for all her mockery of intellectualized and Freudian interpretation, one has the sense that there is a mystery or two up her sleeve, a power of vision that is not at all simple.

An honorific, hero biography, this film interprets O'Keeffe's Adult Life Drive as a quest, the continual striving for an independent expression, the realization of herself in art. The opposition is any person, tradition, school, or environment that tries to restrict her in that quest. Born in Sun Prairie, Wisconsin, in 1887, she was brought up in a large family and spent time in a boarding school. At 12, she knew she wanted to be a painter. Although influenced in college by William Mirror Chase, she did not like being taught to paint like others, so she stopped painting for a while. By the time the famous photographer Alfred Stieglitz presented O'Keeffe's first exhibit in New York in 1916, she had deliberately encountered a wide range of environments: The University of Virginia, Columbia University Teachers College, and teaching jobs in South Carolina and Texas. After her marriage to Stieglitz, she spent 10 summers at Lake George with his family, found it "very pretty, but not for me," then began spending part of her year at Abiquiu, New Mexico, at the ranch she bought. Still, in her old age, she likes to wander through the desert, leaving at 7:00 a.m., returning at 5:00. She has young potter Juan Hamilton helping her, but the most telling image of the film is O'Keeffe standing on top of a dune, her back to the camera, alone, looking into the horizon. She has been successful, but there seems to be no end to her quest.

The film offers art by O'Keeffe and O'Keeffe as an art object. Every stage of her life has been documented by the camera. Few subjects have had so much primary source material on them. There are the many sensitive portraits by Stieglitz of her face, body, and hands when she was in her thirties. There is a section of a 1948 film, *Land of Enchantment, Southwest U.S.A.*, made when she was middle-aged. The current film takes up where Stieglitz left off. The woman creates a definite presence, yet there is still mystery to her, and the film is successful in capturing it. The result is a dynamic character portrait of a person who enjoys people but likes her independence, who has strong opinions but couches them in humor and irony.

"I HAVE A DREAM": THE LIFE OF MARTIN LUTHER KING (BFA: 35 min./b&w/1968)

At age 36, Martin Luther King told an Alabama audience that "some things are so precious . . . they are worth dying for." He announced that he intended to practice what he preached and would continue to be active in the cause of black equality in spite of arrests, bombings, and threats. There was something worse than a physical death, he argued: "A man dies when he refuses to stand up for what is right," and a long life would be meaningless after such a spiritual death. Three years later, King was assassinated on the balcony of a Memphis hotel as he was preparing to lead another civil rights march. His demise demonstrated the integrity of his beliefs. This honorific film biography presents King as a saint and a martyr for a cause in a static characterization. The film has two purposes: to document the career of a contributor to civilization, and to create from King's self-sacrifice an emotional group solidarity against the Antagonistic Force, segregationists.

The structure of the life is traditional. Information is given on antecedents (his father was a pastor, had left a tenant farm at 15, and worked his way through college), education (King graduated from high school at 15, then attended Morehead College, Crosier Theological Seminary, and Boston University), and his marriage (to Corretta Scott, who was attending the New England Conservatory of Music and gave up her career), but nothing about his childhood. The Adult Life Drive started in 1955 when Mrs. Rosa Parks, a black seamstress, boarded a bus, found a seat, then was ordered to stand when the bus became crowded. King established a boycott of all city buses by blacks. The Antagonistic Force, the white segregationists, declared itself: they bombed King's home, had him falsely arrested for interfering with free enterprise, and brought him to court. White Montgomery lost, and at age 27, King had taken the "first step to national leadership." After 382 days, the bus boycott ended. For the next three years he continued to preach from his pulpit in the Baptist church in Montgomery, Alabama. After a trip to India, where he placed a wreath on the tomb of his hero, Gandhi, he resigned his pastorate to devote his full energy to the civil rights movement. According to the film, he organized the first sit-in on February 1, 1960, at Greensboro, North Carolina. In 1962 in Albany, Georgia, demonstrations for the desegregation of all public facilities accomplished nothing. From this failure, he learned to "choose a target carefully, and to attack only after thorough preparation." He applied what he had learned to Birmingham in April of 1963. Once again, he was arrested (the antagonists had arrested him in 1960 in Atlanta for driving without a proper Georgia license; in October of the same year, they arrested him again and sent him to a Georgia prison farm), only this time he was put in solitary confinement. Through President Kennedy's intervention, he was freed on bail. His great successes are seen to begin with the "I have a dream" speech given on August 28, 1963, before 250,000 people on the steps of the Lincoln Memorial. A year later, after being arrested in Florida, he received the Nobel Peace Prize. The successes continued to his death.

Using only the primary sources of archive film footage and photographs, the film clearly shows the determination, courage, and charisma of the leader. He has moments of self-doubt and introspection, he loses his sense of direction at times, and he makes some mistakes, but his personality is as consistent as his spiritual commitment. His character as portrayed in this film might be static, but it is without a doubt powerful, as the speeches demonstrate. The words still stir, some 20 years later, and the spirit still lives.

THE PRIVATE LIFE OF KING HENRY THE EIGHTH (Blackhawk Films: 96 min./b&w/1933)

Sometimes the scriptwriter must take liberties with a life in order to create a desired structure—and to entertain. In this classic British film, we watch a comedic encounter between the masculine principle and the feminine mystique. King Henry struts and frets his macho ways, but does not have a chance against the connivings of the women around him. Using no primary source material, the film is a dramatic reenactment of Henry's life from his mid-forties to his "old age" in the mid-fifties. The normal biographical sequences are missing, and the Adult Life Drive is reduced to the king's search for marital happiness. The purposes of the film are to satisfy curiosity and to change our opinion: the man might have been a great leader and a holy terror, but he was only another frustrated human at home. The slant is muckraking, but the debunking is sympathetic, not malicious.

Characterization is the technique used to put Henry in his place. He might be a king, but he is also a human seeking love and happiness, and his search is not always successful. To make matters worse, he is the little boy who never grew up. When he does not get his own way, he goes into rages and he sulks. The most famous scene in the picture is Henry, disturbed by the court gossip suggesting that he should remarry, in full power eating a capon and throwing the bones over his shoulder. "No delicacy nowadays . . . no consideration of others. . . . Refinement's a thing of the past," actor Charles Laughton complains through burps and mouthfuls of food. But he is also vulnerable. To impress his last young wife, he shows off his strength in a wrestling match and almost kills himself in the process. The same man who later tries to strangle a person who has brought bad news is bullied by his old nurse for taking his baby son outdoors. Everyone in the castle knows what Henry is doing at all times, but Thomas Culpeper is quite successful at being seduced by one of the king's wives under Henry's very nose. After that woman, Katherine, is executed, Henry complains that he is alone, with no friends, no love in his life, not even hatred. The film ends with Henry standing weakly before a fireplace as he furtively chews on a capon leg that his last wife, an old shrew, has forbidden him to eat. "Six wives . . . the best of them's the worst," he complains. He might outrage us with his egotism and lust, but he earns our sympathy through the treachery of those around him and the pain he exhibits from having been betrayed in love. The result is a dynamic characterization.

The wives who form the Antagonistic Force in the film are not complex characters but types. Henry sums them up best: his first wife was clever, his second ambitious, and his third, Jane, stupid. The script has nothing more to offer about them (we never even meet his first wife). Anne of Cleves is clever: she outwits the king, beats him at cards on his wedding night, and yet remains his friend. Katherine Howard is ambitious and conniving. Katherine Parr is a nursemaid and a scold. They might be one-dimensional, but they are more than a match for the fearful leader. For all his bluster, his shrewdness, and his many experiences, Henry remains a naif in the battle of the sexes.

PICASSO IS 90 (Carousel Films, Inc.: 50 min./color/1971)

This birthday tribute to artist Pablo Picasso serves many purposes. Among them, 1) it documents the life of a major artist, 2) it tries to change our opinion about the man by reinterpreting sections of his life, and 3) it satisfies the curiosity of the audience for gossip about the private life of a celebrity. The slant is also complex. There is the objective approach wherein Picasso is seen as a product of his natal environment, but there also is a certain amount of muckraking concerning the artist's personal life and his creativity. In spite of this plethora of purposes and approaches, the character of the man appears simple, static, a "type": the emotional, sensual Spaniard.

Documentation of the artist's life is thorough (the only period of Picasso's art that is ignored is that during World War II and shortly thereafter) and consists almost entirely of primary source material. A number of experts and people who know the artist well—biographer Sir Roland Penrose, art dealer Daniel-Henry Kahnweiler, former lover Françoise Gilot, and son Claude, among others—offer commentary or anecdotes. Archive film footage shows both the public and the private individual. Location shots explore the environment that shaped his personality. And of course, there is a handsome portfolio of Picasso's work.

The life is structured into two strands, strands that interact at times. The major Adult Life Drive is to be an artist, and the conservative forces in the culture, as well as political situations, form the opposition. The artist triumphs totally. In his childhood, we learn, the prodigy finished drawing the legs of a pigeon on his father's painting so successfully that his father, an art teacher and museum official, vowed never to paint again. Picasso came of age in Paris, living in poverty with a Bohemian crowd, trying to find his own style. By 1907, he had created the "landmark of twentieth century painting," *Les Demoiselles d'Avignon*, and entered into his artistic maturity. He attacked conservative artistic forces with cubism; he decried the Spanish Civil War with one of his greatest paintings, *Guernica*, an angry statement against the brutal bombing of a small Spanish town. Although he eventually lived in exile, Picasso at 90, as portrayed in this film, enjoys fame and wealth and has celebrity status.

The second strand of the biography deals with the passionate Spaniard's sexual life. The film carefully records the various wives and mistresses (Eva, Olga, Dora, Marie-Therese, Françoise, and Jacqueline) and suggests he remains loyal to his current young wife only because he is now dependent on her in his old age. This strand shows the negative aspects of his personality: he is consumed with himself. Although he likes little children, he coldly dismisses his own when they grow up. At times, he reveals his sexual life in his artistic works, as with the Rose period, the Minotaur drawings, and the many portraits of his loved ones.

It is fairly unusual for a birthday tribute to be critical of its subject, but this one is. Many of the criticisms are merely attempts by the film to be objective and not to gush about this superstar. Some of the negative information, however, is intended to deflate mythic aspects of the hero, to show that he is, after all, just a human. Thus, we learn that the preoccupations of the art of Picasso are the result of the early Spanish environment, not of any unique artistic vision. Narrator Charles Collingwood argues that even cubism is not all that original: he compares a photograph of a country town to a cubist painting and points out that "architecture falls into natural cubist patterns." According to this view, Picasso is not a great intellectual, just a perceptive, emotional Spaniard. His political views are simplistic: he is "merely" against war, suffering, and injustice, and for peace and "pretty girls." His recent art, the film implies, is shallow and glib. Perhaps the same could be said about TV specials, but this one is an exception. The muckraking is restrained, however: the display of the art work and talent is dazzling, and in spite of the off-key notes, the birthday greeting still shows fondness and appreciation.

COLERIDGE: THE FOUNTAIN AND THE CAVE (Pyramid Films: 33 min./ color/1974)

In this biography, the British poet Samuel Taylor Coleridge (1772-1834) is portrayed as a tragic figure: drug addiction destroyed this artistic prophet who predicted through the creation of the Ancient Mariner his own future loneliness and self-loathing. The life, presented both to document a contributor to Western civilization and to change the opinion of an audience by reinterpreting the life, is viewed through a Freudian lens. The need for opium was caused by the death of his beloved father in his childhood, the years of loneliness at Christ's Hospital Boarding School, his problems with rheumatism, and persecution by his peers. The Adult Life Drive is a search for happiness, self-control, and creative fulfillment. Loneliness and addiction are the constant antagonists as they consume the artist.

Using primary source material such as letters, diaries, memoirs, and Coleridge's poetry, the film is rich in detail. The narration gives dates, significant events for all the traditional segments of the poet's life, and anecdotes that suggest his inspirations for certain works. The film includes information about Coleridge's parents (his father was a parson, his mother a good economist), his unhappy childhood, his education (he won a scholarship to Cambridge), and his early (and unsuccessful) attempt with Southey to found a utopian community. For a few years Coleridge found happiness in the friendship of Wordsworth and his sister, a warmth that produced a great artistic outpouring. Then the drug that had been his nemesis gained the upper hand. We learn from the excerpts of personal writings that Coleridge was absorbed in his physical problems and moral decay. He saw himself as a "spirit in hell." The movie implies that the breakup of his marriage and of the friendship with Wordsworth in 1807 was the result of the drug addiction. The life from 1816, when Dr. James Gilman offered to help control the drug problem, until his death is vague—we are given only the image of a brooding Coleridge alone in a room. Details are selected to reinforce this image. We are made aware of his fascination with German metaphysics and his interest in philosophy and religion during the mature years, but we hear nothing of his romantic entanglements or the £150 annuity Thomas Wedgwood gave him early in his career. Perhaps such facts would have made him less the lonely intellectual, the tragic, cut-off figure.

The character of Coleridge in this film is static. We are told the poet destructively brought about the fulfillment of the fears expressed in "The Rime of the Ancient Mariner." Only the egoistic concerns of Coleridge's mind are noted; there are no illustrations of his important literary criticism or of his ideas beyond the images of his poems. Coleridge's tragic, neurotic character is simplified and dramatized until he himself becomes a vivid poetic image.

IMOGEN CUNNINGHAM, PHOTOGRAPHER (Time-Life: 20 min./color/1970)

Director John Korty's biography of Imogen Cunningham stresses the public personality of the famous photographer. His purpose is to document the existence of a contributor to our culture. Although he provides a wide sampling of the work that earned her reputation, such as "Magnolia Flower" (1925), "Cyprus Roots" (1921), and "Unmade Bed" (1957), he is more interested in capturing the artist herself. Her character is revealed through both documentary-style observation of various everyday activities (such as the making of a dessert, cat-napping, reading, and developing her photographs) and a series of studio poses (in which she models the hats she collected from around the world). She exudes energy, good humor, and an enjoyment of life, but the portrait is static: she is the whimsical but normal artist.

Cunningham's Adult Life Drive was to be an artist, and she accomplished her goal, but not much detail is given here, and sections of her life are ignored. At no time does the portrait pry into personal details or private motivations. Born in Portland, Oregon, in 1883, she later learned photography from a correspondence school. By 1915 she had a studio in Seattle. She married Roi Partridge, an etcher, and had three children. In 1917, she moved to California, later divorced Roi, and settled in San Francisco. She helped form Group $f/64$ (a photographer's club) in 1932. In 1967, the National Academy of Arts and Sciences elected her a member. We are told she is not a religious person; we observe how much she enjoys other people. The slant of the biography is objective and shows the public image. Was there an opposition in her life? There is the implication that she had to make her way in a male-dominated world; otherwise, no Antagonistic Force is indicated.

Unlike Georgia O'Keeffe, Cunningham has not been constantly the subject of the camera. This film creates primary source material that can be used in the future for more complex portraits. It documents Cunningham during a work session, photographing a nude model, with family and friends relaxing outdoors, and at a flower show enjoying the exhibits. Such small but revelatory moments are sometimes never captured in more ambitious biographies.

NEWTON: THE MIND THAT FOUND THE FUTURE (Learning Corp. of America: 21 min./color/1970)

The public figure is presented in this biography for the purpose of documenting the contributions of Sir Isaac Newton to civilization. We are shown the past, those pre-scientific, superstitious attempts to explicate the heavens, such as Stonehenge, and the present, the blast-off of modern rockets, in order to appreciate the massive change in thinking that Newton helped produce. Newton's personal life is ignored, and the character portrayed in this film is static, which allows the filmmaker to give stage center to the mental activity of the great man. Scenes with actors present the key moments of discovery, and the device of a narrator with the persona of Edmond Halley of comet fame, allows for the explication of Newton's concepts.

The structure starts with Newton at age 23 when he observes the apple fall (the film acknowledges that the anecdote might be apocryphal), focusing immediately on the Adult Life Drive—scientific exploration and an interest in alchemy. The opposition is Robert Hook, a rival of long standing. According to the film, the world gained the law of universal gravity thanks to Newton's jealousy of Hook, a scientist who argued for traditional beliefs. At the time the apple allegedly fell, Newton worked out his theory but put it aside to concentrate on other problems. Twenty years later, Halley goaded Newton into recreating the proof of the law (and thus changing the course of science) in order to attack the ideas of Hook. The rest of the film traces chronologically Newton's contributions to the modern world: his use of deductive reasoning (one starts with a postulate or generalization, then performs an experiment to prove the postulate, or demonstrates the proof through patterns of logical thought), the invention of differential calculus, improvements on a reflecting telescope, experimentation with white light, and the writing of the *Principia*.

This film shows that not every life automatically lends itself to visual documentation. Since Newton is an intellectual hero, his mental life must be stressed. Much of his mental work is complex, and to explain it to a young audience, the script has to simplify his discoveries. Moreover, an idea does not necessarily provide the basis for an exciting visual presentation. The contrast of the past with the present as well as the conflict between Newton and his conservative peers helps to add melodrama to the scientist's contributions. The filmmaker has had to use some time-honored literary devices to add tension to ideas. Although we see artifacts from the period and watch newsreel footage of rockets taking off, the life scenes are total reenactments. The static character type, the man of genius, is presented entirely through secondary source materials.

THE TRIALS OF FRANZ KAFKA (Films for the Humanities: 15 min./b&w/ 1975)

The purpose of this film is to instruct the audience about a belief that the effects of a hostile environment on a sensitive artist can produce a nightmarish art that seems to predict the future. Narrator Kurt Vonnegut, Jr., asks, "Was Franz Kafka, like the cabalists, so truthful a seer that he could dream reality into being?" The film says "yes," as it documents with primary sources the aspects of the nightmare. Kafka's natal Prague is dark and sinister with its huge clocks, ugly stone gargoyles, death figures, statues depicting violence, empty cobblestone streets, and bleak buildings and landscape. The precocious child had to contend with a doting mother and a pragmatic, robust, demanding father. Kafka wanted to write, his father wanted him to be "more practical"; so the sickly young man took a job at a workers' accident insurance company. Soon came the horrors of World War I. Kafka felt he was an "accomplice in the cruelty of the modern world." In such an environment, writing for Kafka became "a form of prayer." The author died of tuberculosis in 1924 at the age of 41. The images of the artist quickly turned into reality. His three sisters and sweetheart would die in Nazi concentration camps. The film believes Kafka's novel *The Trial* foreshadowed Hitler's reign of terror of the 1930s and 1940s.

According to this approach, the environment opposes the subject's attempts to accomplish his Adult Life Goal, to be a writer. The film gives a great deal of information, but other biographies and the author's writings reveal there is more to his life and personality. Certainly the environment played an important role: he was timid and suffered from being different, i.e., Jewish; his father was a haberdasher in the Prague ghetto; he was terrified of school as a child; to appease his father, he went to the German University to study law in 1901. But Kafka was not always in Prague, and the film ignores the years during which Kafka learned his craft as a writer. Certainly the film is powerful in its evocation of an almost palpably evil environment, but Kafka's character is reduced to a static type in the process: Kafka is the sensitive artist, the outsider, the prophet.

FOLLOW-UP ACTIVITIES

1. Write a biography of someone you know (not younger than 20 to 25 years old). Through interviews, determine the basic facts of his or her life. Combine information gathered from questions with observations you have made on your own over the years. Begin your biography with a general description of the person's physical appearance and personality. Starting with the antecedents, divide the life of your subject into its stages with a separate paragraph for each section. Indicate the Adult Life Drive and any possible antagonists. Include only those facts from the life that show some important aspect of the subject's personality or that show his or her attitude toward life. In the concluding paragraph, state your personal feelings about the person. Do you admire the person or find the subject unusual in any way?

2. To become acquainted with biographical reference sources, indicate in a chart the information you could gather about the following people in at least six different reference works. The famous people are:
   a. Herbert von Karajan, living
   b. Florence Nightingale, died 1910
   c. Sylvia Plath, died 1963
   d. Haile Selassie, died 1975
   e. Albert Schweitzer, died 1965
   f. Maya Angelou, living

   In each reference book, is there an indication of:
   1. Primary or secondary sources for further reading?
   2. Character?
   3. Antecedents?
   4. Childhood?
   5. Education?
   6. Coming of age?
   7. Adult Life Drive?
   8. Antagonistic Forces?
   9. Victory over or defeat by Antagonistic Force?
   10. Old age?
   11. Death?

Choose six of the following (the numbers preceding the citation refer to the entry number in Christine Gehrt Wynar's *Guide to Reference Books for School Media Centers*, 2nd ed. [Littleton, CO: Libraries Unlimited, 1981]).

232 *The McGraw-Hill Encyclopedia of World Biography*. New York: McGraw-Hill, 1973.

236 *Current Biography*. New York: H. W. Wilson, 1940- .

238 *The International Who's Who*. London: Europa Publications; distr. by International Publications Service, 1935- .

240 *Who's Who in America*. Chicago: Marquis Who's Who, 1899- .

241 *Who's Who in the World*. Chicago: Marquis Who's Who, 1970- .

242 *Who's Who of American Women*. Chicago: Marquis Who's Who, 1958- .

243 *Concise Dictionary of American Biography*, 3rd ed., complete to 1960. New York: Scribner's, 1980.

244 *Dictionary of American Biography*. New York: Scribner's, 1928-1977; Supplements.

246 *Dictionary of National Biography: The Compact Edition*. New York: Oxford University Press, 1975.

248 *Notable American Women, 1607-1950: A Biographical Dictionary*. Cambridge, MA: The Belknap Press of Harvard University Press, 1972.

249 *Notable American Women: The Modern Period*. Cambridge, MA: Harvard University Press, 1980.

253 *Biographical Dictionaries Master Index: A Guide to More than 725,000 Listings in Over Fifty Current Who's Whos and Other Works of Collective Biography*. Detroit, Gale, 1975-1976.

254 *Biography Index: A Cumulative Index to Biographical Material in Books and Magazines, 1946-* . New York, H. W. Wilson, 1947- .

3. Write a biography of a famous living artist based on primary sources. Use magazines, newspapers, memoirs, or autobiography to gather information, but also find examples of the person's accomplishments, such as novels, plays, dance, music, movies or TV, song lyrics, poems, and paintings. Make sure you show how the accomplishments reflect the concerns of the artist.

4. Construct a dramatic scene in which a famous person encouters an Antagonistic Force. The famous person might be
    Sir Thomas More
    Socrates
    Niccolò Machiavelli
    Woodrow Wilson
    Margaret Fuller
    Joan of Arc
Research carefully before you start your writing. Obviously, your research must include information about the Antagonistic Force.

III

REFINING THE MESSAGE

FOCUS, EMPHASIS, AND PACING

Focus, emphasis, and pacing are included in a section of the book on refining the message because teachers generally consider them to be higher-order writing skills that should only be taught after the student learns to narrow a topic, develop an assertion, and research evidence. Yet focus, emphasis, and pacing are more than window dressing. If they are not considered part of the writer's conscious strategy, the essay's assertion may very well make little or no impression on the reader. For the purposes of teaching, focus, emphasis, and pacing will be sharply differentiated and explained as decisions the writer should make after limiting the topic and developing the assertion. The *focus* is upon the most alluring or instructive person or item (within the topic) that the writer can describe to convey his or her assertion. *Emphasis* is the aspect(s) of that person or item the writer must highlight in order to convey that assertion. *Pacing* is the speed with which each section of the work unfolds. This, too, can manipulate the audience into accepting the assertion.

Every topic, obviously, includes a multitude of persons or items that could be chosen as the focus. The only criterion is how well the focus will convey the writer's assertions about that topic. An essay stressing the legitimacy of the nuclear freeze movement could focus on a large nuclear freeze demonstration, on an author who has written a book on the subject, on one of the movement's most dynamic leaders, on a small New England town that has just passed a nuclear freeze referendum, a high school where the nuclear freeze issue is taught in social studies classes, or a nuclear chemist who took part in the Manhattan Project but who has now joined the freeze movement. Once the focus is chosen, the aspects of it that will best prove the assertion must be highlighted. The writer focusing on the small New England town might emphasize how typical and traditional this municipality is, how the movement here began slowly in a grass roots fashion, and how the town meeting debate that preceded the referendum vote saw people of all ages and backgrounds call for an end to the proliferation of nuclear weapons. What the writer would probably leave out—or, at least, would not emphasize—are the families whose members are bitterly divided over the issue, the one articulate anti-freeze speaker who argued that the movement was only a fad, and the behind-the-scenes arm twisting that went on to get so many people down to Town Hall to vote on the referendum.

Two more hypothetical examples show how clever pacing can augment a well-considered focus and emphasis. Assume a writer decided to do an essay on teenage drinking, asserting that it simply must be stopped. To convey such an opinion, he or she could focus on a sensational case in which a family of five was killed on the road by a drunk teenage driver. The writer might emphasize the family's innocence and the youth's recklessness. He or she might create a quick and suspenseful pace by juxtaposing short chronological descriptions of the teenager from the time he is thrown out of a house party and of the family from the time they leave a Walt Disney movie. After the inevitable crash, the pace would slow, ending with a series of rhetorical questions such as: "What can be done to stop tragedies such as this before a family you know perishes on a dark highway like this one?" Or let us assume the writer decides to compose an essay on teenage drinking which asserts that society's own traditions cause young people to drink early and heavily. This writer might focus on an average junior high school student. The times during a normal week when the boy receives information about alcohol would be emphasized: The movies he watches featuring big-drinking heroes, the ads he sees that associate drinking with masculinity, the adult party at his parents' house where his uncle lets him sip from his beer while he tells the boy tall-tale drinking stories from his days as a Marine. This essay might have a quickly paced opening and closing and an evenly paced, episodic middle. The beginning would quote a number of adults bemoaning the way kids drink today. This would be followed by the episodes from the boy's life cited above. The ending would repeat one of the opening lines, such as: "I sure wish kids didn't drink so early and so much!" (The pacing of this essay would be influenced by the contrast, or irony, of the opening remarks and the middle episodes.)

These hypothetical examples show that many possible focuses, emphases, and paces are available to every writer with an assertion to sell. To appreciate this in full, however, students should analyze a number of essays in which the authors have made a wide variety of focus, emphasis, and pacing choices. The five films that follow are visual essays that quickly reveal the effects of such decisions. Once students have discussed several films and completed follow-up reading and writing activities, they will understand that a message unrefined by a well-considered focus, emphasis, and pacing may be little more than dust in the wind.

NANOOK OF THE NORTH (McGraw-Hill Contemporary Films: 55 min./ b&w/1922)

The topic of *Nanook of the North* is Eskimos, and the assertion is that, in this race of people, we can see our ancient ancestor—a magnificent noble savage unspoiled by the evils of civilization yet vulnerable to its encroachment. The *focus* is Nanook and his family. *Emphasized* are the man's skills, innocence, bravery, and oneness with nature. The *pace* of the film's episodes varies to achieve suspense. Starting slowly in the spring when Nanook and his family are relatively safe, the movie quickens as it follows the family into the brutal winter, where daily survival becomes more and more unlikely.

Nanook is chosen as the focus of the film because he is the ideal Eskimo and the epitome of the noble savage. A strong and crafty hunter and a gentle and loving father and husband, Nanook is humanity at its best: free of pride, self-pity, and selfishness and unspoiled by the body-softening luxuries of modern civilization. Through him we learn about the Eskimo habits of food gathering, house building, and family living, but even more importantly we learn about the noble Eskimo spirit.

The harmony of Eskimo life, their skill in adapting to their harsh environment, and the slow corruption of their lifestyle at the hands of modern white civilization are all emphasized. To elevate Nanook to a symbol of the noble savage, the film-maker includes nothing specific about the man's individual character. His conversation is not recorded. No attempt is made to capture troubles he may have had with his family or within the tribe. His personal doubts, superstitions, religious beliefs, and feelings about his ancestors are all left out.

Several episodes from the film illustrate its emphases. The way Nanook's family travels shows that they, unlike us, still function as a harmonious and resourceful nuclear family, struggling as a unit against the rigors and demands of their environment. As Nanook paddles the kayak, his youngest son lies atop it within reach of his father, and the rest—his wife, sister-in-law, eldest son, and puppy—are crammed down inside. This arrangement does not cause feuds about discomfort, status, or individual rights; if it does, the filmmaker has not included them. Similarly, when the family joins others to bring their skins and hides to the trading post, the Eskimos are models of industry, innocence, happiness, generosity, and harmony. Even though the Eskimo families wander alone for most of the year, they work together easily in the spring to visit civilization. Nanook, the master hunter, has brought in the best furs and young huskies to trade with, but he does not boast or gloat over his achievement, nor are other Eskimo men shown to resent his prowess. If such discord does occur, the film does not emphasize it. At the post Nanook is shown a phonograph and listens to a recording for the first time. He is enraptured and confused by the gadget, but refuses to believe the sound comes from the little box. In his innocence he bites the record as he would any unknown object in nature, in order to discover its properties and possible uses. The toy is beyond him, however, so he just laughs at the silliness of white civilization, and somehow in his dismissal of it he seems wise to us. His eldest child does not benefit much from his exposure to modern civilization either. He eats too many pieces of bread soaked in lard and gets a stomachache. Mila, Nanook's wife (her name means "the smiling one"), carries her youngest child up to the post inside her clothing to keep him warm, but once there she allows the cherubic boy to roll around naked on the soft skins in and among the huskie pups. As the narrator says, "there is no more loving mother in all the world."

Nanook's natural strength, cunning, and leadership abilities are shown when the Eskimo men capture a walrus. They wait for the one-ton giants to come ashore, then Nanook slowly crawls toward them, his head down and his harpoon ready. Suddenly, the animals sense his presence and scurry toward the water, but not before Nanook is upon the last one. He harpoons it and holds the struggling walrus until the other men join him in the ensuing tug of war. Eventually, the men win and we watch them happily gobble up the raw and bloody meat. Nanook licks his broad hunting knife once he has had his fill. Nanook has clearly been the group's leader during the encounter. The leader of individuals who work alone the rest of the year also shows no fear or indecision as he stalks the great animals, despite their mass, number, and sharp tusks. Consequently, by the time we see the hunter eating the raw meat, his barbarism looks natural and proper enough that it is possible for us to wonder if raw meat doesn't contain more nutrients after all.

The pace of the film, which has obviously been slow and langorous to this point, quickens and intensifies as winter approaches and Nanook's family heads out on a long and lonely nomadic search for food. To create suspense and to quicken the pace, the narrator describes the scene for us. It is the dead of winter now; the sea and land are locked away. The sun is "a mocking brass ball in the sky," and gone are the days of plenty. Ahead are the long months during which Nanook and his family seem to be the only living things on earth. The entire family helps maneuver the sled drawn by half-wild huskies over the mountains of sharp and jagged ice floes that have been pushed up along the shore of the bay. On this day they find food when Nanook leads them to one of his traps in a snow field where we see only blinding whiteness. From the trap buried deep in a hole, Nanook pulls a white fox—they will eat tonight. The day begins to close, and being too far from base camp, Nanook builds an igloo in the hour or so left before dark.

The filmmaker heightens the pace and begins to build toward a climax by emphasizing the terrible wildness and brutality of the northern landscape against which the family struggles. Nanook tries to load the sled, but the dogs begin to fight among one another. Apparently, the lead dog must prove its mastery each morning by fighting all oncomers. During the day, Nanook sneaks up on a tiny hole in the snow, imperceptible to us, fires his harpoon down it, then engages in a fierce battle to keep hold of his line, on the other end of which struggles a 6-foot-long, 2½-foot-wide seal. Eventually, the hunter's family assists him, and among the four of them they succeed. "Thus the cycle of feast and famine goes on," the narrator says as the family gorges itself on raw meat. Soon, however, the vicious dogs are given stage center again. Nanook tosses them pieces of the meat and the camera gives us an unwanted view of their snarling faces. This image cuts short any sense of relief we may have experienced when the family found food again. The dogs begin to fight again as it is time to move on. Nanook hurries to separate them because they have wandered far afield this day, and both darkness and an arctic gale approach. As the group pushes for home (it is too late to build an igloo), the narrator tells us that theirs is one of the dreaded predicaments of winter. Tired and far from home, the family must fight 100-mile-per-hour winds and -90° temperatures to get home. Just when it looks as if the family will certainly perish, it stumbles upon a deserted igloo and the members rush inside, safe against all odds for another day. The camera does not linger on them inside, though. Again, it pictures the dogs as they settle down outside. The driving snow turns them into haunting, ghost-like stumps that huddle together for warmth. As the filmmaker pans the bleak expanse of snow-swept terrain and we hear the dog-wolves bay against the cold, we, along with the narrator, wish Nanook and his family a good night's sleep and exit the scene hoping against hope for their continued survival.

OTTO: ZOO GORILLA (Films, Inc.: 58 min./color/1978)

The topic here is America's zoos. The message is that modern, well-equipped zoos play a crucial role in preserving animals that would otherwise disappear in the outside world. The *focus* is Otto, a gorilla so playful, eccentric, vulnerable, and human that any viewer would remortgage his house to protect him. The *emphasis* is how happy, healthy, and fertile Otto and all other zoo animals become when they are transferred to a new habitat at Chicago's Lincoln Park Zoo. Apart from the middle of the film, when the *pace* drags somewhat, the movie's episodes proceed quickly, spurred on by carefully interspersed shots of Otto at play and by suspense that builds when the keepers move the great ape from his old cage to his new living quarters.

A film arguing that the public should better support the country's zoos could have no better focus than Otto the gorilla. No viewer could fail to identify with and care for this great primate. The opening closeup of Otto is magnetic and intimidating. We hear only stray sounds from the other cages as we see Otto's massive head, gigantic neck girth, ridged forehead, hulking shoulders, Mohegan haircut, and small, jet black eyes. As the camera pulls back, we see that Otto is eating grapes. Sitting quietly in his cage, he gently pulls the grapes from the stemmed bunch and pops them one at a time into his mouth. As the film progresses, Otto begins to resemble King Kong, that other endangered wonder that so desperately needed our understanding and protection.

Emphasized throughout the film are Otto's charm, the unsuitableness of his old, cramped cage, and the benefits of living in his spacious, new habitat. Otto's unusual enthusiasm for water provides the film with its most exuberant footage. Normally, we are told, gorillas hate water; even in the wild they avoid standing water and eat fruit and plants to hydrate themselves. Not Otto, however. While the other great apes dread the daily hosing down of their cells, Otto has turned the ritual into his own vaudeville routine. The other gorillas hang from the top of their cages or bang on the walls in protest as head primate keeper Jim Higgins washes their habitats. Otto sticks his hand in the hose's spray, cups his hands and bangs them loudly on his chest, shuffles sideways through the water on the floor, spins in circles like a top, and opens his mouth as he scampers around, appearing to laugh or smile. He fills his tire (given to the gorillas for play) with water from the hose, then sloppily scoops handfuls of the liquid up into his mouth. When Higgins bends the hose to slow the water to a trickle, Otto sips from the nozzle. Later, when the apes have adapted to their new homes, Otto develops a more complex and funnier water routine. The just-opened, more elaborate habitat has a maze of caged-in corridors above the apes' living quarters. Here the animals sleep at night and retire when their homes are being hosed down. To flush Otto out of the corridors and back down into his habitat, a keeper named Mike shoots blasts of water at Otto and thus plays right into the hands of the quick-witted trickster. Otto cleverly avoids the trainer's blasts as he skips and slides through the wet corridors, his mouth open and his arms pumping. His plan is to avoid the keeper for a while, then suddenly to appear before him at the wall of the cage, seemingly repentant. Then he scurries off again, running and somersaulting through the corridors, only to return at a full-speed slide down the corridor and into the metal mesh nearest to Mike. Only when the ape has frazzled the keeper's nerves and sufficiently exhausted his patience does Otto end the game and return to his habitat below.

The nineteenth century cells where Otto and the other primates are kept are consistently disparaged as unsuitable for the animals. The camera dwells on the darkness and claustrophobia of these environments. Shots showing the apes peering out through tiny peep holes and their hands reaching out from between black metal bars emphasize the inhumanity of these cells built to accommodate the zoo's visitors, not its animals. The filmmaker wastes no opportunity to emphasize the superiority of the gorillas new three-story habitat, which is replete with a skylight, swinging ropes, a metal "tree," and glass walls (instead of bars). The apes fight less here. Otto is eating more and losing weight because the greater space allows him to exercise more. Mumbie, Otto's mate, has another baby.

This feeling of concern for endangered animals' welfare is also engendered by the film's pacing. At the very beginning, the narrator says the animals will be moved to a new home at the zoo. Neither the new habitat, nor the method of moving the animals is explained right away, however, as we are left to wonder and to anticipate. We are told and shown how inadequate and outdated the present facility is. Eventually, we see sections of the new building as construction workers install the heavy pieces of thick glass they say will withstand the gorillas' strength. Having seen the apes' fits of temper and excitement, we wonder. After Otto (and the others) has been anesthetized and examined by a team of doctors, the huge ape is introduced to his new environment. No one knows how the primate will react to the new cell and its accouterments, however, and our anticipation is increased by interviews of the two keepers and the two veterinarians who know Otto best. Each guesses what Otto's response will be. After a cautious moment or two of inspecting his new home, Otto leaps into the air, bangs his chest with his cupped hands, and assertively claims his new turf. Having participated, in a way, in the whole transfer process, the audience finds very gratifying this carefully timed and prepared climax. When the film flashes forward three months, then six months later, we are even more pleased to see how well the new home suits the beasts. The only pacing problem occurs when the filmmakers spend too much time showing the 143 tests the doctors do on the anesthetized apes. Up until and after this portion of the film, however, the well-spaced footage of Otto playing around, the building of tension over the move, the satisfaction in seeing Otto's smooth transition, and the birth of the newest baby gorilla keep the audience interested and concerned.

PRETEND YOU'RE WEARING A BARREL (Phoenix Films: 10 min./color/ 1978)

Canada's Employment and Immigration Department teamed up with the National Film Board of Canada to produce *Pretend You're Wearing a Barrel*, a film about welfare mothers. The movie asserts that such women will be happier and raise healthier children if they leave welfare dependency and find a career. To promote such a message, the filmmakers *focus* on Lynn, a welfare mother who has made it. *Emphasized* are scenes of Lynn at work as an apprentice engineer and with her five daughters, who now look up to their mother as a glowing role model to be imitated.

The filmmakers focus on Lynn because she fought against incredible odds to get off welfare. She was divorced after bearing five daughters. Finding herself with no marketable skills, she went on welfare. Eventually, she tired of her own and her children's dependence and sought out a job counselor. He placed her in a welding course, which she passed. After several months of fruitless job hunting, she landed a position as an apprentice engineer at a small firm. Soon, her self-respect returned, and, buoyed by renewed confidence and prosperity, she and her daughters resumed a happy, independent life.

The only view we get of Lynn and her daughters during their welfare dependence is contained in two snapshots that show them as a glum, down-and-out group gathered around the doorway of a broken-down house. Three tableau sequences in the film emphasize the new Lynn, an independent woman respected by her workmates and loved by her children. In one, we see Lynn perched on top of a large metal drum. A beefy, male workmate hands her a large container of fluid so she can empty it into the drum she straddles. She handles the transfer well, but he almost drops the container when he takes it back from her, swears, and the two share a laugh. Later, Lynn is pictured during a lunch break with the other male workers. Lounging along with them on pieces of machinery at the side of the warehouse which overlooks a nearby river, she looks like one of the guys. Still later, Lynn is pictured after work. As one of her daughters massages her shoulders, Lynn explains what it is like to apply axle grease to the lug nuts of a truck tire. Though slightly digusted by such a prospect, the daughter is clearly impressed by her mother's skills.

The benefits of work are consistently emphasized in the film. Twice Lynn's children are pictured taking turns swinging on a rope that hangs from the bottom of a highway overpass. Although the girls' game of swinging out over a concrete ravine beneath the bridge is not really seen as life-threatening, their mother's voice-over comments play up the game's risk and make it a symbol of the fragility of childhood and the dangers of bringing children up on welfare. "My children began to ask the social worker for things instead of me," she recalls. "That's no way to bring up kids." Later, during the close of the film, the correct way to raise children is emphasized. At the end of her work day, one of Lynn's children comes running up to the welding garage where Lynn is closing up. The child gives her mother a permission slip to sign for several trips the child wishes to take. The mother happily consents. Then the girl shows Lynn an award she has won at school. The two enjoy the achievement together and agree, at the mother's suggestion, that with a little more effort the top prize may be within the girl's reach next year. As her daughter rushes over to close the garage door for her mother, the film emphasizes that the child has found a positive role model in her own mother.

Unlike many other moral-laden films, *Pretend You're Wearing a Barrel* maintains a quick *pace* by cutting from a few shots of Lynn the welfare mother, to many more of Lynn the engineer, and Lynn the breadwinner for her daughters. The opening shot of Lynn lighting her welder's torch is used to grab our attention, then the camera quickly cuts to her kitchen where the mother and her five children clown around as she prepares for another day at work. Looking very content and independent for teenagers, the girls get themselves ready for school. Back at work, we see Lynn crouching inside the hood of a truck, rolling under a truck chassis, and working down in the engine room of a ship. As she goes about her day, we hear her discuss, in voice-over, her attitude toward work. Unlike the men, she says, she does not define herself through her job. She enjoys it, but sees it as a means toward an end—a paycheck that buys the children shoes. Back at home she quietly and bravely discusses the breakup of her marriage and her realization that she had to get off welfare. Here the pace slows briefly to highlight the turning point in her life. Back at the company she works and relaxes with her male workmates. When Lynn next discusses the destructiveness of welfare, the camera is there to view her daughters on their rope swing. The warm scene between mother and daughter at the garage described earlier constitutes the film's slow close. What image could better convince a welfare mother of the benefits of employment?

HOLLYWOOD: THE DREAM FACTORY (Films, Inc.: 51 min./color/1972)

This film *focuses* on clips from MGM movies to assert that three dichotomies have always fascinated Americans: 1) the American Dream and rigid social hierarchies, 2) meteoric rise to glory and the sudden fall to ruin, 3) sexual prohibitions and sexpots. To prove this theory, the filmmaker *emphasizes* only those clips which show these contradictory fascinations. To simulate the wildness of Hollywood's heyday, which the documentary traces, it adopts a fast and furious *pace*.

Hollywood's movies, which have always pandered to America's dreams and fantasies, are the perfect focus for this or any other "social" history. No other source provides a researcher with such an abundance of easily accessible images that convey at a glance a people's fads, fears, and hopes. For a serious history of the United States, film clips would never do, because at best they contain impressionistic recordings, not an accurate account of a period's politics, institutions, religious beliefs, and customs. Yet for a breezy survey of the country's soul, such as this, film clips from the prosperous MGM studios are an ideal focus.

Only the clips of MGM's stars, magnates, and blockbuster films that illustrate the filmmaker's view of America are emphasized. With cogent, literate topic sentences, narrator Dick Cavett introduces each segment of the film—one on MGM's rise, one on the wish-fulfillment films made during the Great Depression, one on Hollywood's strict social hierarchy, etc. He then steps back as the clips prove the documentary's assertions. The social structure of MGM is seen at a glance. We watch stunt men or stand-ins who dream of being discovered one day patiently doing the grit work for their famous counterparts. To show why these dim lights wait around at all, we see footage of Joan Crawford and Clark Gable before and after they were discovered. She was plucked from a chorus line, he from the cast of a grade B movie. We watch travelogues of lavish Hollywood parties and conventions, beginning to understand just how carefully the industry promoted its own self-image. Hollywood's understanding of the country's sexual mores is shown in a quick montage of famous boy meets girl movie clips, followed by hot love and dance scenes that intentionally skirted the line of Hollywood's own moral code. Cavett shows how Hollywood became the world's greatest business enterprise of dream and profit. It was, he says, a place of ultimate American illusions where anything was thought possible. Ruled by ruthless yet sentimental self-made men like MGM's Louis Mayer, the industry's size, success, wealth, and stature grew phenomenally. It fell to ruin just as quickly. Mayer was muscled out, and eventually the grandeur of the backlots at MGM diminished. As the film closes we see once magnificent movie sets and props auctioned off like rusty lawnmowers at two-bit yard sales.

The fast pace of the documentary is suitable to the film's whimsical tone and survey format. Each famous clip is only held long enough to strike a chord of memory in the audience and to make the filmmaker's assertions about America. Even the few lengthier classic film sequences do not seem to alter the speed of the brisk montage. The quick crosscutting is especially effective in suggesting the rise and fall of MGM itself. Within a twinkle, Judy Garland's sparkly red slippers are shown on her feet in the land of Oz, then on the auction block.

VIVE LE TOUR! (New Yorker Films: 18 min./color/1976)

The general topic on the mind of the maker of this film is sports, and his assertion is that athletics and star athletes serve the same functions for society today as heroes and heroic tales did in ancient times. The *focus* is the Tour de France bicycle race, and the *emphasis* is on the reaction of spectators to the cyclists and on the agony and ecstacy of their heroes, who battle nature and human limitations. The film's *pace* can be divided more or less in two. In the first half, the scenes showing the cyclists interacting with the crowds are quick, light, and humorous; in the second half, the pace slows as we see the drama and pain of the riders.

It is hard to imagine a sporting event other than the Tour de France which could be used as the focus for this film's ambitious assertion. What other athletic event has such epic proportions, such tradition, such drama, such spectator participation, and such challenges to human endurance? Even its setting, which takes in the majestic Alps and Pyrenees, seems mythic.

Vive le Tour! is a poet's, not a journalist's, look at the Tour de France. While a journalist might consider the facts of the race—its stars, sponsors, nationalities, course, outcome, history—the poet, or in this case the filmmaker Louis Malle, emphasizes the glory of the race, the valiant struggle of the participants, and the thrill of the spectators. Facts about the race are included, but not stressed. The film emphasizes the mythic struggles of man versus nature and man versus self, and the role the yearly spectacle serves in the lives of the common people. The first half of the film shows people of all sorts in the audience being united and entertained by the spectacle and high jinks of the riders. In the latter half, the spectators are shown suffering with those riders who fail and surging to help and cheer on their heroes who defeat the mighty racecourse.

In the faces and actions of the spectators, we see the entertainment and unity the Tour brings into their lives. Elders, children, nuns, priests, whole families don paper hats announcing their favorites, flash the thumbs up sign, and applaud the racers from both sides of the narrow European lanes. Parades with floats are held in honor of the race. Cafe owners allow the thirsty cyclists to rush into their establishments, rifle their shelves for bottles of liquid, and leave without paying for them. (The Tour reimburses the owners later.) Locals bring out their garden hoses to wet down the overheated cyclists. Everyone unites to support the riders, and all come alive in the carnival atmosphere the Tour brings to their town. As the race becomes more grueling, the heroism of the athletes is emphasized. Even those who pass out while riding or continue while injured are celebrated for their valor, not questioned for their lack of discretion. When one rider falls, huge pileups result—some bikes are destroyed, riders are injured, but many continue, somehow. One rider fractures his skull in such a fall and is rushed to hospital via helicopter. Another, perhaps under the influence of forbidden drugs, pushes himself until he collapses, then remounts with the help of the race officials, then collapses again and is taken away in an ambulance. In one moving scene, we see a bloody-faced cyclist being treated by a man leaning out of a speeding car that keeps pace with the injured but determined rider. Never does the film allow us to question the race because of its tragedies. They are presented as an integral part of the contest.

Nowhere is the heroic function of the riders more apparent than at the close of the film. Struggling through the mountains above the treeline, in and out of clouds, the riders seem like heroes and gods. Here at 5,000 to 9,000 feet, the cyclists stuff newspapers under their shirts to keep warm. And here, the tradition of pushing takes place. Although it is supposedly forbidden by the rules, spectators briefly push some of the struggling riders up the steep inclines. Through pushing, the spectators vicariously become part of the heroic struggle, as ancient men did by hearing epics sung; they suffer with the riders and enjoy or share in their sense of achievement. The leaders or star riders are never pushed, however. These are the gods of the race, the ideal athletes; to push them would be sacrilegious. Their exalted position is made clear by the final sequences of the film. In ones and twos the leaders are shown descending the mountains, their brakes screaming plaintively. They appear like spirits out of the dense clouds. Then the camera focuses on the lean, drenched, and pained faces of the leaders and in brief flashing crosscuts shows the three winners holding bouquets over their heads as they acknowledge the applause of the stadium full of admirers.

The film's pace builds like the race itself. Over half the film is upbeat, light, fast. The crowds cheer and picnic; reporters cover the race from speeding motorcycles. The cyclists collect their knapsacks of food from race officials every three hours and toss the bags onto the road and into the crowd. Subtly, the pace begins to change as we are told that riders can lose up to nine pounds a day and that speeds at the end of a lap approach 40 miles per hour. Riders shown at the end of a lap look miserable; they talk very seriously about the race—no one smiles; streaks of salt and spittle line their faces. The pace then slows as the tragedies and accidents of the race are shown. Then the pace quickens briefly, showing that the tragedies are only part of the picture, as the riders reach the mountains and the light-hearted tradition of pushing is shown. Finally, at the very end, the movie races pell-mell. The leaders are shown descending the foggy mountain, the camera jumps from one dripping slender face to another, then crosscuts rapid-fire to the stadium where the three winners hold bouquets aloft and enjoy the cheers of their admirers.

Vive le Tour! is a paean to the heroics of sport. Focusing on the Tour de France, the filmmakers intentionally ignore the mechanics of the race, emphasizing instead the glory of the cyclist's ritual struggle against human limitations and the benefit the community receives as a witness of the contest. By carefully manipulating the pace of the film, the makers give us vicarious pleasures, too, in an effort to make us say, "Mishaps be damned, Vive le Tour!"

FOLLOW-UP ACTIVITIES

1. Select a feature story in a newspaper, such as one found in the "Living" or "Home" section. In your analysis of the story, identify who or what is being focused on, what aspects are being emphasized, and what the pacing of the piece is. Determine why the author chose the particular focus, emphasis, and pacing.

2. The topics from the films in this section are:
   a. zoos
   b. bicycle racing
   c. welfare for single mothers
   d. Eskimos
   e. Hollywood

   In *The Readers' Guide to Periodical Literature*, find at least three articles on one of the topics. Compare the approach to focus, emphasis, and pacing in the three articles. You can do this most economically if you prepare a chart. Be specific: what is the focus? what is the emphasis?

3. Using one or two elderly people that you know and can interview as your focus, develop your own assertion and write a feature article on one of the problems facing the aged, such as:
   a. social security
   b. Medicare and Medicaid payments
   c. nursing homes and housing
   d. crime
   e. adaptive equipment needed to function independently

   Your interviewee will supply the details to help you achieve the emphasis you want.

4. Compare the pacing found in an article in two or more of the following:
   a. *National Geographic*
   b. the "Travel" section of the Sunday newspaper
   c. John Muir's *The Yosemite* (Garden City, NY: Doubleday & Co., 1962)
   d. Henry David Thoreau's *A Week on the Concord and Merrimack Rivers* (New York: New American Library, 1961)
   e. *Yankee Magazine*

   Determine *why* the author chose a particular pace for the work.

5. Note, as well, in the "Travel" section of the newspaper the number of places that offer free material explaining why one should visit there. Send away. You will receive some very skillfully written material that illustrates focus, emphasis, and pacing.

ORIGINALITY

Originality in art soon becomes cliché. The inventor of the "Tortoise and the Hare" fable no doubt amazed his audience. After delighting in the ironic ending, the listeners (common sense insists they were adults) probably reflected on its truth, which hung with them well into the next day: the slow sometimes does outdistance the fast. The fablemaker, who was feeling a bit impish when he told the story, shook his head with bemusement, we can imagine. Over a bottle of wine that night, he was a little smug. Then awareness struck him like Zeus' thunder: he could change the characters and situations and use the story almost infinitely. The handsome suitor may be rejected for a plainer man; the strong warrior is sometimes bested by the weaker one; the sophist can be tripped up by the student. It seemed to the fabulist that he could invent stories without even thinking now: he could imitate himself.

Today, alas, the story is not quite so compelling. What was once fresh, now seems trite because so many have imitated it. What was unique at one time may seem simply bizarre or foolish at another because of a change in the culture. Originality requires a genuinely fresh approach or insight in combination with skilled writing and sound judgment if it is going to last. There is no doubting audience hunger for the unique. The works of Blake, Shakespeare, and Rabelais still move us as if each never had a thousand imitators. But every era has also had to endure its versions of pop art, op art, participational theater, automatic writing, and 3D movies, all now lying in aesthetic junkyards with religious heresies and nineteenth century utopian theories. Most discerning readers are skeptical enough to agree with Ecclesiastes that "there is nothing new under the sun." Only the truly and meaningfully unique will capture the lasting attention most writers seek.

Obviously there are no rules or formulas for being original, though some suggestions may be helpful. 1) A writer can make us see an old idea in a new way. For example, he or she can change the traditional point of view in a tale or a theory to have us find something different in the material. John Gardner has retold the opening section of *Beowulf* through the monster's, rather than the hero's, eyes in his novel *Grendel* (New York: Ballantine Books, 1971) and has made the beast more sympathetic than the Geat strong man. Exploring the theory of evolution in his short story collection *Cosmicomics* (New York: Harcourt Brace Jovanovich, 1965), Italo Calvino tells stories in which a fish, a mollusk, and a dinosaur become for the first time protagonists and narrators of material from scientific texts. These prehistoric creatures shed new light on the problems of twentieth century humans.

2) Finding an unusual, but organic, structure for a work's ideas is so rarely done that the achievement is always original. Samuel Beckett's *Waiting for Godot* (New York: Grove Press, 1954) captures through its form the confusion, absurdity, and pointlessness of life. Events in the play are not connected by cause and effect; actions have no logical motives and produce no consequences; the characters are unable to understand themselves or what goes on around them. The absurdity the play discusses is the absurdity that it creates. Though different in every respect, T. H. White's *Once and Future King* (New York: Berkley Publishing Corp., 1958) accomplishes the same feat. He recasts Malory's romance in the form of the modern novel. White is primarily concerned with showing that the brutality, injustice, and oppression of feudal times are still present today. Having Merlin travel backward in time to Arthur's court so that he can describe such twentieth century phenomena as fascism and communism, and giving many of the characters modern, at times slang-filled, dialogue facilitates the exploration of White's theme. By emphasizing details and his characters' thoughts at the expense of action, the author describes how social institutions can corrupt, cause pain, and destroy hopes.

3) Works that make abstract concepts concrete in a vivid way are original because they take the theories out of the textbooks and project them into real life. Jorge Luis Borges does this with the idea of luck or fate in his "Lottery of Babylon," a short story in the collection *Labyrinths* (New York: New Directions, 1964). Everyone in Babylon engages in a lottery in which each person's future—anything from the achievement of a wish or sudden wealth to imprisonment, torture, and death—is determined by the drawing of lottery tickets. No one is certain who is in charge of the game, and people often take fate into their own hands by issuing counterfeit decrees to take vengeance on an enemy. Voltaire's *Candide* is original in this sense. His tale—an adventure, horror, and love story that is also a satire—is a working out of

philosopher Gottfried Leibniz's highly generalized tenet, "Everything works out for the best in this best of all possible worlds," in order to mock it. As Candide and his cohorts are pointlessly whacked about, frustrated, and humiliated time and time again, the reader realizes the shallow insensitivity of the philosopher's contention.

4) Sometimes an author's idea, not the form or structure of the work, is original. An artist can take a very unusual or banal topic and show its universal significance. Virginia Woolf, for example, tells the life of Elizabeth Barrett Browning's dog in her novel, *Flush* (New York: Harcourt Brace Jovanovich, 1961). She provides insight into the famous poet while maintaining the story's focus on the pet. She delves into the master-pet relationship to reveal Browning's internal strength (despite her sickly condition) and to show a parallel between the curtailments of her instinctual needs and those of "man's best friend." John Barth's short story "Petition," from the collection *Lost in the Funhouse* (New York: Bantam Books, 1969), also falls into this category. This tale of Siamese twins, told through the eyes of one, uncovers conflicting elements in the human mind, man's dark and light sides. Thomas Huxley uses a piece of chalk to demonstrate the theory of evolution in his essay "A Piece of Chalk," (New York: Oriole Editions, no date). The essay demonstrates the medieval notion, in a sense revived by biologists in the past century and a half, that the macrocosm—or the universe in general—is reflected in the microcosm—individual objects and organisms.

Naturally, the student should not be expected to produce another *Grendel*. The hope is that the films in this unit, the books recommended, and his or her own writing experiments will get the imagination working and demonstrate that the usual limitations of the real world do not apply to literature. The student should begin to develop his or her own concept of originality and learn to distinguish between those inspirations that have creative potential and those that are just bizarre and imitative. The films, essays, stories, and novels will show how an author works with a unique conception to make it meaningful.

POWERS OF TEN (Eames: 8 min./color/1968)

A camera aimed at a sleeping man from one meter above moves progressively back to explore deep space, then returns to examine a carbon atom inside his skin. The result is the sudden awareness that two magnificent universes, one macro-, the other micro-, exist beyond the world we normally perceive. *Powers of Ten* dramatizes how our view of the world changes when our field of vision is dramatically widened or narrowed. In comparison, the fantastic visions of the medieval alchemists pale. The earth, seemingly so large to a single person, is lost in a muddle of stars and galaxies as the camera recedes. Conversely, a single carbon atom, unnoticed in the skin of a person, is revealed as a vast world when seen close up. The film illustrates abstract concepts and converts science into an art. There is no meaning beyond the concepts demonstrated; the originality is in the way beautiful and wondrous abstractions are made concrete.

The basic premise of the film seems simple enough. A camera starting from one meter above a man increases its distance by one power of 10 (10 meters, 100 meters, 1,000 meters, etc.) every 10 seconds. At 100 meters (10 to the third power) the man is barely visible. At 10,000 meters (the distance a supersonic jet can travel in 10 seconds) the outline of the Florida coast is in view. At one million meters (10 to the sixth power), the entire earth is in view (at 10 to the eighth the earth will be gone from sight). The camera must move at 99.93% of the speed of light to cover the distance between 10 billion meters (10 to the eighth) and 100 billion (10 to the ninth) in 10 seconds. When the distance is 10 to the nineteenth power, the entire Milky Way—a swirling cloud of luminous gases in which no individual star can be distinguished—is in view. By 10 meters to the twenty-first power, 210 seconds have elapsed; during that time, 100,000 years have passed on earth. The Milky Way, at 10 to the twenty-third, is a tiny speck of light among several in a sky of almost total darkness. Space at this perspective is nearly a void.

At 10 to the twenty-fourth, the camera reverses toward earth, covering each power of magnitude in two seconds. Space on the way back in is alternately empty and filled with glowing bodies (star clusters, stars, and finally planets). The camera stops at 10 centimeters from the sleeping man and moves closer by one magnitude (called negative powers of 10 because each is a decrease in distance) every 10 seconds. At 10 centimeters to the minus three power, the camera, which is looking through a microscope, examines a capillary in a field of one millimeter. At 10 to the minus sixth, the field of vision is one micron (a millionth of a meter), and chromosomes appear. The four electrons of the outer shell of a carbon atom are seen at 10 to the minus ninth, the inner shell of 10 electrons at 10 to the minus tenth. A great void, seemingly as vast as deepest space, is shown at 10 to the minus eleventh. An "unimaginably dense nucleus of a carbon atom" comes into view, the six protons and six neutrons swirling about each other with great speed and energy.

Relativity of space and time, the geometric progression of distance and numbers when multiplied by exponential powers, the vastness of cosmic space, the complexities of organisms and matter are the abstractions explored by this film. Knowledge of them in varying degrees is possessed by most people, but few are aware of the significance of these concepts in everyday life. Recognizing that significance and translating it into concrete terms is the film's originality. *Powers of Ten* makes scientific truth beautiful.

BEAD GAME (Pyramid Films: 6 min./color/1977)

In this animated film, a single bead is seen against a black background as an Indian tambour plays a primitive beat. The bead multiplies; the resultant beads spin around each other, unite, separate, and then join in a struggle that is both a dance and a fight as the beat continues. From these original bead creatures more complex forms evolve to continue the dance-fight. When they change into a primitive shell-fish and another underwater creature, *Bead Game* identifies itself as a story of evolution expressed in beads that are representative of living cells. But it is not the subject matter that makes this movie different. Rather, it is the concretizing of an abstract scientific concept and the rendering of an old idea anew that make it unique. The beads point out something we often ignore when contemplating evolution: through the deadly trial and error of survival of the fittest, nature produces great splendor.

The evolution depicted in the film is not altogether factual; both real and imaginary beings take part in the development of life. The bright beads, like paint on a pallet, suggest that evolution is nature's art form, which, though crude and violent, has produced wonders. The organisms do not simply devour each other; they absorb one another and merge as well. A fish-like creature with an almost human face consumes a dinosaur. One creature penetrates an egg, leaving the audience to wonder which one has overcome the other. From this clash, a magnificent bird emerges. A fight between two mammals is a whirl of changing life forms; a buffalo, a lion, and a tiger materialize from the confusion. When the buffalo arises triumphant and changes into an ape, the viewer knows that man's time is near. The ape shatters an egg with a rock, the first tool.

The evolutionary dance fight continues with man and his machines. After two primitive men duel with fists and clubs, a familiar renaissance symbol appears: a naked man inside a circle, which represents human domination of the cosmos. Soldiers with spears give way to men with shields and swords who fight on horseback and in chariots. Cannons and guns, then bombs and missiles decimate armies and cities. A man seizes an atom and hides behind a rock (presumably to keep this new power to himself and protect him from a nuclear explosion). A magnificent nuclear explosion of colored beads blends into trees and flowers. A last image shows an atom spinning inside the hands of a man whose fingers hold a cat's cradle. The human intellect is the most potent evolutionary force; we can put an end to the dazzling display of life, or refine nature's art and produce unparalleled wonders.

Though the moral message of *Bead Game* is not new, the film's overall conception and form are. Using mythological creatures to represent extinct life forms and to imply that evolution is an art forces the audience to rethink its relationship to nature. The beads themselves, whose many combinations are the development of life over time, make Darwin's theory—so remote in the textbooks—concrete, immediate, and beautiful.

TOYS (McGraw-Hill Contemporary Films: 8 min./color/1966)

A toy store provides the setting in this film for a look at how innocence in children is destroyed by adults. Opening shots show youngsters talking and laughing in front of the store window while they point to the playthings as if selecting the ones they want the most. Lively music adds to their happy mood. Their bright faces are reflected in the window. The camera pans to reveal the stuffed figures most suited to their gentle nature: a teddy bear, a clown, dolls, a roaring lion, a squawking parrot. The mood abruptly changes when they spot war toys in another section of the display window: a jeep with a cannon, a tank, soldiers with guns. The children sense the seriousness of what they see and grow silent, their faces tense. What ensues is a bloody battle among the soldiers. The message of *Toys* is not new; sociologists have long argued that military toys encourage violence among the young and a premature acceptance of the tribal war ethic. What is original about the film is the way it presents its message. Rather than an impassioned plea or a social survey, the film adopts the form of a battle to condemn the toys it believes corrupt the young.

The make-believe battle is at first exciting, then horrifying and disgusting. The soldiers array themselves into two armies, one on a plain, the other in the surrounding hills. As the opening music stops, planes drop bombs; soldiers hurl hand grenades; toy men die. After fierce combat, night descends on the snow-covered landscape, and the two armies grimly wait. The onlooking children are no longer laughing, but confused and disturbed. A searchlight prowls the ground, which is littered with battered equipment, revealing a dead body floating in a puddle, and armed men in gas masks. The light spies one of the "enemy." There is an explosion and a cry. The man is enveloped in flames; his plastic body melts. Magically, the soldiers, planes, and tanks are next seen in their original spot in the display window; they are whole again as if the battle never took place. The music resumes, lively as before. But the children seem subtly changed; they talk in subdued voices, their former joy arrested by an awareness of war. We cannot help but feel that toys have given them a knowledge they would be better off without.

The message is old; the form used to present it is new and stunning. *Toys* shows how children can be corrupted by adult society and its commercial institutions. It hardly matters if we have heard it all before; an idea presented in a fresh way explodes the cliché and startles us into seeing an old truth anew.

SORT OF A COMMERCIAL FOR AN ICEBAG (Benchmark Films: 16 min./ color/1973)

Modern art is nothing if not a target for controversy. Critics and laypersons alike debate over girders twisted into unrecognizable shapes, sheets spread over miles of the California coast, and paint-splashed canvases. Are these objects art? Staunch proponents say that any object is beautiful if liberated from a utilitarian perspective. The environment abounds in form and texture, the stuff of creative expression. The freed imagination must point out to the world what, in its dulled sensitivity, it misses. Indignant opponents bristle. What, they ask, is the point of such works? Do their makers demonstrate any skill? *Sort of a Commercial for an Icebag* makes hay out of the controversy by documenting Claes Oldenburg's transformation of an ordinary icebag into sculpture. As we take sides, raise weapons, and fire away at each other, Oldenburg soberly contemplates the difficulties of icebag art with an infuriating, Alfred E. Neuman obliviousness. But after a while we realize that he is, in part, playing with us, that the pose is as much ironic as serious. Just as there can be no western without guns, the brawl has become a part of the spectacle of modern art. When the smoke clears, Oldenburg and the film have achieved originality, both of content and form. They have not only shown the artistic potential of an inconsequential object, but have also made a film that is just as problematic and exasperating as its subject.

Oldenburg says that his first intention was to create a sculpture that combines soft and hard features in an outdoor site. In recounting his search for the appropriate subject, he handles a sponge, a tomato, a balloon, a plastic breast, and cookies, but gets his inspiration for the proper texture and color—light red or pink—from lox. Finally, the elasticity of a beanbag leads him to the icebag, which in its ability to rotate, twist, and move up and down adds motion to the original concept. Oldenburg dons an icebag-shaped cap and imitates the potential motion with his head, torso, legs, and arms. Machinery will make it move, giving it a life of its own. He says that his sculpture is not really about an icebag, but about the behavior of materials under tension and release. Is he serious, we wonder? Should we laugh or take notes?

Oldenburg's imagination is stimulated by the icebag, and his sculpture is, at times, strangely beautiful. But his opponents might argue that, like Frankenstein's monster or the Blob, each is out of control. The bag, Oldenburg says without so much as a smile, is like a living animal, a fish that has just been caught, a stomach. Illuminated by soft light, its slowly twisting silver cap looks like a glowing moon. Five bags will be constructed, each 18 by 11 feet, he thinks out loud, but even better, it would be nice if 150 of them were placed along the main air route from New York to Los Angeles. We watch an icebag fall from the sky, presumably dropped from an airplane.

The preposterous suggestions continue, but we cannot help but marvel at the way it forces us to see the environment in a new way. A bag in a city is dwarfed by skyscrapers, one in a desert rests alone in the sand, another floats eerily underwater sending bubbles to the surface like that creature that came from beneath the sea. Using a photograph, Oldenburg shows what it would look like in the piazza of Saint Peter's Cathedral, "where the cupola and the bag would work together." The bag was planned for a street corner in Ohio. As the soundtrack plays a recording of two cars crashing, Oldenburg tells us it was rejected because of its association with headaches and because it would block motorists' view of oncoming traffic. The sculpture has become hydra-like: every time one of its original associations or purposes is rejected, one or more new ones present themselves. Oldenburg now says that his bag is the shape of a head and an upside down fountain, the study of an image in relation to its environment, more of a structural form softened than an actual icebag.

The headache association, emphasized by the cap worn on Oldenburg's head, is one of the few keys to the film. The sculptor says that he does not mind the association with headaches, but not all of us will feel as he does. Thoroughly flogged, we may find the film and the sculpture comic, provocative, or insulting—all personal responses are alright with Oldenburg, as they are with any artist of his ilk. An image of his art in the flesh, Oldenburg makes it impossible to feel secure in our understanding of him. Is he making fun of modern art or educating us about its theories? Is he a wild eccentric or a genius? Is his imagination chaotic or liberated? Oldenburg impishly surrenders himself to the icebag and leaves the questions to us. The film chooses not to help us with the answers, but instead gives itself over to the artist. Both a satire and an encomium, *Sort of a Commercial for an Icebag* becomes its own subject; it is modern sculpture in celluloid.

THE SONNETS: SHAKESPEARE'S MOODS OF LOVE (Learning Corp. of America: 21 min./color/1972)

Poetic analysis is a hotbed of originality. Because its language is so compact and suggestive, a single poem can produce a score of different views, many of them attracting attention by their strangeness, their author's contorted attempts to appear inspired and unique. Shakespeare's sonnets have always challenged the critics. Who is the dark lady or the young male to whom some of the poems are addressed? Is the speaker Shakespeare himself or a fictional voice reacting to imaginary dramatic situations? Are the poems mere exercises in craft, using a popular form and traditional themes as an excuse for poetic flash, or is Shakespeare speaking from the heart? The answers abound. By positing a concrete speaker, audience, and dramatic situation, *Moods of Love* limits the interpretation to its own unique perspective. It arranges 10 of the sonnets into a story of the "eternal triangle" and employs modern clothes and props to suggest the poems are timeless. As the actors dramatize the words, the viewer ignores Shakespeare's twists of word and thought, as well as sonnet conventions, to concentrate on the theme of love. For the filmmaker, ambiguity, form, and technique are not the routes to the unique. Originality is defined here as the new interpretation.

Sonnet interpretation is most strikingly limited in the film's fourth poem, "Two Loves I Have of Comfort and Despair" (sonnet 144). The first three poems introduce the inner conflict of the speaker, a middle-aged man who (as suggested by his home and clothes) has achieved economic success, but now worries over matters of the heart. Respectively, he praises his wife's human—as opposed to a heavenly—beauty (sonnet 130), contemplates from afar the vitality of his young friend in contrast to his own aging (sonnet 104), and advises the friend to reproduce his own beauty through marriage (sonnet 3). In this love triangle, the film's fourth sonnet's good and bad angels become metaphors for the young man and the wife. The speaker thinks that the woman (the bad angel) has seduced and stolen the friend (the good angel). The accusation, however, is only a suspicion, as lines 11 through 13 indicate,

> But being both from me, both to each friend,
> I guess one angel in another's hell.
> Yet this shall I ne'er know, but live in doubt.

In his imagination, the two no longer find him attractive, and their affair might as well be a reality. This interpretation runs counter to the traditional ones and ignores an Elizabethan convention, the fighting of two angels over a man's soul (*Everyman*, *Dr. Faustus*, et al.). The opening lines,

> Two loves I have of comfort and despair,
> Which like two spirits do suggest me still . . .

imply that the conflict is internal, between good and evil. In a broader (admittedly less defensible) view, the two angels are polarities within the artist, his purity in opposition with an inner perversity (seen as pride) that corrupts his poetry. The artist will not recover creative tranquility until the perversity has run its course, "till my bad angel fire my good one out" (line 14). The film gives the poem a different, more modern psychological truth. The affair, whether real or imagined, symbolizes the speaker's yearning for youthful virility, the need to feel worthy of love.

The other poems follow the same pattern. Conventions in force at Shakespeare's time as well as accepted interpretations are cast aside. The last poem (sonnet 71) is a death fantasy. Shakespeare tells his lover not to mourn for him when he dies, but to forget him and live in the real world. In the film the interpretation is quite different. The wife kneels at the speaker's gravestone as his voice recites the poem. The young male touches the woman's shoulder to comfort her. Surrealistically, the roles then change: in rapid shots each of the three takes turns at being the mourner, the comforter, and the dead. The love triangle, divisive on the surface, actually brings them together. This is not a tale of jealousy triumphant, not the medieval tragedy of Tristan, Mark, and Iseult. The characters deal with their inhibitions; they learn to reach out to, rather than close themselves off from, each other. Loneliness, jealousy, and death play havoc with everyone; love is the only solace, despite the trauma.

If on nothing else, critics agree that timelessness is one test of greatness. Like a master jeweler, the filmmaker fits famous (precious) stones into a new setting. Much of the action takes place in a twentieth century version of a Tudor home; the rest, in a countryside that evokes the feeling of sixteenth century England. In contrast with the Elizabethan ambience, such props as cigarettes, a watch (symbolizing the relationship between love and death fears), and a hair brush, as well as modern clothes, secure the bond between Shakespeare and now. Similarly, the reordering of the sonnets in the "love triangle" plot fastens them to the filmmaker's vision. The film molds for the multi-faceted poet another face. Originality may be achieved by seeing the old in a new, compelling way. For now, this is the standard against which *Moods of Love* will have to be criticized.

FOLLOW-UP ACTIVITIES

1. Begin your search for the unique in your own environment. A story told by a relative, a cherished possession, or a common object around the home, may provide the inspiration you need. For example, you may want to describe your family from the perspective of your goldfish—who seems to be swimming in oblivion, but is actually feeling each household tension in its own way. An approach such as this allows you the freedom to let your mind make observations while the familiar characters and surroundings provide a framework to make the story universal and accessible.

2. Much fantasy writing is imitative and formulaic. Witches, magic swords, poltergeists, and vampires have been the stuff of stories for centuries. The test of uniqueness is not the distance between an idea and reality, but what the author does to an idea to make it succeed. There is more to originality than

simply pulling a hare out of a hat. Posit a person who has no magical or super-natural abilities living in a world of Time Travelers, people with telekinetic power, supernatural characteristics, and the ability to change shape. For all of these, the person with no "power" is terrifying! Explore the situation and show why our "normalcy" can be so frightening.

3. Teachers have been telling you for years what a book is *really* about. Take a work that is totally straight-forward and offer a "new" or symbolic interpre-tation of the book. You might reinterpret: any of the Hardy Boys' adventures, any of the Judy Bloom books, any of the Pippa Longstocking works, or any of the adventures of Winnie the Pooh.

4. Take an abstract concept such as "truth is eternal," or "some march to a dif-ferent drummer," or "justice will out," and compose a concrete dramatic situation that will either satirize or praise the concept.

5. Study the painting or etching of a human face, such as:
   "The Scream" by Munch
   "Mona Lisa" by Leonardo da Vinci
   "Self-Portrait" by da Vinci
   "Self-Portrait" by Van Gogh.

Decide what the cause of the look on the face is, and write a monologue from the *portrait*'s point of view.

APPROPRIATENESS OF STRUCTURE, DETAILS, AND TRANSITIONS

There is a great deal of hard work on the author's part between getting an idea for an essay and executing the finished product. At the very beginning, the author must decide what organization will best suit the purpose of the essay. Once the writer has chosen the structure that will allow for the idea's fullest expression, he or she selects the details that will support the idea or make it vivid. Finally, during the actual writing, the essayist must carefully guide the reader from sentence to sentence, from paragraph to paragraph with transitions. Without transitions, the best thought in the world will appear to be clumsy. At each point in the writing process, the author must be flexible enough to rethink, to cast aside, to simplify, or—the ultimate horror—to rewrite completely. Once the author has found the appropriate structure, details, and transitions, he or she will accomplish the task, and the audience might even be impressed by the technique.

The structure of an essay reflects the purpose (*see* "Purpose," page 249) and emphasis (*see* "Focus, Emphasis, and Pacing," page 198) of the author. There are a number of traditional structures at an author's disposal for achieving different goals. 1) A narrative or story allows the author to entertain the audience in the process of making a point. Through the drama of opposition, suspense, and climax, the author seeks to elicit emotional responses. 2) An episodic structure indicates that all sections potentially have equal value, even though the author will make distinctions and stress certain aspects. One example of the episodic is a time sequence of events, as is found in biography, history, or process writing. There can also be a series of items connected by an idea, category, situation, or location. 3) A relationship arrangement—the essay in which the author begins with a premise and proves a point with evidence—stresses interpretation or points out interrelationships. This structure is found in cause-and-effect, comparison-and-contrast, purpose-and-result, and deductive (general to specific) and inductive (specific to general) writing. 4) There are also experimental approaches to writing, such as the probe wherein the author deliberately does not follow through on all the implications of the material or try to have transitions, but presents provocative material and then forces the reader to react. In such juxtaposition, for instance, the author does not spell out what is on his or her mind, but wants the "thinking" to be done by the audience.

The films in this chapter illustrate the types of structure discussed above. *Prisoners of Chance* uses three exempla or stories to prove a point about teenage sex. *Cider Maker* is episodic and offers the process of cider making and a glimpse at the old-time rural life. *Mary Cassatt* through its episodic structure presents not only a number of portfolios of her art, but also her biography. *Growing Up Female* stresses the cause-and-effect relationship between the lives of women at various ages and the values of the culture in order to show that sexist values may limit and hurt her. *Faneuil Hall Markets* utilizes the experimental structure of constant juxtaposition to make a comparison between the past and the present and to prove that urban redevelopment is essential to revive worn-out cities. Each film has a structure that successfully accomplishes the filmmaker's purpose.

No matter how good the structure is, the details the author uses are vital to the effectiveness of the essay. Paraphrasing George Orwell, all details might be equal, but some are more equal than others. For the young writer, there are six warnings, concerning the appropriateness of details. 1) The writer should use major, not minor, examples to prove a point. Too often, the student will concentrate on some small, insignificant item and ignore the material that is crucial. 2) Conversely, small details in description are best as long as the writer presents a clear picture of the entire scene being described. 3) There should be enough detail to convince, but not so much as to bore. Most teachers believe in the "Law of Three": in opinion essays, if the writer offers three examples to support a generalization, the audience usually feels the author has proven the point. 4) The writer should use details that correspond to the opinion and the attitude of the author or mood of the piece. If the writer is praising the subject, the details should support this attitude. 5) In objective writing, there must be a balancing of details. More or less the same amount of time (and words) should be spent on each item. Again, if the author is objectively giving the pluses and minuses of an issue, there should be an equal number of both. The author is definitely showing slant if either the positive or negative side of an issue is over-weighted with detail. 6) The author should point details toward the topic sentence. In other words, the author must show how each detail or quotation connects to the original assertion.

As the author writes, he or she must also make connections between details, sentences, and paragraphs. In school, the student learns to have the order of the proof parallel to the order of the ideas as stated in the topic paragraph. Each new paragraph starts with a sentence that clearly identifies the section of the topic under discussion. This approach is necessary for any pressure writing in class, but does not produce the smoothest writing possible. The "Law of Transition" is that the writer be like the Roman god Janus and look both backward and forward. Ideally, the writer forces the reader to take note of what he or she has done, indicates briefly the relationship of the new material to the previous, and then moves on. Perhaps the most paradoxical thing about transitions is that when they are done well, they do not call attention to themselves. In general, most transitions between details, sentences, or paragraphs, can be accomplished briefly through a connecting word or phrase such as the ones that follow:

Situation	Transition Word(s)
All items have the same value	and
	in addition
Information is in a series	first, second, third . . .
	first, next, later, finally
	in the beginning, during, at the end
Initial information is modified, contradicted, negated	but
	unfortunately
	yet
	on the contrary
Emphasis is on the relationship between initial and subsequent information	consequently
	therefore
	hence
	accordingly
	similarly
	likewise
Additional information is given on the same topic	moreover
	furthermore
	also
	besides

Repetition is another transition technique. For example, the author can start a new paragraph by repeating the name of the person or thing that is the subject.

Reading can be helpful in showing how appropriateness of structure, detail, and transition contribute to the effectiveness of an essay. The following books exhibit a wide variety of approaches to these skills: Richard Selzer's *Mortal Lessons* (New York: Simon and Schuster, 1976) stresses the narrative. Edward Trapunski's *Special When Lit: A Visual and Anecdotal History of Pinball* (New York: Doubleday and Co., 1979) uses an episodic approach that stresses history, personal anecdotes, and atmosphere. Alan W. Watts' *The Way of Zen* (New York: Random House, 1957) shows that a difficult subject can be made quite clear through a historical survey of a concept. Barry Holstun Lopez wants to change the opinion of his audience about wolves in *Of Wolves and Men* (New York: Scribner's, 1978) and is convincing in his episodic gathering of material about the animal. The traditional essay structure with cause-and-effect relationships is employed in Paul Goodman's *Growing Up Absurd* (New York: Random House, 1960). Marshall McLuhan and Quentin Fiore produced in *The Medium Is the Massage* (New York: Bantam, 1967) an experimental "probe" work.

PRISONERS OF CHANCE (FilmFair Communications: 23.25 min./color/1979)

The "prisoners of chance" in this film, based on fact, are teenagers who have had to deal with premarital pregnancy. Basically, the structure consists of three interviews, each of which presents a different resolution of the problem. Maureen remained single and gave her baby up for adoption. Lynn, still single, kept her baby but soon had interference from her mother in raising the child. Anna married Rick when she became pregnant, but they have been forced by economic reasons to separate, and she has returned to her parents' home. The three exempla show the various problems facing those willing to "take a chance." The message of the film is delivered by Rick: "If I had it to do over again, I would have waited." To bring home this point, details are carefully selected to show the negative aspects of the three situations. The transitions connect sequences smoothly, and in themselves make an important contribution to the film's message.

Obviously, the details supporting an interdiction will stress the punishment that will result from breaking the commandment. A home movie shows Maureen's cute 18-month-old baby playing with a beach ball. The film is allowed to run out as the narrator tells us she put her baby up for adoption. The brief scrap of film is all Maureen has left. The device emphasizes the emotional pull of the separation on the mother. In Lynn's case, the emphasis is on the child's constant demands as she changes him, tries to stop him from crying, comforts him, and plays with him on the carpet. She admits, "Sometimes I even hate him . . . I wish I could come home and he wouldn't be there. . . ." The film vividly captures the claustrophobia she feels from the baby. A sound of irritation comes into her voice as she tells the crying child, "Don't be so paranoid." The crying does not stop; she continues to try to calm him down; both mother and child maintain their hostility. Lynn never lets Greg, the father, see the child because of his insulting comments and behavior when she told him of her pregnancy. Greg tells us he would like to see if the baby looks like him (a fairly egotistic motivation), but he felt he was "off the hook" when Lynn's mother forbade him to come around anymore. In the third case study, at least the two young people love each other—but that seems to be their only asset. Both left school before graduating. Since Rick's job is pumping gas, the young couple has trouble making ends meet. When they try to rent an apartment, the landlord demands a $200.00 security deposit plus two months' rent, a demand that places the apartment out of their reach. The young couple really seem to have tried, but the financial problem was too much for them. The evidence in the film is emotionally and intellectually depressing.

Transitions are clever and set up the emotional pull of each sequence. The camera shows pages from a high school yearbook, then zooms in on a photo of the teenager to be interviewed. At the end of the sequence, we see another photo of the person in the yearbook, more shots, then the next subject. Written comments by classmates help emphasize the isolation of these teenagers from a happy, social existence. The function of a yearbook is to sustain memories, and these pages are reminders of what they have lost. The narrator during the transitions always gives information that further depresses. For instance, Anna wanted to be a fashion designer or model; Rick, a musician. The next scene shows Anna ironing, Rick unable to practice the guitar because it bothers the baby. The contrast further stresses the sense of reduction, of failed possibilities. By themselves, the transition sequences would sell the point of the film.

It is to the film's credit that the narrator does not have a preachy tone and the evidence does not seem heavy-handed. The young people are quite charming, very human, and sympathetic. In fact, they seem to have a great deal of intelligence and cool. The movie convinces us that they could have had successful lives if. . . .

CIDER MAKER (ACI Films, Inc.: 18 min./color/1975)

One purpose of this film is to show how Ellis Apgar in the New Jersey hill country makes apple cider, but the filmmaker is just as interested in the values that Apgar represents, the American belief in personal independence, family togetherness, roots in one place, the pride of the worker in the "homemade" product, and the leisurely pace of the country. For many of us, Apgar's world is linked with Norman Rockwell, Grandma Moses, and even Currier & Ives, those portrayers of a landscape that we, in our busy, modern lives look at with nostalgia. *Cider Maker* captures that world for us. Through the easy flow of Apgar's friendly chat, the film unfolds at a leisurely pace. The structure is episodic; details illustrate the way of life of those romantic olden days of rural America; and transitions are those found in an informal atmosphere.

The sequences are arranged as one would the pearls on a necklace—the larger ones are in the center, the smaller are balanced on the ends. The movie opens with Apgar alone picking apples from the trees; it ends with his son and daughter and their families helping him collect the apples. In the second sequence, we study the family photo album and see Ellis and his wife during their early years together, the horse-drawn carriage, then the auto, the family outings and picnics. Ellis observes that "everybody had lots of time" back then, they were friendlier and not so driven to make money as nowadays. In the next to last sequence of the film, the entire clan sits down to a turkey dinner, says a prayer while the radio is droning on in the background, and enjoys each other's company just like in the old days. The past of the old photos still lives. The core of the film is three sequences. In the first, Ellis shows us the process of making homemade apple cider. The second documents a number of customers helping Ellis out at the press, customers who are being neighborly and, perhaps, acting out a fantasy of life in primitive America. As Ellis says, "People . . . like . . . to keep busy, if possible." The third section makes a nice ecological point that nothing in the homemade process is wasted—the leavings are dried and used as fertilizer, or dairy feed, or winter food for the deer.

Details on cider making show us the process of a homemade product, the way things were done before the factory machines took away human pride in work. All the apples are sent through a brush machine to get rid of leaves and other residue, then they are hand sorted, the larger, nicer ones set aside for roadside sale, the smaller ones for the cider. The cider apples are immersed in water outside the barn, then carried up a small elevator belt; at the top, the apples fall into a grinder. Inside the barn, Apgar spreads the "apple sauce" evenly across a large cloth, carefully folds the cloth to seal in the ground apples, then places the rack on top, and spreads out another cloth. Once the layers of sealed cloths and racks have been built up high enough, Ellis turns on the press that rises and squeezes the juice from the cloths. The cider is forced through a filter and put in kegs. The juice is the real thing, not a chemical concoction of preservatives and taste enhancers. The sequence also shows that one person can run the operation alone, that Ellis can be truly independent.

The down-home atmosphere is partially accomplished through an avoidance of formal essay techniques. No formal connectors are used; instead there are blackouts— the equivalent of triple spacing between paragraphs in writing. The narration is similar to E. B. White's personal farm essays in that the author gives asides while discussing a problem. In the middle of the cider-making process sequence, Apgar delivers a short treatise on the glories of not working on an assembly line—where one does the same small job day after day—and of not having to keep a time schedule. Similarly, during the old photo sequence, Apgar delivers a criticism of modern life with its emphasis on making money and its loss of social encounters during the day. The lack of transitions works because all his opinions are consistent and form a single ideology. Like the rich, autumnal colors of the photography, that leisurely, informal world view is irresistible.

MARY CASSATT—IMPRESSIONIST FROM PHILADELPHIA (Films, Inc.: 30 min./color/1977)

Normally, an art book includes a portfolio of representative works, plus an essay by an authority that contains biographical information, pertinent anecdotes by contemporaries, an analysis of the artist's style, and a critical evaluation. This film has all those ingredients. Its chronology begins in 1874, not the year of Cassatt's birth, but later, at the time of the first exhibit of the Impressionist paintings in France. This sequence accomplishes many things. First, the jokes made then about the exhibit show the condemnation of the style by conservative tastes and function as an attention-getting device. Second, the moment was extremely important in the determination of Cassatt's life because she realized then that her "own work was in agreement with their [the Impressionists'] aims." Third, the section establishes the central thesis of the film: Cassatt had the courage to find a way of expressing herself, her own way even if it meant leaving America and adapting controversial techniques. At the end of this sequence, the film moves to the beginning of Cassatt's life, and the structure is a normal chronology. Details concentrate not on the artist so much as on her artistic career and her defiance of conventions. Actually, the biographical details form the transitions between the extended samplings of her art and the critical approaches to it.

Details carefully prove a central thesis. There is a great deal of information about her battles against the establishment to form her own style and to live her own life. From Cassatt's memoirs comes a typical anecdote. After a salon rejected one of her paintings, she muddied the background, resubmitted it, and they accepted the "new" work. The moral for her was "acceptance on someone else's terms was worse than rejection." Both Anne Dayez, curator of the Impressionist collection in the Louvre, and Adelyn D. Breeskin, curator of the National Collection of Fine Arts, Washington, DC, emphasize how courageous and independent Cassatt was. When she insisted on going to France to pursue her career, her father, one of the socially elite of Philadelphia, told her, "I almost would rather see you dead." She left.

Cassatt's career is divided into the early influence of Degas, the portraits of Lydia, the Mother-Child works, her interest in Japanese art, and the introduction of Impressionism to America, among others. These sections are connected through gossipy biographical information. Thus, a patronizing comment by her brother Alexander about her art leads to the sequence on her relationship to Degas, his influence on her art, his high esteem of her talents, the portraits he painted of her, and their friendship. An interviewer asks Breeskin if they had an affair. The answer is no; Mary Cassatt was a Victorian lady, and her family would have been shocked. Breeskin comments on Cassatt's use of her family as models. We then see the portraits of sister Lydia. Alexander's wife Lois was put off by her sister-in-law, but her children enjoyed their aunt. This family relationship becomes the transition to the Mother-Child works. These transitions obviously have quite a bit of irony: brother mocks and an artist praises; the response of other people's children to Mary leads to the single lady's most famous works, the relationship of the mother to the child.

The film presents the last part of Cassatt's life in a way she would approve—without sentimentality. By 1923, she had lost her dear friend Degas and her sight, but not her courage. An unnamed visitor recounts how the artist held the faces of two children close to her own and observed that she would have enjoyed painting them.

The anecdote captures a final, ironic Mother-Child. The anecdotes are part of the texture of an American life that found fulfillment in another country, a person living alone, but always aware of family, a seeker of controversy whose art exhibits profound serenity.

GROWING UP FEMALE (New Day Films: 50 min./b&w/1971)

This classic film on the socialization of the American female has value for its construction as well as its content. The thesis, that cultural constraints and false values have robbed the American woman of her potential, receives a formal essay presentation with an introduction, six sequences that show different passages in a girl's life (nursery school, the tomboy years, the mid-teens, the early twenties, and the mid-thirties), and a conclusion that recaps the main points of the proof. An abundance of details proves the thesis, and the script carefully connects its "paragraphs" with clear transitions. As a result, the film is more than a powerful work of persuasion, it is an exemplum of good writing.

Made long before Gail Sheehy's *Passages*, *Growing Up Female* argues that the American culture has reduced the possibilities in a woman's life in the various phases of her growth. She is taught by parents and teachers to be "feminine," meaning to curb her enjoyments, to see fulfillment in terms of a male, and to be receptive to his every need. Since success can only mean marriage and children, the girl becomes competitive with other girls over males, and thus has trouble relating to other women. Dissatisfaction with such a life surfaces. Teenaged Terri wants to live someplace else because "the farther away I get, the better it might be." Mrs. Russell, the housewife with three children, a veritable workhorse during the day, sits alone at a table at night and answers "no" to the question, "If I had my life to live over, would I do it the same way?" She has been molded into a type who "attends everyone else's needs except her own."

The audience is convinced through a bombardment of audiovisual proof. We hear such song lyrics from the period as "I will follow him wherever he may go," "Any day now I shall be released," and "The girl that I marry. . . ." A sampling of TV and magazine ads alternates with the interview of an advertising executive (male) who explains the techniques of hooking the female customer. A guidance counselor gives a sermon to Terri on the qualities of an ideal wife, the climax of which is the statement that she should help her husband "to be a healthy, happy, successful man." During this, the camera concentrates on symbols of femininity, the flower-designed Kleenex box, the ornamental dish, the manicured fingernails. The mother of tomboy Ginelle worries that her 12-year-old does not like to wear dresses and is not feminine enough. The mother's bejeweled eyeglasses and fancy sandals show her own signs for femininity. An employer explains that girls make the best key-punch operators (presumably because they are patient, neat, and good at details), but that males do the more important jobs. In contrast, we soon realize that Jessica, who turned down a full college scholarship because she had to support her daughter, is a very bright, articulate woman who has a parts assembly job that uses very little of her ability. The accumulation of such detail is very convincing.

Transitions show a knowledge of and skill in writing conventions. The outstanding transition is between the sequences of Ginelle and Terri. The narrator sums up Ginelle's situation, then concludes "she is on the brink of femininity, but is resisting it . . . In the next few years, something will happen. . . ." The next shot is of Terri and her boyfriend sitting together talking. In effect, the filmmaker has ended a paragraph by introducing an aspect of the next one. At the end of her sequence, a marketing executive discusses the impact of advertising on lifestyle, and concludes that advertisers are now trying to cope with the attitudes of "the flower child, the hippie . . . the hip woman. . . ." Tammie is the next interviewee, and her opening remark is that if she had her choice, right now, she would "probably be in bed with Dave. . . ." She is the hip young woman, and the camera prowls about her room showing that the advertisers have hooked her as well, through her posters, trinkets, and furnishings. At the end of the sequence with Jessica and her daughter is a closeup of Mrs. Russell, who announces she has been married twelve years. This is the only abrupt transition in the film, but it is calculated to show the contrast between the divorced mother and the so-called "happily married" one.

The highest compliment that can be paid a persuasion film is that after a decade, it still works. *Growing Up Female* is a film many of us have grown older teaching, and it still packs a wallop. Its skill and care in construction have been partly responsible.

FANEUIL HALL MARKETS: 1826-1970 (Urbanimage Films: 12 min./color/ 1970)

In 1970, the Faneuil Hall Market was about to undergo a dramatic redevelopment. At that point, things were only at the planning stage. Most of the meat and poultry markets had already posted closing or moving signs. In this film, Monsignor Francis J. Lally, the chairperson of the Boston Redevelopment Authority at the time of the film, stresses that the Authority will "use the old in a thoroughly modern way" in order to make a place that people can relate to and that will be a "living part of the city." The film captures Lally's aims through its technique of juxtaposition, one that has been popular in films since McLuhan's *The Medium Is the Massage* and that suggests energy, intelligence, and hipness. Constant juxtaposition might sharply contrast past and present, but it also soon makes them appear to be harmonious. Since the technique forces the audience to concentrate on details and to make connections (otherwise there would just be confusion), images become highly connotative. The details in this film—the people of the market, archive photography, the blighted look of the area just before redevelopment—have emotional overtones that help to sell Lally's point. The formal structure is juxtaposition. There are no transitions between the film's four sections: the reason for the change, the origin of the market, the heyday of the market, and the current changeover. Like the elements of the redevelopment, they simply coexist. The approach forces the audience to think.

Filmmaker Lawrence Rosenblum has some clever ideas as to how to present details. In one sequence, color shots of market workers today are followed by archive black-and-white photographs of workers of yesterday. There are nine sets of these contrasting portraits, and some sets appear to be of the same person at two different ages. The contrasts give a feeling of continuity, that nothing has really changed in terms of people. John Carroll, a North Market Street merchant, observes that everybody knew everybody else in the old days, that they were all "like a big family." As he reminisces about the teamsters who handled the horse-drawn beef wagons, a series of photos shows the market in 1904, 1920, 1925, 1928, 1930, 1935, 1945, 1967, and, in color, the era of the film. The series shows how busy the market areas were. We also feel that we have had a peek at the "big family's" home photo album. As Monsignor Lally talks about the redevelopment, there are color shots contrasting the weather-beaten, shoddy, empty buildings of the area to modern, busy produce shops, the brick city hall plaza, and the specialty shops. The implication is that redevelopment will turn the old eyesores into a thriving and handsome area, the way it used to be. The contrasts in all three sequences are extremely convincing and suggest a warm, nostalgic approach to rebuilding.

Over a decade later, the Faneuil Hall Market area has become a major tourist attraction. The North and South Market buildings now contain specialty shops and restaurants, while parking garages, hotels, and condominiums have replaced the buildings surrounding the market. Monsignor Lally's comment that the old will be used in a thoroughly modern way has certainly come true. Inadvertently, however, Jack Carroll's comment that the Market district was one big happy family now has an ironic ring to it. For "outsiders," the film is a persuasive argument for redevelopment; for the older Bostonians, the film is a painful reminder of the days before the inundation of the tour bus and the swarming of the hip. As in the film, there was no transition.

FOLLOW-UP ACTIVITIES

1. Read a feature article in a magazine, such as *National Geographic*, *The Atlantic*, *Harper's*, or *The New Yorker*, and analyze the structure, details, and transition techniques that the author uses.

2. Read an entry on the same topic from two encyclopedias in your school or community library, such as *The New Encyclopaedia Britannica*, *Encyclopedia Americana*, *The New Columbia Encyclopedia*, or *World Book Encyclopedia*, and compare the structure, details, and transition techniques that the author uses. Are both authors trying to accomplish the same thing?

3. Read one or more of the following to note the way a skilled writer accomplishes the three skills of appropriateness of structure, details, and transitions:

    Henry Beston, *The Outermost House* (Middlesex, England: Penguin Books, 1976).

    Leon Wolff, *In Flanders Fields* (Alexandria, VA: Time-Life Books, 1963).

    Washington Irving, *The Sketch Book* (New York: New American Library, 1961).

    Ruth Benedict, *Patterns of Culture* (Boston, MA: Houghton Mifflin, 1959).

    J. R. R. Tolkien, "On Fairy-Stories," in *The Tolkien Reader* (New York: Ballantine, 1966).

4. Write an essay on a topic of your own choice. Before you begin, clearly indicate the purpose for the essay, then choose the most appropriate structure and determine the details. Be sensitive as well to your transitions.

IV

READING COMPREHENSION (SAT SKILLS)

MAIN IDEA

The question that is probably most frequently asked the student in class and one that appears on the reading comprehension part of the College Board is "What is the main idea of the selection?" Variations on the question are "What is the topic sentence?" and "What is the major emphasis?" When we want to be more subtle, we ask, "What would be a good title for this selection?" or "The essay primarily answers what question?" In all its various manifestations, it is the bread-and-butter question for secondary English. There are a few pointers that students should keep in mind when taking the SAT.

The "main idea" is more than the discovery of a topic. When looking for the main idea, the reader is dealing with something that is directly stated. In expository writing, the author is trying to do something, such as to prove a point, or to convince the audience about an assertion. If there is more than one paragraph in the SAT selection, the assertion usually will be found in the first paragraph. The author might be claiming a relationship exists, showing evidence for a generalization, or proving that something happened.

English teachers inadvertently create a stumbling block for finding that main idea. To make sure the student does not digress (or avoid formulating an assertion), we tend to insist that the topic sentence of the essay—that single sentence statement of the main idea or assertion—be the first sentence the student writes. The justification for the approach is that sooner or later the student gets into the habit of pre-planning what he or she is trying to prove. However, in most formal writing—science is sometimes an exception—the main idea is rarely the first sentence in the paragraph. The writer gets the attention of the audience, then leads carefully to the assertion. The so-called topic sentence, then, often appears at the *end* of the opening paragraph.

The student should be aware of the nature of the material that the SAT uses in testing reading comprehension. The selections are drops for objective information which offer,

1. descriptions or definitions of an activity, historical moment, or intellectual concern
2. profiles of famous people
3. encyclopedia-like distillations of material on a specialized topic
4. musings on an abstract concept.

The questions on the excerpt might ask the student to recall the main idea of the total passage or of a section of the material. The main idea in such readings might be

1. the uses or functions of something
2. the most important thing to remember about the topic
3. the aspect of the topic the writer wishes to emphasize

It does not hurt for the student taking the SAT to check briefly the questions on the reading comprehension passage before doing the reading. If there is a main idea question, the student should note the statements offered as possibilities, then read the passage.

The films in this section contain a great deal of specific information. Although they are quite well made, they are not primarily "visual" and emphasize texts with the images. The vocabulary in each film is demanding, with specialized words, metaphors, and complex descriptions. Each film has a main idea and offers details to support the idea. Because the texture of the writing—not to mention the subject matter—is what is found normally on the SAT, questions on words in context have been included. For this skill, the more demanding the film, specialized the subject, and difficult the vocabulary, the better.

JOHN MUIR'S HIGH SIERRA (Pyramid Films: 28 min./color/1972)

In his journal, John Muir claims he no longer envies Adam his stay in Eden because at Yosemite he has lived "in creation's dawn" and finds that "the world becomes more beautiful every day." The beauty he extols is shown throughout the film in exquisite photography of the Sierra Mountain range, the famous Yosemite Valley, the seasons. In addition to the homage to the beauties of nature, two points are made. First, Muir is categorized as a conservationist out to save the Sierra from the dangers of lumbermen and sheep. His message is for modern industrial society to leave the wilderness alone. Second, Muir talks of the Sierras as a temple in which one can actually have religious experiences. Muir is the "seer" who writes a kind of paradox that would have made both Thoreau and Emerson proud: "Going out," he says, "I was really going in." The secret is to lose one's identity, as the rain drop does when it falls into a pool of water: "One seems to be dissolved, absorbed, sent pulsing onward, we know not where." The filmmaker successfully captures this mystical experience.

Just as a verbal description of this film is difficult for a writer to catch, so the description of Yosemite proved to be a problem for Muir in his books. He resorted to metaphors. During his first spring in the Sierra he wrote, "one seems to be in a majestic domed pavilion in which a grand play is being enacted with scenery and music and incense. . . ." For him, the glacier-torn rock of Half Dome is "by far the grandest of all the special temples of Nature." The sheer precipices near the great Yosemite Falls are "noble walls sculptured in endless varieties of domes and gables, spires and battlements. . . ." Like many an artist, Muir admits "little can I do beyond mere outlines." Yet he tries. He stresses architecture in the images quoted above, along with religion, drama, and sculpture, but he finds other cultural comparisons helpful in his attempts to describe the ineffable. The pine trees at the north fork of the Merced River are "hieroglyphics written with sunbeams." In the summer, he crosses "glacier-polished pavements," and enjoys the "lace-like fabric of streams." With delight, we find that when Muir describes humans he turns to Nature for the comparison; thus, Emerson is "serene, majestic, Sequoia-like."

In one sequence of the film, narration stops altogether, and the filmmaker produces a visual essay on the transcendental progress of a drop of water from the melting of a piece of ice until it becomes part of a mighty waterfall. Concerning the film's photography, one can only echo Muir's words about Yosemite: "I hopefully pray I may see it again."

ACTIVITIES FOR THE STUDENT

1. The filmmaker does all of the following EXCEPT:
   a. present biographical information about Muir
   b. attempt to convey the beauty of Nature
   c. give historical information about the creation of the mountain range
   d. give details concerning the seasons in the mountains
   e. describe the problems facing lumbermen in the Sierras
   [Answer: e]

2. An important point that the filmmaker wishes to make regarding the Sierras is that. . .
   a. certain animals are becoming endangered
   b. it is a heritage to be guarded and protected by all of us
   c. it is a resource of energy that we should tap
   d. many sports can be enjoyed there
   e. tourists are careless in the way they treat the place
   [Answer: b]

3. By describing Half Dome as "the Sanctum Sanctorum of the Sierra," Muir probably means. . .
   [Answer: that the place is "the grandest of all the special temples of Nature."]

4. When Muir tells Emerson, "Insist on yourself, never imitate," he means. . .
   a. he does not want to be like Emerson in his lifestyle
   b. he does not want to grow a beard
   c. he resented Emerson's staying with him
   d. he thought Emerson was stealing his best ideas
   e. he felt he was the top philosopher in the country
   [Answer: a]

5. When Muir states that in Yosemite one lives in "creation's dawn," he is probably referring to. . .
   [Answer: the fact that the glacier cut out the valley so many centuries ago, it could have been at the time of Eden.]

6. Muir describes Emerson as a "Sequoia-like man." He probably means that. . .
   a. Emerson is very tall
   b. Emerson is wooden in his behavior
   c. Emerson had tough, gnarled features
   d. Emerson has an aura of majesty similar to the tree's
   e. there are not many other people like Emerson around
   [Answer: d]

THE JACKAROO (Stuart Finley: 19 min./color/1962)

A jackaroo is "a cadet or trainee station manager" for a sheep ranch in Australia. Although the film never explains the origin of the term, it does show various aspects of the jackaroo's life, or at least the life as young men lived it in 1960 in the outback. The narrator, David Johnson, tells us about his job with a good-natured enthusiasm that is very appealing. He admits there are drawbacks: we see men swatting away flies as they work in the terrific heat of the sheep yards; some drovers bring in a "mob" of sheep amidst a suffocating dust cloud; the ranch is huge, but only a few people run it. But Johnson tells us he is "helping the country to grow" and is happy to be "part of the pioneer settlers' work," still he seems to enjoy most being something of a cowboy as he chats with his "mates" (or buddies) around a campfire under an open sky.

A ranch, however, is not run on romanticism, but by hard work, and Johnson points out the various jobs that need to be done. A trapper is given rewards for the number of dingos (wild dogs) and foxes he kills. A mill expert has the responsibility of keeping the various water-pumping windmills in working order. A boundary rider on his bicycle checks and repairs the fences of the paddocks and makes sure there is enough water for the animals. Some herders on horseback drive the sheep to the yards ("muster a paddock") and others sort the sheep into drafting yards, according to their age, in preparation for the shearing. The shearing contractors break into subcategories of shearers (they are paid by the fleece), pickers, wool rollers, piece pickers (they go over the discard material), and wool classers. Part of Johnson's job in learning to be a manager is to be a good host and to entertain, so he and his mates have to spend occasional nights at the manager's homestead when there is company, where he wears a white shirt and tie that "feels like a hangman's rope." Although obviously uncomfortable in the boss' home, Johnson approaches the unpleasant task with his usual good cheer.

A jackaroo, we are told, must be a horseman able to "muster a paddock," and a manager able to run a station, but he also must be an agronomist, veterinary surgeon, and a businessperson. More important, he must be self-sufficient in the wilderness. With great pride, Johnson tells about the "flying doctor," whose routine visits to the station by plane become social events. The doctor's need for a plane only points up all the more the vastness of the space these few people function within. For this reason, we accept Johnson's remark that the neighbors of his boss, sitting around the dinner table in a formal, polite setting, exhibit "freedom and independence." They would not otherwise survive.

ACTIVITIES FOR THE STUDENT
1. The film is primarily concerned with. . .
    [Answer: showing the aspects of running an Australian sheep ranch.]
2. The film provides information about each of the job categories on a sheep ranch EXCEPT:
    a. shearing contractor
    b. boundary rider
    c. cook
    d. mill expert
    e. trapper
    [Answer: c]
3. When the narrator says there are "drawbacks" to the life of the jackaroo, he would probably include. . .
    [Answer: the isolation, the heat, the dust, the flies, the hard work, loneliness.]
4. The narrator's phrase "muster a paddock" would best be interpreted to mean. . .
    [Answer: "collect a group of sheep" to bring them in for the shearing.]
5. The narrator uses the word "mob" probably to refer to
    a. jackaroos
    b. aborigines
    c. sheep
    d. cattle
    e. gangsters
    [Answer: c]

VERBAL COMMUNICATION: THE POWER OF WORDS (CRM/McGraw-Hill: 30 min./color/1981)

Language, we are told, is a "tool" that "allows us to work together in all the activities of life." The definition is not a metaphor. This film is concerned primarily with language on the job, and offers some ways by which we can use that tool more effectively in getting a job done. Although the intended audience is probably management trainees, the movie can also be very helpful for students who take language "for granted." The main idea of the film is that "mastery of the world begins with our mastery of the word."

The responsibility for complete communication rests on the speaker, the narrator tells us. There are four aspects to a successful communication:

a. The speaker must articulate a thought.
b. The language that expresses the thought should be "appropriate" (to the situation and the knowledge of the audience) and clear.
c. There should be a warm, tolerant, unhostile climate for the communication.
d. The listener must be receptive (or must be manipulated to be receptive).

To avoid possible "static" that might distort the message, the senders should:

a. say what the sender means
b. avoid "double messages" that gestures, tone of voice, indirect, or disguised statements produce
c. avoid "impenetrable jargon," clichés, bureaucratic double-talk, and unnecessary qualifiers
d. establish a psychological climate conducive to good listening, one that avoids "trembling" (the receiver backs away from making a point because the sender has frightened or intimidated him or her) through two-way communication that includes "feedback"

In conclusion, the narrator states that it is "in our own self-interest to find out what is on other people's minds and show what is on our own." If we do this, we will get our jobs done successfully.

ACTIVITIES FOR THE STUDENT

1. The author provides information that answers each of the following questions, EXCEPT:
   a. How can we determine if the audience has understood our message?
   b. How can we be clear and appropriate in our message?
   c. How can we establish a climate conducive for listening?
   d. How do we formulate our ideas in the brain?
   e. How do we avoid sending "double messages"?
   [Answer: d]
2. The narrator's use of the phrase "double message" could best be interpreted to mean. . .
   [Answer: the message we intend plus the conflicting message sent through gesture, tone of voice, indirect statement, disguised statement, or modified statement.]
3. In terms of management communications, the word "trembling" would mean. . .
   [Answer: the receiver backs away from what he or she wants to say because of feeling intimidated by the boss.]
4. By "impenetrable jargon" the narrator apparently means. . .
   [Answer: the specialized words of a profession or job or activity.]

5.   The phrase "magic of the word" could best be interpreted to mean. . .
       [Answer: the ability to have our words understood by others and to have them
             bring us what we want.]
6.   The most important point that the author wishes to make regarding directions
       being given to others is. . .
       [Answer: that feedback will ensure the audience's understanding the point.]
7.   The author is mainly concerned with what aspect of language under what
       conditions?
       [Answer: the communication system in a management-worker relationship.]

EGYPT'S PYRAMIDS: HOUSES OF ETERNITY (National Geographic Society:
      22 min./color/1978)

This film is primarily concerned with the evolution of pyramid building from
the Step Pyramid of King Djoser at Saggara to the climax of the form in the three
pyramids at Giza. In addition, it considers the elements of the tomb complex, the
ritual of entombing a king, and conjecture on the techniques of pyramid construction.
Thanks to a lucid script and excellent photography, this lesson about the ancient
past can also stand up well to the ravages of time.

Most of the film documents how pyramid building developed. The earliest
Egyptian graves were shallow ones placed beyond the flooding areas of the Nile. In
Saggara, there are rectangular bench-shaped tombs (or *mastabas*) that contain an
underground burial shaft, a mount, and the brick structure on the surface that gives
the tomb its name because of its shape. For King Djoser, the architect Imhotep constructed a six-step tomb, the first to be in the pyramid shape and to be entirely of
stone. The camera prowls from the vertical grave shaft of the main tomb to the
identical one in the cenotaph (the Egyptians built a dummy tomb, perhaps as a decoy
for robbers). At Meidum, the core of an eight-step pyramid that has lost its outer
casing still stands. At Dahshur is the bent pyramid, so named because the builders
"changed their minds" halfway up the construction and reduced the angle of incline
by 11 degrees, and the Northern one, the first "true" pyramid. At Giza are the Great
Pyramid of King Cheops, the pyramid and sphinx of King Chephren, and the small
pyramid of King Mycerinus. After that, the pyramids were smaller and less well built.

There was more to the tomb than just the pyramid. The king "embarked on a
glorious new adventure" in the afterlife when his people brought the body by boat
to the valley temple (there was one for each king) located on the bank of the Nile.
A causeway connected the valley temple to the mortuary temple in front of the
pyramid. Small *mastabas* and cenotaphs were also part of the complex. It was believed
the king, after his death, needed the complex surroundings so that he could continue
to perform his functions forever.

How were the pyramids built? Herodotus, quoted as saying, "Egypt is the gift
of the river" (a gift because the annual flooding allowed people to produce food),
was fascinated by the gift of Egypt to eternity. He conjectured that it took 10 years to
construct the road to the site and 20 more to do the actual pyramid building. He
assumed that masses of slave labor were needed to accomplish the job, a deduction
that is now considered false. Although the film offers the latest theory on construction techniques (the use of ramps and a limited labor force), the pyramids still retain
their aura of mystery.

ACTIVITIES FOR THE STUDENT
1. The film is primarily concerned with which of the following?
    a.   the significance of the Sphinx
    b.   the evolution of pyramid construction
    c.   the details of workmanship in the pyramids
    d.   Egyptian techniques of burying the dead
    e.   the duties in eternity of the pharaohs
    [Answer: b]
2. By calling Egypt the "gift of the river," Herodotus apparently means. . .
    [Answer: that the flooding of the Nile allowed life to be maintained on the
        desert.]
3. The king, we are told, after death "embarked on a glorious new adventure,"
    a phrase which probably means. . .
    [Answer: that the king did not "die" and would be experiencing new events.]
4. The author provides information about each of the elements of the pyramid
    complex EXCEPT:
    a.   the causeway
    b.   the valley temple
    c.   queen's pyramid
    d.   mortuary temple
    e.   cenotaph
    [Answer: c]
5. The phrase on the Sphinx's steele, "I am your guide," probably means. . .
    [Answer: that the spirit of the ancient king is still active and concerned with
        events in the present.]

CELL DIVISION: MITOSIS AND MEIOSIS (CRM/McGraw-Hill: 20 min./
    color/1975)
This film on the processes of mitosis and meiosis is extraordinary in its ability
to convey its main idea: the difference between the two types of cell division.
Cinemicroscopy and animation are employed to illustrate both types of cell division,
and key information sequences are repeated . . . and repeated. The film presents each
process, summarizes the steps in each, then recaps everything once again as it compares
the two. The result is a model for providing information on a difficult subject, for
making a comparison, and for presenting a complex point clearly.
    What is the difference between mitosis and meiosis? In mitosis, the usual process
of cell division, two identical cells emerge from an original cell. The important stages
of mitosis are the following:
    a.   During interphase (the so-called resting phase), the cell duplicates its
         DNA.
    b.   The chromosomes become visible when the DNA coils.
    c.   The chromosomes align themselves in the center of the cell.
    d.   Chromosomes split and move to opposite sides of the cell.
    e.   Single division produces two new cells, both with DNA identical in com-
         position and amount to the original cell.

Meiosis is the cell division necessary to accomplish sexual reproduction. Since half the
46 chromosomes in the offspring will come from the mother, half from the father, a
different cell must be formed for the sperm and the egg. The significant stages of
meiosis are:

a. During interphase, the cell replicates its DNA.
b. Crossing over begins when look-alike chromosomes pair.
c. After crossover is complete, the pairs partially separate and line up in the center of the cell.
d. Splitting occurs with each chromosome still containing two DNA molecules. The genetic composition of these molecules has been changed.
e. Two new cells have been created; the cells enter a resting period (in which no DNA is duplicated).
f. The chromosomes appear and line up; no crossover occurs at this time.
g. After splitting, each chromosome has a single molecule of DNA.
h. At the end of the second division, each cell has half the amount of DNA and half the chromosome number as the original cell.

The film, to simplify its explication, ignores the nuclear proteins involved.

In addition to the clear outline and instant-replay segments, the script also uses metaphor and analogy. To explain the composition of the DNA, the script turns to the world of drafting: the "blueprint" of "each living thing . . . for its species" is found in the DNA. An analogy is made between DNA and the alphabet: just as combinations of the same letters make up books, so "most traits are the interactions of many genes." These are only a few examples of the many techniques this splendid film uses to allow for maximum comprehension.

ACTIVITIES FOR THE STUDENT

1. As used, the word "blueprint" can best be interpreted to mean. . .
[Answer: the information needed by cells for manufacturing the proteins needed by all living beings.]
2. The phrase "alphabet of life" is part of an analogy that compares. . .
[Answer: books made up of combinations of letters to traits that are the combinations of various genes.]
3. The term "interphase" has mistakenly been labeled. . .
[Answer: a period in which no growth occurs.]
4. In the presentation of the film, the author does all of the following EXCEPT:
a. recap the information immediately after the explication of each process
b. present all the material again for the final comparison
c. explain the role of nuclear proteins
d. offer animated sequences to illustrate each process
e. offer instant replay of key moments
[Answer: c]
5. The movie is mainly concerned with. . .
[Answer: showing the process of two types of cell division.]
6. The most important point that the author wishes to make regarding meiosis is that. . .
[Answer: the final cells, after the second division, contain half the amount of DNA as the original cell.]
7. The term "centromeres" can best be defined as. . .
[Answer: the point where the DNA separates.]

TONE

One of the most difficult skills to learn is the easiest to define. Thanks to the insistence of linguist and critic I. A. Richards, we define tone as the attitude of the author toward the subject matter and toward the audience. The difficulty comes in the determination of what exactly those attitudes are. Each work offers a new challenge, and sometimes no two readers of one text can agree on what its tone is. Although few people have trouble understanding the tone of a speaker in everyday conversation (the sound of the voice and the look on the face contribute to understanding), tone in writing is more difficult to discern. Because readers ordinarily cannot see, hear, or become acquainted with the author of a work, they must rely on the clues within the text itself; if they do not understand the attitudes of the author, they can miss the point of the selection completely. The difficulty of the skill makes it a favorite technique of the College Board to determine a student's reading comprehension. The test makers, however, have simplified the problem: as far as the SAT is concerned, tone ususally only means the attitude of the author toward the subject matter.

If the teacher is patient, students can gain sensitivity to tone. Their competency with the skill can be improved by their becoming familiar with the terms that summarize attitudes, by their becoming aware of the methods authors use to convey attitude, and through their encountering a wide range of materials with tone in mind.

What are some of the words used in the exam to identify a particular tone? Frequently, test takers give a wrong answer to a tone question because they are unsure of the meanings of the words in the choices. The larger the repertory of category terms, the more efficient the student will be in pinpointing the attitude. Dictionary work will help to clarify the meanings of these commonly used tone words and to determine the "shades of gray" between terms. The words that appear most frequently on the SAT can be grouped in the following way:

1. those that are definitely *positive*:

admiration	optimism
approval	acceptance
respect	endorsement
interest	encouragement
sentimentality	appreciativeness

2. those that are definitely *negative*:

distrust	derision
alarm	disparagement
contempt	skepticism
indignation	bitterness
dissatisfaction	disapproval
suspicion	jealousy

3. those that show *superiority* of the author to the material:

condescension	pomposity
patronization	aloofness
mockery	sarcasm
complacency	flippancy

4.   those that show *a lack of conviction* or *inferiority*:

anxiety	worthlessness
bewilderment	defensiveness
conciliatoriness	tentativeness
inadequacy	resignation

5.   those that show *other attitudes*:

non-commitment	ambivalence
pedantry	apathy
indifference	surprise
wryness	detachment
irony	neutrality
amusement	concern
despair	astonishment
disinterest	doubt

To be even more demanding, the test makers are fond of combining words to qualify an attitude. For example, the student could encounter:

unalloyed approval
tentative rejection
overt dissatisfaction
muted disdain

Students should begin by identifying attitudes that have not been listed above. In the dictionary, they should find synonyms for the words they do not understand on the list.

The young reader should also be aware of the devices that authors use to convey attitude. The following are some of the more frequently found techniques:

1.   *Writing with an open bias.*
The content of the statement is overtly condemning or praising; name-calling is sometimes found; for example:

> Field work for a folklorist is actually the most exciting part of the discipline. An informant is a complex, compelling human being, not a cold series of statistics, nôr a brief citation in a decaying tome.

There is no ambiguity here: the author does not think much of laboratory research and uses clearly disparaging terms to describe it; conversely, there is open praise for interviewing the informant.

2.   *Stacking the deck.*
The selection of data indicates an attitude; the author can ignore data, or give only positive or only negative information; for example:

> In folklore, good field work can easily be accomplished. The main skills needed are a sensitivity to the feelings of the informants, the ability to listen to what is actually being said, and the sincerity that will allow the informant to trust the worker.

The author ignores the problems facing the fieldworker. The most sensitive persons in the world would produce nothing if they did not know how to question, how to direct conversation toward a goal, and how to record data without making the informant self-conscious. The author has minimized the skills and difficulty of fieldwork.

3. *Objectivity*.

    The complete absence of tone is in itself tone—the scientific, the impersonal, the detached. In such writing, the author carefully keeps personal bias out of the evidence, balances the pro and con arguments, and uses no emotive words or words with strong connotations; for example:

    > The copying machine has had an effect on one area of folklore, the joke. In many offices today, people duplicate a number of jokes and distribute them. Is such material folklore? There are many arguments on both sides of the issue. . . .

    The author has started what will be an extended analysis of a controversial issue. No emotional words are used. We do not know what the author feels about 1) the issue, 2) the people who pass around jokes, or 3) the duplicating machine. NOTE: if the pro arguments outweigh the con (or vice versa), the author, regardless of the most impersonal tone, is showing a judgment as discussed in 2 above

4. *Loaded terms*.

    The words used in the selection have connotations (emotional overtones) that are insulting or complimentary; for example:

    > This variation of the Cinderella story seems to be the result of a novice storyteller overindulging in crowd-pleasing, plebeian details.

    A *novice* is a beginner, one who has not had much experience; we assume that the older, more experienced person has more talent. *Plebeian* suggests vulgar, commonplace, or low class.

5. *Comparison*.

    A value judgment is contained in any form of comparison, whether it be an analogy or a metaphor (*see* "Comparison," page 32); for example:

    > When we compare genuine folktales to the so-called improvements of Hans Christian Andersen, we find the original ones have more power and vividness. Andersen's tales are examples of fake lore, the work of a counterfeiter.

    The comparison obviously attacks Andersen's writings. There is a negative value judgment expressed in the terms "fake lore" and "counterfeiter."

6. *Irony*.

    The author means the opposite of what the words say on the surface (*see* "Irony," page 108); common types of irony include:
    a. sarcasm (the author praises with the intention of insulting)
    b. understatement (the author minimizes an important event or attitude)
    c. overstatement (the author maximizes an important event or attitude)
    d. antithesis (the second half of a sentence opposes the message or attitude of the first half)

    For example:

    > His many decades of field work, his hundreds of published articles, and his countless file drawers filled with data produced one contribution to the study of the folktale; a new variation to the ending of the Cinderella story.

    The contribution is disproportionate to the activity of the folklorist. Such antithesis implies that the author does not think much of this folklorist's ability, is not impressed by the volume of his work.

In the following films, students should look for the "clues" that indicate tone.

TOP OF THE WORLD: TAIGA, TUNDRA, ICE CAP (LCA: 20 min./color/ 1971)

Top of the World accomplishes many things in its brief running time. There is a geography lesson about the terrain, climate, peoples, and natural resources of the area that includes Northern Canada, Alaska, Russia, Iceland, Sweden, Greenland, and the Arctic. There is the vicarious thrill of exploring the frontier, the region beyond the routine travel agent packages. There is also a thoughtful warning that industrial cultures might be on the verge of destroying the ecological balance and resources of the North. That warning, found throughout Ian MacNeill's script, produces a tone of anxious concern for the area and a thinly-disguised disapproval of the technological activities now taking place in the frontier.

Students should have little trouble identifying those sentences that convey the script's attitudes. We are told that "technological man is moving north to one of the last horizons . . . of rich resources. . . ." In the taiga, the "world of wood and water," the first white men were interested in furs. The trapper is vanishing now as a result of "fur farms, overkill, changing fashions," and the belief that trapping is cruel. The hunters are now mostly businesspeople who kill deer "to fill suburban freezers." The remark contains the innuendo that such meat is not a necessity. This technological age might have lost interest in large-scale trapping and hunting, but has not lost interest in "cutting forest wealth." Since the "chain saw can't feed the hunger for pulp wood," the harvester or processor now "eats up the forest with speed and efficiency." To make sure we pick up the negative connotations of the ungoverned appetite metaphor, the film carefully points out that trees grow slowly in the taiga, and that tree farms must regulate the growth of the future. We watch the wood pulp being turned into the product most demanded, newsprint, which will "end up finally in the trash." The statement is ironic: trees that take so very many years to grow are cut down to form a product that loses its value in one day. In the tundra, the world of water and land, the caribou have been depleted thanks to "disease, predators, and the guns of hunters." The "ancient way of life" of the Eskimo has been changed by white "newcomers." In a sentence that tries to sound fair by balancing pros and cons, MacNeill writes, "If the white man brought disease, he also brought cures." But the remark is still a slap: if there were not the diseases, there would be no need for cures. In the ice cap, the area of perpetual ice and snow, a large oil spill could destroy the "fragile ecological balance." The oil tanker S. S. *Manhattan*, the largest ship ever, tried to carry oil across the frozen territory. The first trip was successful, the second less so because of an accident that almost caused an oil spill. The film ends with the question that reflects the anxious concern of the filmmaker: "Will technological man . . . destroy this final frontier?"

The comments that exhibit the attitude of the author toward the subject matter are not sermons or even asides. The attitude is revealed through metaphor, antithesis, directly stated facts, and innuendo. The very selection of data is significant. The film does not explore, for instance, the cultures of the Laplanders or Eskimos. Have they, in any way, affected the "fragile ecological balance" of the North? Is there more to show about the ice cap than the S. S. *Manhattan*'s invasion of the territory? Such questions are not criticisms but a way of showing how the chosen data indicates the author's tone. Normally in a geography film we find analytical objectivity, in the adventure film, breathless intrepidity. The insistence of the critical attitude indicates the priorities of the filmmaker: he is interested in protecting the northern wilderness.

ACTIVITIES FOR THE STUDENT
1. The film's tone suggests that the author's attitude toward the future of the Top of the World is one of. . .
    a. anxious concern
    b. skeptical reserve
    c. flippant sarcasm
    d. enthusiastic optimism
    e. aloof disinterest
    [Answer: a]
2. The author's attitude toward the activities of "technological man" would best be described as one of. . .
    a. astonishment
    b. resignation
    c. disapproval
    d. bewilderment
    e. amusement
    [Answer: c]
3. What would be other possible "tones" the filmmaker could have adopted toward this particular subject? Explain what data would have to be shown to display such tones.
4. Read a selection from any school geography book and determine the tone of the author toward, say, China, Russia, or Cuba.

THE TRULY EXCEPTIONAL CAROL JOHNSTON (Walt Disney Educational Media: 15.50 min./color/1979)

Unqualified admiration is the attitude of this filmmaker toward young Carol Johnston. In spite of her handicap—she has only one arm—Johnston became a successful gymnast for Cal State Fullerton. At one point in her career, while dismounting from the uneven parallel bars, she fell, injured her knee, and underwent surgery. During her recovery period, as she moved about on crutches with her leg in a cast, Johnston made the amazing remark, "I know what being handicapped is now." Six weeks later, Johnston returned to the team and won first place on the parallel bars. Throughout the film, this young lady, who stands only 4 foot 9½ inches, shows the courage and determination that made her a champion.

The filmmaker offers only honorific information about Johnston. The camera records the grace, beauty, and coordination of her award-winning routines, and captures her commendable independence in and mastery of everyday situations. She recalls that when she first came to California from Canada, her roommates helped her out, but she soon showed she could take care of herself. And *that* she certainly can do: we watch her tying her shoelaces or a ribbon in her hair; we see her struggle up a flight of stairs on crutches with one leg in a cast; we learn from a teammate that Johnston sewed her own leotards; we see her tape up her feet and ankle before performing; and we observe her doing sit-ups on the floor with her feet (one leg still in a cast) raised to the top of the bed. At one point, after she has fallen and injured her knee, she cries in frustration at the possibility of having to quit gymnastics. The audience will agree with the filmmaker's tone of sympathy; she has earned the right to feel that moment of dejection: gymnastics, she tells us, has been her whole life. And more is involved than just the awards—through gymnastics kids had accepted her as normal. Dejection does not last long. True to character, she dries her tears and sets about "adjusting to her *new* disability."

The reaction of the coach to Johnston is worth noting for its demonstration of tone. His attitude changed from disbelief to admiration. When he first encountered her, he thought, "You're kidding!" He was astounded that a one-armed person was on the team. To relieve the tension, he started calling her "Lefty." After the accident, he stated he was optimistic that her knee would heal and she would come back: "If not, she'll win at whatever she does." His prediction has so far been correct.

The coach's attitude is shared by the filmmaker. There is no doubt that Johnston is being praised for her sunny disposition and admired for her spirit in overcoming obstacles. For many in the audience there will be a pull on the heart strings when she starts on the comeback trail that leads to the NBC Sports coverage of her gymnastic victory. The real victory, however, is the one over her handicap.

ACTIVITIES FOR THE STUDENT

1. The attitude of the film toward Carol Johnston is best described as one of. . .
   a. aloof disinterest
   b. unqualified admiration
   c. ironic respect
   d. patronizing encouragement
   e. skeptical acceptance
   [Answer: b]
2. For each of the wrong answers to question 1 above, explain what the phrase means, then demonstrate how the film would have to be presented to exhibit such a tone.
3. The coach's first attitude toward Johnston can best be described as. . .
   a. derision
   b. amusement
   c. incredulity
   d. ambivalence
   e. defensiveness
   [Answer: c]

THE WOLF AND THE WHITETAIL (Marty Stouffer Productions: 26 min./ color/1979)

The attitude of scriptwriter Paula Joan Smith toward her subject matter, the timber wolf and the whitetail deer, is one of analytical objectivity, the tone we normally associate with scientific writing. For all its beautiful photography and charming scenes of wolf pups and young deer at play, the film is unflinching in showing the way in which these animals "take [their] ultimate places in nature's plan" as the predator and the prey. Indeed, the climax of the film shows a few adult wolves killing a "weak and unhealthy" buck in front of both wolves and other deer. The narrator explains that "predators . . . keep the herd in top condition, like a gardener pulling weeds." The comment demands a distancing from the event, a withdrawal of sympathetic feelings for the helpless deer, an acceptance of the inevitable. Fully aware of the feelings of the audience, the narrator states "animals are not burdened with the knowledge that they too will someday die." The scientific analysis shows that our emotional reactions are empathetic—we fear our own deaths and project that fear onto the deer. The film asks that we view nature with detachment.

The script is consistent in its objectivity: there are no favorites in nature, only the survival of the fittest. After watching a wolf kill, we are told, "killing for the wolves is as natural and inevitable as the passage of the sun across the sky," and we learn later that, "for deer, each day is a matter of how to eat without being eaten." A buck forces an attacking wolf to back off, and the narrator calls him "a graduate of the school of survival." At the film's end, we hear, "wolf and whitetail are halves of one whole. The deer feeds wolves . . . [and] wolves keep the deer strong. . . ." There is no sentimentality for the death of the weak, no false heroism in the animals, no attempt to create the emotional atmosphere of Bambi. Those cute little wolf pups at play are learning the techniques of hunters. The charming, two-week-old fawn scampering around its mother is building a skill necessary to survive as the hunted.

In a world without heroes, there is also an absence of villains. The film is careful to debunk our more popular prejudices concerning the wolf: the animal is only a predator, not the embodiment of malevolent forces. Through a series of rather disconcerting comparisons to human behavior and customs, the wolf is shown as a societal being with family responsibilities, awareness of class distinctions, and the need to participate in ceremonies. The wolf can even express joy in an aesthetic way, through non-utilitarian howling. The creature is cursorial, not lycanthropic, one that learns how to track, chase, corner, and kill. Like a human, it learns to survive—there is no darkness driving it on.

ACTIVITIES FOR THE STUDENT
1. The author's attitude toward the subject of the wolf and deer is best described as one of. . .
   a. violent indignation
   b. self-rightous patronization
   c. optimistic sentimentality
   d. analytical objectivity
   e. unalloyed disapproval
   [Answer: d]
2. Back up your answer to the question above with at least five statements from the film that show that attitude.
3. Indicate the changes in the film that would be necessary for the tone to be any of the alternatives listed above. (In other words, what would the film have to do to show a tone of "violent indignation"?)
4. Copy down the figures of speech in the script, and note what these images contribute to the author's tone.
5. With the same tone as the film, retell the plot of a Hollywood werewolf story. (Keep in mind that the attitude embodies the scientific theories that the fittest of the species survive and that nature has a reason for everything.)

NOBODY'S VICTIM (Ramsgate Films: 20 min./color/1972)
One of the factors that make tone difficult to determine at times is that different people might arrive at different conclusions about the same text. *Nobody's Victim* is a case in point. The intended audience for the film is the woman who needs help in coping with the threatening living conditions in today's violent society and who needs to build self-confidence. At the end of the film the thematic statement is made: "Don't accept the idea that you are helpless in the face of danger just because you are a woman." Based on F. Patricia Stock's *Personal Safety and Defense for Women*, 2nd ed. (Minneapolis: Burgess, 1975), the movie has a tone that is probably best categorized as concerned, reassuring, and admonitory. However, since much of the advice is of the same common sense variety as that given to Little Red Riding

Hood, one could argue that the attitude toward women is "parental," patronizing. One thing is certain: the discussion of the film's tone will soon be a heated one.

The movie is concerned that a woman be "nobody's victim." The "nobody" of the title is the aggressive male, and the victim must worry about being robbed, harassed, assaulted, raped, or murdered. The film's seriousness of purpose and concentration on its topic make living in the city appear to be a terrifying experience. A woman seems to be on the edge of danger at all times, in all places. To keep alive, she must always be paranoid, on the alert. The film opens with a young lady recalling a hitchhiking experience that ended with her being raped. The possibility of sexual attack is omnipresent. A woman who has had her purse snatched returns home to find her apartment ransacked (presumably by the purse thief). Implied is the possibility that the victim might find an assailant waiting.

Defense tactics are dramatized with a concerned, but reassuring tone. Narrator Beverly Moss warns women not to become hysterical: "If confronted, stay calm, give your purse and valuables to the assailant." Other advice: bring a big dog for protection; if walking alone at night, keep in well-lit places; check the back seat of the car before getting in; never give information about yourself to a stranger on the phone; keep your car in good condition at all times to reduce the possibility of a breakdown. A woman should always have a potential weapon with her, such as a rolled up magazine, a sharply pointed brush, or car keys; she should move fast to take the assailant by surprise so that she can escape. The film also recommends that women take a course in self-defense to build self-confidence.

Some female viewers might find the narrator's tone to be condescending. Since common sense would dictate that a woman not walk alone late at night in dark places or tell a stranger on the telephone that she is alone in the house, the warnings seem to assume members of the audience do not have survival instincts and need help. If a woman followed the advice of the film as to what to do if the car breaks down (do not leave the car or accept rides from strangers), she might well spend a very long time in that car. Such advice can rub a person who prides herself on independence the wrong way.

ACTIVITIES FOR THE STUDENT

1. The author's attitude toward the "personal safety and defense of women" could best be described as...
   a. indifferent
   b. flippant
   c. concerned
   d. pedantic
   e. vacillating
   [Answer: c]

2. For a woman who feels self-confident about handling the dangers of the city, the movie's tone might be interpreted to be...
   a. immature
   b. patronizing
   c. erudite
   d. pompous
   e. whimsical
   [Answer: b]

3. Examine a few books that explain the martial arts and other forms of self-defense. Do all these works have the same tone? Try offering the information in this film using a different tone.

4.   Look up in the newspaper those columns designed to give advice. Some print letters from readers asking for a solution to a problem; some refer indirectly to questions from the readers; some assume there is an audience out there that wants advice in their field, such as cooking, parenting, gardening, etc. For each one, note the area of expertise, the type of audience (male, female, young, old, etc.) and the tone the author has toward the material.

SEAMUS HEANEY: POET IN LIMBOLAND (Films for the Humanities: 27 min./color/1972)

In this film, as Irish poet Seamus Heaney walks through the countryside and through the city of Belfast, his complex attitudes toward the film's various subjects emerge. First, he recites early poems about his childhood from *Death of a Naturalist* (London: Faber & Faber, 1966) in which he shows, for the most part, nostalgia. Second, the poet discusses his love-hate relationship with Ireland. Third, he shows in his narration contradictory views of himself through a wry humor, a tongue-in-cheek mockery. Finally, the film's narrator is sympathetic toward the poet and sees him as trapped: a part of a torn culture, yet unable to change it.

Heaney seems to be quite nostalgic about his childhood in *Death of a Naturalist*. The poems, for the most part, harken back to Heaney's roots as a member of a family of cattle dealers and small farmers. Heaney remembers with open admiration his grandfather's ability to cut sod, the strength of his father as he plowed the fields, the shrewdness of the males in his family at evaluating cattle. Since the film indicates the tone of many of these early poems, the teacher would do well to have the students read them first and determine the tones on their own. The following poems from *Death of a Naturalist* are read by the poet (the asterisks indicate the film's analysis of the tone of each):

"Digging" (pp. 13-14; admiration for his grandfather)

"The Early Purges" (p. 23; *revulsion at the death of some puppies)

"Follower" (pp. 24-25; *dispassion toward his father)

"Ancestral Photograph" (pp. 26-27; nostalgia for the traditions of the past)

"Mid-term Break" (p. 28; *deep grief at the death of his brother)

"Docker" (p. 41; condemnation of the violent Protestant bigot)

"Poor Women in a City Church" (p. 42; *respect for the Catholic church)

"Personal Helicon" (p. 57; nostalgia for the past and self-mockery)

The poet probes the emotional images of the past "to see myself." He feels the "strength" of Irish writing is its poetic images.

Heaney's attitude toward Ireland is very complex; he seems to have a love-hate relationship with his homeland. Although he feels a need to keep in contact with his poetic roots, he finds during the 1969 religious crisis in Belfast that he is living in a "polluted atmosphere" that "shrivels people's generosity" and makes them "alert to the mote in the eye of their brother." He refers to the endless political grafitti he passes as "poison on the walls," and describes as "ugly" the extreme Protestantism, the ghettos, and the "injustices the civil rights people are trying to address." He sums up the situation with the unambiguous remark that the people must "crawl out of the bog of their history." The remark is in contradiction to his comment that he gains poetic strength from the literary images—a part of that history.

The poet's complex relationship with his homeland mirrors his contradictory feelings about himself. At the time the movie was made, Heaney was a lecturer at Queen's University, Belfast. No longer a farm boy, he seems uncomfortable as the university intellectual. The poet is in a "limboland" that would exist whether or not there was a civil war. He is aware of his situation and displays it through self-mockery. His grandfather, as portrayed in the poem "Digging," was a powerful sod cutter; Seamus "digs" with his pen. Obviously, the intellectual does not "work" the way the farmer does. In "Personal Helicon" he gently mocks his poetry as a form of narcissism. At one point, he recounts a few of the jokes of the detached intellectuals; the jokes are not funny, but the mockery of his fellow intellectuals is.

The narrator of the film is sympathetic with the poet. The film shows the author brooding at landscapes and the rubble of the city and offers the visible portrait of the sensitive artist observing the problems of his environment. For the writer alive in such an atmosphere, there is a paradox of needing both to "swim free" of the situation and to draw on the traditions of the culture. Heaney carefully states he has written "journalism" about the war, but implies that he finds the subjects for his poetry elsewhere. There is sympathy toward the poet's plight in the film, a sympathy that Heaney himself does not solicit. He is too busy trying to find meaningful replacements for the "old mythologies" that are crumbling away.

ACTIVITIES FOR THE STUDENT
1. Determine the tone of the following poems from *Death of a Naturalist*: "Digging," "Ancestral Photograph," "Docker," "Personal Helicon."
2. Determine the attitude Heaney has toward the civil war in Belfast.
3. Determine the attitudes Heaney has toward himself as revealed in his poems and in the observations he makes in the film.
4. Determine the attitude the filmmaker has toward the poet in this film.

OPINION

The College Board often asks for an identification of an opinion the author has stated either directly or indirectly. Thus the student will likely encounter the following question:

> Which of the following best states the author's opinion of [a particular subject] . . . .

At times, the opinion is held by a character or famous person who is being discussed in the passage:

> Charles Darwin, according to the passage, holds the opinion that. . . .

The SAT assumes that, once he or she has determined the opinion of an author in a passage, the student can apply the opinion to other statements:

> The author would probably agree with which of the following statements [about a subject] . . . ."

> The author would probably disagree with those who [have a specific opinion on a particular subject] . . . .

> Which of the following would the author probably recommend as [a solution to a problem or a course of action] . . . .

Frequently, the opinion is stated in the passage as if it were a fact. For instance,

> The vocabulary on the College Board is not democratic—and it never has been. We know that the recognition and use of words based on Latin or Greek have always been the signs of the upper class, educated person.

Both remarks are generalizations and both could easily be debated. The reader expects the authority on this subject to have been careful in the construction of the statements, but both comments are only opinion.

To find an opinion that is not directly stated (or prefaced with the remark "in my opinion"), the reader must play the detective and look for clues in the writing. First, students can analyze the descriptive words or figures of speech the author has used to see if they contain honorific or pejorative connotations. Second, students can look at the examples the author uses to prove the point. Could any other examples be given? By discarding or ignoring material, the author is slanting evidence to make a point, and is thus expressing an opinion. Both techniques could be used to reveal the opinion in the following:

> I am amazed at the number of youngsters who take that travesty of a course, College Board Review. They allow the teacher to lecture mumbo-jumbo over their heads for a few weeks, half-heartedly do a few exercises, learn the difference between *supine* and *prone*, and feel that—"presto"—they have been turned into SAT whizzes.

"Travesty" means "a grotesque parody." The activities of the teacher are being compared through metaphor to those of a shaman or magician ("mumbo-jumbo" and "presto"). The only example of what is learned in college board review classes is "the difference between *supine* and *prone*." The first means "lying face upward"; the second, "lying face down." The words are commonly confused. The implication is that the course teaches nothing but a few pedantic distinctions. Anyone who has taken a college board review class realizes there are exercises on vocabulary building, analogies, reading comprehension, etc. The author has trivialized the course by reducing its scope.

Sometimes, an author offers statistics, graphs, charts, facts, or lists, but does not state an opinion about the material; however, the reader can infer opinion from the data provided. Consider the following:

> In my analysis of the Preliminary Scholastic Aptitude Test for October 25, 1980, I found students had to know the meanings of the following words: credulous, pragmatic, obfuscate, anomaly, atrophy, and esoteric.

By listing only difficult words that most teenagers would not know, the author implies that students must work hard on vocabulary to do well on the PSAT. The opinion might be implied, but it is still there.

The following films give practice in identifying directly stated and implied opinion as discussed above. The students should look for the opinions of both the filmmakers and the characters within the films.

VIRGINIA WOOLF: THE MOMENT WHOLE (ACI Films, Inc.: 10 min./color/ 1972)

This film relies solely on Virginia Woolf's own words to convey her opinions about the female artist. Actress Marian Seldes both poses as Woolf and narrates excerpts from *A Room of One's Own*, *The Waves*, and Woolf's diary and letters.

Seldes sits at a desk, stares into space, then leaves the house and walks to the edge of a stream. During this time, we hear Woolf's perceptive, witty, and vivid comments as she sorts out the problems facing the woman who wants to be a writer. It is obvious that the filmmaker holds the opinion that Woolf is a spokesperson for the feminist movement. The unfamiliarity of Woolf's writings for the average student taking the SAT makes this film a demanding but worthwhile experience in determining opinion. Some of the comments are difficult because of the metaphors or irony—but so are the sentences in the College Board reading passages.

Woolf expresses her opinions both directly and indirectly. For the woman who wishes to write, there are four obstacles. Independence and concentration are important. "A writer is a person who sits at a desk and keeps his eyes fixed as intently as he can on a certain object." Obstacles block that fixed gaze. Her statement, "A woman must have money and a room of one's own if she is to write fiction," translates that she must have financial security and independence to give her time to write, and that she must have privacy to concentrate without interruption. Woolf's words imply that males do not face the same obstacles. The third obstacle is the demeaning role society demands that a woman play. Using a metaphor, Woolf calls this role "the angel of the house," the person "who never had a mind of her own," who "sacrificed herself daily" in a man's interest. "Angel" is so negative a word here that we realize she is being sarcastic and that she implies that males dominate society. Woolf says of the "angel" inside all women, "If I had not killed her, she would have killed me." The use of either/or argument reveals her opinion: a woman must fight to be independent of men's demands and views, or she will not have a mind of her own, let alone a creative one. The "angel" wants to flatter the male, to imitate his style, to fawn over his ideas. The final obstacle to the female writer is the artistic tradition that is based on masculine style. The creative power of women, in Woolf's opinion, is different from men's, and that power must be kept distinct: "It would be a thousand pities if women wrote like men. . . ."

When the writer has removed those four obstacles, she can concentrate on the art of capturing that "certain object" of interest to her. Woolf announces her own goal: "What I want to do now is to saturate every atom . . . to eliminate all the waste, deadness, superfluity . . . to give the moment whole." The selections from *The Waves* of the dramatic soliloquys of Susan, Jenny, and Rhoda illustrate the writing style Woolf achieved. As the author does, the three "voices" express their inner feelings through figures of speech. Through metaphor, the author asserts that the normal writing traditions must be cast aside to allow for the exploration of the female character.

In the film, Woolf implies her opinion that once the obstacles are removed, writing is not so tough. One day, she tells us, she decided to send out a review, and it was accepted a month later. So began her life as a journalist. There is no hint in the wording of painful career choices, difficulty in writing, or apprehension at having one's work rejected. Her understatement makes it all sound so easy.

ACTIVITIES FOR THE STUDENT

1. Virginia Woolf would probably agree with which of the following statements about the woman writer:
    a. "It is impossible for a woman to express herself in English in a way that would be different from the style or creativity of a male."
    b. "A woman must not rely on figures of speech to express her innermost thoughts."

    c.   "A man does not face the same obstacles that face a woman if she wants to write."

    d.   "The artistic objective of a woman should be denouncing the opinions of men."

    e.   "A woman should directly express all her views if she is to be understood and to help other women."

    [Answer: c]

2.   List five figures of speech from the film and indicate the connotations of each image. Explain how the image conveys an indirect opinion.

3.   From the film, indicate the examples Woolf uses of the four blocking forces that a woman who wants to write encounters. From these examples, determine Woolf's opinion of the average woman's life.

4.   What is the implied opinion of the filmmaker concerning the writings of Virginia Woolf?

    [Answer: Woolf is a spokesperson for the feminist movement.]

5.   Read Virginia Woolf's *Three Guineas* (New York: Harcourt Brace Jovanovich, 1966) and determine her opinions about

    a.   biography

    b.   education

    c.   suffrage

    d.   intellectual liberty

    e.   war

FOR PARENTS ONLY: WHAT KIDS THINK ABOUT MARIJUANA (National Audiovisual Center: 28 min./color/1980)

This film offers the full range of opinion expression. The informal, directly stated opinion? We see a number of clean-cut, good-looking young people "turning on" and commenting positively about the experience. Except for one young girl, none intends to change this behavior, none feels guilty, and all state very strongly their opinion that marijuana is good for them. The directly stated professional opinion backed up by scientific findings, statistics, and examples? We hear the arguments of a number of experts—a child psychiatrist, a drug abuse prevention counselor, a coordinator for youth drug treatment, a principal at a school—that "heavy use can cause serious mental and physical harm." The implied or indirectly stated opinion? At the end of the film, a printed statement appears proclaiming that "it is important for parents to understand what many young people think and feel about the drug." What is the opinion? When dealing with a controversial issue, the film implies, if we know what the emotional opinions of the opposition are, we can persuade more effectively and, hopefully, alter those opinions. A second implied opinion in the statement is that parents do not really understand their kids.

The filmmaker is fair in that he allows the teenagers to express opinions without any overt editorializing. We are not shown any potheads, degenerates, or lost souls. The young drug users are likeable, intelligent, and even humorous—one comments about smoking that "nothing comes out of it except ashes." They all look very healthy. Certainly few films have accomplished interviews with teenagers that are as natural or so clearly unstaged. Implied in the presentation is the opinion that these well-heeled, middle-class teens can be reached by the film—and changed. Also implied is that pot is a problem for the middle-class suburban area as well as for the ghetto.

The informal opinions of the teens are expressed directly. One young man smokes because peer pressure makes him do it. Another states that he appreciates music more when he is stoned. One holds the opinion that homework is easier when he is high. Finally, a teen argues that each person "should find out for yourself" about drugs. None of the opinions is backed up with concrete proof; all are stated as if they were facts. It must also be noted that the filmmaker does not press the teenagers to supply proof details. On this issue, there is the implied belief that the teens would not be able to give any worthwhile data, that these young people are wrong in their opinions.

Support data appears in abundance in the professional opinions. First, we learn the reasons youngsters take drugs, then the harmful effects of marijuana. The experts present their ideas as facts, in reasonable voices, with conviction. Child psychiatrist Mitchell S. Rosenthall, M.D., calls the drug problem difficult to solve because "our culture tells kids it's okay to get high, even super high" thanks to the million-dollar head shop business, the rock stars' lifestyles, and drug-oriented literature and magazines. In essence, then, he feels the kids are victims of Madison Avenue. Khalelah Abdul-Kareena, coordinator for youth drug treatment, has the opinion that kids "find life is pretty boring" in school and that marijuana "makes dull lives exciting." The implied opinion is that if the boredom were eliminated, the drug problem might be solved. Dr. Rosenthall stresses the destructive cumulative effect of the drug on the nervous system. Implied is that marijuana is as bad as other drugs.

What is a parent to do? The film believes that a young person needs what one principal calls "tough love," that is, affection combined with direction. We are told that love is what convinces the child most, and that the parent must "operate from the position that you have the right to take a position and not leave it to someone else." The repeated emphasis on this point implies that in the opinion of the filmmakers, parents have been too permissive and that possibly one of the reasons for smoking marijuana is to get attention. In other words, the parents have not lived up to their responsibility in bringing up their children. In the implied opinion of the filmmakers, for the parent, the first step is to understand the problem; the second is to join a parent support group in the immediate neighborhood; third is to get up-to-date information on the subject; the last is to give direction to the teenager, to say through a clear authority role that "I care enough about you . . . not to allow you to injure yourself."

ACTIVITIES FOR THE STUDENT

1. Which of the following would the filmmaker probably recommend as a solution to the teenage drug problem:
   a. a drug rehabilitation center
   b. a series of presentations to parents of this film
   c. a class in high school on drug abuse
   d. a visit to the home of a convicted drug user
   e. group experimentation with drugs to learn the truth about them
   [Answer: b]

2. Which of the following best states the filmmaker's opinion about the comments made by the drug takers in the film:
   a. They really do not have accurate information about drugs.
   b. They do not take enough drugs to be affected by them.
   c. They do not take enough drugs to be considered a problem in our culture.
   d. They should be punished for breaking the law.
   e. They are hopeless cases that demand compassion.
   [Answer: a]

3. Explain the meaning of the opinion stated at the end of the film: "It is important for parents to understand what many young people think and feel about
the drug."
[Answer: knowing what the teenagers feel can help in getting them to kick the
habit.]

4. What is the implied opinion of the filmmakers concerning the views of the students on the use of marijuana?
[Answer: the teens would not be able to give any worthwhile data, and they are
wrong in their opinions.]

THE PERFECT MOMENT (Pyramid Films: 11 min./color/1979)

In any extended definition of an abstract term (*see* "Definition," page 20),
we are, in effect, offering an opinion. What is the perfect moment? Class discussion
before the viewing of this film will produce a wide range of answers, a plethora of
informal opinions. As this particular filmmaker directly states, the perfect moment is
the exhilaration an athlete feels when engaging in a sport that requires coordination,
willpower, and the courage to take risks. We are told that few can experience that
moment. The film offers as proof for the opinion the testimonials of three athletes,
who reenact their perfect moments, and quotations from two famous authors. All
statements in the script are presented as facts—as if there were no other way to define
the term.

Narrator Orson Welles tells us openly that the perfect moment is not for everyone. Corky Fowler, a professional skier; Chris Price, a champion hang-glider; and Jan-
Michael Vincent, a surfer (and a Hollywood star), are the examples of "those among
us who accept the challenge." Each athlete is of the opinion that the moment requires
physical preparation, extraordinary courage (the athlete must take risks, must be
"close to disaster"), self-confidence, and determination. When the moment has been
achieved, there is an "expanded state of awareness." Welles announces that once we
have passed through "the barrier to a higher place . . . we cannot rest until we return
once more." Such poetic phrasing and the beautiful photography suggest the filmmaker's implied opinion that for such individuals sport involves a mystical experience,
a moment of epiphany.

To support these opinions, the film opens with a printed statement by Samuel
Johnson and closes with one by William Blake. The implication is that the two British
authors are defining the term "perfect moment" the same way the filmmaker does.
When Johnson says

> To catch the good that is within our reach is the great art
> of life,

he is talking about moral values, not sports. The filmmaker can justify applying the
quote to the film because of Johnson's belief in self-discipline. Blake's comment,
"Oh that men would seek immortal moments," probably is an appeal to humans to
try to attain a transcendental, religious experience. The remark, as the film uses it,
urges people to explore, but suggests possible disappointment. The athletes in the film
admit that the moment does not always come, that it is "elusive" and depends on
many variables; yet one must be "constantly ready." The quotations by the two
famous authors might be on other subjects, but they add prestige to the filmmaker's
view. Perhaps, we might add, the considerable verbal presence of Orson Welles, that
world-famous eccentric, talented artist, and risk taker, is there for the same reason.

The perfect moment is not an ordinary, run-of-the-mill experience. Visually
we are dazzled by Price hang-gliding through a notch in a mountain as he descends

toward the ocean, and by Vincent surfing through a pipeline wave tunnel, his right hand extended to touch the moving wall of water. The idealism of the movie is contagious.

ACTIVITIES FOR THE STUDENT

1. The filmmaker would probably agree with which of the following statements:
   a. "It is a beauteous evening, calm and free;
      The holy time is quiet as a nun
      Breathless with adoration. . . ."
   b. "Yet all experience is an arch wherethro'
      Gleams that untravel'd world whose margin fades
      For ever and for ever when I move. . . ."
   c. "Music soothes the savage beast. . . ."
   d. "He that hopes to be a good angler [fisherman] must not only bring an inquiring, searching, observing wit, but he must bring a large measure of hope and patience . . .; but angling will prove to be so pleasant, that it will prove to be like virtue, a reward to itself."
   e. "The perfect moment occurred when first I saw you . . ."
   [Answer: b]
2. State the opinion the filmmaker has of the nature of the perfect moment.
3. List the figures of speech the filmmaker uses in verbally describing the perfect moment. Why have they been used?
4. What is the implied opinion of the filmmaker concerning the chance of every person's attaining a mystical experience in a sport?

A DANCER'S WORLD (Phoenix Films: 31 min./b&w/1957)

A "paradox" appears to be self-contradictory or absurd, but makes sense if one delves deeper into it. An audience can become so involved working through the non-logical surface of a paradox that it can overlook the fact that the statement is often a cleverly phrased, directly stated opinion. In her attempt to explain her views on dancing, world famous dancer and choreographer Martha Graham relies heavily on paradox to express her opinions. Her strong views are backed by years of experience and success, but that does not make her statements either factual or right. In essence, she feels that freedom, the dancer's goal, is achieved through rigorous, self-imposed discipline and conformity. The filmmaker is interested in presenting Graham's philosophy of the dance and treats her every word as truth.

In Graham's opinion (stated in this film as she prepares herself in her dressing room for her role as Jocasta), art should be taken very seriously. "You give all your life to accomplish one thing," Graham tells us. One must go through at least 10 years of study in which one "submits to the demands of the craft" before one can be considered a dancer. This view suggests the indirect opinion that the choreographer is a god, and insists that the novice must squash ego and originality to accomplish anything worthwhile. At the peak of the dancer's power, after those years and years of training, one achieves "two fragile things": spontaneity and simplicity. The paradox raises the question as to how a puppet can achieve freedom. Graham goes on to a directly stated opinion: there is no competition in a dancer's world, there is only the striving to "speak clearly and beautifully and with inevitability." Her remark implies the opinion that a serious artist is only in competition with him- or herself to achieve "perfection." She seems to believe this perfection is a universal truth, one with which all would agree. Another paradox is that the dancer should return frequently to the studio "to work among many to be reborn as the one." The mysticism of the remark indicates her unstated belief that dancing is a religious experience.

According to Graham, the artist must be submerged in universal inner truth, must become that truth and then project it to others. The individual is only a medium. We watch her dancers perform dances that are supposed to reveal these inner universal truths. If nothing else, there will be strong differences of opinion among the student audience as to what the dancing reveals. In Graham's opinion, the dances accomplish her goal. At the end of the film, Graham in full makeup for her role of Jocasta can look into the mirror and find that Jocasta "looks at you and recognizes herself": in her ideal, the being of the dancer has merged with the role she performs.

ACTIVITIES FOR THE STUDENT
1. Martha Graham would probably agree with which of the following statements about dancing:
    a. The dancer should improvize and be different.
    b. The dancer should respond to the tastes of the audience.
    c. The dance is an equal sharing between performer and choreographer.
    d. The dancer must tightly control her ego and spontaneity.
    e. The great dancer is born, not made.
    [Answer: d]
2. What is the opinion of the filmmaker about Martha Graham?
3. What are the implications of Graham's remark that a serious artist is only in competition with him- or herself to achieve perfection?
4. For a comparison of Graham's opinions about dance to those held by others, read one of the following:

    De Mille, Agnes. *Dance to the Piper* (New York: Da Capo, 1980).

    Fonteyn, Margot. *Margot Fonteyn: Autobiography* (New York: Knopf, 1976).

    Greco, Jose, and Ardman, Harvey. *The Gypsy in My Soul: The Autobiography of Jose Greco* (Garden City, NY: Doubleday & Co., 1977).

    Magriel, Paul, ed. *Nijinsky, Pavlova, Duncan: Three Lives in Dance* (New York: Da Capo, 1977).

THE DIVIDED TRAIL: A NATIVE AMERICAN ODYSSEY (Phoenix Films: 33 min./color/1978)

An odyssey can be the epic exploration of the hero in search of home, or it can be, as Doris Lessing suggests in *Briefing for a Descent into Hell*, the travels through inner space in a symbolic search for self. Betty Chosa Jack, her brother Michael Chosa, and her friend Carol Warrington live through both kinds of odyssey. Uprooted from the Chippewa Indian Reservation at Lac de Flambeau, Wisconsin, the three move to Chicago, become leaders in the Indian Rights Movement in the mid-seventies, endure personal crises, and move inward in an attempt to become whole human beings again. The very comparison of their experiences to Homer's *Odyssey* indicates filmmaker Jerry Aronson's opinion of his subject. He feels they are heroic people who, through suffering, have completed a difficult quest. Within the film are many opinions, in many forms. Some are directly stated, others implied.

From confrontation, painful lessons were learned and some opinions were changed. To show others their living conditions in the Chicago slums, the Indians constructed teepees to form the first Chicago Indian Village and chose Michael Chosa as chief. Three months later, they were evicted. For two years, they demonstrated to publicize their plight, then in 1971 they squatted on the abandoned Belmont Harbor Missile Base. After three weeks, the police removed them from government property. Before the fracas, Warrington tells the camera, "I don't care what happens to me, anymore . . . What have they done to our minds?" Betty Jack, in tears, waves away a camerman as she sobs, "We'll die here for this land, right here and now." All three express directly the opinion that confrontation was the only way to effect a change; they believe strongly in the cause and are willing to go to any lengths to defend it. Ironically, their own opinions seem to have changed more than those of the "enemy," white people. The confrontation was violent, and the Indians lost against the tear gas of the police. The impact of defeat led these two women to alcoholism, then to self-awareness. Jack learned that "we think of ourselves as strong people, but we're not." She further discovered: "I am as good as anyone else . . . and I can speak up for myself." Chosa's comment that "the power of the movement comes from people, not the individual," implies a self-condemnation of his years as chieftain. Chosa now puts his energies into helping teenage Indians stay in high school: if the kids keep up their studies, they receive training in the martial arts. It is obvious that Chosa has curtailed his ego. Warrington entered a halfway house to overcome her drinking problem (at one point, Betty Jack asks, "Who's going to stop it?" and Warrington answers quietly, but firmly, "I am"), then became a case worker in the Phoenix Indian Outreach Center, offering her insights into her own problems to help others.

Betty Jack sums up the experiences with a provocative opinion: "What we had to go through, we had to go through to become what we are today." Through pain, she feels, she has gained understanding and an approach to living that she otherwise would not have had. Many in the audience will agree with the filmmaker that Betty and her family have exhibited the epical strength of heroes. Villains have been exterior (exploitive whites) and interior (psychological problems), but they were faced in whatever shape they took—faced, and overcome.

ACTIVITIES FOR THE STUDENT
1. What is the opinion of the filmmaker about Betty Chosa Jack, Michael Chosa, and Carol Warrington?
2. What is the implied opinion contained in Michael Chosa's remark, "The power of the movement comes from people, not the individual"?
3. Explain Betty Jack's opinion concerning the events she lived through.
4. Read Chapters 3-6 in William T. Hagan's *American Indians* (Chicago, IL: University of Chicago Press, 1961) and determine his opinion about the way the U. S. government has handled the Indians.
5. Read the hero tales in Stith Thompson's *Tales of the North American Indians* (Bloomington, IN: Indiana University Press, 1966), pp. 78-125. The storytellers had what opinion about the characteristics of the Indian?

PURPOSE

To determine mastery in reading comprehension, the College Board frequently asks questions about the author's purpose. The questions start in the following ways:

The author's main purpose is_____

The primary purpose of the passage is _____

mentions
The author describes } (something) in order to_____
does

The subject's primary purpose in (doing something) is to_____

These questions ask the student to determine *why* the authors wrote the passages.

An examination of the verbs in the answer choices will help the students to determine the answers. The following verbs, for instance, indicate that the author is concerned mainly with conveying content to an audience:

analyze	describe
explain	report
examine	relate
point out	pinpoint
show	demonstrate

As the students reread the passages, they can ask themselves the following questions. Has the author merely gathered information together about a subject? If so, the correct verb is probably "report" or "relate." If there are several items in the passage, does one item have more emphasis than the others? Then "point out" or "pinpoint" is the correct verb. Is the author giving causes, effects, or implications of the various features of one subject? Then "examine" or "analyze" is the answer. Is the author trying to have the reader visualize something? "Describe," "demonstrate," or "show" designates this purpose. In such passages, the giving of the information is the end in itself.

Other verbs show the author is trying to accomplish a more complex goal: not only presenting material, but also evaluating it. With the following verbs, the author wants the audience to form a conclusion about the material or to change an opinion:

expose	criticize
challenge	encourage
suggest	urge
persuade	convince
condemn	exemplify

compare

The author might be attacking for some reason (criticize, condemn, challenge, expose), offering a new interpretation or change in behavior (suggest, urge, convince, encourage, persuade), making the audience see the material as an example of an idea or as something typical (exemplify), or want the audience to note similarities or differences (compare).

There are many possible pre-film activities. Passages can be given the student to analyze, preferably passages from disciplines other than English. Some suggested essays are Ron Jones, *The Acorn People* (New York: Bantam, 1980); Susan Sontag, *Illness as Metaphor* (New York: Farrar, Straus & Giroux, 1978); R. Buckminster Fuller, *Operating Manual for Spaceship Earth* (New York: Pocket Books, 1972); Farley Mowat, *People of the Deer* (New York: Bantam, 1981); Loren Eiseley, *The Immense Journey* (New York: Random House, 1957); Matthew Josephson, *The*

Robber Barons (New York: Harcourt Brace Jovanovich, 1962); Ruth Benedict, *Patterns of Culture* (Bonston, MA: Houghton Mifflin, 1959); and Julius Fast, *Body Language* (New York: M. Evans & Co., 1970). The students can find the purpose in selections from the textbooks actually being used. On any one day, a typical newspaper would have samples of all the functions possible for writing, especially in editorials and letters to the editor. The student could easily cut out and identify articles from the paper for a bulletin board display. Instead of a normal montage, the youngsters could attach the items to an explication of the purpose for each.

The function of these films is to have the students start identifying purpose, so that when they approach the College Board, they can easily recognize the range of answers possible to such *why* questions. In some respects, the films are easier than the passages encountered on the SAT; in others, more difficult (the data is visualized but given quickly, and cannot be "reread"). The demands on the reader's comprehension of sentences might be difficult in a College Board passage, but there is no ambiguity as to purpose. The following films, however, frequently have more than one purpose (all are obviously intended to educate). As in the College Board, the students are asked to distinguish between the filmmaker's (author's) intended purpose, and, within a passage, a subject-character's purpose.

THE CITY THAT WAITS TO DIE (Time-Life: 42 min./color/1971)

The city that waits to die is San Francisco. In 1906 an earthquake that lasted 60 seconds devastated the city. At the time this documentary was made in early 1970, there were predictions that the activity of the San Andreas Fault would soon bring on another major earthquake that would once again destroy the city. Showing what geophysicists have learned about the fault and about earthquakes in general, the film questions why the city's citizens, building codes, and planners do not take into account the predictions of the scientists. At first glance, the purpose of the film would be to alert the citizenry to the potential danger, to incite them to depart from a deathtrap. The amount of data given about earthquakes and the discussion of some potential ways of controlling the San Andreas Fault suggest that the film is an educational and scientific work about earthquakes. However, the original audience were viewers of the BBC television network in England, and the filmmaker seems to have been treating them to entertainment in the same genre as the catastrophe movie, such as *The Towering Inferno* or *The Poseidon Adventure*.

Certainly the film uses devices not normally associated with a science film. The earthquake of 1906 is shown as if a photographic slide show is being given; we hear the audible click of the machine. Then comes the film title, a highly dramatic one. As the title fades, five motorcyclists zoom over the crest of a hill, speed through the city, leap into space as a musical group called "Thanksgiving" sings a song about the destruction of the city. Are the cyclists angels of death? At the end of the movie they are riding again toward the city, and we hear the song in the background. Do they represent the recklessness of people who ignore the signs of danger and continue to live in the city? Are the cyclists tracing the line of the San Andreas Fault? Whatever else they might be, they are dramatic. Archive film footage of the 1906 quake is followed by shots of the rebuilt city to the music of Bach's *Toccata and Fugue in D Minor* for organ (dramatic music associated in films with madmen like Captain Nemo in *Twenty Thousand Leagues Under the Sea* and Bela Lugosi in *White Zombie*).

Tension is increased as we are told that if a major quake hit San Francisco during the rush hours, the city's death toll would be equal to the total number of Americans who died in Vietnam, maybe even more. The reason is that the fault line south of

San Francisco has been shifting at about an inch a year, whereas the land under San Francisco is bottled up; when the land in the city does move, it will move as violently as it did in the earlier quake. In a single community, 13 public schools have been built on the fault, as well as a police department, a hospital, and a civil defense center. As we comprehend the scale of the potential disaster, any feelings of security about modern building codes are wiped out by the film's portrayal of the effects of the Caracas, Venezuela, earthquake on high-rise buildings that followed American anti-quake specifications. Our terror is further enhanced by film footage a sailor took of the Good Friday earthquake in Anchorage, Alaska, in 1964. His camera records the disappearance into a chasm of some children and dogs who were standing on the dock.

In addition to getting maximum power out of a dramatic subject, the film activates, through thinly veiled implications, our suspicion about the motivations of those in control of the city. We are told it was called the San Francisco *fire*, not earthquake, a euphemism to hide the fact that the city was in trouble. (By whom? and why?) A scientist states that his and his fellow scientists' major duty is to step beyond the "official responsibilities to our employers" to warn the public. (Does that mean the employers are trying to keep information from the public? Why?) A specialist announces that "when public officials, engineers, speculators refuse to listen to [the facts] . . . we have found the place where the responsibility rests." (Are they all in a cabal to make money off naive citizens? Where do these money-makers live?) Finally, we see shots of people going about their business in the city that waits to die. They are the innocent victims.

What are the scientists doing about earthquakes? They have been recording the "events" that precede an earthquake in order to predict future disturbances more accurately. To study the movement of the earth they used geotolites, laser measuring devices. They have also been examining possible ways of relieving "tensions" in the fault. One possibility is underground nuclear explosions. The film is not optimistic about this approach: a scientist admits that they are possibly as dangerous as the quake itself. Another is to raise the fluid level deep underground, the way the Army did by accident at Denver, Colorado, through the subterranean disposal of nerve gas, an action that triggered a series of small earthquakes in the area. The scientists are also warning against building houses on the fault itself, or in the bay mud areas, which have no bedrock under them. We are shown evidence of the effect of the fault on the town of Hollister, where street curbing has shifted. The warnings of the specialists are vivid enough to give cause for genuine alarm for anyone living in the Bay area. For the rest of us, there is the sinister and delicious tension of tragedy about to happen.

ACTIVITIES FOR THE STUDENT
1. What is the purpose of the film for those who originally saw the film in England on BBC TV?
2. What is the purpose of the film for Californians?
3. What is the purpose in the film of showing the Army problem with nerve gas in Colorado?
4. What is the purpose in the film of the motorcyclists?
5. What is the purpose of the geotolite, the laser measuring device used by the scientists?
6. What is the purpose of showing the incident in Alaska?

GOODNIGHT MISS ANN (Pyramid Films: 28 min./color/1978)

This boxing film does not present the sentimental world of *Rocky*, that paean to the American Dream in which the naive little guy has a chance at the big time. The title, *Goodnight Miss Ann*, the verbal signal of the fighter to the trainer that the towel should be thrown in, captures the film's purpose. This documentary focuses on the Los Angeles Main Street Gym and the Olympic Arena to expose to us that boxing is a tough life that takes a tremendous toll on the body and face at an earning rate of about $0.10 per hour, to show us that the young Mexicans now, like the minority groups that preceded them in the arena, are trying, through boxing, to get out of the slums, to avoid skid row (an area that is right outside the door of the gym), to make something of themselves. The trouble is, only one fighter in about 500,000 ever makes it. The emotional jolt of this movie comes from the irony that for all the bleakness of the sport, the fighters, managers, and trainers are hooked on it. There is also an entertainment purpose.

Bobby Chacon is an example of an actual success story. He admits that before he tried boxing, he had been in trouble with the police, had done some street fighting, and had taken drugs. At 18, he started boxing; by 22, after 24 fights, he was a champion in the featherweight division. He lost the title, then started back. Bobby is now somewhat cynical about success itself. He had spent a lot of money by the time he won the title, had had fans around him, had signed autographs. On the comeback trail, he distrusts the fans' worship and adds, "When you get it [success], you wish that it'd never come. . . ." In spite of his reservations, he still seems to enjoy the congratulations after a triumph.

For most, however, boxing proves to be a brutal experience. One fighter complains that "all he does is get beat up for a living. . . ." A black manager explains that now there are not many white fighters because "white boys can get a job." An articulate blond fighter tells us the Mexicans will "risk their lives to make a hundred bucks to send . . . to their mother and father in some small province in Mexico. . . ." The interviewed fighters agree that a good manager is important; too often, a manager will throw the fighter to "the wolves" or destroy the fighter's health. The effects of boxing are shown through a sequence of closeups of boxers' faces starting with the young and moving through middle age to the old: as the series progresses the nose, mouth, and eyebrows become more battered; on some, there are cauliflower ears.

For all the tragic overtones, the documentary shows the powerful attraction to boxing, one that is not easy to get out of one's system. Bobby reports that in the gym there are no middle-aged people, just the kids who are fighters and the oldtimers, those who are trying to "make something out of themselves," something they didn't accomplish when they were fighting. A trainer tells us that boxers are born, not made. They have to have a "meanness . . . a willingness to take punishment . . . to sacrifice . . . to stand and deliver." It takes guts, because when "you start to lose, no one is going to help you . . . you're alone." Bobby complains that he doesn't want "to come back all my life," but he is still in there giving everything he has. The blond boxer admits he really enjoys the sport. And at times, so do the filmmakers.

The ambiguity of approach makes the function of the film interesting. It is partly educational in that the film shows the "realistic" and unglamorous aspect of a sport, but it is also entertaining as we watch the process of training, the desperation of some, the courage of others in confrontations that are, we are told, "violent, raw . . . classic." The spokespersons in the film are quite articulate, anecdotal, and likeable; they might criticize, but they are also hooked.

ACTIVITIES FOR THE STUDENT
1.   The filmmaker's main purpose in this film is to do what?
2.   The film shows a series of closeups of fighters' faces in order to make what point?
3.   Bobby Chacon's primary purpose currently in fighting is to do what?
4.   The film shows bums sleeping it off on skid row for what purpose?

TRAGEDY OF THE RED SALMON (Doubleday Multimedia: 24 min./color/ 1975)

Fertilized salmon eggs were placed by scientists in Frazer Lake in Alaska. For one year, the young fish built up strength, then they migrated to the ocean. After four years, the surviving fish returned to Frazer Lake to spawn. The camera crew of Jacques Cousteau followed the spring run of the salmon back to the original spawning ground. Their film shows the drive and courage of the fish as they fight their way upstream against tiers of rocks in a waterfall. The spawning ritual and the death of the fish soon follow. The purposes of the film are 1) to report on the life cycle of the sockeye salmon, 2) to demonstrate the universal law of the survival of the fittest, and 3) to show the "heart of the hero" (in this case, the salmon) that drives it toward the achievement of a difficult quest. Except for a few shots of the fish eggs developing and the narrator's brief summary of the five-year life cycle, the film reports on the last season of the salmon's life. They return upstream to spawn only once. To acclimatize themselves, they find an area where fresh water mixes with salt water. During that time, physiological changes take place, such as the body turning red, the head green, the female body bulging from the roe, the male's teeth protruding, and his mouth becoming a hooked snout. What allows the salmon to find their source? Scientists conjecture they might have scent compasses, or be sensitive to magnetic fields, or be aware of variations in gravity. Whatever the cause, they will try to return, no matter how dangerous the trip. To make their jumps of up to six feet at about 15½ miles per hour, the fish wait for backwash at a falls to swirl in the proper direction, then take advantage of its propulsion.

The life cycle of the fish demonstrates the universal law of survival of the fittest. Those fish that make it past the human predators, the falls, the various weirs, and the animal predators, are near exhaustion because they have used up the fat in their bodies, but they are the strongest of the lot, a fact that helps to improve the species. Out of the 5,000 eggs a female lays in fresh water, only 10 will hatch, develop, and live to come back to the spawning ground. The courtship and mating last for a few weeks, then the salmon, with fungus spreading across their bodies, die in less than a fortnight.

The purpose that makes the film extremely powerful is Cousteau's wish to pay homage to the "heart of the hero." The film documents the bravery of the fish as they fulfill the purpose of their lives. We watch them hurtling themselves upward at the foot of the falls, only to crash into rocks. Cousteau observes that they could just as well mate downstream, but must reach their goal, and they will commit suicide in their attempts. Cousteau and his crew lie on their stomachs on the bank by the spawning ground and watch the "elected ones dash forward" to the mating ceremony. There are a "few days of supreme excitement," then their bodies undergo an aging that would take 20 to 40 years in a human. The arena of pleasure soon becomes a graveyard. "The heart of the hero is the last to die," Cousteau comments. But the images that haunt are not those of the dying and dead; they are those of the bodies hurtling out of the swirling water, those leaps of bravery that make the famous scientist exclaim in awe, "Incredible."

ACTIVITIES FOR THE STUDENT

1. Choosing the correct verb, complete the following sentences:
    a. For the filmmaker, the purpose is to. . .
        (1) urge _____
        (2) condemn _____
        (3) report _____
        (4) pinpoint _____
        (5) persuade _____
    [Answer: 3]
    b. For the scientists, the purpose is to. . .
        (1) demonstrate _____
        (2) encourage _____
        (3) compare _____
        (4) urge _____
        (5) challenge _____
    [Answer: 1]
    c. For Cousteau, the purpose is to. . .
        (1) praise _____
        (2) criticize _____
        (3) expose _____
        (4) describe _____
        (5) challenge _____
    [Answer: 1]
2. What is the purpose of using this film in a science class?

DEMAGOGUES AND DO-GOODERS: NOISY VOICES OF THE DEPRESSION
(Time-Life: 18 min./b&w/1972)

Segments of the old weekly newsreel *The March of Time* from 1935 to the early 1940s have been "edited and rearranged" to show the influence on the American people of Huey Long, Gerald Smith, Father Coughlin, Father Divine, and Dr. Frances Everett Townsend. During the Great Depression, the people turned to "anyone who could offer them a future," but the newsreel editors suggest that the first four definitely had things on their minds other than the salvation of the country. The film is infuriating in its utterance of value-judgements, its assumption that the audience already knows something about the period, its abridgment of biography, and its lack of detail in the explication of a belief, but as a film for the analysis of purpose, it offers fantastic riches. For the modern filmmaker, the purpose is to convince the audience that extremists or dissident groups are necessary to keep the country honest. For *The March of Time*, the purpose was to expose the leaders as self-serving. For the followers of the do-gooders, the leaders served the purpose of showing them how to escape from the Depression.

What is the purpose for the modern filmmakers? If the main purpose were to educate, the film would have had to offer many more facts. If it were to entertain, there would be longer excerpts from the speeches, more evidence of wit or charm. No, there seems to be something else on the filmmakers' minds. We are told that the "lunatic fringe had a lasting effect on the country." "Lunatic fringe" is an insulting phrase, but it is being used with irony. The final comment on Townsend is that his actions "forced the New Deal to speed up social reform." Good did come from these people, then. For a present-day audience, the film suggests that dissident groups are part of the democratic system, that they serve an important function. One has the feeling that the "we" now includes that "lunatic fringe." (They serve as the gadfly to keep "us" on the right track.) The film warns, though, that leaders of dissident groups might have other interests at heart. Last, but not least, in the film's purpose there is a desire to create pride in a period of history when America was on the ropes but was preparing for a comeback.

The original purpose of *The March of Time* newsreel clips is totally different. The newsreel commentator suggests that the leaders really were on quests for personal power, that their motives were self-serving. Indeed, the newsreel is quite open in its condemnation of some leaders: Long is a "self-styled kingfisher," a "grass-roots radical," and a person of "ruthless ambition." One can assume the purpose of the original newsreel is to debunk, to show the "truth" to the public. There is also the establishment of a "we" and a "them" attitude; the "them," the "lunatic fringe," is aligned with the outsiders who threaten democracy, such as the fascists, Hitler, gangsters, and imposters.

Finally, for Americans at the time, what purpose did these "demogogues and do-gooders" serve? For the public, each of the figures was a means of getting out of the Depression: Huey Long presented the "Share Our Wealth" movement; Gerald Smith saw himself as Long's political heir and, according to a newspaper headline, pictured himself as "America's Hitler"; Father Coughlin sponsored a powerful political lobby that "smacked more and more of fascism" through his Single Voice National Union of Social Justice; Father Divine, whose followers believed him to be God, gave them "black pride and an early form of black power"; Dr. Townsend pressed to have pensions of $200.00 per month for everyone over 55, an increase in buying power that would end the Depression and give security to the old. Long challenged FDR for the presidency but was assassinated. Smith, Coughlin, and Townsend united to challenge FDR but were defeated. Father Divine's followers carried placards advertising his political platform (we are not told where, when, or why) that stated, "Abolish All Tariffs," "Doctors Must Pay if Patients Die," "God Has as Much Right in Politics as in Church," but he, too, lost.

The film is a challenge to students who are looking for purpose because of the three different purposes discussed above. It will also make them want to know more about the leaders and about the era in general.

ACTIVITIES FOR THE STUDENT
1. What are the filmmakers' primary purposes in collecting the newsreel footage?
2. What is the purpose these leaders served to the American people of the thirties?
3. What original purposes did the newsreel footage serve for the American public in 1935-1940?
4. What is *The March of Time* suggesting as the real purpose for these leaders in attracting a following?
5. What function did Townsend serve in American history?
6. What is the purpose in showing the later years of Coughlin, Smith, Divine, and Townsend? (Their endings are ironic commentaries on their lives. A doctor assassinated Long; Coughlin ended up in "a parish backwater." The war "shut up" Smith, who later built a 200-foot statue of Jesus in the Ozarks as a tourist attraction. Father Divine died in great wealth, owning over 40 homes. Townsend died at age 91, no longer famous.)

———

A MEASURE OF CHANGE (Urbanimage Films: 28 min./color/1975)

The problems of urban renewal are illustrated in this study of Newburyport, Massachusetts. Plans made in the 1960s to make the downtown a "catalyst for economic development" required the razing of a number of old buildings. Historian Truman Nelson explains that when the people saw the "dustbowls" created by the demolition work, it was as if "a bomb dropped." A small coalition of citizens formed to argue for a different approach: to renovate the buildings, to keep the beauties of the past, and to make the new buildings compatible with the old aesthetic. Although at times there have been major disagreements within the community, the approach seems to have worked. The main purpose of this film is to convince the audience of the validity of an approach to urban renewal that is sensitive to the heritage of a community, the needs of the citizens, the economic survival of the downtown, and the quality of life in an urban area.

The key to Newburyport is the awareness of "the importance of history as a communal experience." A town that made its money from the waterfront, shipbuilding, trade, and privateering, Newburyport originally maintained both common space held in trust for public use (for cattle grazing) and public access to the water's edge. Over time, patterns of industrial use built a "wall" of buildings between the public and the river. Such selfish behavior has produced a problem for the town today, namely the reconstruction of the waterfront area and the maintenance of the public access to the water's edge. In other ways, Newburyport has shown an admirable sense of community spirit in solving problems. Part of the town's tradition was that after the fire of 1811, the business community would adhere to such standards for new construction as the use of brick and granite, and the building of firewalls and chimneys above the roof line. In the redevelopment of the 1970s, the town prohibited cars in some areas to offer pedestrian walkways, made lighting more compatible with the era of the buildings, buried utility lines, put in brick paving, and restricted business sign size to allow for a unified character. This working together of the business community and the citizens with the return to a concern for the public's comfort and safety led to the upgrading of private property in the rest of the town. Although "increasing property values compelled older residents to leave" (the film's euphemism for "the tax rate went up"), there has been an increase in community pride as some have spent "thousands of hours [on their homes] stripping away caked-up paint . . . exposing original detail." Toward the end of the film are shots of the town enjoying a parade, picnic, and community games that link the people to their past.

The film suggests honestly the problems that are involved in urban renewal. What about the people who are forced to move out because of increased taxes? Should new buildings merely copy, rather than express new ideas in architecture? What about car congestion in the downtown? What concessions can be made concerning parking? Updating the film, through research, on Newburyport since 1974, when the film was made, would be illuminating. For all the questions, the purpose of the film is still clear; it convinces that urban quality can be achieved.

ACTIVITIES FOR THE STUDENT

1. What is the purpose for the filmmaker in making this film?
2. What were the original purposes of the waterfront in Newburyport?
3. What is the purpose in urban renewal of preserving original constructions?
4. What is the purpose of showing in detail the qualities of compatibility for constructing new buildings?
5. What was the purpose of the Friends of Newburyport Waterfront in blocking the construction of the new building proposed by the Redevelopment Authority?

DIRECTLY STATED FACTS

Surely the easiest question of all to answer in terms of a reading passage is one that asks for the facts actually stated in a selection. It is the bread-and-butter question for any teacher, the subject of ridicule on the part of public school satirists, and a staple of the College Board.

The range of questions on the SAT that require recall of facts is actually impressive. There are, of course, the simple pinpointing questions that ask only for data, such as:

According to the passage, a quarterback must exhibit what qualities?

At times, the reader is asked to give evidence for the major idea of the reading selection:

The author's theory that spiders changed their way of hunting to keep up with the evolution of insects is based on what information?

This type of question sometimes requires an awareness of a comparison or of cause-and-effect relationships as shown in the following three examples:

1. "According to the passage, modern cities compared to those in the medieval period are. . ."
2. "According to the passage, a quarterback will have more endurance and can take more punishment if. . ." (The search is for a cause or condition.)
3. "According to the passage, the study of the language capabilities of chimps accomplishes what goal? (The search is for the effect of a series of actions.)

Even though the text will clearly establish the comparison or cause-and-effect relationship, the answer rarely is worded the same way. The questions require a scanning of a passage for content. One approach is for the student to read the questions, read the text, then answer the questions.

At times, the Board quizzes students on directly stated facts by asking them to distinguish between accurate and inaccurate paraphrases. To make sure the student decodes the question correctly, the key word is placed in bold-faced type:

1. "According to the passage, which of the following statements about a computer is FALSE?"
2. "All of the following are specifically mentioned in the passage as the stages of language development of deaf children EXCEPT:"

Test takers must be alert for such twists in the directly stated facts game.

Another convolution asks the readers to juggle in their minds several stated facts at once. Two such examples follow:

1. "The author provides information on language development to answer which of the following questions?"

Here the reader must search for an answer in the text for each question that has something to do with the topic of the selection.

2. "According to the passage, the standards for public housing in Poland include which of the following?"
    a. Size of the apartment depends on the size of the family.
    b. No apartment may have less than 1½ hours of sun in the winter months.

c.   Windows must have insulation.

d.   Everyone has equal right for a balcony.

[Answer choice: (1) a only; (2) a and c only; (3) b and d only; (4) a, b, and d only]

It is worth noting again that the reading comprehension section of the Boards rarely includes fiction; rather, they use passages found in science or social studies essays. Consequently, assignments where students read novels and look for the theme or main idea are not a good preparation for these kinds of SAT questions. Nonfiction selections should be assigned and read for their proof data and logic. Students should also be exposed to the range of SAT questions.

In dealing with each of the films in this sequence, let the students have the questions before the film is shown. If the movie is long, stop the projector at the end of a sequence to give them a chance to answer the questions while the content is fresh.

THE MAKING OF A QUARTERBACK (Learning Corp. of America: 30 min./ color/1979)

This film explains what it takes to be a quarterback. The concrete, detailed information given by Roger Staubach and Dan Reeves has the same density as an SAT reading passage. For some students, the subject matter might be as "alien" as the subject matter on the test about economics, biology, anthropology, or geology; for others, their fondness for the sport might ensure better recall and thus build confidence in the skill of restating concrete data.

What makes a quarterback great? We are told that perseverance, self-discipline, and self-confidence are important. As the film progresses, hard work, good habits, a consistent training program, endurance, strength to take punishment, and a competitive spirit are added to the list. Not stated directly, but definitely implied, is the need for intelligence—the ability to look around, to size up a situation, to prepare an emergency plan and to plot ahead. At the end, the narrator states that the superior quarterback is willing "to give all there is to give," wants to win, and knows how to lose.

The film suggests ways to get to the top, offers illustrations, then repeats the major points at the end of the film. For our purposes, the film's cause-effect information is especially important. 1) Warm-up exercises done correctly help to avoid injuries. For the quarterback, there can be less injury to the back and arms if consistent exercises are done. Leaping exercises help to build stamina and strength; shoulder rolls teach the player to come up off the ground running. 2) Strong hands are important. Dropping the ball and quickly catching it in midair, first with one hand and then the other; passing the ball around the body and legs faster and faster; flipping the ball between the hands with the arms extended are three ways to build strong hands. 3) Working with a medicine ball builds strength. Either standing seven or eight yards apart or throwing while tilted back on inclined boards, one player to another, strengthens the arms. Occasionally, the ball is heaved at the partner's chest (rather than overhead) to simulate the impact of a charging player in a game. 4) Weight lifting helps Roger Staubach to have a stronger throwing arm and to have more endurance to take punishment. 5) Throwing techniques can be improved either by hurling the ball from a kneeling position to a partner 10 or 20 yards away or by throwing in a stationary standing position, the legs shoulder width apart. We are told the partner should form a target with his hands to help improve accuracy. 6) Throwing on the run requires that the shoulders be squared with the line of scrimmage: the ball must not be thrown across the body. (At this point in the film, there is an aside about developing leadership ability in the huddle. Keep the others in line; only one person, the quarterback, does the talking. He takes control, sticks to the game plan, steps into the huddle only after his plan of attack is set, and breaks huddle once the play is called.) 7) Practicing taking the snap from the center is crucial. With hands under the center, the quarterback looks in both directions to pick up information. He should avoid looking into the back of the center. The ball should be snapped against the top hand to avoid the chances of a fumble. Without tipping off the opposition, the quarterback barks out the count in a loud voice with a distinct cadence. 8) When running with the ball, the quarterback must keep both hands on the ball. When he hands the ball off, the quarterback must keep the fake going, not stand around watching the rest of the play. 9) Before passing, he must keep his head turned downfield and then throw the ball high. He must practice the various set-ups: three steps back for a quick pass; five steps back for a medium distance pass; seven steps for a long pass.

ACTIVITIES FOR THE STUDENT

1. Shoulder rolls during warm-up exercises teach the player what skill?
2. Working with a partner while doing hand strengthening exercises accomplishes what?
3. According to the film, Roger Staubach works out with weights to accomplish what?
4. According to the film, the quarterback avoids looking into the back of the center for what reason?
5. According to the film, the quarterback establishes his leadership ability through what behavior?
6. All of the following qualities are specifically mentioned as being necessary in a good quarterback EXCEPT:
   a. self-discipline
   b. endurance
   c. intelligence
   d. competitive spirit
   e. the willingness to give all there is to give
   [Answer: c]

COME INTO MY PARLOUR, SAID THE SPIDER. . . (Arthur Mokin Productions, Inc.: 20 min./color/1977)

A film wholly devoted to the hunting techniques of spiders? Certainly this is a subject that in essence has limited appeal. In the hands of some very creative Australian filmmakers, however, the material becomes extremely engrossing. A clear, well-written script, handsome photography, and a soundtrack of humorous and exciting noises do the trick. As with a horror film, the youngsters might cringe, but their attention surely will not flag.

The spider is presented as a predator whose "job" is keeping the insect population from becoming "intolerable" through their sheer numbers or their stripping of the earth's vegetation. The spider is thus one of nature's built-in checks and balances. As the lifestyles of insects evolved and diversified, so did the hunting techniques of the spiders. The narrator suggests some insects evolved wings "perhaps to escape from the spiders." The spiders took countermeasures by following the insects upward, building webs to catch them in flight.

The film offers everything you ever did or did not want to know about its subject. 1) Spiders that make webs are shortsighted. They rely on the vibrations of the web felt through their feet to give them information. 2) The spider wraps its insect catch with thread to immobilize it, preventing the victim from hurting the attacker. 3) The spider kills by injecting a lethal dose of poison through its fangs. 4) Spiders can feed only on liquids. A strong fluid in their mouths allows them to predigest their victims externally by turning them into a fluid meal. Spider enthusiasts will be disappointed to learn that the film avoids discussion of this bug's enemies (except for the fact it can scare off an assassin bug), mating habits, and life span. The concentration is on the activities of a killing machine.

Although some spiders use the simple stalk and pounce technique, others build elaborate traps and snares. Flower spiders will stay perfectly still on the blossom so as not to deter insects from approaching the nectar. Then they pounce. Similarly, the tama spider makes itself inconspicuous on a tree trunk, waits, rushes around the victim girdling it with silk, bites it, then carts it off for a future snack. The trap-door spider makes a camouflaged, weather-proofed lid out of silk and soil and attaches one end of it to the opening of the burrow; vibrations alert it to the approach of an insect, then out it pops. The dianopis spider takes a good half hour to make a rectangular-shaped net that can be stretched with its claws; after a series of tests to make sure the net holds together, it drops the net on its victim. The most elaborate snare is created by the magnificent spider which feeds only on male moths of a particular species; it emits a scent that is similar to that of the female moth and lures the male to its trap line: a long strand with sticky globules that the spider rotates with one leg until the victim blunders into it.

The film follows the conventions of the classic horror show. There are near misses. In the early part of this study, one wonders how the hunter keeps alive, because the spiders keep missing their prey. The climax is the capturing of the moth by the magnificent spider. The poor moth, led on by the female scent, ends up in the terrifying embrace of the killer spider, and there is no escape. The music at that point is a hollow organ sound associated with early thrillers.

ACTIVITIES FOR THE STUDENT
1. According to the film, some insects evolved wings for what reason?
2. According to the film, if the insect population explosion were not curtailed, the result would be what?
3. All of the following data about spiders is specifically given in the film EXCEPT:
   a. the web-making spiders are short-sighted.
   b. spiders can feed only on liquids.
   c. the spider kills by injecting venom into its victim.
   d. the life expectancy of a spider is only a few months.
   e. the spider wraps up its victim with its thread.
   [Answer: d]
4. According to the film, which of the following statements about the hunting techniques of spiders is FALSE?
   a. some spiders stalk and pounce.
   b. some spiders rely on camouflage and remain motionless.
   c. some spiders hypnotize their victims.
   d. some spiders build trap doors to hide behind.
   e. some spiders emit a scent to attract their victims.
   [Answer: c]

5.   According to the film, some spiders have specialized tastes, such as the magnificent spider, which feeds only on what?

AMAZULU—PEOPLE OF THE SKY (FilmFair Communications: 23.25 min./ color/1979)

An old chieftain tells the young a story of the Zulu past in his native language. The narrator of the film suggests, in English, that the events during a typical day in any current Zulu settlement would be the same as in that glorious past of the old man's memory. Thus starts this study of the Zulu culture. Using a small village near a river as its example, the film explores the values, activities, and folklore of the People of the Sky.

The day begins with the herd boys of the village (kraal) letting out the cattle. We are told that cattle are "Zulu gold": the number of cattle determines a man's wealth, and they are the payment to his future father-in-law for a wife. Each animal has a name. The boys use pointed sticks to protect the herd from leopards, lions, or other predators. If any of the cattle are lost, the boys are called to account. From age six until the rite of passage (the time when he learns to use a spear), the young male's role in the village is that of herder. He spends his day, once the animals are grazing by the river, in games such as shooting his stick at a rolling target, or stick fighting with the emphasis on footwork and agility, or in acquiring information about the quality of the plants and animals around him. Such observation tells the boys, for instance, that the Zulu plum is edible because small bucks eat them. They also spend their time bragging about their chief's wealth to boys from other kraals.

Women have a variety of jobs to perform during the day. While the maidens fetch water in clay pots that are covered with lids of leaves, they sing of "husbands to be and lovers lost." The married women plant the maize, crush the grain into flour with stone pestles, prepare two meals (noon and evening) of maize porridge cooked in giant black pots. They also feed the children, sweep the dance area in the village, make bead necklaces and bracelets that have the identifying mark of the village on them, and put straw roofs over the shells of new houses. Late in the day, the women bring back dry wood for the fires and feed the men.

The adult males are the providers and defenders of the village. They hunt, build fires started with twirling sticks, make weapons such as spears and shields, and build new huts. The narrator suggests the weaver bird's nest probably served as the inspiration for the men's hut building techniques. Pliant long sticks are thrust into the ground, then curved over until the other end can be imbedded in the earth. Specialists in the village are the herb doctor, who lives apart from the others, and the metals worker, who produces spear tips. In the afternoon, the men dance out the stories of past glories, those confrontations for cattle and honor. The music for the dance includes singing and whistling.

In the late afternoon, the cattle are returned to the village pen. In the evening, the old man tells his story about Shaka, the Black Napoleon who came to power one year after Waterloo. Shaka could kill a rabbit with a spear at 50 yards. In the old man's story, Shaka is killed by his half-brother before the fulfillment of his prophecy about the coming of the swallows (the white men who defeated the Zulu). As the old man talks, a youngster falls asleep.

In the Ruth Benedict tradition (*Patterns of Culture* [Boston, MA: Houghton Mifflin, 1959]), the film delineates the general character of the people. 1) Nature provides everything they need (except, it would seem, beads, cooking pots, and the metal in their spears) and serves as a model for the people. 2) They have a rich folklore that continues the traditions of the past. 3) They are fond of boasting and fighting, and their games, dances, and stories reinforce their values.

ACTIVITIES FOR THE STUDENT
1. According to the film, what are the rules of stick fighting between two herd boys?
   [Answer: they do not use the point; they parry with the left hand, strike with the right; the footwork is most important, and they do not become angry or try to hit on the knuckles.]
2. According to the film, what information does the design on the men's large shield reveal?
   [Answer: rank, experience, and regiment]
3. According to the film, how is a spear made?
   [Answer: the iron ore is smelted; the metal is shaped by being hit with a stone while hot. Once honed to razor sharpness, it is inserted in the wooden shaft while the metal is hot, glued by silla juice, and bound with bark, the tail of an ox, and magic.]
4. What are some of the animals photographed in the film?
   [Answer: bucks, giraffes, zebra, kudu antelope, rhinoceros, and weaver bird]
5. According to the film, how do the Zulu eat?
   [Answer: there are no implements other than the pots, so they form a ball of maize with their fingers, then eat it.]
6. According to the film, the Zulu fashioned their homes after what item in nature?
   [Answer: the nest of the weaver bird]
7. What is the source of the old man's pipe?
   [Answer: a cattle horn]

LANGUAGE DEVELOPMENT (CRM Educational Films: 19 min./color/1973)
Before five years of age, all normal children have mastered the basics of their native language, an intellectual feat all the more remarkable in that they have not had any formal language instruction. In order to determine the way children accomplish this, linguists have analyzed the stages of language growth, made comparison studies of language development in the deaf, and experimented with chimpanzees to determine their language capabilities. The findings of the experts have shed light on the process of language development, but have not explained fully the cause of this phenomenon. Instead, we are offered two conflicting theories concerning the nature of language acquisition. Thanks to the many shots of children playing in the Arroyo Elementary School (in Simi Valley, California), cartoons that illustrate the stages of language development, and scenes of deaf children practicing sign language, there are a charm and warmth to this film that raise it above ordinary linguistic primers. The effect of the film on secondary students is usually to prompt a flood of anecdotes about what they have observed in their own experience, a reaction that is a sign of a successful movie.

With great clarity, the script makes the following points about language acquisition:

a. In over 30 cultures representing 30 different languages, children showed that they learned to speak in the same sequence of steps at the same rate.
b. The first stage of "language" is *crying*, the sound a baby makes to express basic needs for food and comfort.

c.   From three to four months, a baby is *cooing*, the stage when he or she first experiments with sound (which increases in frequency and variety).

d.   By six months, the baby is *babbling*, a stage that shows an increase in the type and number of sounds; up to this point in their development, all babies in all language communities sound the same.

e.   By 10 months, the baby's experiments with stress and pitch patterns produce *echolalic babbling*, an imitation of adult language; at this stage, deaf infants cease to vocalize.

f.   At 12 months, a baby reaches the *one word* stage, where he or she identifies tangible objects; one word functions as a sentence and intonation gives meaning; language is now used to define the environment.

g.   When *two words* are given together, there is the start of syntax; as in a telegram, nonessential words are left out; experiences are now being shared through language.

h.   From two to three years, the child combines *three words* and starts using consistent rules to form sentences; the youngster knows grammar intuitively and masters most of the basics of the adult language.

i.   During the next stage, the child suffers from *over-generalization*, where a rule of grammar is applied to a situation in which it does not apply (past tense of hurt: hurted; the plural of mouse: mouses). Before entering this stage, the child actually uses irregular verbs correctly. The child develops a conception of number (otherwise plurals could not be made) and of time (otherwise verb tense could not be understood). Research reveals that over-generalization occurs in the "signing" of deaf children, too.

j.   Using plastic symbols that stand for words, trained chimps can make statements and ask questions and are able to view a plastic object literally and in terms of its symbolic meaning.

Theorists differ sharply on whether the human mind is genetically predetermined to learn language or if language is learned through imitation and reinforcement. The film leans toward Noam Chomsky's view that language is biologically programmed in humans. The film also proves that linguistics can be presented in a lively, caring way if the filmmaker has artistic sensitivities, a control over language, and the desire to communicate clearly to a wide public audience.

ACTIVITIES FOR THE STUDENT

1.   According to the film, deaf children go through what language stages?
2.   According to the film, chimps do all of the following EXCEPT:
     a.   decode the literal features of a plastic object
     b.   decode the symbolic meaning of a plastic object
     c.   vocalize a one-word sentence
     d.   answer questions with plastic symbols
     [Answer: c]
3.   According to the film *echolalic babbling* is an imitation of what?
4.   According to the film, learning the rules of number and tense produces what stage in language development?
5.   Linguists are divided over what issue of language development?
6.   Youngsters have mastered the basics of language by what age?

———————

A COMPUTER GLOSSARY: OR COMING TO TERMS WITH THE DATA PROCESSING MACHINE (Encyclopaedia Britannica: 10 min./color/1968)

This fast-paced cartoon by Charles and Ray Eames offers in a brief period of time a great deal of information about an electronic, digital computer. It does so by explicating some of the special words in the computer field. Because the film is short, it can be shown twice and discussed within a class period. The second viewing will also reveal more of the movie's wit.

The thesis of *A Computer Glossary* is that the "key to understand a new or special field is to get to know something of its mood, its particular flavor." This can be done by learning the field's jargon. (This approach also justifies the "coming to terms" pun in the film's title.) The computer, in this film, is the servant of humans, not their master and not a threat. The value of the machine is that it can quickly solve problems—as long as the programmer states them in terms of the Boolean Logic of "yes" or "no" choices. To illustrate the way the computer sorts information into those "yes" or "no" decisions, the cartoon diagrams at the bottom of the screen the computer choices of a man's daily routine from the alarm going off to his eventual return to bed. We soon realize that the "flavor" of the computer world in this film is the intellectual excitement and wonder at the speed and efficiency of the machine.

The terms forming the glossary are legion. An *electronic digital computer*, we are told, accepts instruction and information; following the instructions, it performs operations on the information and reports the results. *Hardware* refers to the devices themselves, while *software* means the programs and the procedures. A *program* is a set of instructions for performing computer operations, and a *flow chart* is a graphic version of a program in which symbols are used to represent operations. A *subroutine* is a larger problem and can itself be part of a larger unit. A *mnemonic* is an easily remembered code word for one or more computer instructions; *language* is a collection of mnemonics selected and organized to allow convenient expression of a problem. *Boolean Logic* is the symbolic way of stating a problem in terms of "yes" or "no" decisions. A *nanosecond* is one one-thousandth of a millionth of a second, the amount of time in which a basic operation can take place. *Simulation* is the use of a computer program as a model of a real situation. *Pattern recognition* is the automatic identification and classification of shapes, forms, and relationships, such as: a) listening to a spoken phrase and recognizing the words, b) inspecting a fingerprint and identifying the owner, c) scanning satellite photographs and locating a possible hurricane, d) reading a photomicrograph and identifying an abnormality, and e) examining a chessboard and choosing a good next move. Finally, *algorithm* is the step-by-step procedure designed to lead to the solution of a problem. (All these definitions are statements taken directly from the film's soundtrack.)

The glossary shows the overall definition of the "computer": the terms for feeding information to the computer, the way the machine works out problems, the length of time the operation takes, and the practical uses for the machine. Not bad for 10 minutes.

ACTIVITIES FOR THE STUDENT

1. According to the film, if one knows the key terms or jargon of a special field, then one achieves what?
2. According to the film, pattern recognition includes all of the following EXCEPT:
   a. inspecting a fingerprint
   b. examining a chessboard

c.   scanning satellite photographs
d.   diagnosing the treatment for a disease
[Answer: d]
3.   The film defines all of the following terms EXCEPT:
a.   mnemonic
b.   nanosecond
c.   interface
d.   algorithm
e.   software
[Answer: c]
4.   According to the film, can a computer program be evolved if it does not make use of Boolean Logic?

INFERENCE/IMPLICATION

A large number of questions on the SAT reading selections require the student to identify *inferences* or *implications*. The skill demands that the test taker determine information the passage does not directly state. Unfortunately, these key words are used carelessly in everyday speech. Properly used, to *imply* is to suggest or to state indirectly; to *infer* is to draw a conclusion from evidence. The sender of the message *implies* certain things, and the receiver of that message must do the *inferring*. The College Board especially enjoys using the passive construction "It can be inferred that. . . ." Obviously, the test taker is the one who does the inferring. The error made repeatedly by the students is to read a question, such as "It can be inferred that Sebastian believed his mother's religious views were. . . ," then to reread the passage looking for a direct statement that answers the question. Indeed, frequently one of the wrong answers to an inference question will be a statement actually printed in the reading passage.

Offering the student examples of inference and implication is fairly easy. No matter how careful we are, a great deal of unstated material always forms part of our speech. Without our ability to determine inferences, we would never be able to respond to a call for help. We immediately infer from the sound that the sender has encountered some sort of unexpected problem, that the sender desires others to come to the rescue and that the sender does not feel capable of handling the situation alone. If a newspaper review of a concert series states that "Beethoven's *Symphony No. 9* should be played only on special occasions by a conductor with a special interpretation," then we can infer that the reviewer feels 1) there is something "bad" about listening to Beethoven's *Symphony No. 9* too frequently, 2) a conductor with a traditional approach to the music should not deal with that particular symphony, and 3) a special occasion is not a regular series concert. Actually, the best material for practicing inference is contained in movie and music reviews. There authors frequently imply their value judgments.

By and large, the College Board looks for six types of inference:

1.   connotations of a word or phrase:
     stated: The person was *high strung*.
     implied: The person was nervous, full of energy, temperamental.

2.   unstated details or traits:
     stated: The congressman ate a late breakfast, then walked around the mall, before having his afternoon nap.

implied: He was not in his office much of that day; he was not doing his job.

3. unstated opinion, interpretation, or value judgment:
   stated: I left the Boston Symphony concert wanting to hear some music.
   implied: I did not enjoy the music I actually heard at that concert.

4. unstated cause or effect:
   stated: She replied to her angry boss that if she had heard the phone she would have answered it.
   implied: The boss is angry at missing an important call. His secretary is saying that missing a call does not mean that she is stupid.

5. converse of stated facts or ideas:
   stated: I like only primary colors.
   implied: I dislike secondary colors.

6. prediction of outcomes/determination of preceding arguments:
   stated: Marcy put her hands up when she realized she was surrounded by police.
   implied: She was arrested shortly afterwards. Marcy had committed a crime.

Exercises are easy to construct to illustrate these examples. Here is a sample:

Infradig finally found success at age 31 when he published his first novel, *The Sacred and the Profane*. In his resignation to the School Committee, Infradig wrote, "I have corrected my last student theme. This was my first job, and I have red inked my youth. I can now do something that is actually read and might actually change behavior." For a year he worked on *Origins of Rashtra Buntley*, the second volume of the trilogy. His fans were not hostile to his creation of a bizarre religion and a culture that did not have compulsory education. They were soon buying Rashtra Buntley T-shirts.

From such a paragraph, the following questions could be asked:
1. It can be inferred that Infradig's biography would include information about what pieces of writing?
2. It can be inferred that the critics of Infradig's novels were disturbed by what material?
3. It can be inferred that Infradig supported himself in what job prior to the publication of his first novel?
4. It can be inferred that Infradig means what by the phrase "red inked my youth"?
5. It can be inferred that three of the drawbacks to Infradig's first job were what?
6. It can be inferred that the author of the passage felt what about the fans of Infradig?

One final point: the fact that something is implied in the message by the sender does not make the data suspect. In the movies that follow, the student is not looking for underhanded and hidden attempts to "sell" something. The filmmaker's implications are a legitimate and an artful part of the final message.

NOTES ON THE POPULAR ARTS (Pyramid Films: 20 min./color/1978)

Someone is typing "An Essay: The Popular Arts Today." The camera moves in to show the keys imprinting the words on the page, the beginnings of sentences found in the traditional essay, phrases that are immediately x-ed out and rejected: "When we consider the popular arts . . . Much can be said about the . . . As Emerson so wisely pointed out. . . ." Then the film launches into colorful vignettes that comment on five of the popular arts: TV, music, comics, books, magazines, and movies. At the film's conclusion, the typist starts a letter to "Sis," complaining about his inability to write the essay: "I dread my publisher's call . . . What can he do, shoot me?" Immediately, there is a firing squad. The essay writer, placed against the wall, makes his last statement. He explains the point of the vignettes in a speech that employs big words the guards cannot understand. A male soldier chases a dancing girl, others eat, gamble, daydream. The writer is shot but still utters one more sentence before the soundtrack drowns out his voice with "Toot toot tootsie, good-bye." Saul Bass, the filmmaker, seems to be implying that words produce clichés, whereas the cinema artist can find more creative ways of making commentary.

If the teacher stops the film before the firing squad sequence, the students can discuss the inferences of each section. There will be much to discuss.

a. Television: A balding man in an office tries to do his job. The electric pencil sharpener eats up his pencil; the plastic rotary dial comes off the phone and the cord pulls the handset back to the base; the stapler starts working on its own. In frustration, he turns on the TV and watches a detective hero, himself, exchange gunfire with a villain in an underground parking garage. After a hyperbolic car chase, the villain's car goes off a cliff, the hero dives in, saves the villain's girl, and they both swim off across the ocean. (Implied: The man made to feel inferior by technology regains his manhood through TV adventures.)

b. Music: A young girl in a white nightgown stares narcissisticly into a mirror and imagines herself a beautiful adult. As excerpts from four popular songs are played (with lyrics such as "I'm walking in channels . . ." and "I have felt the joy behind the pain . . ."), her fantasy life and dreams of a future husband and children are explored. (Implied: Popular music permits personal teenage fantasies.)

c. Comics: A young boy is a failure at the violin but imagines himself as the heroic Superfiddle, a cartoon figure who foils some safecrackers through his bad playing. (Implied: Superheroes provide small children feelings of superiority and strength.)

d. Books and Magazines: The timid young woman waiting in the doctor's office sees herself as a successful doctor ("The Prime Minister will live. There will be no revolution") and a successful lawyer standing in front of an all-male jury and audience. Her imaginary personae can do everything but get her into the doctor's office quickly. (Implied: Magazines allow the adult to transcend everyday frustrations.)

e. Movies: Inside a theater, an audience sees a one-minute film called *The Monk* in which a hooded figure walks out of the fog toward the camera, turns, then walks away. The audience is unanimous in its praise of the film. (Implied: Movies allow adults the chance to be "intellectuals.")

The final speech in front of the firing squad sums up the vignettes:

> Popular arts bring new meaning, new experiences, and stimulation
> to the imagination of the people. And answer the need to recreate

life on a heroic scale, enabling the mind to soar in transcendental flight above the moribund existence that technological man is heir to. They synthesize the hope, the dreams and aspirations, giving life to the yearnings of those seeking the meaning of diurnal experiences. They embody the dialectic contradictions expressed in the tastes and preferences of an entire culture. But I put it to you. What indeed is culture? That is an enigma—a conundrum worth considering. One may say culture is the communal expression of people in a particular place at a particular point in time. Does culture call forth the popular arts or popular arts the culture? . . . Culture and the popular arts exist in a dynamic unity of opposites. . . .

ACTIVITIES FOR THE STUDENT

1. Look up the following words before the film begins:

acculturational	enigma
conundrum	communal
dialectic	synthesize
technological	moribund
holistic	transcendental
diurnal	aspirations

   What implication is the scriptwriter making by having his main character use such words in the essay and before the firing squad? (What unstated prejudice about words is the film revealing?)

2. The section on television implies that the balding man identifies himself with the TV detective hero for what reasons?

3. In the section on music, the script implies the songs have what effect on the young girl?

4. In the section on comics, the activities of Superfiddle imply that the young boy enjoys comics for what reasons?

5. In the section on books, the fact that the woman earns the applause of an all-male courtroom implies what about her everyday associations with males?

6. The criticism offered on the one-minute movie implies what about the critics?

7. What is the implication of the author's not being able to write the essay?

8. What is the implication of the firing squad's behavior during the final words of the essayist?

THE DREYFUS AFFAIR (Texture Films: 15 min./b&w/1970)

Composed entirely of sketches, photographs, newspaper ads, and a few political cartoons, this film recounts the Dreyfus Affair from its beginning in the court-martial trial of 1895 to the acquittal in 1906. Enough cultural and historical information is offered along with the events of the trials to allow inferences to be made about the cause of the first trial, the motivations of those who gave false evidence, the eventual change in the verdict, and the nature of justice.

The script does not stint on facts, however. In an "ambience of super patriotism," the court found Alfred Dreyfus, an Alsatian, a Jew, and an unpopular army officer, guilty of treason based on one piece of evidence, a list of classified documents he was reputedly offering to the enemy. Dreyfus was stripped of his rank, publicly degraded, forbidden to bear arms again, and sentenced to exile on Devil's Island. There six jailers guarded Dreyfus day and night and did not allow him to speak. In 1896, Lt. Col. Georges Picquart tried unsuccessfully to prove in court that Major Esterhazy and Lt. Col. Henry had submitted false evidence against Dreyfus in the original trial.

Novelist Émile Zola wrote a series of articles in which he also accused the court of condemning Dreyfus without evidence and called Esterhazy and Henry liars. In 1898, Zola was convicted of criminal libel and Picquart was arrested for his comments during the trial. Soon after, Lt. Col. Henry confessed and committed suicide. This caused the trial to be opened again. "Militarists, rightists, and anti-Semites" were still against Dreyfus and Zola. On August 8, 1899, before a military tribunal, the prosecutor blocked the attempts to prove there were forgeries and found Dreyfus guilty once again with extenuating circumstances. The president of France offered Dreyfus a pardon, however. After the trial there were disturbances that exhibited antimilitarist and anticlerical feeling. In 1902, Zola died and Dreyfus attended the funeral. In 1903, a new investigation of the dispute began, and by 1906, the court finally declared Dreyfus innocent. He was once again an officer in the army and was made a Knight of the Legion of Honor. The narrator tells us the crowds chanted during the ceremony, "Long live Dreyfus, long live justice." This preposterous scenario obviously implies that justice is blind.

The social context of the trials as presented by the film implies further that the whims of society prevent justice. At the beginning, we are shown a country troubled by anarchy. The president of France was assassinated for refusing to grant pardons for two bomb-throwing radicals. France had just suffered defeat in the Franco-Prussian war and the army vowed to regain its glory. Under the new president, patriotism was being rebuilt. At that moment, the Dreyfus Affair started, thus making Dreyfus a logical scapegoat. During the second trial in 1899, the established right wing saw the new trial as a "blow aimed at the army." We are told that "demagogues harrangue the crowd and incite them to violence. France is near the boiling point." Drefus was found guilty again. By 1900, France had become strongly antimilitarist and anti-clerical. A church was sacked. In such an atmosphere, justice slowly reversed itself, declaring Dreyfus innocent. For such fickle behavior, the film finds against justice.

ACTIVITIES FOR THE STUDENT
1. The script implies that the emotional atmospheres surrounding the various Dreyfus trials were caused by what?
2. If the militarists, rightists, and anti-Semites in 1899 were against Dreyfus, the film implies that those for Dreyfus would be whom?
3. The script implies that the motivation of Esterhazy for forging the document was what? (Esterhazy is described as a man of "dwindling fortunes who lived by squalid means.")
4. What is the film implying about the nature of justice?
5. The film implies what about Zola's values?
6. What can we infer about society's influence on justice?

MEN'S LIVES (New Day Films: 43 min./color/1974)
What choices are open to men growing up in America? Josh Hanig and Will Roberts, both young men, explore in this film the "roots of masculinity" in an attempt to answer the question. They find that an "aggressive, profit-oriented society" has imposed a traditional image on man, one that it "is in our interests to change." Their argument is carried through the implications of the inclusions and exclusions of the various interviews they record.

The chronology of the phases of a man's life holds the film together: childhood, adolescence, young manhood, marriage, the working years. An elementary school teacher feels boys like to "show off, hit, take the ball." She admits she expects more from the boys because they will have to be the breadwinners. Mr. Wiseman, the teacher of Health and Social Living and the head basketball coach in a secondary school, feels that the man is primarily responsible for the financial burden in the family, that satisfaction comes from achieving goals, and that if men "lose and it doesn't bother them, they will be failures." A radio host announces that competition is the most important part of men's lives: "without competition, there's nothing." Man should make the final decision in a marriage; he quotes the Bible to prove that man is superior to woman. With such views held by those who influence a young man's life, it is not surprising to hear a teenage football player announce, "I like to kill . . . Either you kill them or they kill you." A youngster holding a pool cue announces that he wants a "pretty blue . . . cadillac of my own" and a teenager confirms the feelings of masculinity and power he gets from his car. At a college mixer, a male categorizes college girls into those who want a quick pickup and those who want a year-long commitment. He then openly makes a move on the girl beside him. After the ritual of sex comes marriage. After marriage comes the job for the rest of one's life. A factory worker, Joe Carpenter, explains that all his employer wants is his labor, not his "emotional satisfaction." Joe does not want his wife to work; he is the breadwinner, even though, he admits, he has not always been happy about his breadwinning ability.

The film offers a great deal of insightful material and documents a wide range of masculine activity, but it also implies through its inclusions and exclusions a number of attitudes of the filmmakers about masculinity. Sensitive, open males seem to be a definite minority in the film. Other than the two filmmakers, there is a ballet dancer/gymnast who is self-conscious about dancing and is bothered by the derisive comments made by the audience. He says his father let him do what he wanted, but later admits his father would rather he were a lawyer. A barber offers wisdom while cutting the hair of one of the interviewers. He feels males are frightened about opening up, are afraid of intimacy, are too concerned with material possessions. He announces there should be a liberation of all "mankind." To make this point, the filmmakers do not talk to a psychiatrist, a symbol of the establishment, but to a man of the people, the barber. The implication is that he is more insightful, more honest. An articulate, charming factory worker admits he drinks too much at times and the film then shows unhappy males at a bar: one drinks to escape one's failures, is the implication. A TV sequence shows western shootouts, John Wayne, a body building contest, a handsome male preparing for a big date while telling an admiring little boy that his girl is a real centerfold type. The sequence implies that TV pushes only one version of a male (not mentioned are the many shows in which the father is a sensitive wimp and dullard). The interview of the basketball coach implies that there will be a sexist approach to the Health and Social Living course because his job is to mold winning teams.

The value of the film is its final challenge: if males can be open, caring, affectionate, and vulnerable, they might actually find happiness. To exercise this option, they will have to be less competitive, rely less on material possessions, and be more sensitive to the real needs of women. The most depressing remark in the film is Carpenter's: "If a man has really and truly one friend, that is all he can expect." There must be more than that. For all the detail, there are still things missing. There are no interviews of authors, rock stars, actors, social workers, business executives, cooks, interior decorators, secretaries, farmers, politicians, clothiers, military personnel. The very poor and the very rich are ignored. There are no representatives of the marriage in which both members work. And there is no interview to reflect the middle phases of a man's life—contrary to rumor, it just ain't one long day, no changes, until retirement comes.

ACTIVITIES FOR THE STUDENT
1. What is the implication of choosing a barber rather than a psychologist to comment on men's problems?
2. What is the implication about the teacher who is also the head basketball coach?
3. What does the film imply would be better life traits for males?
4. Juxtaposing the scenes at a bar with the factory worker's admittance that he drinks too much at times has what implication?

A WALK IN THE FOREST (Pyramid Films: 28 min./color/1976)

On its surface, this film extols the beauty of the forest and the beneficence of British Columbia's MacMillan Bloedel Company, a lumber firm that cuts and replenishes nature's trees. Along the way, however, the filmmaker implies that this company represents the epitome of today's new lumber industry, that yesterday's image of such companies as destroyers of the wilderness is no longer true (if it ever was), that lumber firms are actually more kind to the forest than are its freeloading wild animals, and finally, that the forest and its animals are better off now that such companies are around to protect and tend to them.

Part of the unstated thesis of this film is that animals consume, but only people can replenish. "Only man consciously creates his future," Richard Harris narrates, then adds somewhat condescendingly that the lives of the animals "fulfill a purpose secret in themselves . . . their mission instinct commands." In the winter, "each animal, stirred by ancient memory, prepares for the change to come." A squirrel gathers conifer cones; later a mouse in its burrow devours its winter store. In contrast, the MacMillan Bloedel workers harvest cones in the fall and in the dead of winter in the Forest Service Nursery, plant the seeds. "Man does not rest . . . [he] prepares to replace what he has cut." When fire starts, the animals can only flee; humans gather forces to stop the fire (there is some exciting footage of a plane spraying a fire out). Left to its own devices, an old tree is overcome by a "mounting tangle of brush and fallen trees . . . [as] disease hastens its decay." Humans have no cure for age, but they can farm and tend the forest. The implication is that humans are needed by the forest to remove its debris.

The film defends the lumber companies against arguments that are never directly stated. The statement "in a single generation, we have learned to invest new life for what we take," implies there was a time when firms cut down forests with no regard for the future. This company plants replacement trees that in 80 years may stand 100 feet tall: "those who planted the seeds will not see the trees, but their children will." At the end we are told that "man, too, seeks to endure" and has learned that ruthless survival of the fittest, driven only by the instinct to stay alive, is not the best way; today, lumber companies know they must take the responsibility of maintaining the balance of nature.

A final visual portrait of a magnificent forest, given its position in the film, implies that this Eden is the product of this company's loving care. The forest is a world of butterflies, hummingbirds, dragonflies, squirrels, mice, and small animals. There are predators, but they are never shown eating the kill. The camera moves slowly through a threatening forest at night, but the owl with sharp claws misses its tiny prey. A raccoon on a stream bank and a bird hopping about in the shallow water are both unsuccessful at fishing. In the spring, we watch cubs of various sorts encountering life. A number of small raccoons cross a stream by way of a teetering dead limb; one does fall in but finally makes it to safety. During the fire sequence we watch the deer flee to safety. Best of all is the snowy sequence that shows the quiet snow-engulfed forest, then the closeup of the snug little home of a mouse. Such animals, the film seems to imply, need our protection.

The film is very successful in presenting its message. There is the school of forestry (at Yosemite, for instance) that believes the forest knows how to take care of itself and that the balance of nature is better served by humans keeping out of its way, but this walk through the forest is breathtaking, and the MacMillan Bloedel Company and, by implication, other lumber companies seem to be nature's benevolent partners.

ACTIVITIES FOR THE STUDENT
1. The sentence "Man, too, is a guest upon this planet" implies what?
2. What does the film imply would happen to the forests without the services of humans as custodians?
3. What does the film imply is the drawback of the fact that the animals work on instincts that force them to survive?
4. If the old trees suffer from growth around them, what does the film imply the caretakers should do? Why?
5. What does the film imply is the "silent contract" between humans and the forest?
6. If "in a single generation we have learned to invest new life for what we take," what does the film imply about the past?
7. What does the film imply in its juxtaposition of the mouse devouring its winter store and the Forest Nursery during the winter?
8. What is the film implying by not showing any of the predators of the forest achieving a kill?

THE CITY AT THE END OF THE CENTURY (Arthur Mokin Productions, Inc.: 19 min./color/1977)

After showing the conditions of the modern city, the narrator asks four questions: "Can our cities be saved?" "Should our cities be saved?" "What do cities contribute to our lives?" and "Are they vital to our civilization?" The first and second questions are answered (affirmatively) through implications; the last two are answered through direct statements. The entire film, shot in various locations in New York City (some the familiar landmarks and some more difficult to identify), is an homage to a great city. As seen through director Arthur Mokin's eyes, the city has never been lovelier. The rhetorical question never asked, but always implied through visual implication, is, "If the city is that beautiful now, what would it be like if its problems were solved?"

Mokin opens by discussing the ideal concept of the city as visualized by ancients. This approach implies that today's cities, the embodiment of those dreams, must be, and can be, saved. In the beginning, the city was a "metaphor for paradise . . . the visible promise of heaven and the hereafter." For the Greeks, the core of the polis contained the sacred temples and the locus of political power: the "citizen, freed from the routine of gathering food, building shelter, and bearing arms, could turn . . . energy to pursuits of the mind and spirit," the pursuits that fostered the glory that was Greece. The ancient Greeks were intelligent enough to establish organic limits to the growth of the city and to set up colonies around it when it threatened to overflow. Then can the cities be saved? Mokin implies through comparison that such an approach will indeed save our cities, and that the dreamers, those who first conceived this forceful metaphor, will be able to solve the problems. He implies that our cities should be saved in order to continue to offer freedom for the individual and to offer stimulation for the dreamers since "only the city is the proper setting for what they have to give."

Mokin disagrees with the Melting Pot theory; for him, the city is a "magnet that draws people together where they can live, work, worship, recreate with freedom in accordance with individual custom." The variety is the city's strength. He defines the ideal city as a place where "people of different persuasions, backgrounds, and interests come together to pursue mutual interests." The ideal is not the city of mass conformity. The camera illustrates the thesis with a variety of activities: attending church, relaxing at the beach, shopping, playing games, going to the zoo or amusement park, horseback riding, jogging, even walking one's dogs. The visual display convinces us that a number of people in a city can do their own thing without any outside hassle. Even the dreamer can find the space for meditation, the walk in the rain, the visual inspirations, such as the Statue of Liberty, the lights going on at the top of the Empire State Building at dusk, the beautifully lit fountains and buildings. For such possibilities, our cities should definitely be saved; they do make contributions to our lives.

Is the city vital to our civilization? Mokin implies that the answer is "yes." He sees it as a center for communication and transportation, a meeting place, a "storehouse" of our knowledge so that "we can draw on the past and, thus enriched, move into the future." We can still attain that ancient dream of paradise, that spiritual, moral, and intellectual ideal of the ancient Greeks. The film is unusual in that it stresses the potential City of God rather than the problems of urban renewal, integration of minorities, poverty. Twice in the film we are shown the signs of decay and squalor, but the stronger impression is the beauty he shows us in New York. Shot after shot displays aspects of the city that we have overlooked, that we have not realized are right there in front of us. Confronted by the vision of this filmic dreamer, we cannot help but see some possibilities for improvement and wish to share in the richness of that dream.

ACTIVITIES FOR THE STUDENT

1. By showing the range of activities in the city, the film implies what about the small community in the suburbs?
2. What is the author implying by concentrating the camera on the various buildings and landmarks of New York City, some famous, some not, all handsome?
3. If the dreamers will be the salvation of the city, then what is the film implying about the functions of the other categories into which people fall?
4. What does the author imply is the cause of the city's downfall?
5. From the visual display, what does Mokin imply when he says "the city is a place for dreamers . . . here, anything is possible"?
6. By stressing the details of the Greek polis, the script is implying what in terms of the problems facing the modern city?
7. What is the implication of the author's ignoring the other cradles of ancient civilization, such as Carthage or Rome or Jerusalem?

V

RESEARCH SKILLS

The thrust of this section is locating and organizing information in common reference sources to support the writing process. Four segments are arranged by broad discipline areas: General Reference Sources, the Humanities, the Social Sciences, and Pure and Applied Science. Each segment is prefaced by a bibliography of reference sources, contains annotations for three to five films, and includes a range of student activities. The activities include a documented short paper.

The films selected for each segment are broad in scope, provide a wide range of subtopics for investigation, and imply or state only partial information about these subtopics. The films serve to focus attention and to provide a general context for the information. The bibliographies included here reflect the content of the selected films. Thus, though the third segment is entitled "Social Sciences," the reference materials cited are U.S. history sources, and those under "Humanities" are primarily literature and art sources.

The bibliographies for each segment have been compiled from:

Wynar, Christine Gehrt. *Guide to Reference Books for School Media Centers*, 2nd ed. (Littleton, CO: Libraries Unlimited, 1981).

The number before each entry is the entry number in Wynar. The bibliographies are broad to account for differences in local collections; however, each reference tool has been cited only once, even though it may also be used in later sections. Each media specialist will need to reproduce bibliographies that reflect the local collection. Each student should have copies of these bibliographies. Adding annotations to each local bibliography and citing the source(s) from which it was generated will reinforce the method one follows when locating reference tools as well as make the bibliography more useful both for these activities and for future consultation.

The student activities have been designed both with library logistics and research methodology in mind. We have eschewed the "right answer" type of activity designed to highlight the characteristics of a particular reference tool, for such questions inevitably force entire classes to converge on a single volume. Rather, we have focused on the research process, constructed the bibliographies to increase awareness of the range of information tools available, and directed attention to standard bibliographies, guides, and indexes as avenues to further information. The research skills include:

retrieving from the local collection	structuring information
scanning for an overview	verifying information
identifying a topic	footnoting
taking notes	writing a short documented paper

The bibliographic format in the student activities is based upon (Wynar, 996) Turabian, Kate L., *Student's Guide for Writing College Papers*, 3rd enl. ed. (Chicago: University of Chicago Press, 1977). However, any standard guide, including most English grammar texts, will provide the necessary consistency. Both faculty and students would benefit if a single bibliographic practice were followed throughout the school. This section presumes that research and writing are common to the English, social studies, and science curricula. Since filling in blanks is a reflex for most of us, bibliographic forms are suggested both to ensure that students gather all of the information requested and to make them aware of bibliographic format. Placing a supply of these cards near the catalog, encyclopedias, and indexes should encourage students and faculty to use them regularly, and may help avoid the horrors of fugitive dates and pagination, a perennial midnight crisis.

GENERAL REFERENCE SOURCES

The activities in this section introduce the mechanics of the research process by requiring from the outset that students cite sources in standard bibliographic form. They also learn to survey the resources immediately available and to practice scanning information for an overview. Reference sources include: desk and general encyclopedias, general periodical indexes, and almanacs.

The activities are designed to increase student familiarity with the general resources of the local collection, the characteristics of its card catalog, and the locations of general reference sources. To heighten their awareness of the differences between sources, activities require students to compare and contrast various general encyclopedias as well as to use almanacs, chronologies, and college guides. The list of reference sources could include the following titles.

170　*Reference Books for Small and Medium-Sized Libraries*, 3rd ed. Larry Earl Bone, ed. Chicago: American Library Association, 1979.

172　Sheehy, Eugene P., comp. *Guide to Reference Books*, 9th ed. Chicago: American Library Association, 1976.

189　*Information Please Almanac*. New York: Simon and Schuster, 1947- .

191　Kane, Joseph Nathan. *Famous First Facts: A Record of First Happenings, Discoveries and Inventions in the United States*, 3rd ed. New York: H. W. Wilson, 1964.

197　*The World Almanac and Book of Facts*. New York: Newspaper Enterprise Association, 1863- .

210　*The New Columbia Encyclopedia*, 4th ed. William H. Harris and Judith Levey, eds. New York: Columbia University Press; distr. by J. P. Lippincott, 1975.

211　*The Random House Encyclopedia*. James Mitchell, ed.-in-chief. New York: Random House, 1977.

212　*Academic American Encyclopedia*. Princeton, NJ: Arete Publishing, 1980.

215　*Collier's Encyclopedia*. William D. Halsey, editorial director, Louis Shores, ed.-in-chief. New York: Macmillan Educational Corp., 1949- .

217　*Encyclopedia Americana*. Bernard S. Coyne, ed.-in-chief. New York: Grolier Educational Corp., 1829- .

218   *Merit Students Encyclopedia*. William D. Halsey, editorial director, Louis Shores, senior library advisor. New York: Macmillan Educational Corp., 1967- .

220   *The New Encyclopaedia Britannica in 30 volumes*. Chicago: Encyclopaedia Britannica Educational, 1978- .

221   *The World Book Encyclopedia*. William H. Nault, ed. Chicago: World Book-Childcraft International, 1917- .

226   *The Magazine Index*. Menlo Park, CA: Information Access. Monthly.

229   *Readers' Guide to Periodical Literature*. New York: H. W. Wilson, 1900- .

1872   *Encyclopedia of Careers and Vocational Guidance*, 4th rev. ed. Garden City, NY: Doubleday & Co., 1978.

1873   *Occupational Outlook Handbook*. Division of Manpower and Occupational Outlook. Washington, DC: Government Publication Office, 1949- .

The following films offer overviews of broad topics. *To Fly* moves swiftly through a history of transportation toward the glory of flight. *Future Shock* surveys the directions of modern technology and its impact on society. *The Invisible World* offers a scientific perspective of modern photographic techniques that have made heretofore invisible parts of our world visible. Activities follow each film.

TO FLY (Conoco: 25 min./color/1976)
   This film, designed for projection on the giant screen of the National Air and Space Museum of the Smithsonian, both reflects and promotes the museum's collection. Urgently building toward the conclusion that "human destiny has ever been and always must be to fly," it surveys transportation landmarks on the path to flight. It provides students with topics that are easy to locate and that are covered amply in general reference sources.
   The film starts on the July 4th celebration in 1841, when a curiosity occurs: a balloon lifts above the rural landscape. Its passenger extols the beauty below as the camera pans forests, hillsides, and rivers. America was catching its first vertical glimpse of itself and the next 100 years would alter rural lifestyles radically. At a pace symptomatic of these changes, we sweep over vast waterways; below, a solo canoeist paddles. We cross the prairies behind covered wagons and chase a locomotive racing with a stagecoach. The country is crossed. In the new century space shrinks as the motor car and the flying machine burst on the scene. The vertical world becomes increasingly familiar to people throughout the country and the planes evolve . . . single wing, cargo, jet, helicopters, passenger ships, and fighters. Barnstorming becomes the rage in the twenties, and the camera dives with the stunt men. The screen splits, quadruples, and divides again as aircraft after aircraft soars into space. The human scale has disappeared. Through a fish-eye lens we pivot over the skyscrapers of New York and launch out across the country that took the pioneers months, years to cross. As the century draws to a close, land's end is no longer the end of the line, and Hawaii beckons. The narrative directs our attention to the heavens above and the mysteries beyond. At the space center a rocket blasts off and the narrator asks, "What will we find where all human scale has vanished?" At the film's end, we move past Mars, Jupiter, Saturn, toward silence or answers.

ACTIVITIES FOR THE STUDENT

Among the modes of transportation shown are the balloon, canoe, wagon, locomotive, automobile, airplane, helicopter, and rocket. Select one of the above and check the following resources to see what information could be gathered on the topic.

1. Check the card catalog:
    a. Give the complete bibliographic citation to one book in the collection on the selected topic. (Use the following form for this activity.)

Book by author, association or institution—Bibliographic form

Author(s) _ _ _ _ _ _ _ _ _ _ _ _ _ _ , _ _ _ _ _ _ _ _ _ _ _
                 last,   first

Title _____ . _ _ _ _ _ _ _ _ _ _ .
               underlined   edition

_ _ _ _ _ _ _ _ _ _ _ : _ _ _ _ _ _ _ _ _ _ , _ _ _ _ _ .
       place published: publisher,   year.

---

    b. Scan the book; take brief notes (25-30 words) on content.
2. Consult three general encyclopedias (Wynar, 212, 215, 217, 218, 220, 221).
    a. Give the complete citation to each article in bibliographic form. (Use the following form.)

Encyclopedia—Bibliographic form

_____ , _ _ _ _ _ _ _ _ _ _ .
encyclopedia title (underlined),   edition or date.

" _ ," by
              "article title,"

Author _ .
(if given)   first   last.

---

    b. Scan each article in each encyclopedia; take brief notes on coverage.

3. Check a periodical index (Wynar, 226, 229).
   a. Provide a complete citation to one article in bibliographic form. (Use the following form.)

```
┌─────────────────────────────────────────────────────────────┐
│                                                             │
│            Periodical article—Bibliographic form            │
│                                                             │
│                                                    "        │
│   Author _ _ _ _ _ _ _ _ _ , _ _ _ _ _ _ _ _. "_ _ _ _ _ _ _ _ │
│              last,              first.              "Title   │
│                                                             │
│                            ."                               │
│   _ _ _ _ _ _ _ _ _ ."    _____ ,  │
│        of article."         Title of periodical (underlined), │
│                                                             │
│   _ _ _ _ _ _ , _ _ _ _ _, pp._____ .                │
│      month,         year,       pages.                      │
│                                                             │
└─────────────────────────────────────────────────────────────┘
```

   b. Scan one article; take brief notes.
4. To show the kind of information available from these different types of sources, compile an annotated bibliography of them. Arrange it alphabetically by the first word on each of the bibliographic forms. Describe, in no more than 25 words, the information in each source.

FUTURE SHOCK (McGraw-Hill Contemporary Films: 30 min./color/1972)

Scenes of pastoral serenity are juxtaposed with scenes of urban squalor and violence to show a culture victimized by technology, surfeited with consumer options, and sickened by impermanence. This society, warned Alvin Toffler, is in *Future Shock* (New York: Random House, 1970). It suffers from the premature arrival of the future, from change: too much, too fast.

Some of the film's predictions, such as the test-tube baby, are already a reality. Other of its observations reflected the sixties and have diminished as social issues. Much has changed since the production date, so the film is ripe with topics to research.

People are bombarded by products and information. Which brand of precooked instant, canned, frozen, condensed, or dried commestible from the supermarket are we to choose? Which turntable, amplifier, audiocassette, or videotape deck is closest to state-of-the-art technology? Two-thirds of the chemicals now used have been discovered since the 1930s. Technology feeds on knowledge. Over 1,000 books per day, or 365,000 per year, are published internationally. How do we keep up? Computers give us information at a faster and faster rate.

Nothing is permanent. Buildings once made to last a lifetime are torn down. Others are built to be erected, used, disassembled, and moved elsewhere. Thirty-six million Americans move each year. Telephone directories are rewritten daily. A race of nomad hitchhikers has been reared on high-speed changes, seeing home as a place to leave. The narrator laments temporary relationships, instant intimacy, and the loss of a sense of belonging. Everything is becoming disposable. On October 26, 1968, Carl Shaefer underwent a heart transplant; the disposable body had arrived. A doctor speculates that since the artificial kidney exists, the heart and ultimately the modular body will follow. Rapidly specialists describe advances in prosthetics (stepping stones to the artificial person), plastic surgery (to alter physical appearance), and genetic engineering (to manipulate the entire structure and the characteristics governed by the genetic code). Cloning, artificial intelligence, robotics, and test-tube babies are all potential.

Traditional sources of security are under attack. The family is crumbling, for the likelihood of a couple's achieving confluent growth and development is strained by the pace of change. Evolving alternatives are: group marriages, communes, and homosexual marriages. Religious and educational institutions and societal standards are in flux. Witness student, teacher, civil servant, and police strikes. Witness the women's and gay rights movements. Collective protests are giving birth to new turbulence. The result? Stress.

The pace of the scientists is relentless. The scenario projects a future where drugs raise IQs and control memory processes; battery packs stimulate body movement; and man, the victim of biotechnology, is essentially without free will. Toffler urges that we not accept the future blindly, that we say no to some technology.

ACTIVITIES FOR THE STUDENT

1. Both *To Fly* and *Future Shock* concern developments that radically altered society. The narration of *To Fly* indicates that the 100 years following July 4, 1841, would radically alter rural lifestyles. Likewise, Alvin Toffler wrote, "In the three short decades between now and the twenty-first century, millions of ordinary, psychologically normal people will face an abrupt collision with the future" (*Future Shock* [New York: Random House, 1970], p. 11). His conclusions reflected recent developments as well as future forecasts.

   a. Since one way to structure information is to approach it chronologically, you are going to construct a simple time line which identifies at least 20 events that accelerated the pace of change. The time line format could be the following:

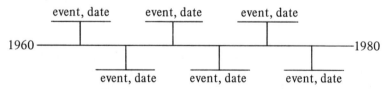

   b. Select the time span 1841-1941 or 1960-1980.
   c. Consult an almanac (Wynar, 189, 191, 197) or a general encyclopedia (Wynar, 212, 215, 217, 218, 220, 221); take notes.

2. Much has changed since *Future Shock* was produced in 1972. Investigating any of the topics would require checking numerous sources. Select a topic such as urban renewal or unrest; air, water, or noise pollution; trends in the publishing, food, chemical, or home electronics industries; the status of organ transplants, prosthetics, genetic engineering, cloning, or robotics; the status of collective movements such as the Civil, women's, gay, Chicano, or student rights movement; the effects of collective protests by the above groups or by teachers, civil servants, or police; alternatives to the nuclear family; or changes in religious, educational, or social organizations.

a. Check the card catalog, the general encyclopedias (Wynar, 212, 215, 217, 218, 220, 221), almanacs (Wynar, 189, 191, 197), chronologies (Wynar, 893, 897), and the periodical indexes (Wynar, 226, 227).
b. Locate 3-5 sources which provide information.
c. In two paragraphs, summarize the current status of your topic and project the impact on the future of this community.

THE INVISIBLE WORLD (National Geographic Society: 60 min./color/1979)

The human eye is a limited device. Much around us is too small, fast, or slow to see unaided; much is too far away or beyond the spectrum of visible light. Cameras and other optical devices have expanded vision beyond the limits of the naked eye. Though this film summarizes many discoveries made possible by optical and electrical technology, it also shows people involved in a number of professions and in a variety of institutional settings. Since professions pose basic reference questions for many students, this film is used to investigate institutions as well as professions.

With the invention of the microscope nearly 400 years ago, more of the surrounding world became knowable. In 1694 came the discovery of bacteria by Leeuwenhoek. Through modern microscopes equipped with cameras, one can now observe the cellular structure of a leaf and the movement of blood corpuscles. Optical magnification is limited to 2,000x; the scanning electron microscope raises magnification to 100,000x. On a finger we can see fierce dust mites consume sloughed-off skin particles; at the Fermi Institute in Chicago, Dr. Albert Crewe demonstrates an electron microscope that can magnify 10-20 million times, something like blowing a basketball up to the size of the earth. Through this, one sees single uranium atoms.

We were once exiled from another world by time. In 1870 photographer Eadweard Muybridge settled a wager about a horse's stride. Motion pictures, when transferred to a computer, make it possible for Dr. Gideon Ariel to measure the force, acceleration, and velocity of physical motion and thence to improve athletic performance. At MIT in 1931, Dr. Harold Edgerton dissected time and motion when he invented the strobe light in order to observe the motion of motors. Now with the strobe flashing at less than one-millionth of a second and with a high-speed camera, he freeze-frames a bullet traveling at 2,800 feet per second as it cuts a playing card. The technique stretches time.

The eyes can see only through a narrow spectrum of light waves which have been analyzed into colors from red to violet. A camera with a filter can record ultraviolet light unapparent to the human eye. On the other end of the spectrum, red light becomes energy, which can be recorded as heat through ultrared photography; each color zone represents $\frac{1}{2}°$ difference in temperature. X-rays with a much shorter wavelength than visible light were discovered in 1895 (Roentgen) and have been used not only in medicine but also by archaeologists examining mummies. Sound waves can be captured by sound-imaging cameras, which have revolutionized prenatal care with their ability to "see" tissue.

Another whole area hidden from the naked eye is energy. Discovered around the turn of the century, the *Cirlian aura* is still being investigated. A bio-energetic field appears to emanate around the body and can be caught on a photographic plate; at present little is understood of its import. Under heavier investigation at the Fermi Nuclear Research Institute are quarks, any of three types of elementary particles, believed to form the basis of all matter. In machinery designed to shatter atoms, cameras track the tiny particles, and scientists theorize that quarks may be composed of something even smaller. At Kitt Peak National Observatory astronomers using a colossal telescope with computers and cameras study the energy in our own as well as other galaxies. They theorize that the universe contains 100 billion galaxies and question whether the universe has an end. The telescope magnifies six million times greater than the eye can see. Finally, research into the connection between human optics and electrical energy continues. At the University of Utah's Salt Lake City campus, scientists bypass the optic nerve totally. By attaching 64 electrodes directly onto the cortex of a blind man, and linking the electrodes to a video camera with a computer system, they can project braille dots directly onto the brain. The man can see the dots, and researchers foresee the day when cameras will actually provide artificial vision.

ACTIVITIES FOR THE STUDENT
Select either one of these activities:

1. *The Invisible World* reflects work done in laboratories, observatories, and research centers throughout the world. Select one of these institutions: Kitt Peak National Observatory, The Hale Observatories, Lick Observatory, Lowell Observatory, McDonald Observatory, Mauna Key Observatory, National Radio Astronomy Observatory, Yerkes Observatory, U.S. Naval Observatory, Enrico Fermi Institute for Nuclear Research, National Astronomy and Ionosphere Center, Argonne National Laboratory, or Brookhaven National Laboratory.

   a. Use an almanac (Wynar, 189, 197), a desk encyclopedia (Wynar, 210, 211), or a general (Wynar, 212-21) encyclopedia.

   b. Use notecards to record the answers to the questions below:
      (1) When was the institution established?
      (2) Where is it located?
      (3) By whom is it sponsored and administered?
      (4) What special resources does it provide?
      (5) What is the principal focus of its work?

   c. Give a complete bibliographic citation for the sources that provided the information.

2. Many universities provide highly sophisticated resources and facilities for advanced scientific research. Select one of these institutions: The University of California, Chicago, Utah, New Mexico, Michigan, or Wisconsin; Harvard, Indiana, Pennsylvania State, Cornell, Johns Hopkins, Ohio State, or Columbia University; Massachusetts Institute of Technology.

   a. Use the sources cited above (Wynar, 189-97, 210-21).

   b. Use notecards to record the following information:
      (1) institution mailing address and date of charter
      (2) name and address of admissions officer
      (3) composition of student body and enrollment
      (4) number and types of colleges within the university
      (5) size of library collection(s)
      (6) types of special facilities on campus(es)
      (7) undergraduate admission requirements.

   c. Give a complete bibliographic citation for the sources that provide the information.

FOLLOW-UP ACTIVITIES
1.   People in the films *To Fly*, *Future Shock*, and *The Invisible World* represent a
     variety of professions: architecture; medicine; ministry; electrical, mechanical,
     or civil engineering; computer science; biological research; advertising; journal-
     ism; social work; criminology; photography; education; and aeronautics, to name
     a few. Most of these professions require at least an undergraduate degree; many
     require advanced study. Select one profession.
     a.   Consult *The Encyclopedia of Careers and Vocational Guidance* (Wynar,
          1872) and *The Occupational Outlook Handbook* (Wynar, 1873).
     b.   Prepare a brief oral report which covers the following information:
          (1)   What career title did you choose?
          (2)   What is the employment outlook for the future?
          (3)   What is the earning potential in this field?
          (4)   What undergraduate major(s) is (are) common preparation for the
                field?

THE HUMANITIES

The *American Heritage Dictionary* defines the humanities as "those branches of
knowledge concerned with man and his culture, as philosophy, literature and the fine
arts." The sources included here, however, reflect only literature, painting, and Greek
mythology. Students will be using sources of quotations, *Essay and General Literature
Index*, and subject encyclopedias, dictionaries, bibliographies, and handbooks. They
will locate and identify quotations, take notes, use footnotes, and write a short paper.
The supporting bibliography could include the following titles.

260   *New Century Cyclopedia of Names*. Clarence L. Barnhart and W. Halsey, eds.
      New York: Appleton-Century-Crofts, 1954.

275   *Bartlett's Familiar Quotations: A Collection of Passages, Phrases and Proverbs
      Traced to Their Sources in Ancient and Modern Literature*, 15th ed. Boston,
      MA: Little, Brown, 1980.

281   *Magill's Quotations in Context*, Frank N. Magill, ed. Englewood Cliffs, NJ:
      Salem Press. First Series, 1966. Second Series, 1969.

286   Stevenson, Burton, ed. *The Home Book of Quotations: Classical and Modern*,
      10th rev. ed. New York: Dodd, Mead, 1967.

287   Tripp, Rhonda Thomas, comp. *The International Thesaurus of Quotations*.
      New York: T. Y. Crowell, 1970.

711   Gardner, Helen. *Art Through the Ages*, 6th ed. Rev. by Horst de la Croix and
      Richard G. Tansy. New York: Harcourt Brace Jovanovich, 1975.

712   Janson, H. W., with Samuel Cauman. *History of Art for Young People*, 2nd
      ed. rev. and enl. New York: Abrams, 1980.

723   *Encyclopedia of Painting: Painters and Painting of the World from Prehistoric
      Times to the Present Day*, 4th rev. ed. Bernard S. Myers, ed. New York:
      Crown, 1979.

726   *McGraw-Hill Dictionary of Art*. Bernard S. Myers, ed. New York: McGraw-Hill,
      1969.

727 *McGraw-Hill Encyclopedia of World Art.* New York: McGraw-Hill, 1967.

729 *Phaidon Dictionary of Twentieth Century Art,* 2nd ed. New York: Phaidon, 1977.

731 *Praeger Encyclopedia of Art.* New York: Praeger, 1971.

1198 *The Reader's Advisor: A Layman's Guide,* 12th ed. New York: Bowker, 1974-1977.

1202 Brewer, Ebenezer C. *Brewer's Dictionary of Phrase and Fable.* Centenary ed. Rev. by Ivor H. Evans. New York: Harper & Row, 1970.

1203 *Cassell's Encyclopedia of World Literature,* rev. and enl. ed. John Buchanan-Brown, general ed. New York: William Morrow, 1973.

1206 *Cyclopedia of Literary Characters.* Frank W. Magill, ed. New York: Harper & Row, 1963.

1208 *Encyclopedia of World Literature in the 20th Century.* New York: Ungar, 1967-1971.

1209 Freeman, William. *Dictionary of Fictional Characters.* Rev. by Fred Urquhart. Boston, MA: The Writer, 1974.

1212 *The Reader's Encyclopedia,* 2nd ed. William Rose Benet, ed. New York: T. Y. Crowell, 1965.

1231 *Crowell's Handbook of Classical Drama.* By Richard Y. Hathorn. New York: T. Y. Crowell, 1967.

1257 *Literary History of the United States,* 4th ed. rev. Robert E. Spiller and others, eds. New York: Macmillan, 1974.

1269 Wright, Andrew. *A Reader's Guide to English and American Literature.* Glenview, IL: Scott, Foresman, 1970.

1287 *The Concise Cambridge Bibliography of English Literature, 600-1950,* 2nd ed. George Watson, ed. New York: Cambridge University Press, 1965.

1306 *Crowell's Handbook of Classical Literature.* By Lillian Feder. New York: T. Y. Crowell, 1964.

1307 *The Oxford Classical Dictionary,* 2nd ed. N. G. L. Hammond and H. H. Scullard, eds. New York: Oxford University Press, 1970.

1308 *The Oxford Companion to Classical Literature,* 2nd ed. Sir Paul Harvey, comp. and ed. New York: Oxford University Press, 1966 (c 1937).

1408 *New Grove Dictionary of Music and Musicians,* 6th ed. Washington, DC: Grove's Dictionaries of Music; St. Martin's Press, 1980.

1409 *The International Cyclopedia of Music and Musicians,* 10th rev. ed. Oscar Thompson, ed. New York: Dodd, Mead, 1975.

1455 *Crowell's Handbook of Classical Mythology.* By Edward Tripp. New York: T. Y. Crowell, 1970.

1456 *Funk & Wagnalls Standard Dictionary of Folklore, Mythology, and Legend.* Maria Leach, ed. New York: Funk & Wagnalls, 1949-1950; dist. by New York: T. Y. Crowell, 1972.

1458 *Mythology: An Illustrated Encyclopedia.* Richard Cavendish, ed. New York: Rizzoli International, 1980.

The selected films introduce a breadth of information quickly. *The Humanities: A Bridge to Ourselves* is an essay built on short quotes, dramatic excerpts, and visual montages which becomes a sampler of cultural heritage. *Meaning in Modern Painting* shows the range of attitudes toward modern art. *The Greek Myths*, Parts I and II present segments from a number of myths and refer to even more.

THE HUMANITIES: A BRIDGE TO OURSELVES (Encyclopaedia Britannica: 29 min./color/1974)

Throughout this segment of the EBEC Humanities program, Clifton Fadiman, general editor of the series, advocates respect for and an awareness of our cultural heritage as "an escape from the labyrinth of a mechanical world." Quotations are often included in writing to express an idea more eloquently or adequately than could the writer. They are also used to substantiate a writer's thesis. This film posits that the humanities are necessary bridges between people and the outer world and pursues the thesis directly, substantiating throughout with quotations.

The film asks general questions, offers specific quotations, and mentions numerous authors and books. The questions are those normally asked in a humanities course: What is the nature of human character, of good, of evil? What is history? What is the value of the past, of life, of religion? Relying heavily on quotations as answers (or at least as opinions on the subject), Fadiman moves chronologically from pictograms to Pascal's comment that a person is a "thinking reed." Almost all of the quotations are unidentified in the narrative, but any quoted in the first student activity can be verified through Bartlett's (Wynar, 275). Finally, various forms of the arts that have sent out signals are reviewed. The theater starts with its Grecian origins, then moves to Shakespeare's *Macbeth*, Ionesco's *Rhinoceros*, and Giraudoux's *Madwoman of Chaillot*. Charlie Chaplin as the little clown gives a nod to the movies. The opening lines from *A Tale of Two Cities*, *Adventures of Huckleberry Finn*, *Gone With the Wind*, *Moby Dick*, *Anna Karenina*, and *The Old Man and the Sea* represent the novel. All culminates pessimistically on a note from Arnold's "Dover Beach": we are left ". . . on a darkling plain . . ." in a technocratic society with a need for bridges to our own humanity through the humanities.

ACTIVITIES FOR THE STUDENT

1. In writing, sources of quotations (Wynar, 275, 281, 286, 287) are often useful: to identify or verify specific passages, to locate additional quotations on a specific subject, and to find more quotations by the same person. Each student need not do all three exercises (a-c) on page 286; rather, three small groups could each do one and discuss their approaches or methods. If the number of quotation sources is limited, two groups could start exercise 2. In each section on page 286 (a-c) select a quotation, a subject, or an author; consult a source of quotations and locate a quotation; provide a complete bibliographic citation to the original source of the quotation; and copy the *exact* content provided by the quotation source.

a. Identify one of the following quotations:

— "What is man, that thou art mindful of him?"
— "Man is the measure of all things."
— "And now abideth faith, hope, charity, these three."
— "What a piece of work is man!"
— ". . . the bulk of your natives to be the most pernicious race of little vermin. . . ."
— "Man is but a reed, the weakest in nature but he is a thinking reed."
— "Athens, nurse of man."
— "Whose woods these are I think I know."
— "Tomorrow and tomorrow, and tomorrow . . ."
— "And we are here as on a darkling plain. Swept with confused alarms of struggle and flight."

b. Locate an additional quotation on one of these subjects:

— What is the nature of human character, of good, of evil?
— What is history?
— What is the value of the past, of life, of religion?
— History is bunk.
— The business of America is business.
Posit your own statement; write it on a note card.

c. Find another quotation from the works of one of these *novelists*:
Jonathan Swift, William Faulkner, Fyodor Dostoyevsky, Charles Dickens, Samuel Langhorne Clemens (Mark Twain), Herman Melville, Count Lev Nikolayevich Tolstoi, and Ernest Hemingway;

poets:
Matthew Arnold, Robert Frost, and William Blake;

dramatists:
Sophocles, William Shakespeare, George Bernard Shaw, Jean Giraudoux, and Eugene Ionesco;

or *philosophers*:
Blaise Pascal, Martin Luther King, and Albert Einstein.

2. When this film was made, someone had to select the authors whose works would be included as representatives of "man's cultural heritage." From the novelists, poets, dramatists, and philosophers listed above, select one. Presume you are the author's agent.

Before proceeding, scan an article about the person in a general encyclopedia. Note, you can save hours and avoid frustration in any search for information by examining closely the titles and annotations on your bibliography or in Wynar. From the encyclopedia article, you already know the generation and the nationality of the author. Therefore, you can eliminate many reference sources. For instance, the French dramatist Giraudoux will not be treated in the *Literary History of the United States* (Wynar, 1257).

a. To locate essential biographical data, you would need to consult the sources cited in section "A Sign Model: Biography," page 197 of this book.
(1) Consult at least two sources.
(2) Take notes.

b. Many sources provide a bibliography of an author's work as part of the descriptive or critical entry on the author, but the following five sources in Wynar take particular care to do so: 1198, 1203, 1257, 1269, and 1287. If available and appropriate, check the *Cambridge Bibliography*, complete edition.

   (1) Consult at least two sources.

   (2) Take complete bibliographic citations to no more than five titles by this author.

c. In a short (125-200 word) memo, based upon your research, delineate why your client should be included in the film. Append to the memo a bibliography, compiled alphabetically by title, of no more than five works by this author.

MEANING IN MODERN PAINTING? (Encyclopaedia Britannica: Part I, 23 min./color/1967)

Is there meaning in modern art? In this film painters comment about meaning in their works. Only the paintings and the observations provide information. A viewer without an art history background would need to see more of the work and know more about the artist to appreciate the survey. Does Van Gogh, for instance, use red and green predominantly? Who was he? When did he live? Who were his contemporaries? Where does one find such information? While the camera pans two or three paintings of each artist, the narration records their observations.

Vincent Van Gogh: "I have tried with red and green to express the terrible passions of humanity."

Paul Cézanne: "To paint is to grasp a harmony among numerous relationships."

Paul Gauguin: "Art is an abstraction."

Henri Matisse: "A work of art has in itself its own absolute meaning."

Pablo Picasso: "Art is not truth. Art is a lie that makes us realize truth."

Georges Braque: "The senses deform. The mind forms."

Wassily Kandinsky: "He who looks at a painting ought to see it not as a reproduction of the exterior aspect of things."

Marc Chagall: "The interior is perhaps more real than the apparent world."

Georgio de Chirico: "One should not forget that a painting ought always to reflect a profound feeling and that profound means strange, and strange means not known."

Kurt Schwitters: "Anything an artist spits is art."

René Magritte: "A pure and powerful sentiment saved me from the traditional chase after formal perfection. My interest lay in provoking an emotional shock."

Piet Mondrian: "Isn't art concrete logic?"

Paul Klee: "The aim is to reveal the invisible."

Joan Miró: "Painting is made as we make love."

Salvador Dali: "Systematize the confusion."

Jackson Pollock: "I want to be in the picture."

Georges Mathieu: "A real avant-garde has deep roots in tradition."

Robert Rauschenberg: "I'm in the present. I try to celebrate the present."

Victor Vaserely: "Art will stimulate the human .biochemical complex."

As a montage of paintings by these artists sweeps across the screen, the narrator observes that little positive agreement exists between the artists about the meaning in modern painting; however, they do agree that art need not mirror reality.

ACTIVITIES FOR THE STUDENT
1. The artists quoted in *Meaning in Modern Painting?*, Part I agree that art need not mirror reality. If you were to refute or support any of the opinions expressed, you would need to gather information about each artist's body of work.
    a. Select an artist quoted in *Meaning*.
    b. Consult first a general encyclopedia (Wynar, 212-21) or a general art history (Wynar, 711, 712), then at least two art dictionaries or encyclopedias (Wynar, 723, 726, 727, 729, 731). If available, one source must be 727. Look for information, such as places and dates of birth/death; location(s) of adult residence(s); titles, subjects, media, dates, and present location of major works; association with or influence by a particular style, movement, artist, or patron. Take notes.
    c. Based upon your research, offer a short interpretation of how the artist's statement does or does not reflect his experience and work.

GREEK MYTHS, PART I: MYTH AS FICTION, HISTORY AND RITUAL
(Encyclopaedia Britannica: 27 min./color/1971)

The narration indicates that some myths evolved as stories to entertain; others evolved to explain rituals, and still others to explain history. Three segments reflect these categories, and each segment contains an example of at least one myth.

Snatches of the stories of Apollo and Daphne, Hyperion, and Artemis tantalize the viewer. Oedipus explains the riddle of the Sphinx. Then an animated sequence tells the story of Orpheus and Eurydice. This was a poetic reflection of love and bereavement, perhaps told for its own sake, notes the narrator.

As an example of a myth explaining ritual, the next segment uses animation as well as reenactment of the ritual. The animation tells of Demeter's search for Persephone and the deal mother Demeter struck with Hades. In Persephone's absence the mother earth would be barren, but fertile with her return. Thus in the spring, we see the reenacted sacred ritual, with oratory and chorus, welcoming back the daughter and awakening the mother earth with plows to receive the daughter grain.

Finally, there is the myth which the narrator says may have evolved to explain history, in this case the story of Theseus, whom the Athenians believed to be their first strong king. The drama is reenacted. Every nine years the Cretan King Minos threw a tribute of Athenians, seven men and seven women, to the half bull, half man Minotaur, which reigned in the labyrinth beneath the palace. No one ever emerged until Theseus marked his way with thread given him by Ariadne, slew the Minotaur, and escaped the impenetrable maze.

GREEK MYTHS, PART II: MYTH AS SCIENCE, RELIGION AND DRAMA
(Encyclopaedia Britannica: 25 min./color/1971)

A more apt subtitle for Part II would be "Myth as Science and Religious Drama," for the second segment of this film treats religion and drama as a unit. One must remember that these figures were indeed the Greek gods and goddesses; what we term myth was Greek religion.

Many myths, the narrator states, are close to science. Could it be that once a blazing comet entered the atmosphere, altering the balance of nature? Mythologies worldwide concern cataclysmic events, he notes. Another animated sequence tells of Hyperion's daily, steady drive of the golden chariot across the zodiac until, tricked by his son Phaethon, Hyperion reluctantly lets the boy drive the chariot. The team escapes; fires rage; mankind faces destruction; then Zeus aims his thunderbolt to kill Phaethon.

The final segment deals with religious issues and drama through some scenes from *Prometheus in Chains*, by Aeschylus. The drama concerns wars between the gods, and the narration identifies specifically the question, "How can gods be evil, all-powerful, but unjust?" In the play, the dramatist confronts moral and religious questions. Prometheus has angered Zeus by snatching a holy brand of fire and delivering it to man, for whom Zeus had planned eradication. Zeus decrees punishment, and the filmed sequence opens with the agent Hephaestus, aided in this version by Power and Violence, chaining Prometheus to a rock, driving a spike through his chest and leaving him to die. "I am a god; see how the gods torment me. . . ." The selected scenes telescope the play into barest plot.

ACTIVITIES FOR THE STUDENT

Since many English teachers require students to write documented thematic essays or to do research on specific authors or artists, students need to understand how to locate, use, and footnote quotations in the body of a paper. They also should be aware of a range of reference tools. Therefore students will need a handout on the system followed locally for citing quotations and for using footnotes.

For the purposes of this exercise, it will probably be easier for students to place all footnotes on a separate sheet. They will probably need a sample to follow. The sample on page 290 might help.

The Greek Myths, Parts I and II, relate a number of myths briefly and mention many characters. Among those who appear are Actaen, Apollo, Ariadne, Artemis, Daphne, Demeter, Eurydice, Hades, Helios, Hephaestus, Hermes, Hyperion, Minos, Minotaur, Narcissus, Oceanus, Odysseus, Orpheus, Persephone, Phaethon, Prometheus, the Sphinx, Theseus, Typhoes, Vulcan, and Zeus.

Select one character. Research the character as directed below. Write a short, perhaps 250-word, essay that identifies the character's place in mythology and shows how the character has entered today's world. Footnote the locations of information; number the footnotes sequentially throughout the paper; place all on a separate sheet at the end.

1. Through standard dictionaries and encyclopedias of mythology (Wynar, 1455, 1456, 1458) you will assemble enough information to identify this figure. Look for parentage, offspring, and major deeds.
2. Determine how these figures have entered our culture. Some have become words, trade names, or places; others have inspired poems, novels, plays, sculpture, or music. Additionally, constellations, stars, and space flights have taken their names. Check as many sources as time permits, but do include the following if they are available: a source of quotations (Wynar, 275, 281, 286, 287), an art reference (Wynar, 711, 712, 723, 726, 727, 729, 731), Brewer's (Wynar, 1202), a dictionary that includes fictional characters (Wynar, 1206-09), a classics handbook (Wynar, 1231, 1306, 1307, 1308), and a music source (Wynar, 1408, 1409). You would do well to check drama and literature sources as well as general encyclopedias and dictionaries.

Type of work:	Format for Footnotes
If a book, then:	——————————, ——————————————, author: first last, title (underlined), (————————————————————), pp. ——————. (place published: publisher, date), page(s).

If an encyclopedia, then:	————————————————, ————————————,
	    encyclopedia title (underlined), edition or date,
	
	s.v. "——————," by ——————————————.
	     "article title," author (if given) first last.

If a periodical, then:	——————————, "——————," —————— author: first last, "title of article," title of ————————————, ———— ————, pp. ————. periodical (underlined), month year, page(s).

If a newspaper, then:	——————————————, "——————————
	   author: first last (if given), "article title
	
	——————————," ————————————————,
	   (if given)," newspaper title (underlined),
	
	———— ———, ————, ——————————, ————.
	month day, year, section (if given), page(s).

If a signed essay from an edited volume, then:	——————————, "——————————————"
	   author: first last, "title of essay or chapter,"
	
	in ——————————————, ed. by ——————————,
	    title of work (underlined), first last,
	
	(——————: ————————, ———), p (pp). ——— .
	(place: publisher, date), page(s).

SOCIAL STUDIES

All of the films selected for this section explore issues in U.S. history. Therefore, the reference sources in the bibliography will support research in this area. Sources of statistics, primary sources, and subject encyclopedias, dictionaries, atlases, and handbooks are included. The first student activity is suggested to clarify the arrangement of U.S. history subject cards in the catalog. The others continue to combine research and writing. Students can select from a range of topics which will determine the sources required. Some topics are more difficult than others; teachers and media specialists may need to guide some choices. The supporting bibliography could include the following titles.

623 *Harvard Encyclopedia of American Ethnic Groups.* Stephan Thernstrom, ed. Cambridge, MA: Harvard University Press, 1980.

627 *The Ebony Handbook.* Ebony Editors and Doris E. Saunders, eds. Chicago: Johnson Publishing, 1974.

633 *The Negro Almanac: A Reference Work on the Afro-American.* Harry A. Ploski and Warren Marr, eds. New York: Bellwether, 1976.

634 *The Negro in American History.* Mortimer J. Adler, gen. ed.; Charles Van Doren, ed.; George Ducas, exec. ed. Chicago: Encyclopaedia Britannica Educational Corp., 1972.

645 *The American Indian: A Chronology and Fact Book*, 2nd ed. Henry C. Dennis, ed. Dobbs Ferry, NY: Oceana, 1977.

652 *Handbook of North American Indians.* William C. Sturtevant, ed. Smithsonian Institution; distr. by Washington, DC: Government Printing Office, 1978- , 20v (in progress).

658 *Ethnic Chronology Series.* Dobbs Ferry, NY: Oceana, 1971-1977.

848 Shepherd, William R. *Historical Atlas*, 9th ed. rev. and updated. New York: Barnes and Noble, 1973.

879 Gilbert, Martin. *American History Atlas.* Cartography by Arthur Banks. New York: Macmillan, 1969.

880 Lord, Clifford L., and Lord, Elizabeth H. *Historical Atlas of the United States*, rev. ed. New York: Holt, 1953; rep., New York: Johnson Reprint, 1969.

881 Paullin, Charles O. *Atlas of the Historical Geography of the United States.* J. K. Wright, ed. Washington, DC: Published jointly by Carnegie Institute of Washington and the American Geographical Society, 1932; repr. Greenwood Press, Westport, CT., 1975.

882 Cassara, Ernest. *History of the United States of America: A Guide to Information Sources.* Detroit, MI: Gale, 1977.

886 *Harvard Guide to American History*, rev. ed. By Frank Freidel, with the assistance of Richard K. Showman. Cambridge, MA: Belknap Press of Harvard University Press, 1974.

893 *The Encyclopedia of American Facts and Dates*, 7th rev. ed. Gordon Carruth, ed. New York: T. Y. Crowell, 1979.

896   *Dictionary of American History*, rev. ed. New York: Scribner's, 1976.

897   *Encyclopedia of American History*, Bicentennial 5th ed. Richard B. Morris and Jeffrey B. Morris, eds. New York: Harper and Row, 1976.

900   Hochman, Stanley. *Yesterday and Today: A Dictionary of Recent American History*. New York: McGraw-Hill, 1979.

903   *Record of America: A Reference History of the United States*. Joseph F. X. McCarthy, ed. New York: Scribner's, 1974.

904   *America: History and Life*. Eric H. Boehm, ed. Santa Barbara, CA: ABC-Clio, 1974- .

908   *An American Primer*. Daniel J. Boorstin, ed. Chicago: University of Chicago Press, 1966.

909   *The Annals of America*. Mortimer J. Adler, Charles Van Doren, and others, eds. Chicago: Encyclopaedia Britannica, 1976.

910   *Basic Documents in American History*, rev. ed. Richard B. Morris, ed. New York: Van Nostrand Reinhold, 1965.

912   *Documents of American History*, 9th ed. Henry S. Commager, ed. Englewood Cliffs, NJ: Prentice-Hall, 1974.

915   *Makers of America*. Wayne Moquim, ed. Chicago: Encyclopaedia Britannica Educational Corp., 1971.

1639   Ireland, Norma Olin. *Index to America: Life and Customs*. Westwood, MA: Faxon, 1978.

1643   U.S. Library of Congress. *A Guide to the Study of the United States of America: Representative Books Reflecting the Development of American Life and Thought*. By Donald H. Mugridge and Blanche P. McCrum. Washington, DC: Government Printing Office, 1960. Supplement, 1956-1965, 1976.

1768   *Historical Statistics of the United States: Colonial Times to 1970*. Bureau of the Census. Washington, DC: Government Printing Office, 1976.

1773   *Statistical Abstract of the United States*. Bureau of the Census. Washington, DC: Government Printing Office, 1878- .

Each U.S. history film presents a different historical period. *American Time Capsule* flies from the revolution to Ford's inauguration. (Pyramid added the final segment without re-copywriting the film, so the production date stands correct at 1968.) *The Immigrant Experience* tells the story of a Polish family through the eyes of Janek, the son. *America: Gone West*, episode 5 of Alistair Cooke's *America* series, chronicles the westward movement from Daniel Boone to the Louisiana Purchase to the gold rush. *The Life and Times of Rosie the Riveter* juxtaposes archival film footage with observations by five women regarding the home front during World War II.

AN AMERICAN TIME CAPSULE (Pyramid Films: 3 min./color/1968)

Two hundred years of American history leap off the screen chronologically in visuals which last only 1/12 to 2/3 of a second and include documents, paintings, cartoons, and photographs. Essentially framed by wars, the film begins with the Declaration of Independence and concludes with the inauguration of Gerald Ford.

In rapid succession flow the Revolutionary battles, Constitutional Convention, War of 1812, and the burning of Washington; Indians, wilderness, and farm life; Jackson, the frontier, and emerging blacks; the railroads west, abolitionists, slavery; Lincoln, and the Civil War, the *Monitor* and *Merrimack*; the Black Army, Fort Sumpter, and battle after battle; the assassination of Lincoln, the first Unknown Soldier, and *Huck Finn*; the battles west, the Indians, the railroads, and the calvary; the growth of cities, Philadelphia's Centennial Exposition, balloons, and airplanes. Then, at an incredible pace, the film covers TR and the Spanish American War; Uncle Sam and WW I; the Depression, Mickey Mouse, and FDR; WW II, planes, cemeteries, and Generals Eisenhower and MacArthur. The swirl continues through President Ford.

The trip is breathtaking. Taking notes the first time through will be impractical. Students might pool their observations as a group and then amplify them on a second viewing. Glimpses appear of Hancock, Jefferson, Washington, Adams, Franklin, Sitting Bull, Lee, Grant, John Wilkes Booth, Cochise, Custer, Wilson, Truman, Dewey, Nixon, JFK, Jackie, RFK, King, Humphrey, and LBJ—to name a few. Your students and you will spot others.

ACTIVITIES FOR THE STUDENT

1. Most U.S. history teachers assign several papers each year which require some student research. Much of this relies on the general collection. However, most students need to understand more about the system for filing U.S. history subject cards to use the local card catalog effectively. Since the basic arrangement is chronological and since *American Time Capsule* whisks from 1776 to 1974 in three minutes, projecting the film is a quick and painless way to emphasize chronological arrangement. Because the breakneck speed can be overwhelming, it needs to be projected once with the only requirement being careful observation. Then, depending on local resources, provide students with copies of pages from *Sears* (Wynar, 1134), a transparency thereof, or a typed outline of locally used subject headings. They should be able to discuss the parallels of chronological approach. Now ask them to view the film a second time and to match in the margins as many events to dates as possible.

THE IMMIGRANT EXPERIENCE: THE LONG, LONG JOURNEY (Learning Corp. of America: 31 min./color/1972)

Who came? Thirty-five million people in under 100 years: Slavs, Jews, Germans, Italians, and Irish. The story of this Polish family, narrated by the 12-year-old son, represents the patterns of many. The father works three years in a slaughterhouse for their passage. Two weeks aboard an overcrowded steamer begins their odyssey. Tired and confused, they struggle against a language barrier to pass inspection. In 1907, Ellis Island was flooded with such families; some were separated and detained. Others, like this one, were reunited and free to make their way up the endless flights of stairs to the tenements of Bedford Street. Janek goes to school. In America he learns that he is a greenhorn. He talks wrong: "th's" won't come. He dresses wrong: he exchanges the treasured cap with the used clothes pedlar. He eats wrong: boys snatch his potato and shriek as he chomps through an unpeeled banana. "The Irish got here first," he observes, "and think they own the country." Janek resolves to become an American. Painfully, he learns to read. The teacher, comparing his father to a work horse, urges him to rise above his background. No more Polish at home, he pronounces; the family reverberates. Within six months Janek has conquered the "th's" and much of the language.

Disaster strikes: the father is permanently disabled at work, and the slaughterhouse replaces him immediately. The family is without recourse. Janek leaves school just before his thirteenth birthday to work in the slaughterhouse. He'll return to school one day, he says. "No," responds the teacher, "It never happens that way."

As the film closes, we meet Janek, the man, who reminisces. The father never worked again. He and his mother persevered. And, after 52 years, Janek has retired from the slaughterhouse. With pride he tallies a home and garden, a pension and social security, a son (a salesman) and a grandson in college. The American dream, notes Janek, was a long, long journey, one taking a lifetime.

ACTIVITIES FOR THE STUDENT

1. As noted in *The Immigrant Experience*, over 35 million people entered the United States in just under 100 years; those would be the years between 1881 and 1971. By 1880, the census already stood at 50,155,783, so many had already joined the native American population. The immigration rate since 1871 has continued apace. The history of groups within the country varies widely. *The Immigrant Experience* speaks of Slavs, Jews, Italians, Irish, and Polish immigrants. Select an ethnic group. Research the following sources and write a report which indicates when and where the majority of the group entered the country, significant problems they encountered, where the majority settled, and how they have adapted. Cite bibliographical information completely and take notes. If you intend to quote directly from a source, be sure to take the page number. All sources cited below will not be appropriate for every group, so be selective.

    a. Some reference sources cover general U.S. history. Check Wynar, 896, 897, 900, and 903 as well as a general encyclopedia (Wynar, 212-21) to determine what information they provide on the history and contributions of your group.

    b. Other reference sources have been designed to amplify information about ethnic groups. Check Wynar, 623, 627, 633, 634, 645, 652, and 658 as appropriate to your topic.

    c. Statistical information could be important. Check Wynar, 1768 and 1773 both under your group and under immigration.

    d. Quotations from primary sources could be especially important in determining the problems groups faced. Check compilations of primary source material (Wynar, 908, 909, 910, 912, 915).

    e. Indexes to articles or essays in books (Wynar, 225, 1639) or periodicals (Wynar, 904) should be consulted. Of equal importance are selected bibliographies, which you will find especially valuable in doing research in college. First among these is the *Harvard Guide* (Wynar, 886); also useful would be Wynar, 882 and 1643.

AMERICA: GONE WEST (Time-Life: 58 min./color/1972)

The American West, claims Alistair Cooke, began 200 years ago in the ridges of Appalachia, where people began moving, "bound for the promised land." During the 100 years between the discovery of the Cumberland Gap in 1750 and the discovery of gold in California, they crossed the continent.

The Cumberland Gap, which became part of Daniel Boone's Wilderness Road, opened a route west through which hunters, trappers, and surveyors moved. It was Indian country, where only the self-sufficient could survive. Some travelers, mostly of English, Irish, and Scottish stock, cleared land and settled. Others pushed further into the wilderness. On the rivers, Frenchmen plied a trade between Canada and the Gulf of Mexico.

In 1803, the Louisiana Purchase doubled the country's land mass and Jefferson immediately commissioned the Lewis and Clark expedition (1803-1806), guided by the Indian woman Sacajawea, to survey it. The results of the expedition, notes Cooke, must have been painful for Sacajawea, who lived until 1884, for it led the way to dispossessing the Indians from their homelands.

The initial stimulus west was cotton. The pioneers began farming the delta soils of Mississippi. By 1830, Alabama, Georgia, and Mississippi outlawed Indian tribes, for they interfered with farming. Jackson ordered their complete removal west of the Mississippi.

To the Rockies came trappers in search of beaver pelts. Here the eighteenth century British class system and Jeffersonian democracy met in conflict. In the British hierarchy, the English and Scots managed the trading; the French Canadian canoeists transported; the Indians trapped. The Americans, however, set their own traps and paid the Indians three to four times as much for theirs. The original trading or rendezvous areas on the river plains gradually became stockades, actually private forts later purchased by the U.S. Cavalry.

At such a fort, John Sutter in 1847 hired James Marshall to set up a saw mill. Soon thereafter, while routinely cleaning a sluice, Marshall spotted gold. The decade after Marshall's discovery saw a rush across the prairies, for although one could take other routes, each was arduous and more expensive. Thus most jumped off from St. Joseph, Missouri, where the railroad ended. Each June, between 1850 and 1860, reports Cooke, one-quarter of a million people passed through the Wyoming hills. By July 4, most parties had reached Independence Rock. The trip continued across the scrub desert of western Wyoming to Pacific Springs, along the Humbolt River into Nevada. The remaining hurdle was to pass through the high Sierra Nevada before early September, when the snows began. One early party (the Donner Party, unnamed in the narrative), hemmed in for the winter, resorted to cannibalism.

Once through the mountains, they could proceed unimpeded down the foothills toward the gold fields. Few found the wealth they sought. In 1852, Sutter's mill burned; John Marshall died penniless, but the port of San Francisco burgeoned.

ACTIVITIES FOR THE STUDENT

1. *America: Gone West* speaks of the route west through the Cumberland Gap, the river route opened by the Lewis and Clark expedition, the routes west to California from St. Joseph, Missouri, and alternate routes around the Horn, through Panama or Nicaragua, or across Mexico and up the coast. Consult a historical atlas (Wynar, 848, 879, 880, 881) as well as general reference sources. Select a route, and locate a map of the route.

a. Reproduce the map as either a transparency or a class handout. Footnote its source on the copy.

b. Be prepared to discuss the advantages, disadvantages, and importance of this route.

2. Several events receive but glancing treatment in *Gone West*. Select and research one of the following. Write a short documented essay (250-500 words).

a. Why did Thomas Jefferson "advise and consent" with no one over the Louisiana Purchase?

b. What really happened when Andrew Jackson ordered the Cherokees moved west of the Mississippi; from whence comes the term "Trail of Tears"?

c. The early party trapped in the Sierra Nevada was the Donner Party. What happened to them, when, why?

d. Cooke notes that as a result of the Lewis and Clark expedition, the Indians were dispossessed from their homelands by 1884, when Sacajawea died. Can you substantiate this statement?

e. Cooke also cites the American fur trappers in the Rockies, who purchased pelts from the Indians, as examples of Jeffersonian democracy. What was Jeffersonian democracy? Why would the term be used here?

THE LIFE AND TIMES OF ROSIE THE RIVETER (Clarity Educational Productions: 65 min./color/1980)

This film shows the home front during World War II. Rosie was the collective name, taken from the lyrics of a popular song, for the women who worked in the factories, shipyards, and mills. Meticulously selected segments from government films, screen newsclips, newspapers, magazines, and popular songs encapsulate the flavor of the times and are juxtaposed with the perceptions of five women representative of 700 women interviewed prior to the production. During the war the issues were: recruitment, training, safety, unionism, absenteeism, child care, prejudice, and patriotism. After VJ Day, they were: layoffs, unemployment, and the baby boom. The interviewees are: from Brooklyn, Lola Weixel, party favor assembler; from Los Angeles, Margaret Wright, kitchen mechanic; from Richmond, California, Gladys Belcher, farmer's widow; from Detroit, Wanita Allen, domestic; and from San Francisco, Lyn Childs, single parent. The untrained recruits of the hidden army were not the white middle class women consistently featured in the film clips; they were, as Weixel notes, working people. Not patriotic fervor but the opportunity for training and earning power motivated these women.

The women, declared the newsclips, were as safe in the workplace as at home, doing a man's job for a man's pay and enjoying the company of others. Yet the *New York Times* clipping of January 21, 1944, announced 37,600 industry deaths since Pearl Harbor, exceeding by 7,500 the war deaths. Pay, too, was an issue, but it was unionism, not "the company of others," which they found valuable. Weixel recounts the lockout that occurred when they joined the United Electrical Union and that the National Labor Relations Board adjudicated.

The women testify to the difficulties of life beyond the workplace. Groceries, meals, cleaning, laundry, and child care were constants in their lives; their roles as women at home did not change with the assumption of jobs.

They speak, too, of long hours, double shifts, and unresolved grievances. Pride and esprit de corps were part of the workplace but so, too, were dissension and hardship. Margaret Wright recalls the times; it was unpatriotic, she muses, to complain, much less to speak of unionism. Lyn Childs tells of using a torch to rescue a Filipino from racial harassment by a young white officer. Lola Weixel speaks of the long hours amid bleak surroundings. The war was taking a long time, and the men were gone for the duration.

In a newsreel clip as the war was closing, Bill Jacks informed his workers, "You women have been employed because your husbands have been called to war . . . Each returning serviceman will get his job back and you women and girls will go home to be housewives and mothers again as you promised to do. . . ." The layoffs began: first the women, then the black men, and finally some white men. Seventy thousand a month were discharged, and despite film forecasts of jobs for all, even the combination of new consumer goods and overseas markets could not provide enough employment. Weixel notes it was not "like a dance in an opera. We were no longer comrades in arms, but competitors . . . in the workplace."

Concurrently the media urged women back into the home, warning of unsupervised children, financially independent wives, and the erosion of femininity. Many needed to continue working, but their choices were limited to jobs with long hours and little pay. In that time period 1.5 million households were established and 4 million babies were born. Without rancor, Weixel muses, "We believed we were new women . . . I think that they prepare women psychologically for the role that society wants them to play . . . America wanted babies and we did, too . . . but for that we gave up everything."

ACTIVITIES FOR THE STUDENT

Choose for investigation one of the questions below or develop a question to investigate. Check any individually developed questions with your teacher or media specialist. Research may require the use of your general collection as well as any of the previous reference sources. Write your findings in a short essay (250-500 words). Document your information with footnotes on one sheet at the end.

1. The women speak of silk stockings "before they got away" and of prices that rose astronomically. What kinds of items were rationed during World War II? What other restrictions did civilians encounter? What efforts were made to control prices? What was the Office of Price Administration?

2. The effort to mobilize the hidden army was massive. What part was played by: the War Manpower Commission, the National War Labor Board, the National Defense Mediation Board, the Office of Production Management, and the War Production Board?

3. The women speak of unions and higher salaries, also of lockouts and discrimination on the job. What was the Federal Wage and Hour law? How many women were employed during the war, and what were their average salaries? Did union membership increase during this time? Were work stoppages and strikes common? Do you find records of racial disturbances in the war plants?

4. What were landmarks in the fields of entertainment and the arts between 1940 and 1945 (Wynar, 893 will help)? Were they regulated in any way? What movies, books, or songs were popular or won awards? The women speak of the change in the media after the war. Can you document this change?

5. What happened to the birth, marriage, and employment pictures between 1941 and 1944 as compared to the period 1945-1948? What kinds of consumer goods became available after the war? What happened to the cost of living?

PURE AND APPLIED SCIENCE

Each of the films selected for this section represents a field where ongoing research has brought rapid changes. To understand developments, students need a command of a specialized vocabulary, an overview of the topic, and access to the latest information. The activities all appear at the end of the section and are based on subject dictionaries, encyclopedias, yearbooks, and periodical articles. The supporting bibliography could include the following titles.

340 *Illustrated Encyclopedia of Astronomy and Space*, rev. ed. Ian Ridpath, ed. New York: T. Y. Crowell, 1979.

342 Tver, David, and others. *Dictionary of Astronomy, Space and Atmospheric Phenomena*. New York: Van Nostrand Reinhold, 1979.

343 Burnham, Robert, Jr. *Burnham's Celestial Handbook: An Observer's Guide to the Universe Beyond the Solar System*, rev. ed. New York: Dover, 1978-1979.

345 Hitching, Francis. *The Mysterious World: An Atlas of the Unexplained*. New York: Holt, Rinehart and Winston, 1979.

348 Moore, Patrick. *The Rand McNally New Concise Atlas of the Universe*. Chicago: Rand McNally, 1978.

351 Murdin, Paul, and Allen, David. *Catalogue of the Universe*. New York: Crown, 1979.

354 *Cambridge Encyclopaedia of Astronomy*. Simon Mitton, ed. New York: Crown, 1977.

355 Moore, Patrick. *The A-Z of Astronomy*. New York: Scribner's, 1976.

362 *A Dictionary of Life Sciences*. E. A. Martin, ed. New York: Pica Press; distr. by New York: Universe Books, 1977.

363 *The Encyclopedia of Biological Science*, 2nd ed. Peter Gray, ed. New York: Van Nostrand Reinhold, 1970.

364 Gray, Peter. *Student Dictionary of Biology*. New York: Van Nostrand Reinhold, 1973.

365 *McGraw-Hill Dictionary of the Life Sciences*. Daniel N. Lapedes, ed.-in-chief. New York: McGraw-Hill, 1976.

366 Steen, Edwin B. *Dictionary of Biology*, 2nd ed. New York: Barnes and Noble, 1975.

372 *Biological and Agricultural Index*. New York: H. W. Wilson, 1916- .

817 *Dorland's Medical Dictionary: Shorter Edition*. Philadelphia, PA: Saunders; distr. by New York: Holt, Rinehart and Winston, 1980.

1592 *McGraw-Hill Dictionary of Scientific and Technical Terms*, 2nd ed. Daniel H. Lapedes, ed. New York: McGraw-Hill, 1978.

1593 *McGraw-Hill Encyclopedia of Science and Technology*, 4th ed. Daniel W. Lapedes, ed. New York: McGraw-Hill, 1977.

1596   *Van Nostrand's Scientific Encyclopedia*, 5th ed. New York: Van Nostrand Reinhold, 1976.

1598   *McGraw-Hill Yearbook of Science and Technology, 1966-* . New York: McGraw-Hill, 1967- .

1601   *Science Year: The World Book Science Annual*. Chicago: World Book-Childcraft International, 1965- .

1602   *Yearbook of Science and the Future*. Chicago: Encyclopaedia Britannica, 1968- .

1603   *General Science Index*. New York: H. W. Wilson, 1978- .

1606   *American Men and Women of Science*, 14th ed. Jacques Cattel Press, ed. New York: Bowker, 1979.

1608   *Dictionary of Scientific Biography*. Charles Coulson Gillispie, ed. New York: Scribner's, 1970-1978.

1611   *McGraw-Hill Modern Scientists and Engineers*. New York: McGraw-Hill, 1980.

Each of the selected films represents a different scientific discipline. *Man: The Incredible Machine* is a travelogue through the body, made possible by medical technology that utilizes photography. *The Green Machine* surveys current research regarding plant growth and physiology. *Universe* covers recent discoveries and theories about the nature of celestial bodies including stars, galaxies, quasars, pulsars, and black holes.

MAN: THE INCREDIBLE MACHINE (National Geographic Society: 26 min./ color/1976)

The incredible machine is perhaps no more celebrated in this film than the techniques that have made visible its parts. Both bear equal attention. In a travelogue of the human body, the filmmakers explore parts of the body systems. Beginning with the senses, we see the skin as a cooling mechanism and sense organ, the eyes as an information source to the brain and as an emotional outlet, the ears as receivers and transmitters of sound to the brain. The film moves through the respiratory, circulatory, digestive, muscular, skeletal, and nervous systems.

Medical techniques utilizing photography have produced some unusual footage. The electron microscope magnifies pores by 2,400x. Thermography shows the heat generated in the body by exercise. An indirect laryngoscopy shows a singer's vocal cords. TV endoscopy captures the action of red blood cells in the lungs as well as the churning action of the stomach walls. Cinemicrography shows leukocytes consuming invaders in the bloodstream. Cinefluorography reveals the chewing process as someone eats candy; it also shows the joints in the hand.

Further medical techniques and mysteries are noted in the narration. Scientists still cannot record, nor do they understand, how the brain decodes images that the lens of the eye inverts onto the retina. Even though scientists understand that the brain receives sound as electricity, electronic implantations on the brain have produced only a perception of sound by deaf people, not normal hearing. Finally, through attaching an electroencephalograph to a man emitting Alpha waves and then to an electric train, the train moves. The longer the Alpha waves, the faster the train; the Alpha waves are unexplained.

THE GREEN MACHINE (Time-Life: 48 min./color/1978)

Using the classification system established by Linnaeus, botanists have classified and stored over half a million distinct plant specimens, as proven by the last count of the herbarium of the Royal Botanical Gardens at Kew. There is more to botany than classification, however. This film examines the growth, respiration, circulation, digestion, sight, muscle, and nerve systems in plants. Through time-lapse photography, the electron microscope, and biochemical analytical techniques, scientists around the world are researching plant physiology and are beginning to draw hesitant comparisons to like systems in animals. For all the research, mysteries regarding plant physiology still exist.

Plant growth continues to mystify the scientists. Shoots use light to guide their directional growth, as proved by Darwin over 100 years ago. Not until 1973 did scientists isolate from the tips of plants the hormone auxin, which travels down the side of a shoot and makes the cells more permeable to water. Cells enlarge, become heavy, and the plant bends. Other hormones discovered since the 1950s are the gibberellins, growth hormones; cytokinins, which cause rapid cell division; abscisic acid, a growth inhibitor; and ethylene, which effects ripening. At the University of Glasgow biochemists suspect that more than the five identified groups of hormones exist.

The Glasgow investigating team measured the suction power of leaves by reversing the respiration process and forcing sap backward through a leaf. This required placing the leaf under 180 pounds of pressure per square inch, 15 times greater than atmospheric pressure. Plants withstand this pressure only because of their geodetic structure. All leaves are capable of photosynthesis, but the process is still a mystery.

In the 1950s Melvin Calvin and an English biochemist further unraveled the mystery. By adding radioactive carbon dioxide to plant cells and analyzing samples, they were able to observe the chemical reactions that occur when a plant assimilates carbon dioxide and produces carbohydrates. The animated sequence, which demonstrates carbohydrate manufacture, indicates in summary that still no one understands how this chemical process produces life.

Plants appear to see light; this, too, is a mystery. The search for color receptors began 25 years ago. The blue receptor has not yet been found, but the red has been identified as phytochrome, which acts like a botanical light meter. This substance detects the long red waves that penetrate shady areas, changes chemically to stimulate rapid growth toward the light, and converts again to prompt normal growth as the plant reaches shorter waves. Somehow, phytochrome senses light and interacts with the internal clock.

Climbing action in plants appears to be governed by another clock. Bean shoots in search of support revolve once every 1½ hours. Dr. Mark Jaffe discovered that the twining response in pea tendrils, which can occur within 20 seconds, is somewhat similar to the molecular response of contracting muscle cells in animals.

At Cambridge, a scientist explains that plant cells are like batteries. Using a giant single cell alga, she has recorded primitive nerve action in response to mechanical stimulation such as pinching. She suggests that the response is similar to that in animals but a thousand times slower, and that thus basic communication between cells is possible. In St. Louis, morning-glories have produced on chart recorders repetitive signals too random to interpret but too regular to ignore. These instances may be evidence of a nervous system in plants, but research in the field is still in its infancy.

None of the scientists will accept the theories advanced by Clive Baxter, a lie detection expert. Baxter attached his equipment to a philodendron that he claimed reacted to his thoughts of fire; he concluded that plants could detect danger and respond, as well, to injury to other organisms. In 1968, a plant hormone specialist tried to verify Baxter's findings with a controlled experiment. He found no evidence of plant reaction. To date, whether or not plants have extrasensory perception remains a question.

UNIVERSE (National Audiovisual Center: 27 min./color/1977)

Produced by NASA, *Universe* packs a lot of information into an exciting promotion for continued space exploration. After an explanation of the creation of the universe via "The Big Bang" theory, the film moves from the familiar sun, solar system, and galaxy out into the unfamiliar universe where quasars, pulsars, black holes, Red Giants, and White Dwarfs exist.

In the beginning, all the matter of the universe was contained in one primordial pattern of cosmic concentration of elemental particles. After hundreds of millions of years of cooling, the galaxies we now observe began to evolve. Inside the galaxies, whirlpools of gravity condensed hydrogen into incredibly hot stars, which sustained the thermonuclear reactions transforming hydrogen into heavier elements. Our sun is one of those stars.

Astronomers study the sun to understand the structure and energy of the stars. Spectroscopic analysis of the sun shows a visible signal of dark lines cutting across the color bands; each line is the signature of a chemical element like sodium, iron, or calcium. The sun's core is a violent nuclear furnace where hydrogen is converted into helium, producing great energy that radiates out as a gas and convects as a bubbling liquid beneath the surface. On the surface, sun spots, regions of intense magnetic fields, appear. From the surface, the greatest explosions are flares, which move hundreds of miles per second and emit the light of a billion hydrogen bombs. Dark areas, coronal holes, may provide clues to the sun's interior and may be the source of the solar winds. On earth these winds produce auroras and disrupt radio communication.

A half century ago, we thought our galaxy was alone. Now we know that we are part of a local group of 20 galaxies, but that 10 billion galaxies grouped in clusters exist as far as present instruments can reach. Little is known about the evolution of galaxies. Less is known about the galactic core and its role in the evolution and structure of galaxies. Some galaxies are in a state of extreme disarray, exploding; some interact with each other. Even more puzzling are quasars, star-like objects that emit as much radio energy every second as the sun does in 10 million years. They appear to be among the most remote objects in space.

All stars, including our own, are born, live their life span, and die. They are the victims of two opposing forces. Pressure from the energy in the core of the star pushes out, while gravity pulls inward. When the pressures are balanced, the star shines steadily. As the hydrogen fuel is depleted, the release of energy is insufficient to withstand the compression of gravity, and the exterior collapses. But compression by gravity raises the temperature in the core and the helium ash rekindles, lifting the outer core against gravity. Now the star becomes a Red Giant.

In its final evolution the mass of a star seems to determine its fate. The sun is a medium-sized star. In 10 million years it will expand to four times it size and engulf the inner planets of Mercury, Venus, Earth, and Mars and create a nebula extending beyond the outer planets. After millions of years, its reserves of nuclear fuels will be exhausted. Its outer areas and layers of air will have dissipated, and only an ashen White Dwarf star will remain. The temperature will drop to zero, and it will become a black stellar corpse.

When stars larger than the sun reach the Red Giant state, the collapse of the core raises temperatures billions of degrees and trips a spectacular detonation. At the center of the explosion the residue is crushed to a neutron core so dense that 10 billion tons of it would fill only a tablespoon. It spins, rapidly generating radio signals in a strong magnetic field. Since the radiation beam swinging past earth is observed as a pulse, the stars are called pulsars.

Stranger ends are predicted for very massive stars. According to the laws of gravity as presently understood, nothing can stop them from collapsing. These stars disappear and are seen as black holes, which distort the gaseous shapes of their neighbors with gravitational pull and emit X rays that can be detected in space. Neither light nor matter can leave the field of these cosmic abysses. The physical laws governing them are totally unknown to us.

This evolving universe itself must come to an end. If it continues to expand indefinitely, the light of every star will in time be extinguished. If gravity halts its expansion, the universe will fall back on itself; galaxies will lose their separate identities; stars will explode; and the skies again will be a blaze of light. Finally, all matter will be engulfed in a fireball like that from which it emerged.

ACTIVITIES FOR THE STUDENT

The three films *The Green Machine* (1978), *Man: The Incredible Machine* (1976), and *Universe* (1977) include terms, summarize research, quote scientists, and state assumptions that bear investigation.

1. Subject dictionaries and encyclopedias are especially useful in the sciences, where new vocabulary often evolves with new knowledge. Select three terms; examine your bibliography; identify likely sources; and cite the most recent definitions. Define each in layman's terms which your classmates can understand.

endoscopy	ethylene	sun spot
bronchoscope	geodetic	coronal hole
microcirculation	phytochrome	solar wind
electroencephalograph	cosmic	asteroid
electron microscope	thermonuclear	primordial
chloroplast	galaxy	cyclonic
extrasensory perception	heliostat	nebulae
leukocyte	spectroscope	quasar
thermography	microcosmic	Red Giant
auxin	cineflurography	White Dwarf
gibberellin	laryngoscopy	pulsar
cytokinin	cinemicrography	black hole

2. Although biographies of major scientists appear in general biography sources, subject biographies include more people and emphasize their professional contributions. Remember that the *Dictionary of Scientific Biography* (Wynar, 1608) includes no living scientists. Use Wynar, 1606, 1608, 1611, 253, or 254, or a general source.

The following scientists are mentioned in the two films:

from *The Green Machine*: Charles Darwin, Carolus Linnaeus, Melvin Calvin

from *The Invisible World*: Anton van Leeuwenhoek, Enrico Fermi, Albert Crewe, Harold Edgerton, and Wilhelm Roentgen.

Select one person, do research, and summarize your findings in a paragraph. Cite your source in bibliographic form.

3. The following statements represent the status of information at the date of production for each film. The world of science changes rapidly. Select a statement, research its background, and determine if the sentence is still considered accurate. Be certain to check periodical and newspaper coverage (Wynar, 372, 1603, and 226, 227, 229) as well as scientific yearbooks (Wynar, 1598, 1601, 1602). Document your findings in a short paper (300-500 words); be certain to footnote quotations. Provide a separate bibliography of sources used.

    a. Scientists in Glasgow have identified five groups of plant hormones and suspect that more exist.

    b. Electrical pulses in morning-glories and the primitive nerve action in a single cell alga may be evidence of a nervous system in plants, but research in the field is in its infancy.

    c. Coronal holes may provide clues to the sun's interior and may be the source of the solar winds.

    d. The probe of Mars has shown a dynamic and evolving planet.

    e. Drifting on the surface of Jupiter is a mysterious red spot that radiates more energy than the planet receives from the sun.

    f. Little is known about the evolution of galaxies; less is known about the galactic core and its role in the evolution and structure of galaxies.

    g. Quasars appear to be among the most remote objects in space.

    h. According to the laws of gravity as presently understood, nothing can prevent the collapse of very massive stars, which disappear and are seen as black holes; the physical laws governing them are unknown to us.

    i. All things on earth, living and inert, are formed from the elements forged in some distant star.

    j. It is reasonable to believe that somewhere in the universe there are stars where conditions favorable to life exist.

    k. The skin is a sense organ; humans require touching almost as much as food.

    l. Muscles work predominantly in pairs.

    m. The medical applications for thermography have evolved rapidly.

    n. We are only beginning to understand the connection between electricity and the functions of the brain.

FILM TITLES INDEX

l'Adolescence, 30
Aging, 82
Amazulu—People of the Sky, 262-63
America: Gone West, 295
American Character: Aunt Arie, The,
181-82
American Time Capsule, An, 293
Amish: A People of Preservation, The, 16-17
Ancient Games, The, 84-85
Anything You Want to Be, 145-46
At 99: A Portrait of Louise Tandy Murch, 181

Bach to Bach, 119-20
Basic Law Terms, 15-16
Battle of Culloden, 40-41
Bead Game, 210-11
Beauty Knows No Pain, 117-19
Black History: Lost, Stolen or Strayed,
112-14
Braverman's Condensed Cream of Beatles,
166-68

Campaign, 148-49
Castles of Clay, 85-86
Cell Division: Mitosis and Meiosis, 230-31
Chick, Chick, Chick, 26-27
Child Abuse: Cradle of Violence, 140
Churchill—the Man, 187-88
Cider Maker, 219-20
City at the End of the Century, The, 273-74
City That Waits to Die, The, 251-52
Close Harmony, 147-48
Coleridge: The Fountain and the Cave,
193-94
Come into My Parlour, Said the Spider...,
260-61
Computer Glossary: Or Coming to Terms
with the Data Processing Machine, A, 265
Cooking of France: An Alpine Menu, The,
83-84
Critic, The, 120-21

Dancer's World, A, 247-48
Day in the Life of Bonnie Consolo, A, 80-81
Decisions, Decisions!, 15
Demagogues and Do-Gooders: Noisy Voices
of the Depression, 255-56
Dinosaur, 106-7
Divided Trail: A Native American Odyssey,
The, 248-49
Doubletalk, 114-16
Dreyfus Affair, The, 269-70

Egg, The, 160-61
Egypt's Pyramids: Houses of Eternity, 229
End of One, The, 150-51
Escargots, Les, 170-72
Evolution, 49-50

Fable of He and She, The, 127-28
Family That Dwelt Apart, The, 69-70
Faneuil Hall Markets: 1826-1970, 222-23
Fantasy, 163-64
Feminine Mistake, The, 94-95
Fireworks, 128-29
Flight of the Gossamer Condor, 82-83
For Parents Only: What Kids Think About
Marijuana, 244-45
For Tomorrow We Shall Diet, 144-45
Frank Film, 19
Franklin D. Roosevelt: The New Deal, 189
Friend or Foe, 71-73
From Courtship to Marriage, 37-39
Future Shock, 279-80

Georgia O'Keeffe, 189-90
Girl with the Incredible Feeling, The, 180-81
Glass, 56-57
Goodnight Miss Ann, 253
Great Society, The, 98-99
Greek Myths, Part I: Myth as Fiction, History
and Ritual, 288
Greek Myths, Part II: Myth as Science, Religion
and Drama, 288-89

Green Machine, The, 300-301
Growing Up Female, 221-22

Heartbeat of a Volcano, 45-46
Henry Ford's America, 74-75
Hollywood: The Dream Factory, 204-5
Humanities: A Bridge to Ourselves, The, 285

"I Have a Dream": The Life of Martin Luther King, 190-91
Icarus Montgolfier Wright, 48
Immigrant Experience: The Long, Long Journey, The, 293-94
Imogen Cunningham, Photographer, 194
Invisible World, The, 281-82
Iran, 159-60
Italian American, 50-51

Jackaroo, The, 226-27
Job Interview: I Guess I Got the Job, 104-5
John Muir's High Sierra, 225-26

Knud, 182-83
Kudzu, 25

Language Development, 263-64
Leisure, 27-28
Life and Times of Rosie the Riveter, The, 296-97
Listen to Britain, 172-73
Log House, 59-62
Look Before You Eat, 39-40

Magic Machines—and Other Tricks, 126-27
Magic Rolling Board, 104
Making of a Quarterback, The, 259-60
Man: The Incredible Machine, 299
Marketing the Myths, 138-39
Mary Cassatt—Impressionist from Philadelphia, 220-21
Matter of Survival, A, 149-50
Meaning in Modern Painting?, 287-88
Measure of Change, A, 257
Men of Bronze, 131-33
Men's Lives, 270-71
Metamorphosis, 54-55
Metric America, A (2nd Edition), 139
Metropolis, 169-70
Middle Years, The, 28-29
Mr. Gimme, 29-30
Mistons, Les, 31
Moonwalk, 95-96

Nanook of the North, 199-201
Newton: The Mind That Found the Future, 194-95
Night and Fog, 142-43
Nobody's Victim, 238-39
Noise Pollution, 93-94
Notes on the Popular Arts, 268-69

Olympia Diving Sequence, The, 165-66
Otto: Zoo Gorilla, 201-3

Perfect Moment, The, 246-47
Picasso Is 90, 192-93
Pillar of Wisdom, 158-59
Pinter People, 129-31
Plow That Broke the Plains, The, 102-3
Powers of Ten, 209-10
Prelude to War, 143-44
Pretend You're Wearing a Barrel, 203-4
Prisoners of Chance, 218
Private Life of King Henry the Eighth, The, 191-92
Problem Solvers, 55-56

Resurrection of Bronco Billy, The, 161-62
Run!, 168-69

Sea behind the Dunes, The, 46-47
Seamus Heaney: Poet in Limboland, 240-41
Secrets, 162-63
Separate But Equal, 141-42
Set of Slides, A, 17-18
Shopping Bag Lady, The, 73-74
Skating Rink, The, 149
Snowbound, 70-71
Soccer, U.S.A., 140-41
Solo, 57-59
Sonnets: Shakespeare's Moods of Love, The, 213-14
Sort of a Commercial for an Icebag, 212-13
Spider, 179-80
Spivey's Corner, 81-82
Star Spangled Banner, 173-74
Street Musique, 164-65
Sunday Dinner, 174-75

To Fly, 277
Top of the World: Taiga, Tundra, Ice Cap, 235-36
Tops, 80
Toys, 211-12
Trader Vic's Used Cars, 105-6
Tragedy of the Red Salmon, 254
Trials of Franz Kafka, The, 195-96

Truly Exceptional Carol Johnston, The, 236-37
Two Cities: London and New York, 35-36
Two Factories: Japanese and American, 36-37

Universe, 301-2

Verbal Communication: The Power of Words, 228
Virginia Woolf: The Moment Whole, 242-43
Vive le Tour!, 205-6

Walk in the Forest, A, 272-73
What Do You Do When You See a Blind Person?, 146-47
What Is Poetry?, 97-98
Wolf and the Whitetail, The, 237-38
Worshipping, 116-17

Your Credit Is Good, Unfortunately, 68-69

Allegory, 168-72
Allusion, 45, 79, 90, 170, 248-49
Anecdote, 79, 81, 89
Appeal to reader. *See* Devices, attention-
     getting
Archetype, 57-58, 155-56, 158-63, 165-68
Aside, 79, 219
Assertion, 88, 89-100, 198
     in comparisons, 34
     implied, 80
     readings, suggested, 92, 100
     selection of, 91
Audience, 89-100. *See also* Communication
     assumptions about, 88
     readings, suggested, 92, 100
     student consideration of, 91

Bias, 34, 233
Bibliographic form, 276, 278-79, 282-83,
     285, 289, 294. *See also* Research
Bibliographies
     general, 276-77
     humanities, 283-85
     sciences, pure and applied, 298-99
     social studies, 291-92
Biography, 176-97. *See also* Character;
     Character type; Profile
     adult life drive, 185
     antagonistic force, 185
     chart of types, 186-87
     chronology, 42, 185
     fictionalizing, 191-92
     life structure, 183-97
     purpose, 184, 186-95
     sign model, 157, 176, 183-84
     slant, honorific, 184, 187-91
     slant, objective, 185, 194-96
     slant, pejorative, 184-85, 191-94
     sources, primary, 184, 186, 189, 191-93
     sources, reference, 186, 197, 302
     sources, secondary, 184, 186, 195

Categories, 11-20, 227
     classification, 11, 12
     in comparison, 33

Categories (cont'd)
     in definition, 20, 21-22
     in exposition, 78, 81
     function of, 15
     general to specific, 14
     subcategories, 11-12
     taxonomy, 13, 16
Cause and effect, 62-78
     in exposition, 78, 85-86
     function of, 62
     inference of, 267
     misuse of, 67
     pattern 1, forward looking, 63-64, 70-73,
          76-77
     pattern 2, backward looking, 63, 65, 73-74,
          76-77
     pattern 3, both forward and backward
          looking, 63, 66-67, 68-69, 69-70, 74-76
     revealed through chronology, 44
Character, 176-83, 184. *See also* Biography;
     Character type; Profile
     categories of, 176-77
     definition of, 176
     dynamic, 176-77, 181-83, 187-92
     function of, 176
     personality types, 176-77
     static, 176-77, 179-81, 189, 190-91, 192-96
     techniques for revealing, 176-78
Character type, 176, 178-79. *See also* Biog-
     raphy; Character; Profile
     examples, 178-82
     function of, 178-79
     readings, suggested, 178
Chronology, 42-52, 280, 293
     in biography, 42, 185
     in cause and effect, 42, 44, 62
     embellishments, 45
     example of, 43-44
     in exposition, 78, 82-83
     function of, 42, 50
     in scientific writing, 45-46, 280
     selecting facts for, 43-44, 50
     structural variations, 42, 44-45
     time line, 43-44, 280
Classification. *See* Categories

Communication, 7, 114-16. *See also*
    Audience; Persuasion
  message distortion ("static"), 228
  relationship of sender, message, and
    receiver, 86, 106, 123-24, 134
Comparison, 32-42
  assertion development in, 34
  balance in, 34
  bias, 34
  categories in, 33
  in exposition, 78, 84
  faulty, 33
  function of, 32
  structural variations, 32-34
  in tone, 234
Composition. *See also individual terms*
  assertion, 34, 80, 88, 89-100, 198
  conclusions, 62, 82-83, 155
  details, 21, 80-81, 215-23
  devices, attention-getting, 88, 89-100
  emphasis, 198-207
  exposition, 78-87
  focus, 198-207
  originality, 207-15
  pacing, 198-207
  persona, 88, 122-33
  refining the message, 198-223
  structure, 215-23
  tone, 31, 89-90, 100-103, 232-41
  topic, 12, 14, 91, 198, 199, 216, 280
  topic sentence, 28, 224
  transitions, 89-91, 215-23
  voice, 88-90, 100-108
Conclusions, 82-83, 155
  of process writing, 62
Critical thinking, 7, 11-78. *See also* Cate-
    gories; Cause and effect; Chronology;
    Comparison; Definition; Process
    ("how-to") writing

Definition, 20-32
  category/subcategory/details, 20, 21-22
  dictionary, 20, 24, 27
  etymology, 20, 24
  in exposition, 78, 81
  extended, 20, 23, 25, 26-27, 246-47
  negation, 20, 24
  operational, 20, 22
  readings, suggested, 23, 32
  simile, 20, 23
  tautology, 20
Description, 79, 83
Details, 21, 80-81, 215-23
  in definition, 20, 21-22
  inference, 266-67
Devices, attention-getting, 88, 89-100
  anecdote, 89
  allusion, 90
  kicker, 89
  in persuasion, 134

Devices, attention-getting (cont'd)
  in process writing, 62
  question, 90
  readings, suggested, 100
  symbol, 90
  in tone, 89-90
  transitions from, 89-91
  types of, 90-91
Dictionary, 20, 21, 24, 27
  criticism of, 20, 25
  standard, 288, 289
  subject, 302
  tautology in, 20

Emphasis (in writing), 198-207
  of assertion, 198
  definition of, 198-99
  examples, 198-99
Essay. *See* Literature, types of
Exposition, 78-87. *See also* Exposition,
    structure of; Exposition, techniques of
  definition of, 78
  proof, thorough, 80-81
  use of authorities in, 82
Exposition, structure of. *See also* Exposition;
    Exposition, techniques of
  categories, 12, 78, 81
  cause and effect, 78, 85-86
  chronology, 42, 78, 82-83
  comparison, 41, 78, 84
  deductive, 78, 81
  definitions, 23, 78, 81
  inductive, 78, 79, 82
  process ("how to"), 78, 80, 83
  quest, 78, 82-83
Exposition, techniques of. *See also* Exposition;
    Exposition, structure of
  allusion, 78, 84
  anecdote, 79, 81
  aside, 78, 84, 85, 219
  description, 79, 83
  evidence, 80, 82
  fact and example, 79, 80, 81
  figurative language, 78, 85
  interviews, 81
  quotation, 79, 80-81, 84
  repetition, 79, 80, 81-82
  statistics, 82
  variations, 79, 80

Facts, directly stated, 258-66
  accurate paraphrases, 258
  in cause and effect, 258
  types of, in SAT, 258-59
Figurative language, 78, 79, 85
  hyperbole, 48
  metaphor, 45, 48-49, 85-86, 90, 97-98,
    225
  personification, 48
  simile, 20, 23, 85, 113

Focus (in writing), 198-207
   definition of, 198
   examples, 198-99
   support of assertion, 198
Folklore
   functions of, 81
   informants in, 81-82
   proverbs, 86-87

"How to" writing. *See* Process ("how-to")
   writing
Humor, 27, 31, 45, 69-70, 84-86, 106-7,
   114-16, 145-46. *See also* Character
   type; Satire
   absurdity, 49-50
   comic diction, 127-28
   exaggeration, 69
   mockery, 51, 112-13, 127-28
   parody, 127-28
   puns, 45, 48-49, 94, 119

Images, 48-49. *See also* Figurative
   language; Signs; Symbols
Implication. *See* Inference
Inference, 266-74
   connotation, 266
   definition of, 266
   distinction from implication, 266
   incorrectly stated facts, 267
   prediction of outcomes, 267
   unstated cause and effect, 267
   unstated details, 266-67
   unstated interpretation, 267
   unstated opinion, 267
   unstated value judgment, 267
Irony, 108-22. *See also* Satire
   chart of functions and types, 111
   dramatic, 49-50, 109, 114-16, 119-20,
   136
   function of, 110
   as persuasion technique, 98-99, 136,
   143
   situational, 109, 116-17, 117-19
   in tone, 234
   verbal, 109, 112-14, 120-21

Library. *See* Reference sources; Research
Literature, types of
   allegory, 168-69, 170-72
   autobiography, 19
   biography, 176-97
   character type, 176, 178-79
   diary, 78, 82-83
   essay, expository, 53
   essay, humorous, 52
   essay, persuasive, 88, 134-51
   essay, scientific, 45, 303
   exemplum, 149-50
   folklore report, 81-82, 86-87

Literature, types of (cont'd)
   journal, 78, 82-83
   parable, 29-30, 68, 139
   parody, 127-28
   poetry, 97-98, 213-14, 240-41
   process ("how to"), 53
   profile, 74-77, 80-81, 176, 179, 183
   proverbs, 86-87
   research paper, 82, 84, 282-303
   satire, 69, 110, 158, 178-79
Logic in writing, 7, 11-78. *See also* Categories;
   Cause and effect; Chronology; Comparison; Definition; Process ("how-to")
   writing
   deductive, 78, 81, 195
   inductive, 55, 78, 79, 82
   scientific method, 55, 194-95

Message. *See* Communication
Mood, 31
Moral in writing, 68-69

Note taking, 52, 280-81, 282, 288, 294

Opinion, 241-49
   through allusion, 248-49
   clues that determine, 242, 246-47, 248-49
   through definition, abstract word, 246-47
   directly stated, 241-42, 244-45
   indirectly stated, 242
   through paradox, 247-48
   in process writing, 56-57
   readings, suggested, 244, 248, 249
Originality (in writing), 207-15
   examples in literature, 208-9
   types of, 208-9
Outline, 12, 27, 67-68

Pacing (in writing), 198-207
   climax, 201, 202-3
   connection to focus and emphasis, 198-99
   definition of, 198
   examples, 198-99
   suspense, 200-201
Paradox, 225. *See also* Rhetorical devices
   to express opinion, 247-48
Persona, 88, 122-33. *See also* Voice
   clues to, 123, 126, 127
   definition of, 122-23
   examples of, 123-24
   labels for, 125-26
   of narrator, 124
   readings, suggested, 133
Persuasion, 88, 134-51, 197. *See also*
   Persuasion, devices of; Persuasion,
   structure of
   distinction from propaganda, 134
   function of, 135

Persuasion (cont'd)
  motivational techniques, 134, 136-37,
    139-51
  techniques to avoid, 134
Persuasion, devices of, 135-51. *See also*
    Persuasion; Persuasion, structure of
  card stacking, 136, 149
  connotation, 136, 143-44
  either/or, 135, 143-44, 145-46, 149-50
  glory by association, 95-96, 136, 140-41,
    143-44
  irony, 142-43
  irony, dramatic, 136, 143-44, 150
  juxtaposition, 95-96, 136, 142-43, 150-51
  legitimacy, 136, 140-41
  minimizing or maximizing, 136, 139,
    148-49
  name calling, 136, 143-44
  parable, 139
  presence of hero, 136, 140-41
  reduction to absurdity, 135, 145-46
  shock, 94-95, 135, 142-43, 146-47
  stereotyping, 136, 147-48, 149
  straw man, 135, 144-45, 146-47
  testimonial, 136, 140, 144-45
  understatement, 142-43
  voice of science or reason, 136, 141-42,
    144-45
Persuasion, structure of, 134-35. *See also*
    Persuasion; Persuasion, devices of
  exemplum, 134-35, 146-51
  pro-and-con argument, 134, 139-45
  satire, 134-35, 145-46
Process ("how to") writing, 53-62
  devices, attention-getting, 62
  directions, 53
  in exposition, 78, 80, 83-84
  function of, 53-54
  opinion in, 56-57
  steps for technical clarity, 53
Profile, 74-78, 80-81, 176, 183. *See also*
    Biography; Character; Character type
  examples of, 181
  function of, 179
Proof techniques, 91
Propaganda, 134. *See also* Persuasion
Purpose, 249-57
  SAT verb choices for, 250

Quotation in exposition, 79

Reading comprehension, 224-74. *See also*
    Scholastic Aptitude Test (SAT)
  facts, directly stated, 251-66
  inference, 266-74
  main idea, 224-31
  opinion, 241-49
  purpose, 249-57
  tone, 89-90, 232-41

Receiver. *See* Communication
Reference sources, 186, 197, 302
  almanac, 280, 282
  art, 288, 289
  atlas, historical, 295
  bibliographies, 276-77, 283-85, 291-92,
    294, 298-99
  biography, 197, 286-87, 302-3
  classics handbook, 289
  criticism, 287
  dictionaries, standard, 288, 289
  dictionaries, subject, 302
  encyclopedias, desk, 276, 282
  encyclopedias, general, 276, 278, 280-83,
    286, 288
  index, article and essay, 294
  index, periodic, 279
  index, subject-heading, 293
  music, 289
  newspapers, 303
  periodicals, 303
  quotation, 285-86, 289, 294
  yearbooks, scientific, 303
Report, oral, 283
Research, 275-303
  bibliographic form, 276, 278-79, 282-83,
    285, 289, 294
  bibliography, annotated, 275, 279
  card catalog, 276, 278-79, 280-81, 293
  footnoting, 289-90, 297, 303
  local collection retrieval, 278-79, 280-81,
    282-83
  note taking, 280-81, 282, 288, 294
  paper, documented, 82, 84, 282, 287, 288,
    289, 294, 295-96, 297, 303
  scanning for overview, 23, 278-83
  source citation, 276, 278-79, 282-83, 285,
    289, 294
  structuring information, 280, 293
  topic selection in, 280
  verification of information, 285-86
Rhetorical devices, 102-3. *See also* Irony
  juxtaposition, 40-41, 80, 93, 95-96, 98-99
  paradox, 225, 247-48
  puns, 45, 48-49, 94, 119
  question, 113

Satire, 110, 178-79. *See also* Character type;
    Irony
  examples in films, 49-50, 69-70, 98-99,
    116-21, 158-59
  parody, 127-28
  persuasion structure, 134-35, 145-46
Scholastic Aptitude Test (SAT). *See also*
    Reading comprehension
  vocabulary, 45, 101, 225, 232-33, 250,
    265, 268-69
  words in context, 225-31, 262

Signs, 152-76
    archetype, 57-58, 155-56, 158-63,
        165-68
    context, 153
    conventional, 152-53, 164
    dynamic, 153-54, 158-63, 170-72,
        173-74
    functions of, 157-58
    models, 88, 157-58, 161, 164-69, 171,
        173, 176
    paradigmatic line, 154-57, 159-60, 162-69,
        174-75
    personal, 152-53
    readings, suggested, 175
    set, 153, 163, 168
    signified, 152-53
    signifier, 152-53
    static, 154, 163-68, 172-73
    as symbol, 152ff
    syntagmatic line, 154-57, 159-60, 162-69,
        174-75
    universal, 152-53
    words as, 21
Sources, primary, 184, 186, 189, 191-93
Sources, secondary, 184, 186, 195
Stereotypes, 162
Structure (in writing). *See* Biography; Chrono-
    logy; Comparison; Composition;
    Exposition; Persuasion; Research
Suspense, 83
Symbols, 48, 90, 103, 152ff. *See also* Signs

Taxonomy, 13, 16
Tone, 31, 89-90, 100-103, 232-41. *See also*
    Persona; Voice
    comparison, device of, 234
    connection to attention-getting devices,
        89-90
    definition of, 100-101, 232
    irony, device of, 234

Tone (cont'd)
    loaded terms, device of, 234
    objectivity, device of, 234
    open bias, device of, 233
    readings, suggested, 107-8, 240-41
    SAT words for, 232-33
    stacking the deck, device of, 233
Tone of voice. *See* Voice
Topic selection, 12, 14, 78, 91, 198-99, 216,
    280
Topic sentence, 78, 224. *See also* Assertion
    implied assertion, 80
    question as, 78, 82
Transitions. *See* Composition

Values clarification, 70-74
    cause and effect in, 70-74
Voice, 88-90, 100-108. *See also* Persona; Tone
    connector of sender to audience, 101, 104-5
    definition of, 100-101
    labels for, 101
    readings, suggested, 107-8
    of science and reason, 136, 141-42, 144-45

Words. *See also* Definition; Dictionary
    abstract, 21, 25, 26-27, 246-47
    concrete, 21, 27, 29-32
    connotation, 266
    etymology, 20, 24
    as signs, 21
Words in context. *See* Scholastic Aptitude
    Test (SAT)
Writing. *See* Composition
Writing, types of. *See* Literature, types of